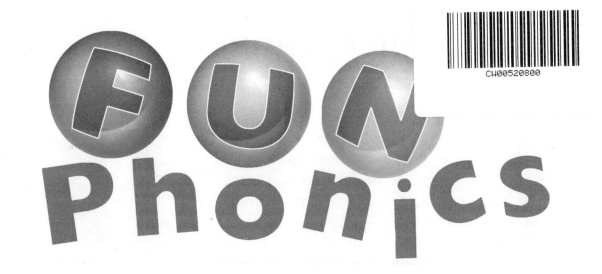

Teacher's Handbook

CONTENTS

About the authors	ii
A guide to using *Fun Phonics*	iii
How *Fun Phonics* works	iv
Unit 1 Concept of Rhyme	1
Unit 2 Identifying Alphabet sounds	30
Unit 3 Blending and Segmenting	129
Unit 4 Blending and Segmenting	219
CVC and CVCC words	
CV + *ck* and CV + *ng* words	
Unit 5 Blending and Segmenting	263
CCVC words	
Digraphs	
Trigraphs	
Word lists	337
Glossary	344

ABOUT THE AUTHORS

Joyce Sweeney is Deputy Head Teacher at Braidbar Primary School in East Renfrewshire, Scotland, with responsibility for language, support for learning and special educational needs. She has 20 years' classroom teaching experience, most of which has been spent with the early stages of the Primary School. She has additional qualifications in infant and nursery teaching.

She has always been a strong proponent of phonics skills teaching.

> *'I have always believed that phonics is a skill to be taught in a systematic and structured way and a strategy to be used by children to become successful readers.* Fun Phonics *has its roots in twenty years' experience of successfully teaching children to read.'*

Carol Doncaster is a Primary School Teacher with 20 years' primary teaching experience. At present, she works in Renfrewshire as a home link teacher, identifying and developing appropriate strategies to help raise achievement and to sustain young children in education. Carol says of her key responsibilities:

> *'I encourage parents to become involved in their child's learning and in the life of the school.'*

Joyce Sweeney and Carol Doncaster co-authored the long-selling, successful *Key Phonics* and *New Key Phonics* phonic workbook series.

A GUIDE TO USING FUN PHONICS

LAYING THE FOUNDATIONS OF LEARNING TO READ

To learn to read and write, children need to be phonologically aware and have a functional understanding of the alphabet along with an understanding of the purpose and value of print. Successful reading and writing depends on their ability to make the association between all three of these skills.

Learning to read should be treated as an enjoyable problem-solving activity. Children must be encouraged to use a wide range of strategies to help them read unknown words. Many educators now advocate that children who rely on one or two strategies aren't as successful in learning to read as those who use several. The National Literacy Strategy (NLS) stresses the importance of teaching children to tackle texts from both ends: from the text down and from the sounds and spellings up.

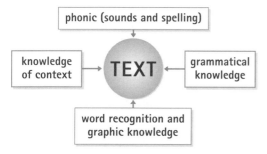

The *Fun Phonics* programme fosters a steady development of phonological and phonemic awareness using a systematic, structured teaching programme. The teaching is in the context of lively, fun-to-read rhyming texts.

THE FRAMEWORK FOR TEACHING FUN PHONICS

Fun Phonics has a framework of five units that supply the essential tools for reading and writing. These units provide the know-how for children to learn how to blend phonemes into words for reading, and how to segment words into phonemes for spelling.

IN UNIT 1:

Children develop the skills necessary to generate rhyme. The unit focuses on the rhythm and rhyme of language and sets out to increase the child's awareness and understanding of it. The three elements of rhyme are: an awareness of rhyme, the ability to recognise and identify rhyme and the ability to generate rhyme.

IN UNIT 2:

Children begin to appreciate alliteration and learn how to identify onsets in words. To do this, they need to acquire a knowledge of initial sounds. The smallest unit of sound in words, namely the phoneme, is taught in this unit. These phonemes are: the initial sound as in *hat* and *pat*; the medial sound as in *hat* and *hot*; and the end sound as in *hat* and *had*. Onsets of more than one sound: *sh* as in *shop* are also taught at this stage.

IN UNIT 3:

Work now starts on developing children's ability to make reading and spelling analogies. They are given the opportunity to build words with letters using their sense of analogy and to see the resemblance between certain words. This involves reading new words by changing the initial sound (onset) and by using the rime from the original word. For example, *hat* can be used for making *bat*. They are also systematically taught how to develop an appreciation of blending individual sounds to make words.

IN UNIT 4:

Reading is ultimately about getting meaning from text. To do this well, children need to develop fluency in reading words (automaticity). Plenty of practice of this is given in both *Dexter Dog's Big Book of Rhymes (CVC)* and Workbook 4.

IN UNIT 5:

As the complexity of the texts increases, so does the complexity of the phonemic knowledge required. Onsets develop from single consonants to consonant blends, e.g. *c* to *cr*. Rimes require a knowledge of long vowels and letter strings, e.g. *ran* to *rain*. All the work now concentrates on developing automaticity in these skills, so that children can use their knowledge of phonemic awareness to read and understand texts.

FUN PHONICS AND OTHER READING PROGRAMMES

Fun Phonics is a supplemental course. It may be used with other reading programmes to teach phonics as a strategy for reading.

HOW FUN PHONICS WORKS

INSTRUCTIONAL MATERIALS

TEACHER'S HANDBOOK

The practical step-by-step teacher's manual has been designed for daily desk-top use. It is easy to use because everything is provided and all the lessons are pre-planned. The book contains the programme overview and 150 lessons. These cover all the National Literacy Framework (NLF) progression in phonics requirements from YR to Y2.

Each lesson has the following features:

- *Before You Start*
  This is vital pre-lesson preparation. It recommends the resources needed to teach the lesson and outlines the aims and outcomes.

- *The Lesson*
  Each lesson is approximately 15 minutes long. It starts with a quick review of the skills previously learned. Lessons develop the course incrementally and follow the skills progression requirements laid down in the NLF. They are compatible with the Scottish 5-14 Guidelines. Lessons are scripted with questioning techniques to help pupils participate fully and interact with the teaching. We advocate that following the lesson format is essential to the success of the programme. Lessons contain appropriate activities such as learning about rhyme; developing phonemic awareness; alphabet naming activities and blending and segmenting.

- *Further Practice*
  This provides follow up suggestions for consolidation and reinforcement of skills learned. The handy "Note" feature gives advice/suggestions related to the particular lesson.

- *Planning*
  Planning can be done using the index to the NLF for each lesson. The index has the following features:

  The NLF Year/Term Reference recommends when, during the calendar year, a child may learn a particular skill. There is no obligation to follow the year planner. Each teacher will assess their pupil's progress and move through the skills at a pace matching the pupil's need. The Year/Term Reference is a useful "barometer" for measuring and comparing progress against NLF guidelines.

  The Key Skill being taught, e.g. Identifying End sounds.

  The Specific Skill being taught, e.g. – the rimes *og, op*.

COURSE MANAGEMENT VIDEO

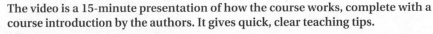

The video is a 15-minute presentation of how the course works, complete with a course introduction by the authors. It gives quick, clear teaching tips.

The video shows how to:

- Teach a lesson

- Assess a child's progress and learning.

A very useful addition is the glossary of sounds.

The glossary demonstrates how to:

- pronounce initial consonant sounds correctly without distortion

- say the long vowels as well as other vowel phonemes.

The correct pronunciation of the sounds demonstrated in the glossary is invaluable for effectively communicating a most vital part of phonics instruction: accurate auditory discrimination of sounds in words.

SUPPORT AND ASSESSMENT

The Support and Assessment Masters provide photocopiable material for a range of assessment, practice and reinforcement work. There are masters for both pupil and teacher. The teacher's masters are in Section E.

- *Section E: Phonic Assessment Record Sheets* allow the teacher to keep a record, with comments where appropriate, of all assessments undertaken by the children.

BIG BOOKS

Each of the four big books contains a wide selection of rhymes: traditional rhymes; alliterative rhymes which introduce the alphabet sounds as onsets; rhymes focusing on CVC words in the context of two lively stories and rhymes focusing on consonant clusters as onsets. They are also a delightful way to make children excited about reading and encourage them to use a variety of strategies to read continuous text.

At the same time, the big books help the teacher assess how well the children understand the basic concepts of print, their attitudes to reading and their reading skills.

They can be used for Whole Class interactive work.

- *Candy Cat's Big Book of Rhymes (Traditional)* helps children follow the progression of rhyming skills outlined in the NLF. These are: listen and enjoy; listen and join in; listen and anticipate; listen and identify rhyme; identify rhyme from a choice of three and volunteer words that rhyme with a given word.

- *Hector Hedgehog's Big Book of Rhymes (Alphabet)* uses alliteration to help children differentiate the initial sounds in words and to read the letters that represent the sounds.

- *Dexter Dog's Big Book of Rhymes (CVC)* gives practice in blending phonemes to read CVC words in continuous text. This is in the form of two lively rhyming stories.

- *Freda Frog's Big Book of Rhymes (Consonant Clusters)* gives practice in identifying initial consonant clusters in words and reading the letters that represent these clusters. It provides a text for children to use a number of strategies to read.

PUPIL MATERIALS

WORKBOOKS

The workbooks help children build on the skills learned. The workbook activities extend their grasp of a new concept. Ongoing practice helps them assimilate these concepts.

Workbook use is specifically indicated in the programme – where applicable. The workbooks are a vital part of reinforcement and consolidation work on the programme but not a substitute for direct teaching/active learning.

- *Workbook 1 (Unit 2)* gives practice in phoneme-grapheme correspondence. It provides a resource to develop the relationship between initial sounds in words and their written representation.

- *Workbook 2 (Unit 2)* also gives practice in phoneme-grapheme correspondence. It provides a resource to develop the relationship between initial sounds in words and their written representation.

- *Workbook 3 (Unit 3)* provides a resource to practise onset and rime as a reading and spelling analogy using CVC words. It also gives practice in blending phonemes to read words.

- *Workbook 4 (Unit 4)* provides a resource to develop speed and accuracy in reading and writing CVC and CVCC words.

- *Workbook 5 (Unit 5)* provides a resource to practise consonant clusters as onsets. It also gives practice in the different representations of the long vowels and the letter strings.

SUPPORT AND ASSESSMENT

As previously outlined, the Support and Assessment Masters provide photocopiable material for a range of assessment, practice and reinforcement work. The pupil's masters are in Sections A, B, C and D.

- *Section A: Additional Support Copymasters* provide more practice in essential skills for those who need it.

- *Section B: Copymasters* are a set of photocopiable sheets for use with Unit 1. They provide practice in the skills necessary to be able to produce a rhyming string.

- *Section C: Homework Masters* allow children to practise skills at home to increase the speed and accuracy of word recognition.

- *Section D: Pupil Phonic Assessment Sheets* comprise lists of words in discrete units for assessment of reading and spelling.

SKILLS ACTIVITY PACK

The Skills Activity Pack is a box of cards and games to develop phonological awareness, phonemic awareness, auditory discrimination, automatic word recognition and vocabulary building. It includes picture cards, word and phrase cards and games to ensure assimilation and the ultimate mastery of reading skills.

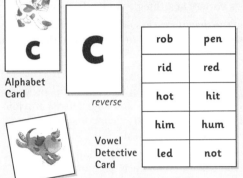

Alphabet Card

reverse

Vowel Detective Card

rob	pen
rid	red
hot	hit
him	hum
led	not

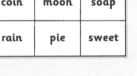

Picture Rhyming Card

The bag has a big zip

Read-me-Write-me Card

Rhyming Bingo

coin	moon	soap
rain	pie	sweet

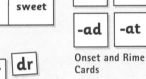

-ag   -an

-ad   -at

Onset and Rime Cards

tr br cr dr

pr sl bl

Quick Cards

g   oal

b   oat

Flash Cards

ck ee oe

- *Alphabet Cards* are individual alphabet letter cards for the teacher to use in direct teaching. Each card has an alphabet letter on one side and a smaller alphabet letter plus associated character in colour, on the other.
- *Vowel Detective Cards* are CVC word cards for the pupil to use to practise quick recognition of CVC words where only the vowel is different e.g. *hat, hot, hut*.
- *Picture Rhyming Cards Sets A, B, C* are colourful picture cards which can be used to develop rhyming skills as suggested in the "Developing Skills" section of Units 3 and 4.
- *Read-me-Write-me Cards* are cards with CVCC words embedded in phrases. They can be used for scanning to quickly identify the CVCC word; for reading practice and for identifying rhyming CVCC words within each phrase. They are also a resource for dictation.
- *Rhyming Bingo Sets A, B, C* give practice in developing the skills of rhyming and reading words out of context.
- *Onset and Rime Cards Sets A, B, C* are cards to help develop the skill of manipulating the onset to create new words.
- *Quick Cards Sets A, B, C* are letter cards to facilitate quick identification of the letter that represents the initial, final or medial sound in words. A fourth set of quick cards shows the written representation of consonant clusters.
- *Flash Cards* are in two sets. The first set shows the written representation of all the digraphs and trigraphs in the programme. The second has regular phonetic word flash cards needed for flash card practice and the activities suggested in the skills practice sections.

CLASSROOM MATERIALS

The Classroom Materials provide related material for the classroom walls. They ensure continued exposure to and reinforcement of key skills that children need to assimilate while learning to read.

ALPHABET FRIEZE

- *The Alphabet Frieze* features the characters associated with each letter in *Hector Hedgehog's Big Book of Rhymes (Alphabet)*. The frieze helps children contextualise and memorise phonics skills. It can be displayed either as a poster or in a strip.

5 LONG VOWEL POSTERS

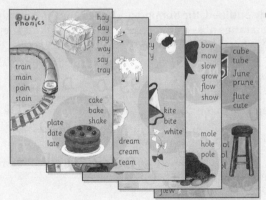

- *5 Long Vowel Posters* provide lots of opportunities for pupils to see and reflect on the different representations of the long vowels.
  ay, ai, a_e words are displayed
  ee, ea words are displayed
  igh, i_e, ie, y words are displayed
  ow, oa, o_e words are displayed
  u_e, ue, oo, ew words are displayed

UNIT 1

CONCEPT OF RHYME

> Instilling a concept of rhyme is essential for the development of children's phonemic awareness.
> **When children experience singing, chanting and learning rhymes, they gradually develop a script for building rhyming skills through imitation and experimenting.**

INTRODUCTION

Unit 1 of *Fun Phonics* covers the NLF Word Level Work required for Reception Year in which pupils should be taught:

■ to recognise when two words rhyme
■ to continue a rhyming string.

The focus of the unit is on the rhythm and rhyme in language through interactive teaching using *Candy Cat's Big Book of Rhymes (Traditional)*.

Many activities are suggested for you to help raise the children's awareness of rhyme and to develop the skills necessary to be able to continue a rhyming string.

Please note that some activities in the book require you to provide your own materials. These are:

■ Magnetic letters

■ Children's name cards

■ Collections of pictures representing initial sounds

■ Headbands with slits (this simple device is a strip of paper, or preferably light card, that fastens from behind with tape. A slit just wide enough to allow a Letter Card to be put in is cut out at the front.)

Concept of Rhyme

THE NLF AIMS

- Recognise when two sounds rhyme.
- Work towards being able to continue a rhyming string.

WHAT YOU NEED

RESOURCES

- *Candy Cat's Big Book of Rhymes (Traditional)* pages 2 to 9

KEY LESSON POINTERS

VOCABULARY

rhyme   sounds the same   end word   line

THE CHILDREN should throughout the lesson:

- listen to and focus on the rhythm and rhyme of the language.

YOU should throughout the lesson:

- emphasise the rhythm and rhyme by tapping to keep the rhythm and encouraging the children to clap on the rhyme
- focus on one-to-one correspondence between the spoken and the written word.

STARTING THE LESSON

- Show the children *Candy Cat's Big Book of Rhymes (Traditional)*.

  Open the book at pages 2 and 3.

  Ask the children to look at the pictures carefully. Tell them that you want everyone to tell you about one thing they can see in the picture.

  Discuss the picture emphasising the teapot, its appearance and its use. You should be familiarising the children with the vocabulary in the rhyme and ensuring that they understand it.

TEACHING THE LESSON

LESSON 1

- Read "I'm a little teapot".

  Reread emphasising the rhythm and rhyme. (*As you read, gently tap your foot or tap on your thigh to keep rhythm, and clap on the rhyming words.*)

  Ask the children to "read" the rhyme with you, inviting them to clap when you do: on the rhyming words.

  Reread with the children in the same way.

- Ask the children to listen while you read the rhyme one line at a time.

  Tell the children that they have to listen carefully and be able to tell you the words on which you clap.

  Confirm *stout, spout, shout, out.*

  Ask the children to listen while you read the rhyme and join in by clapping on the rhyming words.

  Ask the children which words they clapped on.

  Confirm *stout, spout, shout, out* respectively.

  Ask the children what they notice about these words.

  Repeat the words *stout, spout, shout, out* with emphasis on the rhyme. Confirm that they all sound the same at the end: they rhyme.

- Ask the children to "read" the rhyme with you again. (*Use pointer to draw children's attention to direction of print for reading and the return sweep in continuous writing. Also introduce them to the idea of the relationship between the spoken word and the written word.*)

  Point to and emphasise the rhyming words. The children may continue to clap on the rhyming words.

- Reread "I'm a little teapot".

  Ask: "What are the rhyming words?"

  Confirm *stout, spout, shout, out.*

Say: "These words sound the same at the end."

Ask: "What do we call words that sound the same at the end?"

Confirm rhyming words.

■ Tell the children that you are going to say three words and two of them rhyme (sound the same at the end). Invite the children to tell you which two words rhyme:

out   go   shout   spout out play
apple stout out   shout big spout

When the children give a correct answer, repeat the correct words, for example, *out* and *shout*.

Say: "Yes, *out* and *shout* sound the same at the end, they rhyme."

■ Reread "I'm a little teapot".

LESSON 2

■ Repeat the above procedure for "Wee Willie Winkie", pages 4 and 5.

Rhyming words: *town* and *gown*, *lock* and *clock*.

Ask: "Which two words rhyme?"

down up   town   green gown   brown
sock lock shoe   rock   sweet clock

LESSON 3

■ Repeat the above procedure for "Twinkle, twinkle", page 6.

Rhyming words: *star* and *are*, *high* and *sky*.

Ask: "Which two words rhyme?"

far car bus   moon bar   star
fly sky boat   tie   shirt high

LESSON 4

■ Repeat the above procedure for "Dan, Dan", page 7.

Rhyming words: *man* and *pan*, *hair* and *chair*.

Ask: "Which two words rhyme?"

man   boy fan   pan   ran   walk
chair dog bear   hair stair cat

LESSON 5

■ Repeat the above procedure for "Here is the sea", pages 8 and 9.

Rhyming words: *sea* and *me*, *below* and *go*.

Ask: "Which two words rhyme?":

tree out sea   bee me   look
go   leg sow   he   grow blow

DEVELOPING SKILLS

Some or all of these activities must be done to ensure progress:

■ **Paint and display**

Large picture of the main focus of the rhyme with the accompanying written rhyme.

Rhyming pictures – sets of pictures of things that rhyme.

Suggested sets of pictures:

mug   jug   rug
van   man   can
sock   lock   clock
ring   king   swing
snail pail   whale
boat   goat   coat

■ **Complete the rhyme**

Recite a rhyme, missing out a rhyming word. Encourage the children to provide it.

■ **Spot the mistake**

Recite a well-known rhyme and substitute a non-rhyming word for the rhyming word. Ask the children to provide the correct rhyming word. Example:

"Humpty Dumpty sat on a wall,
Humpty Dumpty had a great jump . . ."

■ **Listen for the rhyme**

Stick or draw a picture on the board, for example a flag.

Say a list of words and ask the children to raise their hands when they hear a word that rhymes with the picture.

Suggested words:

bell   bag   book jag rag teddy
chair wag   doll tag sag rain

■ **Let's rhyme**

Listen to, recite, sing and learn nursery, playground and other rhymes.

ACTIVITIES AT HOME

■ Encourage the children to ask their parents or other adults to tell them a rhyme they learned when they were young.

■ Look for two objects or pictures of things that rhyme to take to school.

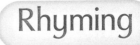

Rhyming

3

Concept of rhyme

THE NLF AIMS

- Recognise when two sounds rhyme.
- Work towards being able to continue a rhyming string.

WHAT YOU NEED

RESOURCES

- *Candy Cat's Big Book of Rhymes (Traditional)* page 10
- Copymaster 1

KEY LESSON POINTERS

VOCABULARY

rhyme   sounds the same   end
word   line

THE CHILDREN should throughout the lesson:

- listen to and focus on the rhythm and rhyme of the language.

YOU should throughout the lesson:

- emphasise the rhythm and rhyme by tapping to keep the rhythm and encouraging the children to clap on the rhyme
- focus on one-to-one correspondence between the spoken and the written word.

STARTING THE LESSON

- Show the children *Candy Cat's Big Book of Rhymes (Traditional)* and open at page 10.

  Ask the children to look at the pictures carefully.

  Discuss the contents of the picture. Familiarise the children with the vocabulary in the rhyme and ensure that they understand it.

TEACHING THE LESSON

- Read "One, two, three, four".

  Reread emphasising the rhythm and rhyme. (*As you read, gently tap your foot or tap on your thigh to keep rhythm, and clap on the rhyming words.*)

  Ask the children to "read" the rhyme with you, inviting them to clap when you do: on the rhyming words.

  Reread with the children in the same way.

- Ask the children to listen while you read the rhyme one line at a time.

  Tell them that they have to listen carefully and be able to tell you the words on which you clap.

  Confirm *four, door, eight, plate* respectively.

  Ask the children to listen while you read the rhyme and to join in by clapping on the rhyming words.

  Ask the children which words they clapped on.

  Confirm *four, door, eight, plate.*

  Ask the children what they notice about *four* and *door*.

  Confirm that they sound the same at the end, that is, they rhyme.

  Ask the children what they notice about *eight* and *plate*.

  Confirm that they sound the same at the end, that is, they rhyme.

  Ask the children to "read" the rhyme with you again. (*Use pointer to draw children's attention to direction of print for reading and the return sweep in continuous writing. Also introduce them to the idea of the relationship between the spoken word and the written word.*)

  Point to and emphasise the rhyming words. The children may continue to clap on the rhyming words.

- Reread "One, two, three four".

  Ask: "What are the rhyming words?"

4

Confirm *four* and *door, eight* and *plate* – words that sound the same at the end.

Ask: "What do we call words that sound the same at the end?"

Confirm rhyming words.

■ Tell the children that you are going to say three words and two of them rhyme (sound the same at the end). Invite the children to tell you which two words rhyme:

four   shore two   core door window
garden eight date   plate cup   date

When the children give a correct answer, repeat the correct words, for example, *four* and *shore*.

Say: "Yes, *four* and *shore* sound the same at the end, they rhyme."

Reread "One, two, three, four".

NOW OR LATER

■ Distribute Copymaster 1.

Section 1

■ Ask the children to identify the first three pictures.

Confirm *window, door, chimney*.

Tell the children that you will read "One, two, three, four" and leave out a rhyming word.

Recite "One, two, three, four,
          Jenny at the cottage _ _ _ _". (*door*)

Ask the children to point to the picture that completes the rhyme.

Ask the children to circle the picture.

■ Repeat the procedure for
"Five, six, seven, eight,
Eating cherries off a _ _ _ _ _". (*plate*)

Section 2

■ Ask the children to identify the pictures.

Confirm *plate, tree, flower, gate*.

Ask the children to draw a circle around the plate.

Ask the children to point to the picture that rhymes with *plate* and draw a circle around it. (*gate*)

■ Tell the children that they should now colour the pictures that they have put a circle around.

Check that the children understand the instructions by asking questions like:

"Will you colour the chimney?"
"Will you colour the plate?"
"How many pictures will you colour?"

DEVELOPING SKILLS

Some or all of these activities must be done to ensure progress:

■ **Paint and display**

Large picture of the main focus of the rhyme with the accompanying written rhyme.

Rhyming pictures – sets of pictures of things that rhyme.

Suggested sets of pictures:
seat	sweet	feet
stone	cone	bone
ball	fall	wall
chick	brick	stick
book	cook	hook
snake	cake	rake

■ **Complete the rhyme**

Recite a rhyme, missing out a rhyming word. Encourage the children to provide it.

■ **Spot the mistake**

Recite a well-known rhyme and substitute a non-rhyming word for the rhyming word. Ask the children to provide the correct rhyming word. Example:

"I'm a little teapot, short and stout. Here's my handle, here's my lid . . ."

■ **Listen for the rhyme**

Stick or draw a picture on the board, for example a cake.

Say a list of words and ask the children to raise their hands when they hear a word that rhymes with the picture.

Suggested words:
bake	car	name	rake	lake
bus	wake	spade	take	shake
sheet	flake	snake		

■ **Let's rhyme**

Listen to, recite, sing and learn nursery, playground and other rhymes.

ACTIVITIES AT HOME

■ Encourage the children to ask their parents or other adults to tell them a rhyme they learned when they were young.

■ Look for two objects or pictures of things that rhyme to take to school.

Rhyming

Concept of rhyme

BEFORE YOU START

THE NLF AIMS

- Recognise when two sounds rhyme.
- Work towards being able to continue a rhyming string.

WHAT YOU NEED

RESOURCES

- *Candy Cat's Big Book of Rhymes (Traditional)* page 11
- Copymaster 2

KEY LESSON POINTERS

VOCABULARY

rhyme   sounds the same   end   word   line

THE CHILDREN should throughout the lesson:

- listen to and focus on the rhythm and rhyme of the language.

YOU should throughout the lesson:

- emphasise the rhythm and rhyme by tapping to keep the rhythm and encouraging the children to clap on the rhyme
- focus on one-to-one correspondence between the spoken and the written word.

THE LESSON

STARTING THE LESSON

- Show the children *Candy Cat's Big Book of Rhymes (Traditional)* and open at page 11.

  Ask the children to look at the pictures carefully.

  Discuss the contents of the picture. Familiarise the children with the vocabulary in the rhyme and ensure that they understand it.

TEACHING THE LESSON

- Read "The elephant goes like this".

  Reread emphasising the rhythm and rhyme. (*As you read, gently tap your foot or tap on your thigh to keep rhythm, and clap on the rhyming words.*)

  Ask the children to "read" the rhyme with you, inviting them to clap when you do: on the rhyming words.

  Reread with the children in the same way.

- Ask the children to listen while you read the rhyme one line at a time.

  Tell them that they have to listen carefully and be able to tell you the words on which you clap.

  Confirm *that, hat, toes, nose*.

  Ask the children to listen while you read the rhyme and to clap on the rhyming words.

  Ask the children which words they clapped on.

  Confirm *that, hat, toes, nose*.

  Ask the children what they notice about *that* and *hat*.

  Confirm that they sound the same at the end, that is, they rhyme.

  Ask the children what they notice about *toes* and *nose*.

  Confirm that they sound the same at the end, that is, they rhyme.

  Ask the children to "read" the rhyme with you again. (*Use pointer to draw children's attention to direction of print for reading and the return sweep in continuous writing. Also introduce them to the idea of the relationship between the spoken word and the written word.*)

  Point to and emphasise the rhyming words. The children may continue to clap on the rhyming words.

- Reread "The elephant goes like this".

  Ask: "What are the rhyming words?"

  Confirm *that* and *hat*, *toes* and *nose* – words that sound the same at the end.

FUN Phonics

Ask: "What do we call words that sound the same at the end?"

Confirm rhyming words.

■ Tell the children that you are going to say three words and two of them rhyme (sound the same at the end). Invite the children to tell you which two words rhyme:

bat   cat   mouse   mat   door   chat
rose   hose   book   nose   head   grows

When the children give a correct answer, repeat the correct words, for example, *bat* and *cat*.

Say: "Yes, *bat* and *cat* sound the same at the end, they rhyme."

Reread "The elephant goes like this".

NOW OR LATER

■ Distribute Copymaster 2.

Section 1

■ Ask the children to identify the first three pictures.

Confirm *coat, scarf, hat.*

Tell the children that you will read "The elephant goes like this" and leave out a rhyming word.

Recite "The elephant goes like this, like that.
    He's terribly big and wears a _ _ _". (*hat*)

Ask the children to point to the picture that completes the rhyme.

Ask the children to circle the picture.

■ Repeat the procedure for
"He has no fingers, he has no toes,
But goodness gracious, what a _ _ _ _". (*nose*)

Section 2

■ Ask the children to identify the pictures.

Confirm *hat, rabbit, duck, cat.*

Ask the children to draw a circle around the hat.

Ask the children to point to the picture of an object that rhymes with *hat* and draw a circle around it. (*cat*)

■ Tell the children that they should now colour the pictures that they have put a circle around.

Check that the children understand the instructions by asking questions like:

"Will you colour the scarf?"
"Will you colour the nose?"
"How many pictures will you colour?"

DEVELOPING SKILLS

Some or all of these activities must be done to ensure progress:

■ **Paint and display**

Large picture of the main focus of the rhyme with the accompanying written rhyme.

Rhyming pictures – sets of pictures of things that rhyme.

Suggested sets of pictures:
seat   sweet   feet
stone   cone   bone
ball   fall   wall
chick   brick   stick
book   cook   hook
snake   cake   rake

■ **Complete the rhyme**

Recite a rhyme, missing out a rhyming word. Encourage the children to provide it.

■ **Spot the mistake**

Recite a well-known rhyme and substitute a non-rhyming word for the rhyming word. Ask the children to provide the correct rhyming word. Example:

"Dan, Dan, the funny wee man
Washed his face in the frying pot . . ."

■ **Listen for the rhyme**

Stick or draw a picture on the board, for example a ring.

Say a list of words and ask the children to raise their hands when they hear a word that rhymes with the picture.

Suggested words:
swing   bed   king   thing   dinner
shed   church   swing   wing   clock
sting   bath   bring

■ **Let's rhyme**

Listen to, recite, sing and learn nursery, playground and other rhymes.

ACTIVITIES AT HOME

■ Encourage the children to ask their parents or other adults to tell them a rhyme they learned when they were young.

■ Look for two objects or pictures of things that rhyme to take to school.

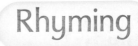
Rhyming

Concept of rhyme

BEFORE YOU START

THE NLF AIMS

- Recognise when two sounds rhyme.
- Work towards being able to continue a rhyming string.

WHAT YOU NEED

RESOURCES

- *Candy Cat's Big Book of Rhymes (Traditional)* pages 12 and 13
- Copymaster 3

KEY LESSON POINTERS

VOCABULARY

rhyme   sounds the same   end
word   line

THE CHILDREN should throughout the lesson:

- listen to and focus on the rhythm and rhyme of the language.

YOU should throughout the lesson:

- emphasise the rhythm and rhyme by tapping to keep the rhythm and encouraging the children to clap on the rhyme
- focus on one-to-one correspondence between the spoken and the written word.

THE LESSON

STARTING THE LESSON

- Show the children *Candy Cat's Big Book of Rhymes (Traditional)* and open at pages 12 and 13.

  Ask the children to look at the pictures carefully.

  Discuss the contents of the picture. Familiarise the children with the vocabulary in the rhyme and ensure that they understand it.

TEACHING THE LESSON

- Read "Pussy Cat, Pussy Cat".

  Reread emphasising the rhythm and rhyme. (*As you read, gently tap your foot or tap on your thigh to keep rhythm, and clap on the rhyming words.*)

  Ask the children to "read" the rhyme with you, inviting them to clap when you do: on the rhyming words.

  Reread with the children in the same way.

- Ask the children to listen while you read the rhyme one line at a time.

  Tell them that they have to listen carefully and be able to tell you the words on which you clap.

  Confirm ***been, Queen, there, chair***.

  Ask the children to listen while you read the rhyme and to clap on the rhyming words.

  Ask the children which words they clapped on.

  Confirm ***been, Queen, there, chair***.

  Ask the children what they notice about ***been*** and ***Queen***.

  Confirm that they sound the same at the end, that is, they rhyme.

  Ask the children what they notice about ***there*** and ***chair***.

  Confirm that they sound the same at the end, that is, they rhyme.

  Ask the children to "read" the rhyme with you again. (*Use pointer to draw children's attention to direction of print for reading and the return sweep in continuous writing. Also introduce them to the idea of the relationship between the spoken word and the written word.*)

  Point to and emphasise the rhyming words. The children may continue to clap on the rhyming words.

- Reread "Pussy Cat, Pussy Cat".

  Ask: "What are the rhyming words?"

  Confirm ***been*** and ***Queen, there*** and ***chair*** – words that sound the same at the end.

Ask: "What do we call words that sound the same at the end?"

Confirm rhyming words.

■ Tell the children that you are going to say three words and two of them rhyme (sound the same at the end). Invite the children to tell you which two words rhyme:

clean   white   mean   king   bean   queen
hair   chair   ribbon   where   go   there

When the children give a correct answer, repeat the correct words, for example, *clean* and *mean*.

Say: "Yes, *clean* and *mean* sound the same at the end, they rhyme."

■ Reread "Pussy Cat, Pussy Cat".

NOW OR LATER

■ Distribute Copymaster 3.

Section 1

■ Ask the children to identify the first three pictures.

Confirm *queen, bride, groom*.

Tell the children that you will read "Pussy Cat, Pussy Cat" and leave out a rhyming word.

Recite "Pussy Cat, Pussy Cat, where have you been? I've been to London to visit the _ _ _ _ _". (*Queen*)

Ask the children to point to the picture that completes the rhyme.

Ask the children to circle the picture.

■ Repeat the procedure for "Pussy Cat, Pussy Cat, what did you there? I frightened a little mouse under a _ _ _ _ _". (*chair*)

Section 2

■ Ask the children to identify the pictures.

Confirm *chair, banana, pear, apple*.

Ask the children to draw a circle around the chair.

Ask the children to point to the picture of an object that rhymes with *chair* and draw a circle around it. (*pear*)

■ Tell the children that they should now colour the pictures that they have put a circle around.

Check that the children understand the instructions by asking questions like:

"Will you colour the queen?"
"Will you colour the table?"
"How many pictures will you colour?"

DEVELOPING SKILLS

Some or all of these activities must be done to ensure progress:

■ **Paint and display**

Large picture of the main focus of the rhyme with the accompanying written rhyme.

Rhyming pictures – sets of pictures of things that rhyme.

Suggested sets of pictures:

seat   sweet   feet
stone   cone   bone
ball   fall   wall
chick   brick   stick
book   cook   hook
snake   cake   rake

■ **Complete the rhyme**

Recite a rhyme, missing out a rhyming word. Encourage the children to provide it.

■ **Spot the mistake**

Recite a well-known rhyme and substitute a non-rhyming word for the rhyming word. Ask the children to provide the correct rhyming word. Example:

"The elephant goes like this, like that. He's terribly big and wears a scarf . . ."

■ **Listen for the rhyme**

Stick or draw a picture on the board, for example a sweet.

Say a list of words and ask the children to raise their hands when they hear a word that rhymes with the picture.

Suggested words:

heat   duck   horse   meat
feet   bag   seat   biscuit
wheat   neat   glasses   beat
greet   basket   sheet

■ **Let's rhyme**

Listen to, recite, sing and learn nursery, playground and other rhymes.

ACTIVITIES AT HOME

■ Encourage the children to ask their parents or other adults to tell them a rhyme they learned when they were young.

■ Look for two objects or pictures of things that rhyme to take to school.

Rhyming

Concept of rhyme

THE NLF AIMS

- Recognise when two sounds rhyme.
- Work towards being able to continue a rhyming string.

WHAT YOU NEED

RESOURCES

- *Candy Cat's Big Book of Rhymes (Traditional)* pages 14 and 15
- Copymaster 4

KEY LESSON POINTERS

VOCABULARY

rhyme   sounds the same   end word   line

THE CHILDREN should throughout the lesson:

- listen to and focus on the rhythm and rhyme of the language.

YOU should throughout the lesson:

- emphasise the rhythm and rhyme by tapping to keep the rhythm and encouraging the children to clap on the rhyme
- focus on one-to-one correspondence between the spoken and the written word.

THE LESSON

STARTING THE LESSON

- Show the children *Candy Cat's Big Book of Rhymes (Traditional)* and open at pages 14 and 15.

  Ask the children to look at the pictures carefully.

  Discuss the contents of the picture. Familiarise the children with the vocabulary in the rhyme and ensure that they understand it.

TEACHING THE LESSON

- Read "Hey diddle diddle".

  Reread emphasising the rhythm and rhyme. (*As you read, gently tap your foot or tap on your thigh to keep rhythm, and clap on the rhyming words.*)

  Ask the children to "read" the rhyme with you, inviting them to clap when you do: on the rhyming words.

  Reread with the children in the same way.

- Ask the children to listen while you read the rhyme one line at a time.

  Tell them that they have to listen carefully and be able to tell you the words on which you clap.

  Confirm *diddle, fiddle, moon, spoon*.

  Ask the children to listen while you read the rhyme and to clap on the rhyming words.

  Ask the children which words they clapped on.

  Confirm *diddle, fiddle, moon, spoon*.

  Ask the children what they notice about *diddle* and *fiddle*.

  Confirm that they sound the same at the end, that is, they rhyme.

  Ask the children what they notice about *moon* and *spoon*.

  Confirm that they sound the same at the end, that is, they rhyme.

  Ask the children to "read" the rhyme with you again. (*Use pointer to draw children's attention to direction of print for reading and the return sweep in continuous writing. Also introduce them to the idea of the relationship between the spoken word and the written word.*)

  Point to and emphasise the rhyming words. The children may continue to clap on the rhyming words.

- Reread "Hey diddle diddle".

  Ask: "What are the rhyming words?"

  Confirm *diddle* and *fiddle*, *moon* and *spoon* – words that sound the same at the end.

Ask: "What do we call words that sound the same at the end?"

Confirm rhyming words.

■ Tell the children that you are going to say three words and two of them rhyme (sound the same at the end). Invite the children to tell you which two words rhyme:

fiddle middle end   riddle lamp diddle

soon June August   prune song tune

When the children give a correct answer, repeat the correct words, for example, **soon** and **June**.

Say: "Yes, **soon** and **June** sound the same at the end, they rhyme."

■ Reread "Hey diddle diddle".

NOW OR LATER

■ Distribute Copymaster 4.

Section 1

■ Ask the children to identify the first three pictures.

Confirm **trumpet, drum, fiddle**.

Tell the children that you will read "Hey diddle diddle" and leave out a rhyming word.

Recite "Hey diddle diddle
        the cat and the _ _ _ _ _ _". (*fiddle*)

Ask the children to point to the picture that completes the rhyme.

Ask the children to circle the picture.

■ Repeat the procedure for
"The cow jumped over the moon.
The little boy laughed
To see such fun
And the dish ran away with the _ _ _ _ _". (*spoon*)

Section 2

■ Ask the children to identify the pictures.

Confirm **spoon, star, moon, cloud**.

Ask the children to draw a circle around the spoon.

Ask the children to point to the picture of an object that rhymes with **spoon** and draw a circle around it. (*moon*)

■ Tell the children that they should now colour the pictures that they have put a circle around.

Check that the children understand the instructions by asking questions like:

"Will you colour the spoon?"
"Will you colour the fork?"
"How many pictures will you colour?"

FURTHER PRACTICE

DEVELOPING SKILLS

Some or all of these activities must be done to ensure progress:

■ **Paint and display**

Large picture of the main focus of the rhyme with the accompanying written rhyme.

Rhyming pictures – sets of pictures of things that rhyme.

Suggested sets of pictures:

seat	sweet	feet
stone	cone	bone
ball	fall	wall
chick	brick	stick
book	cook	hook
snake	cake	rake

■ **Complete the rhyme**

Recite a rhyme, missing out a rhyming word. Encourage the children to provide it.

■ **Spot the mistake**

Recite a well-known rhyme and substitute a non-rhyming word for the rhyming word. Ask the children to provide the correct rhyming word.

■ **Listen for the rhyme**

Stick or draw a picture on the board, for example a chair.

Say a list of words and ask the children to raise their hands when they hear a word that rhymes with the picture.

Suggested words:

bear	cat	garden	hair	stair
tree	wear	pear	stone	fair
bush	bucket	share		

■ **Let's rhyme**

Listen to, recite, sing and learn nursery, playground and other rhymes.

ACTIVITIES AT HOME

■ Encourage the children to ask their parents or other adults to tell them a rhyme they learned when they were young.

■ Look for two objects or pictures of things that rhyme to take to school.

Rhyming

Concept of rhyme

THE NLF AIMS

- Recognise when two sounds rhyme.
- Work towards being able to continue a rhyming string.

WHAT YOU NEED

RESOURCES

- *Candy Cat's Big Book of Rhymes (Traditional)* pages 16 and 17
- Copymaster 5

KEY LESSON POINTERS

VOCABULARY

rhyme   sounds the same   end
word   line

THE CHILDREN should throughout the lesson:

- listen to and focus on the rhythm and rhyme of the language.

YOU should throughout the lesson:

- emphasise the rhythm and rhyme by tapping to keep the rhythm and encouraging the children to clap on the rhyme
- focus on one-to-one correspondence between the spoken and the written word.

THE LESSON

STARTING THE LESSON

- Show the children *Candy Cat's Big Book of Rhymes (Traditional)* and open at pages 16 and 17.

  Ask the children to look at the pictures carefully.

  Discuss the contents of the picture. Familiarise the children with the vocabulary in the rhyme and ensure that they understand it.

TEACHING THE LESSON

- Read "Sing a song of sixpence".

  Reread emphasising the rhythm and rhyme. (*As you read, gently tap your foot or tap on your thigh to keep rhythm, and clap on the rhyming words.*)

  Ask the children to "read" the rhyme with you, inviting them to clap when you do: on the rhyming words.

  Reread with the children in the same way.

- Ask the children to listen while you read the rhyme one line at a time.

  Tell them that they have to listen carefully and be able to tell you the words on which you clap.

  Confirm *rye, pie, sing, King*.

  Ask the children to listen while you read the rhyme and to clap on the rhyming words.

  Ask the children which words they clapped on.

  Confirm *rye, pie, sing, King*.

  Ask the children to "read" the rhyme with you again. (*Use pointer to draw children's attention to direction of print for reading and the return sweep in continuous writing. Also introduce them to the idea of the relationship between the spoken word and the written word.*)

  Point to and emphasise the rhyming words. The children may continue to clap on the rhyming words.

- Reread "Sing a song of sixpence".

  Ask: "What are the rhyming words?"

  Confirm *rye* and *pie*, *sing* and *King* – words that sound the same at the end.

  Ask: "What do we call words that sound the same at the end?"

  Confirm rhyming words.

■ Tell the children that you are going to say three words and two of them rhyme (sound the same at the end). Invite the children to tell you which two words rhyme:

tie   goat   fly   cry   pie   cake
park swing   ring   king queen bring

When the children give a correct answer, repeat the correct words, for example *tie* and *fly*.

Say: "Yes, *tie* and *fly* sound the same at the end, they rhyme."

■ Reread "Sing a song of sixpence".

NOW OR LATER

■ Distribute Copymaster 5.

Section 1

■ Ask the children to identify the first three pictures.

Confirm *cake, pie, bread*.

Tell the children that you will read "Sing a song of sixpence" and leave out a rhyming word.

Recite "Sing a song of sixpence,
    A pocketful of rye.
    Four and twenty blackbirds
    Baked in a _ _ _". (*pie*)

Ask the children to point to the picture that completes the rhyme.

Ask the children to circle the picture.

■ Repeat the procedure for
"When the pie was opened
The birds began to sing.
Wasn't that a dainty dish
To set before the _ _ _ _". (*King*)

Section 2

■ Ask the children to identify the pictures.

Confirm *pie, tie, scarf, glove*.

Ask the children to draw a circle around the pie.

Ask the children to point to the picture of an object that rhymes with *pie* and draw a circle around it. (*tie*)

■ Tell the children that they should now colour the pictures that they have put a circle around.

Check that the children understand the instructions by asking questions like:

"Will you colour the clown?"
"Will you colour the pie?"
"How many pictures will you colour?"

FURTHER PRACTICE

DEVELOPING SKILLS

Some or all of these activities must be done to ensure progress:

■ **Paint and display**

Large picture of the main focus of the rhyme with the accompanying written rhyme.

Rhyming pictures – sets of pictures of things that rhyme.

Suggested sets of pictures:

seat	sweet	feet
stone	cone	bone
ball	fall	wall
chick	brick	stick
book	cook	hook
snake	cake	rake

■ **Complete the rhyme**

Recite a rhyme, missing out a rhyming word. Encourage the children to provide it.

■ **Spot the mistake**

Recite a well-known rhyme and substitute a non-rhyming word for the rhyming word. Ask the children to provide the correct rhyming word.

■ **Listen for the rhyme**

Stick or draw a picture on the board, for example a boat.

Say a list of words and ask the children to raise their hands when they hear a word that rhymes with the picture.

Suggested words:

dress	coat	float	shoes
goat	slippers	watch	note
wrote	ground	vote	shelf

■ **Let's rhyme**

Listen to, recite, sing and learn nursery, playground and other rhymes.

ACTIVITIES AT HOME

■ Encourage the children to ask their parents or other adults to tell them a rhyme they learned when they were young.

■ Look for two objects or pictures of things that rhyme to take to school.

Rhyming

Concept of rhyme

BEFORE YOU START

THE NLF AIMS

- Recognise when two sounds rhyme.
- Work towards being able to continue a rhyming string.

WHAT YOU NEED

RESOURCES

- *Candy Cat's Big Book of Rhymes (Traditional)* pages 18 and 19
- Copymaster 6

KEY LESSON POINTERS

VOCABULARY

rhyme   sounds the same   end
word   line   odd one out

THE CHILDREN should throughout the lesson:

- listen to and focus on the rhythm and rhyme of the language.

YOU should throughout the lesson:

- emphasise the rhythm and rhyme by tapping to keep the rhythm and encouraging the children to clap on the rhyme
- focus on one-to-one correspondence between the spoken and the written word.

THE LESSON

STARTING THE LESSON

- Show the children *Candy Cat's Big Book of Rhymes (Traditional)* and open at pages 18 and 19.

  Ask the children to look at the pictures carefully.

  Discuss the contents of the picture. Familiarise the children with the vocabulary in the rhyme and ensure that they understand it.

TEACHING THE LESSON

- Read "Little Boy Blue".

  Reread emphasising the rhythm and rhyme. (*As you read, gently tap your foot or tap on your thigh to keep rhythm, and clap on the rhyming words.*)

  Ask the children to "read" the rhyme with you, inviting them to clap when you do: on the rhyming words.

  Reread with the children in the same way.

- Ask the children to tell you two words that rhyme in "Little Boy Blue".

  Confirm: ***horn*** and ***corn***, ***sheep*** and ***asleep***,

        I and ***cry***.

  Ask the children: "What do you mean when you say that two words rhyme?"

  Confirm that the words sound the same at the end.

- Tell the children that you are going to say three words and they have to tell you which word is the odd one out, that is, the one that doesn't rhyme.

  Suggested words:

blue	glue	water	horn	pink	thorn
flew	book	chew	stew	born	corn
band	hand	foot	big	wet	get
fix	bowl	mix	pan	flan	soup

  Encourage the children to explain why a certain word is the odd one out, for example, "**Water** *is the odd one out because it doesn't rhyme with* **blue** *and* **glue**."

- Tell the children that they have to think of another word that rhymes with *horn* and *corn*.

  Suggested words:
  born   thorn   torn.

  (*Children may find this difficult at first so help them by giving a choice. For example: "Which word would rhyme with* **horn** *and* **corn** – **born** *or* **go**?"*)

- Encourage the children to put the words into a rap with actions, for example, *horn* and *corn*: "Click left fingers as you say *horn*, click right fingers as you say *corn*." Say: "They rhyme with *born*. Clap hands on *born*."

  Repeat the procedure for words that rhyme with *sheep* and *asleep*.

  Suggested words:
  keep   peep   jeep   weep   deep   sweep

  Repeat the procedure for words that rhyme with *I* and *cry*.

  Suggested words:
  tie   buy   my   fly   shy   try
  pie   die   fry   high   lie

- Reread "Little Boy Blue".

NOW OR LATER

- Distribute Copymaster 6.

- Ask the children to identify the first three pictures.

  Confirm *shoe, mouse, fish*.

- Tell the children that you will read a list of rhyming words and they have to choose and circle the picture of an object that completes the rhyming pattern.

  Read *blue, new, glue*.

  Children circle the shoe.

- Repeat the procedure for
  corn, born, thorn . . . (*horn*).
  sleep, cheep, keep . . . (*sheep*).
  cry, tie, why . . . (*fly*).

- Children colour the circled pictures.

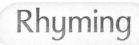

FURTHER PRACTICE

DEVELOPING SKILLS

Some or all of these activities must be done to ensure progress:

- **Paint and display**

  Large picture of the main focus of the rhyme with the accompanying written rhyme.

  Rhyming pictures – sets of pictures of things that rhyme.

  Suggested sets of pictures:

hat	cat	bat
boot	suit	root
hose	rose	toes
chair	bear	pear
handle	candle	sandal
gate	plate	eight

- **Complete the rhyme**

  Recite a rhyme, missing out a rhyming word. Encourage the children to provide it.

- **Spot the mistake**

  Recite a well-known rhyme and substitute a non-rhyming word for the rhyming word. Ask the children to provide the correct rhyming word.

- **Listen for the rhyme**

  Stick or draw a picture on the board, for example a tree.

  Say a list of words and ask the children to raise their hands when they hear a word that rhymes with the picture.

  Suggested words:

we	me	lock	see
wing	ride	three	tea
tame	flee	knee	saw
club	bee		

- **Let's rhyme**

  Listen to, recite, sing and learn nursery, playground and other rhymes.

ACTIVITIES AT HOME

- Encourage the children to ask their parents or other adults to tell them a rhyme they learned when they were young.

- Look for two objects or pictures of things that rhyme to take to school.

Rhyming

Concept of rhyme

THE NLF AIMS

- Recognise when two sounds rhyme.
- Work towards being able to continue a rhyming string.

WHAT YOU NEED

RESOURCES

- *Candy Cat's Big Book of Rhymes (Traditional)* pages 20 and 21
- Copymaster 7

KEY LESSON POINTERS

VOCABULARY

rhyme   sounds the same   end
word   line   odd one out

THE CHILDREN should throughout the lesson:

- listen to and focus on the rhythm and rhyme of the language.

YOU should throughout the lesson:

- emphasise the rhythm and rhyme by tapping to keep the rhythm and encouraging the children to clap on the rhyme
- focus on one-to-one correspondence between the spoken and the written word.

STARTING THE LESSON

- Show the children *Candy Cat's Big Book of Rhymes (Traditional)* and open at pages 20 and 21.

  Ask the children to look at the pictures carefully.

  Discuss the contents of the picture. Familiarise the children with the vocabulary in the rhyme and ensure that they understand it.

TEACHING THE LESSON

- Read "One, two, three, four, five".

  Reread emphasising the rhythm and rhyme. (*As you read, gently tap your foot or tap on your thigh to keep rhythm, and clap on the rhyming words.*)

  Ask the children to "read" the rhyme with you, inviting them to clap when you do: on the rhyming words.

  Reread with the children in the same way.

- Ask the children to tell you two words that rhyme in "One, two, three, four, five".

  Confirm: *five* and *alive*, *ten* and *again*, *go* and *so*, *bite* and *right*.

  Ask the children: "What do you mean when you say that two words rhyme?"

  Confirm that the words sound the same at the end.

- Tell the children that you are going to say three words and they have to tell you which word is the odd one out, that is, the one that doesn't rhyme.

  Suggested words:

five	dive	walk	ten	girl	men
go	row	sing	in	right	light
went	sent	run	belt	jump	lump
fast	swim	last	walk	talk	sing

  Encourage the children to explain why a certain word is the odd one out, for example, "**Walk** *is the odd one out because it doesn't rhyme with* **five** *and* **dive**."

  Tell the children that they have to think of another word that rhymes with *five* and *alive*.

  Suggested words:
  dive drive hive jive live

  (*Children may find this difficult at first so help them by giving a choice. For example: "Which word would rhyme with* **five** *and* **alive** *– **drive** or **swing**?"*)

- Encourage the children to put the words into a rap with actions, for example, *five* and *hive*: "Click left fingers as you say *five*, click right fingers as you say *hive*." Say: "They rhyme with *drive*. Clap hands on *drive*."

  Repeat the procedure for words that rhyme with *ten* and *again*.

  Suggested words:
  men   Ben   den   hen
  pen   when   then

  Repeat the procedure for words that rhyme with *go* and *so*.

  Suggested words:
  no   bow   row   show
  grow flow   blow   mow

- Reread "One, two, three, four, five".

NOW OR LATER

- Distribute Copymaster 7.

- Ask the children to identify the first three pictures.

  Confirm *book, five, telephone*.

- Tell the children that you will read a list of rhyming words and they have to choose and circle the picture of an object that completes the rhyming pattern.

  Read *hive, drive, jive*.

  Children circle the five.

- Repeat the procedure for
  when, ten, men . . . (*hen*).
  go, so, low . . . (*bow*).
  bite, night, right . . . (*kite*).

- Children colour the circled pictures.

FURTHER PRACTICE

DEVELOPING SKILLS

Some or all of these activities must be done to ensure progress:

- **Paint and display**

  Large picture of the main focus of the rhyme with the accompanying written rhyme.

  Rhyming pictures – sets of pictures of things that rhyme.

  Suggested sets of pictures:
  hat   cat   bat
  boot   suit   root
  hose   rose   toes
  chair   bear   pear
  handle candle   sandal
  gate   plate   eight

- **Complete the rhyme**

  Recite a rhyme, missing out a rhyming word. Encourage the children to provide it.

- **Spot the mistake**

  Recite a well-known rhyme and substitute a non-rhyming word for the rhyming word. Ask the children to provide the correct rhyming word.

- **Listen for the rhyme**

  Stick or draw a picture on the board, for example a book.

  Say a list of words and ask the children to raise their hands when they hear a word that rhymes with the picture.

  Suggested words:
  hook   pen   took   look   window
  shook train wind   cook   rook

- **Let's rhyme**

  Listen to, recite, sing and learn nursery, playground and other rhymes.

ACTIVITIES AT HOME

- Encourage the children to ask their parents or other adults to tell them a rhyme they learned when they were young.

- Look for two objects or pictures of things that rhyme to take to school.

Rhyming

Concept of rhyme

THE NLF AIMS

- Recognise when two sounds rhyme.
- Work towards being able to continue a rhyming string.

WHAT YOU NEED

RESOURCES

- *Candy Cat's Big Book of Rhymes (Traditional)* pages 22 and 23
- Copymaster 8

KEY LESSON POINTERS

VOCABULARY

rhyme   sounds the same   end
word   line   odd one out

THE CHILDREN should throughout the lesson:

- listen to and focus on the rhythm and rhyme of the language.

YOU should throughout the lesson:

- emphasise the rhythm and rhyme by tapping to keep the rhythm and encouraging the children to clap on the rhyme
- focus on one-to-one correspondence between the spoken and the written word.

STARTING THE LESSON

- Show the children *Candy Cat's Big Book of Rhymes (Traditional)* and open at pages 22 and 23.

  Ask the children to look at the pictures carefully.

  Discuss the contents of the picture. Familiarise the children with the vocabulary in the rhyme and ensure that they understand it.

TEACHING THE LESSON

- Read "Miss Polly had a dolly".

  Reread emphasising the rhythm and rhyme. (*As you read, gently tap your foot or tap on your thigh to keep rhythm, and clap on the rhyming words.*)

  Ask the children to "read" the rhyme with you, inviting them to clap when you do: on the rhyming words.

  Reread with the children in the same way.

- Ask the children to tell you two words that rhyme in "Miss Polly had a dolly".

  Confirm: *sick* and *quick*, *hat* and *tat*,
  dolly and *Polly*, *head* and *bed*,
  pill and *bill*.

  Ask the children: "What do you mean when you say that two words rhyme?"

  Confirm that the words sound the same at the end.

- Tell the children that you are going to say three words and they have to tell you which word is the odd one out, that is, the one that doesn't rhyme.

  Suggested words:

trick	bow	sick	pig	hat	cat
holly	dolly	teddy	bed	green	red
pill	will	happy	loud	rain	cloud
grin	clown	town	ready	teddy	big

  Encourage the children to explain why a certain word is the odd one out, for example, "*Bow is the odd one out because it doesn't rhyme with* **trick** *and* **sick**."

  Tell the children that they have to think of another word that rhymes with *sick* and *quick*.

  Suggested words:

  trick   thick   stick   flick
  pick   tick   brick   wick

  (*Children may find this difficult at first so help them by giving a choice. For example: "Which word would rhyme with* **sick** *and* **quick** – **trick** *or* **just**?")

■ Encourage the children to put the words into a rap with actions, for example, *sick* and *quick*: "Click left fingers as you say *sick*, click right fingers as you say *quick*." Say: "They rhyme with *trick*. Clap hands on *trick*."

Repeat the procedure for words that rhyme with *hat* and *tat*.

Suggested words:
cat bat flat chat mat rat pat sat

Repeat the procedure for words that rhyme with *dolly* and *Polly*.

Suggested words:
holly jolly lolly brolly Molly

Repeat the procedure for words that rhyme with *pill* and *bill*.

Suggested words:
hill   fill   will   Jill   kill   mill
sill   till   frill   chill   drill   grill

Repeat the procedure for words that rhyme with *head* and *bed*.

Suggested words:
red   Ted   wed   dead   fed   led
said   shed bled   fled   bread spread

■ Reread "Miss Polly had a dolly".

NOW OR LATER

■ Distribute Copymaster 8.

■ Ask the children to identify the first three pictures.
Confirm *dolly, jug, pram*.
Tell the children that you will read a list of rhyming words and they have to choose and circle the picture of an object that completes the rhyming pattern.
Read: *holly, brolly, jolly*.
Children circle the dolly.

■ Repeat the procedure for
jag, flag, rag . . . (*bag*)
bat, flat, chat . . . (*hat*)
floor, roar, sore . . . (*door*)

■ Children colour the circled pictures.

FURTHER PRACTICE

DEVELOPING SKILLS

Some or all of these activities must be done to ensure progress:

■ Paint and display

Large picture of the main focus of the rhyme with the accompanying written rhyme.

Rhyming pictures – sets of pictures of things that rhyme.

Suggested sets of pictures:
hat   cat   bat
boot   root   suit
hose   rose   toes
chair   bear   pear
handle   candle   sandal
gate   plate   eight

■ Complete the rhyme

Recite a rhyme, missing out a rhyming word. Encourage the children to provide it.

■ Spot the mistake

Recite a well-known rhyme and substitute a non-rhyming word for the rhyming word. Ask the children to provide the correct rhyming word.

■ Listen for the rhyme

Stick or draw a picture on the board, for example a star.

Say a list of words and ask the children to raise their hands when they hear a word that rhymes with the picture.

Suggested words:
bat   car   bus   hood   jar
bird   tar   pot   far   house

■ Let's rhyme

Listen to, recite, sing and learn nursery, playground and other rhymes.

ACTIVITIES AT HOME

■ Encourage the children to ask their parents or other adults to tell them a rhyme they learned when they were young.

■ Look for two objects or pictures of things that rhyme to take to school.

Rhyming

Concept of rhyme

THE NLF AIMS

- Recognise when two sounds rhyme.
- Work towards being able to continue a rhyming string.

WHAT YOU NEED

RESOURCES

- *Candy Cat's Big Book of Rhymes (Traditional)* pages 24 and 25
- Copymaster 9

KEY LESSON POINTERS

VOCABULARY

rhyme   sounds the same   end
word   line   odd one out

THE CHILDREN should throughout the lesson:

- listen to and focus on the rhythm and rhyme of the language.

YOU should throughout the lesson:

- emphasise the rhythm and rhyme by tapping to keep the rhythm and encouraging the children to clap on the rhyme
- focus on one-to-one correspondence between the spoken and the written word.

STARTING THE LESSON

■ Show the children *Candy Cat's Big Book of Rhymes (Traditional)* and open at pages 24 and 25.

Ask the children to look at the pictures carefully.

Discuss the contents of the picture. Familiarise the children with the vocabulary in the rhyme and ensure that they understand it.

TEACHING THE LESSON

■ Read "Teddy Bear, Teddy Bear".

Reread emphasising the rhythm and rhyme. (*As you read, gently tap your foot or tap on your thigh to keep rhythm, and clap on the rhyming words.*)

Ask the children to "read" the rhyme with you, inviting them to clap when you do: on the rhyming words.

Reread with the children in the same way.

■ Ask the children to tell you two words that rhyme in "Teddy Bear, Teddy Bear".

Confirm: *nose* and *toes*, *ground* and *around*, *stairs* and *prayers*, *light* and *night*.

Ask the children: "What do you mean when you say that two words rhyme?"

Confirm that the words sound the same at the end.

■ Tell the children that you are going to say three words and they have to tell you which word is the odd one out, that is, the one that doesn't rhyme.

Suggested words:

rose	nose	head	sound	noise	ground
lion	stairs	bears	night	sky	bright
jug	sink	plug	clap	trap	fox
fist	hand	mist	go	crab	no

Encourage the children to explain why a certain word is the odd one out, for example, *'Head is the odd one out because it doesn't rhyme with* **rose** *and* **nose**.*"

Tell the children that they have to think of another word that rhymes with *nose* and *toes*.

Suggested words:

rose   hose   doze   goes
grows   blows   shows   froze

(*Children may find this difficult at first so help them by giving a choice. For example: "Which word would rhyme with* **nose** *and* **toes** – **shows** *or* **like?***")

■ Encourage the children to put the words into a rap with actions, for example, *nose* and *toes*: "Click left fingers as you say *nose*, click right fingers as you say *toes*." Say: "They rhyme with *rose*. Clap hands on *rose*."

Repeat the procedure for words that rhyme with *ground* and *around*.

Suggested words:

sound   found   wound
pound   hound   mound

Repeat the procedure for words that rhyme with *stairs* and *prayers*.

Suggested words:

bears   chairs   pears   fares
cares   wears   tears

■ Reread "Teddy Bear, Teddy Bear".

NOW OR LATER

■ Distribute Copymaster 9.

■ Ask the children to identify the first three pictures.

Confirm *toes, hand, feet*.

Tell the children that you will read a list of rhyming words and they have to choose and circle the picture of an object that completes the rhyming pattern.

Read: *nose, goes, grows*.

Children circle the toes.

■ Repeat the procedure for
stair, care, tear . . . (*chair*)
right, white, light . . . (*kite*)
where, hair, pear . . . (*bear*)

■ Children colour the circled pictures.

FURTHER PRACTICE

DEVELOPING SKILLS

Some or all of these activities must be done to ensure progress:

■ **Paint and display**

Large picture of the main focus of the rhyme with the accompanying written rhyme.

Rhyming pictures – sets of pictures of things that rhyme.

Suggested sets of pictures:

hat   cat   bat
boot   suit   root
hose   rose   toes
chair   bear   pear
handle   candle   sandal
gate   plate   eight

■ **Complete the rhyme**

Recite a rhyme, missing out a rhyming word. Encourage the children to provide it.

■ **Spot the mistake**

Recite a well-known rhyme and substitute a non-rhyming word for the rhyming word. Ask the children to provide the correct rhyming word.

■ **Listen for the rhyme**

Stick or draw a picture on the board, for example a zip.

Say a list of words and ask the children to raise their hands when they hear a word that rhymes with the picture.

Suggested words:

drip run   ship lip pie hip ten
pip   chip go   box tip dip lid

■ **Let's rhyme**

Listen to, recite, sing and learn nursery, playground and other rhymes.

ACTIVITIES AT HOME

■ Encourage the children to ask their parents or other adults to tell them a rhyme they learned when they were young.

■ Look for two objects or pictures of things that rhyme to take to school.

Rhyming

Concept of rhyme

THE NLF AIMS

- Recognise when two sounds rhyme.
- Work towards being able to continue a rhyming string.

WHAT YOU NEED

RESOURCES

- *Candy Cat's Big Book of Rhymes (Traditional)* pages 26 and 27
- Copymaster 10

KEY LESSON POINTERS

VOCABULARY

rhyme   sounds the same   end
word   line   odd one out

THE CHILDREN should throughout the lesson:

- listen to and focus on the rhythm and rhyme of the language.

YOU should throughout the lesson:

- emphasise the rhythm and rhyme by tapping to keep the rhythm and encouraging the children to clap on the rhyme
- focus on one-to-one correspondence between the spoken and the written word.

THE LESSON

STARTING THE LESSON

- Show the children *Candy Cat's Big Book of Rhymes (Traditional)* and open at pages 26 and 27.

  Ask the children to look at the pictures carefully.

  Discuss the contents of the picture. Familiarise the children with the vocabulary in the rhyme and ensure that they understand it.

TEACHING THE LESSON

- Read "Jelly on a plate".

  Reread emphasising the rhythm and rhyme. (*As you read, gently tap your foot or tap on your thigh to keep rhythm, and clap on the rhyming words.*)

  Ask the children to "read" the rhyme with you, inviting them to clap when you do: on the rhyming words.

  Reread with the children in the same way.

- Discuss the rhyming patterns, that is, the repetition of words for rhyming patterns, for example:

  plate, plate   wobble, wobble
  pan, pan   over, over

  Ask the children: "What do you mean when you say that two words rhyme?"

  Confirm the words sound the same at the end.

- Tell the children that you are going to say three words and they have to tell you which word is the odd one out, that is, the one that doesn't rhyme.

  Suggested words:

plate	gate	door		duck	gobble	wobble
pan	sing	ran		over	clover	pink
sink	wink	bath		tent	gran	went
bank	toe	sank		wish	fish	dog

  Encourage the children to explain why a certain word is the odd one out, for example, "*Door is the odd one out because it doesn't rhyme with* **plate** *and* **gate**."

Tell the children that they have to think of another word that rhymes with *plate* and *gate*.

Suggested words:

date hate late mate rate wait great

(*Children may find this difficult at first so help them by giving a choice. For example: "Which word would rhyme with* **plate** *and* **gate** *–* **date** *or* **day***?"*)

■ Encourage the children to put the words into a rap with actions, for example, *plate* and *gate*: "Click left fingers as you say *plate*, click right fingers as you say *gate*." Say: "They rhyme with *date*. Clap hands on *date*."

Repeat the procedure for words that rhyme with *gobble* and *wobble*.

Suggested words:

cobble bobble hobble

Repeat the procedure for words that rhyme with *pan* and *ran*.

Suggested words:

ban Dan fan Jan man
tan van plan gran

■ Reread "Jelly on a plate".

NOW OR LATER

■ Distribute Copymaster 10.

■ Ask the children to identify the first three pictures.
Confirm *fork, plate, pot*.
Tell the children that you will read a list of rhyming words and they have to choose and circle the picture of an object that completes the rhyming pattern.
Read: *gate, wait, late*.
Children circle the plate.

■ Repeat the procedure for
fan, can, ran . . . (*pan*)
stand, land, band . . . (*hand*)
red, head, said . . . (*bed*)

■ Children colour the circled pictures.

DEVELOPING SKILLS

Some or all of these activities must be done to ensure progress:

■ **Paint and display**

Large picture of the main focus of the rhyme with the accompanying written rhyme.

Rhyming pictures – sets of pictures of things that rhyme.

Suggested sets of pictures:

hat	cat	bat
boot	suit	root
hose	rose	toes
chair	bear	pear
handle	candle	sandal
gate	plate	eight

■ **Complete the rhyme**

Recite a rhyme, missing out a rhyming word. Encourage the children to provide it.

■ **Spot the mistake**

Recite a well-known rhyme and substitute a non-rhyming word for the rhyming word. Ask the children to provide the correct rhyming word.

■ **Listen for the rhyme**

Stick or draw a picture on the board, for example a net.

Say a list of words and ask the children to raise their hands when they hear a word that rhymes with the picture.

Suggested words:

let	wet	handle	get	wing
clock	met	boot	bet	jet
cook	box	pet		

■ **Let's rhyme**

Listen to, recite, sing and learn nursery, playground and other rhymes.

ACTIVITIES AT HOME

■ Encourage the children to ask their parents or other adults to tell them a rhyme they learned when they were young.

■ Look for two objects or pictures of things that rhyme to take to school.

CONCEPT OF RHYME

RHYMING WORDS

Rhyming

Concept of rhyme

THE NLF AIMS

- Recognise when two sounds rhyme.
- Work towards being able to continue a rhyming string.

WHAT YOU NEED

RESOURCES

- *Candy Cat's Big Book of Rhymes (Traditional)* page 28
- Copymaster 11

KEY LESSON POINTERS

VOCABULARY

rhyme   sounds the same   end
word   line   odd one out

THE CHILDREN should throughout the lesson:

- listen to and focus on the rhythm and rhyme of the language.

YOU should throughout the lesson:

- emphasise the rhythm and rhyme by tapping to keep the rhythm and encouraging the children to clap on the rhyme
- focus on one-to-one correspondence between the spoken and the written word.

STARTING THE LESSON

- Show the children *Candy Cat's Big Book of Rhymes (Traditional)* and open at page 28.

  Ask the children to look at the pictures carefully.

  Discuss the contents of the picture. Familiarise the children with the vocabulary in the rhyme and ensure that they understand it.

TEACHING THE LESSON

- Read "Humpty Dumpty".

  Reread emphasising the rhythm and rhyme. (*As you read, gently tap your foot or tap on your thigh to keep rhythm, and clap on the rhyming words.*)

  Ask the children to "read" the rhyme with you, inviting them to clap when you do: on the rhyming words.

  Reread with the children in the same way.

- Ask the children to tell you two words that rhyme in "Humpty Dumpty".

  Confirm: ***Humpty*** and ***Dumpty***, ***wall*** and ***fall***, ***men*** and ***again***.

  Ask the children: "What do you mean when you say that two words rhyme?"

  Confirm that the words sound the same at the end.

- Tell the children that you are going to say three words and they have to tell you which word is the odd one out, that is, the one that doesn't rhyme.

  Suggested words:

boy	men	hen	when	bat	ten
wall	day	ball	clock	fall	hall
hill	fill	road	rat	clock	sock
bus	goat	coat	wig	park	big

  Encourage the children to explain why a certain word is the odd one out, for example, *"**Boy** is the odd one out because it doesn't rhyme with **men** and **hen**."*

Tell the children that they have to think of another word that rhymes with *wall* and *fall*.

Suggested words:
ball call hall Paul tall

(Children may find this difficult at first so help them by giving a choice. For example: "Which word would rhyme with **wall** *and* **fall** *– **teddy** or* **ball**?")*

■ Encourage the children to put the words into a rap with actions, for example, *wall* and *fall*: "Click left fingers as you say *wall*, click right fingers as you say *fall*." Say: "They rhyme with *ball*. Clap hands on *ball*."

Repeat the procedure for words that rhyme with *men* and *again*.

Suggested words:
ten Ben den hen Jen Ken pen

■ Reread "Humpty Dumpty".

NOW OR LATER

■ Distribute Copymaster 11.

■ Ask the children to identify the first three pictures.

Confirm ***bridge, wall, fence***.

Tell the children that you will read a list of rhyming words and they have to choose and circle the picture of an object that completes the rhyming pattern.

Read: ***fall, ball, tall***.

Children circle the wall.

■ Repeat the procedure for
men, ten, when . . . (*hen*)
run, fun, bun . . . (*sun*)
take, bake, make . . . (*cake*)

■ Children colour the circled pictures.

DEVELOPING SKILLS

Some or all of these activities must be done to ensure progress:

■ **Paint and display**

Large picture of the main focus of the rhyme with the accompanying written rhyme.

Rhyming pictures – sets of pictures of things that rhyme.

Suggested sets of pictures:

hat	cat	bat
boot	suit	root
hose	rose	toes
chair	bear	pear
handle	candle	sandal
gate	plate	eight

■ **Complete the rhyme**

Recite a rhyme, missing out a rhyming word. Encourage the children to provide it.

■ **Spot the mistake**

Recite a well-known rhyme and substitute a non-rhyming word for the rhyming word. Ask the children to provide the correct rhyming word.

■ **Listen for the rhyme**

Stick or draw a picture on the board, for example a ball.

Say a list of words and ask the children to raise their hands when they hear a word that rhymes with the picture.

Suggested words:

hall	frog	wink	fall	hall	hole
shawl	drink	Paul	clasp	belt	tall
call	bend				

■ **Let's rhyme**

Listen to, recite, sing and learn nursery, playground and other rhymes.

ACTIVITIES AT HOME

■ Encourage the children to ask their parents or other adults to tell them a rhyme they learned when they were young.

■ Look for two objects or pictures of things that rhyme to take to school.

Rhyming

Concept of rhyme

THE NLF AIMS

- Recognise when two sounds rhyme.
- Work towards being able to continue a rhyming string.

WHAT YOU NEED

RESOURCES

- *Candy Cat's Big Book of Rhymes (Traditional)* page 29
- Copymaster 12

KEY LESSON POINTERS

VOCABULARY

rhyme   sounds the same   end word   line   odd one out

THE CHILDREN should throughout the lesson:

- listen to and focus on the rhythm and rhyme of the language.

YOU should throughout the lesson:

- emphasise the rhythm and rhyme by tapping to keep the rhythm and encouraging the children to clap on the rhyme
- focus on one-to-one correspondence between the spoken and the written word.

THE LESSON

STARTING THE LESSON

- Show the children *Candy Cat's Big Book of Rhymes (Traditional)* and open at page 29.

  Ask the children to look at the pictures carefully.

  Discuss the contents of the picture. Familiarise the children with the vocabulary in the rhyme and ensure that they understand it.

TEACHING THE LESSON

- Read "Ding dong bell".

  Reread emphasising the rhythm and rhyme. (*As you read, gently tap your foot or tap on your thigh to keep rhythm, and clap on the rhyming words.*)

  Ask the children to "read" the rhyme with you, inviting them to clap when you do: on the rhyming words.

  Reread with the children in the same way.

- Ask the children to tell you two words that rhyme in "Ding dong bell".

  Confirm: *bell* and *well*, *in* and *thin*, *out* and *stout*.

  Ask the children: "What do you mean when you say that two words rhyme?"

  Confirm that the words sound the same at the end.

- Tell the children that you will say three words and they have to tell you which word is the odd one out.

  Suggested words:

bell	shell	sand	thin	sheet	pin
desk	out	stout	well	wish	fish
hug	win	rug	bath	path	sink
belt	milk	silk	huff	puff	run

  Encourage the children to explain why a certain word is the odd one out, for example, "**Sand** *is the odd one out because it doesn't rhyme with* **bell** *and* **shell**."

Tell the children that they have to think of another word that rhymes with **bell** and **well**.

Suggested words:
fell   sell   tell   shell   swell   spell

(*Children may find this difficult at first so help them by giving them a choice. For example: "Which word would rhyme with* **bell** *and* **well** – **walk** *or* **tell**?")

■ Encourage the children to put the words into a rap with actions, for example, **bell** and **well**: "Click left fingers as you say **bell**, click right fingers as you say **well**." Say: "They rhyme with **sell**. Clap hands on **sell**."

Repeat the procedure for words that rhyme with **in** and **thin**.

Suggested words:
pin   bin   din   fin   tin   win   chin   shin

Repeat the procedure for words that rhyme with **out** and **stout**.

Suggested words:
doubt   shout   spout   grout

■ Reread "Ding dong bell."

NOW OR LATER

■ Distribute Copymaster 12.

Ask the children to identify the first three pictures.

Confirm **sun, star, bell**.

Tell the children that you will read a list of rhyming words and they have to choose and circle the picture of an object that rhymes.

Read: **sell, well, fell**

Children circle the bell.

■ Repeat the procedure for:
pin, thin, win . . . (*bin*)
ready, steady, Freddie . . . (*teddy*)
shook, look, took . . . (*book*)

■ Children colour the circled pictures.

DEVELOPING SKILLS

Some or all of these activities must be done to ensure progress:

■ **Paint and display**

Large picture of the main focus of the rhyme with the accompanying written rhyme.

Rhyming pictures – sets of pictures of things that rhyme.

Suggested sets of pictures:

hat	cat	bat
boot	suit	root
hose	rose	toes
chair	bear	pear
handle	candle	sandal
gate	plate	eight

■ **Complete the rhyme**

Recite a rhyme, missing out a rhyming word. Encourage the children to provide it.

■ **Spot the mistake**

Recite a well-known rhyme and substitute a non-rhyming word for the rhyming word. Ask the children to provide the correct rhyming word.

■ **Listen for the rhyme**

Stick or draw a picture on the board, for example a pot.

Say a list of words and ask the children to raise their hands when they hear a word that rhymes with the picture.

Suggested words:

got	shot	hook	ring	not	house
dot	vest	fence	hot	clap	what
pill	taught				

■ **Let's rhyme**

Listen to, recite, sing and learn nursery, playground and other rhymes.

ACTIVITIES AT HOME

■ Encourage the children to ask their parents or other adults to tell them a rhyme they learned when they were young.

■ Look for two objects or pictures of things that rhyme to take to school.

Rhyming

Concept of rhyme

THE NLF AIMS

- Recognise when two sounds rhyme.
- Work towards being able to continue a rhyming string.

WHAT YOU NEED

RESOURCES

- *Candy Cat's Big Book of Rhymes (Traditional)* pages 30 and 31
- Copymaster 13
- Assessment 1.1, 1.2

KEY LESSON POINTERS

VOCABULARY

rhyme   sounds the same   end
word   line   odd one out

THE CHILDREN should throughout the lesson:

- listen to and focus on the rhythm and rhyme of the language.

YOU should throughout the lesson:

- emphasise the rhythm and rhyme by tapping to keep the rhythm and encouraging the children to clap on the rhyme
- focus on one-to-one correspondence between the spoken and the written word.

THE LESSON

STARTING THE LESSON

- Show the children *Candy Cat's Big Book of Rhymes (Traditional)* and open at pages 30 and 31.

  Ask the children to look at the pictures carefully.

  Discuss the contents of the picture. Familiarise the children with the vocabulary in the rhyme and ensure that they understand it.

TEACHING THE LESSON

- Read "Mrs White".

  Reread emphasising the rhythm and rhyme. (*As you read, gently tap your foot or tap on your thigh to keep rhythm, and clap on the rhyming words.*)

  Ask the children to "read" the rhyme with you, inviting them to clap when you do: on the rhyming words.

  Reread with the children in the same way.

- Ask the children to tell you two words that rhyme in "Mrs White".

  Confirm *fright* and *night*, *shoe* and *two*, *Queen* and *bean*, *bed* and *head*, *town* and *down*.

  Ask the children: "What do you mean when you say that two words rhyme?"

  Confirm that the words sound the same at the end.

- Tell the children that you will say three words and they have to tell you which word is the odd one out.

  Suggested words:

bright	day	night	water	shoe	glue
seen	been	draw	head	green	red
town	brown	big	well	back	tell
hop	thump	bump	cross	boss	sand

  Encourage the children to explain why a certain word is the odd one out, for example, "*Day is the odd one out because it doesn't rhyme with* **bright** *and* **night**."

  Tell the children that they have to think of another word that rhymes with *fright* and *night*.

  Suggested words:

bite	fight	height	light
might	tight	white	flight

  (*Children may find this difficult at first so help them by giving them a choice. For example: "Which word would rhyme with* **bright** *and* **night** *–* **white** *or* **blue**?")

■ Encourage the children to put the words into a rap with actions, for example, *fright* and *night*: "Click left fingers as you say *fright*, click right fingers as you say *night*." Say: "They rhyme with *white*. Clap hands on *white*."

Repeat the procedure for words that rhyme with *shoe* and *two*.

Suggested words:
blue   glue   you   flew
grew   true   new   stew

Repeat the procedure for words that rhyme with *Queen* and *bean*.

Suggested words:
Jean   lean   mean   seen
clean   green   sheen

Repeat the procedure for words that rhyme with *bed* and *head*.

Suggested words:
fed   led   red   said   Ted   wed
bled   Ned   shed   spread   dread   bread

Repeat the procedure for words that rhyme with *town* and *down*.

Suggested words:
brown   gown   drown   clown   frown

■ Reread "Mrs White."

NOW OR LATER

■ Distribute Copymaster 13.

■ Ask the children to identify the first three pictures.

Confirm *tie, vest, socks*.

Tell the children that you will read a list of rhyming words and they have to choose and circle the picture of an object that rhymes.

Read: **nest, rest, best.**

Children circle the vest.

■ Repeat the procedure for:
stage, page, rage . . . (*cage*)
bee, see, knee . . . (*tree*)
lock, sock, knock . . . (*clock*)

■ Children colour the circled pictures.

DEVELOPING SKILLS

Some or all of these activities must be done to ensure progress:

■ **Paint and display**

Large picture of the main focus of the rhyme with the accompanying written rhyme.

Rhyming pictures – sets of pictures of things that rhyme.

Suggested sets of pictures:
hat   cat   bat
boot   suit   root
hose   rose   toes
chair   bear   pear
handle   candle   sandal
gate   plate   eight

■ **Complete the rhyme**

Recite a rhyme, missing out a rhyming word. Encourage the children to provide it.

■ **Spot the mistake**

Recite a well-known rhyme and substitute a non-rhyming word for the rhyming word. Ask the children to provide the correct rhyming word.

■ **Listen for the rhyme**

Stick or draw a picture on the board, for example a kite.

Say a list of words and ask the children to raise their hands when they hear a word that rhymes with the picture.

Suggested words:
balloon   white   fright   brake   game
bright   light   stool   height   bed
tight   bite   knife   flight

■ **Let's rhyme**

Listen to, recite, sing and learn nursery, playground and other rhymes.

ASSESSMENTS 1.1, 1.2

ACTIVITIES AT HOME

■ Encourage the children to ask their parents or other adults to tell them a rhyme they learned when they were young.

■ Look for two objects or pictures of things that rhyme to take to school.

Rhyming

UNIT 2

IDENTIFYING ALPHABET SOUNDS

The powerful reason for looking at alphabet letters as initial sounds is to give children a tool to read words. Encourage them at all times to use the sound of a letter as a reading tool. **It is important for children to know the sounds. It is more important for them to use the sounds as a reading strategy.**

INTRODUCTION

Unit 2 of *Fun Phonics* covers the NLF word level work required for Reception Year, in which pupils should be taught:

■ knowledge of grapheme/phoneme (symbol/sound) correspondence
■ alphabetical and phonic knowledge.

The focus in Unit 2 is on letters as initial sounds. *Hector Hedgehog's Big Book of Rhymes (Alphabet)* uses alliteration to help children differentiate the initial sounds in words. However, you should take every opportunity you can to make the children aware that letters appear anywhere in words.

As each letter is introduced, the children with names starting with that letter are asked to place their name under the appropriate letter on the alphabet frieze. This offers an opportunity to look at the alphabet as a whole by asking "Peek-a-Boo" questions such as: *Is it near the beginning of the alphabet? Is it near the end of the alphabet? Is it in the middle? Does it come before* (name a letter)*? Does it come after* (name a letter)*?*

Throughout the unit, help children differentiate between the *sound* and the *name* of a letter, as they may use either one in their answers. Stress that *c* (*see*) is the name of the letter and that the letter *c* makes the *c* sound. At this stage, emphasis should be on the sound.

The lessons follow the same pattern throughout, making them easy and reassuring to use. You may wish to spend more time on some lessons than others, depending on the needs of your pupils. You may also choose to teach the lessons to the whole class or a group, depending on the class structure, organisation and management.

The term *sound* is used generally rather than the clumsier phrase, "letter that represents the sound".

HOW TO USE THE WORKBOOKS

There are three sorts of activity in the workbooks designed for use with Unit 2. One is matching pictures that start with a given sound to the letter that represents the sound. Another is to circle the letter representing the initial sound of pictures. The third is another type of matching in which letters down the left-hand column of a page relate to pictures down the right-hand column.

- When matching a given sound to its letter:
  Ask the children to identify the pictures on the page.
  Then ask them to draw a line from the pictures that start with the given sound to the letter in the middle of the page.
  Demonstrate on the teacher's copy suggested in Resources.

- When circling:
  Ask the children to identify the pictures on the page.
  Then ask them to choose the sound that the picture starts with and draw a circle around it.
  Demonstrate on the teacher's copy.

- When matching two columns:
  Ask the children to identify the pictures on the page.
  Then ask them to draw a line from the letter that represents the sound to the picture that starts with the sound.
  Demonstrate on the teacher's copy.

HANDWRITING PENCIL GRIP

It is important to encourage children from the earliest stage to hold a pencil correctly and to form letters correctly. As handwriting is a motor skill, poor habits once established are almost impossible to change. While the main focus of *Fun Phonics* is not handwriting, it is better to establish good habits from the start.

Directions have been given for writing the letters without exit strokes (tails). Schools use different scripts so you should adjust as appropriate.

PEEK-A-BOO ACTIVITY

For use in skills practice in Unit 2.

To do this activity, children have to have a good knowledge of the formation of letters and sufficient reasoning ability to allow them to use the visual cues. Peek-a-boo practice will help develop children's reasoning ability. Here is how it works:

Hold a Letter Card behind a blank card of the same size.

Slowly push the blank card down so that a small part of the letter is visible.

Ask the children to predict what sound the letter makes before the whole letter is visible.

Encourage the children to use strategies, not to guess wildly.

Example 1

 Because of the shape that is visible, the letter might be **a**, **c**, **e**, **g**, **o**, **q** or **s**.

 As more of the letter card is revealed, letters **c**, **e**, **o** and **s** and **s** are eliminated. It might be **a**, **g** or **q**.

 This much of the letter eliminates **a**. When fully revealed, the letter will be a **g** or **q**, according to the tail.

Example 2

 Because of the shape that is visible, the letter might be **b**, **d**, **h**, **k** or **l**. (Some children may guess correctly that it cannot be a **d** or **l** because the position of the down stroke is well towards the left of the card.)

 As more of the letter card is revealed, **d**, **k** and **l** are eliminated. It will be **b** or **h**.

SOUNDS BOOK

As each letter is taught, a copy should be stuck into a notebook for each child to take home. This allows parents/guardians to know which letters their children are studying at school and invites them to become involved in their children's learning.

The c sound

THE NLF AIMS

- Hear and identify the initial sound *c*.
- Read the letter that represents the sound *c*.

WHAT YOU NEED

RESOURCES

- *Hector Hedgehog's Big Book of Rhymes (Alphabet)* page 4
- Letter Card *c*
- Alphabet Frieze
- Cards with names of children in class whose names start with *c*

KEY LESSON POINTERS

VOCABULARY

alphabet   letter   name   sound   word
letter shape   capital   rhyme   trace
start/beginning

THE CHILDREN should throughout the lesson:

- distinguish between the letter sound *c* and the letter name *c*, pronounced "see"
- pronounce the pure sound *c* without blurring it by adding a vowel as in *cu*
- focus exclusively on the sound activity and not stray onto unrelated topics.

YOU should throughout the lesson:

- emphasise the *c* sound at all times
- emphasise the difference between the letter sound and the letter name
- ensure correct pronunciation of the pure *c* sound
- encourage the use of examples such as the words *carrot* and *cake* but not *clown* where *c* is part of the *cl* cluster, or *crown* where *c* is part of the *cr* cluster
- ensure that enough time is spent looking at and talking about the book and rhyme
- emphasise starting at the correct point when tracing/writing the letter *c* and moving finger/pencil in the correct direction.

THE LESSON

STARTING THE LESSON

- Show the children *Hector Hedgehog's Big Book of Rhymes (Alphabet)*.

  Ask: "What is the book about?"

  Discuss what the book might be about and then elicit from the children the letters of the alphabet.

  Say that all the letters in the alphabet are contained in this Big Book.

  Tell the children that there are 26 letters in the alphabet.

  Consider with the children which letter might come first.

  Say: "Yes, *a* is the first letter (of the alphabet) but we are going to start with a different one."

TEACHING THE LESSON

- Open the book at page 4 and tell them that this will be today's activity. (*Be sure to spend some time together, looking at the page.*)

  Ask: "What can you see in the picture?"

  Discuss the content focusing on the *c* words such as *cat* and *car*.

  Emphasise the *c* words. (*Ensure the children focus exclusively on the objectives of the activity. Don't let them stray onto unrelated topics.*)

- Read the rhyme, emphasising the *c* words.

  Reread it and encourage the children to join in.

  Ask: "Which animals went out in the car?"

  Confirm **Candy** the *cat* and the *cow*, heavily emphasising the *c* at the start of **Candy**, *cat* and *cow*.

  Tell them to listen carefully and to say what sound they can hear at the beginning of **Candy**.

  Confirm that it is the sound *c*.

  Tell them to listen carefully and to say what sound they can hear at the beginning of **cat**.

  Confirm that it is the same sound *c*. (*Be sure to check that the children pronounce the **c** correctly; not as **cu**.*)

  Ask them to listen for other *c* words while you reread the rhyme.

  Confirm other *c* words: ***car, cow, cardigan, carry, cabbages, coconuts, call, camels, come.***

- Tell them that the letter *c* looks like this in books and birthday cards, on posters and signs (lower case).

  Finger trace the letter on the page.

  Say that this is its shape (*going over the letter again*). Say again that *c* is its sound.

  Ask: "Does anyone knows what its name is?"

- Show Letter Card *c* and finger trace. Confirm that it is the same letter as the one in the book.

  Ask: "What is the name of the letter?"

  Ask: "What sound does the letter make?"

  Ask them, as appropriate, to finger trace over the letter shape *c*. (*Emphasise the correct starting point and the correct formation when tracing over the letter.*)

- Ask them if anyone could be in the *c* set with a name beginning with the sound *c*. (*For example,* **Colin, Caroline.**)

  Ask identified children to select their name cards and stick them under the correct letter on the Alphabet Frieze.

  Ask the children what they notice about the letter at the beginning of their name.

  Confirm that it is a capital letter and explain that it makes the same sound and that it is a very important kind of letter. It always comes at the beginning of people's names.

  Ask them, as appropriate, to finger trace over the capital letter shape.

  Ask: "Does anyone's mummy, daddy, aunties, uncles, cousins have names beginning with the sound *c*?" (*Emphasise names beginning with the sound* **c** *and not the name* **c** *as this could include such names as Charles and Celia. At this point, indicate that sometimes the letter* **c** *makes a different sound. Today's activity is about the letter when it makes the* **c** *sound.*)

- Tell them that **Candy** the **cat** has room in the **car** for other things that start with *c*.

  Ask them to listen carefully and tell you which things can go in the **car**.

  Give examples: ***potato*** or ***carrot, cup*** or ***saucer, caterpillar*** or ***worm, book*** or ***cake.***

- Reread the rhyme, encouraging the children to join in. Track the words with a pointer to focus on the direction of print, the return sweep and the correspondence between the spoken and the written word.

FURTHER PRACTICE

DEVELOPING SKILLS

- **Some or all of these activities must be done to ensure progress:**

- Find the letter *c* on the Alphabet Frieze.

- Find *c* letters in the alphabet rhyme.

- Find the letter *c* in books and around the classroom.

- Cut out pictures from magazines to make a book about *c*.

- **Listening/memory game**

  How to play:

  You: "*Candy* went to the market and bought *carrots*."

  First child: "*Candy* went to the market and bought *carrots* and *cake*."

  Children in turn: "*Candy* went to the market and bought *carrots, cake* and (add another *c* word)."

- **Alliteration**

  Children say a name in the possessive (*Carla's, Colin's* or other) and add another *c* word (*Carla's coat, Colin's cabbage*).

OR

- **Paint/draw vegetable people**

  Name them, for example, *Caitlin carrot, Connor cabbage, Calum cucumber*.

NOTE

When the children line up, ask those whose names begin with the *c* sound to come forward first.

ACTIVITIES AT HOME

- Look for an object starting with *c* to bring to school.
- My Sounds Book.

AUDITORY DISCRIMINATION

IDENTIFYING ALPHABET SOUNDS

C

The c sound

THE NLF AIMS

- Hear and identify the initial sound *c*.
- Read the letter that represents the sound *c*.
- Write the letter that represents the sound *c*.

WHAT YOU NEED

RESOURCES

- *Hector Hedgehog's Big Book of Rhymes (Alphabet)* page 4
- Letter Card *c*
- Whiteboard/chalkboard/easel
- Collection of *c* pictures and other pictures
- Workbook 1 page 1
- Teacher's copy of Workbook 1 page 1
- Alphabet Frieze

KEY LESSON POINTERS

VOCABULARY

alphabet letter name sound word letter shape capital rhyme trace start/beginning middle match

THE CHILDREN should throughout the lesson:

- distinguish between the letter sound *c* and the letter name *c*, pronounced "see"
- pronounce the pure sound *c* without blurring it by adding a vowel as in *cu*
- focus exclusively on the sound activity and not stray onto unrelated topics.

YOU should throughout the lesson:

- emphasise the *c* sound at all times
- emphasise the difference between the letter sound and the letter name
- ensure correct pronunciation of the pure *c* sound
- encourage the use of examples such as the words *carrot* and *cake* but not *clown* where *c* is part of the *cl* cluster, or *crown* where *c* is part of the *cr* cluster
- ensure that enough time is spent looking at and talking about the book and rhyme
- emphasise starting at the correct point when tracing/writing the letter *c* and moving finger/pencil in the correct direction.

THE LESSON

STARTING THE LESSON

- Read the *c* rhyme with the class.
- Review Lesson 1, identifying the initial sound *c* and reinforcing its sound and name.

TEACHING THE LESSON

- Show the children the *c* Letter Card.

  Ask them what sound this letter shape makes (*trace the letter shape with finger*).

  Stick the *c* Letter Card on the board.

- Tell the children that they can only put pictures of objects starting with *c* on the board.

  Select a picture starting with *c*, such as *cake*. (*Remember not to use pictures of words such as* **clown** *where* c *is part of the* **cl** *cluster, or* **crown** *where* c *is part of the* **cr** *cluster.*)

  Ask the children if the picture of the *cake* can go on the board.

  Ask the children to tell you why it can go on the board.

  Repeat using the other *c* pictures. (*Encourage children when answering to give the reason for their answer:* "**Candle** *can go in the* c *set because it starts with* c".)

- Introduce Workbook 1 to the children.

  Show the teacher's copy of page 1.

  Ask: "What sound does the letter in the middle of the page make?"

  Ask them to identify the pictures on the page.

  Repeat the words, emphasising the *c* in the *c* words.

  Tell them that they have to match the pictures that start with *c* to the *c* letter shape in the middle.

  Ask them to choose a picture that will match to *c*.

  Demonstrate matching by drawing a line from the letter to the picture.

  Ask the children to match the *c* to the other appropriate pictures on the page.

- Children complete Workbook 1 page 1 (Matching). (*Remember to remove teacher's copy of workbook before children start work.*)

  You may wish the children to colour one, two or all of the pictures that start with *c*. You may wish the children to cross out the pictures that don't start with *c*.

  Encourage the children to listen to the instructions you give, such as:

  – "Colour one *c* picture."

  – "Colour two *c* pictures."

  – "Colour all the *c* pictures."

  – "Colour any *c* pictures of things you can eat."

  Listening is an important skill and every opportunity should be taken to help children develop it.

NOW OR LATER

- Finger trace the *c* letter shape.

  Demonstrate the correct letter formation giving a commentary as you do so: "Round and down and round." (*Remember to demonstrate the letter so that the children see it from the correct direction.*)

- Ask the children to write the *c* letter shape on their hand, on the desk, on the floor.

  Ask the children to write the *c* letter shape on the board.

  Ask the children to write the *c* letter shape on the sample copy of page 1.

  Ask the children to write *c* letter shapes in Workbook 1 page 1.

DEVELOPING SKILLS

Some or all of these activities must be done to ensure progress:

- Find the letter *c* on the Alphabet Frieze.

- Find *c* letters in the alphabet rhyme.

- Find the letter *c* in books and around the classroom.

- Practise letter formation.

- Cut out pictures from magazines to make a book about *c*.

- **Listening/memory game**

  How to play:

  You: "*Candy* went to the market and bought *carrots*."

  First child: "*Candy* went to the market and bought *carrots* and *cake*."

  Children in turn: "*Candy* went to the market and bought *carrots*, *cake* and (add another *c* word)."

- **Alliteration**

  Children say a name in the possessive (*Carla's*, *Colin's* or other) and add another *c* word (*Carla's coat*, *Colin's cabbage*).

OR

- **Paint/draw vegetable people**

  Name them, for example, *Caitlin carrot*, *Connor cabbage*, *Calum cucumber*.

NOTE

When the children line up, ask those whose names begin with the *c* sound to come forward first.

ACTIVITIES AT HOME

- Look for an object starting with *c* to bring to school.

- My Sounds Book.

AUDITORY DISCRIMINATION

IDENTIFYING ALPHABET SOUNDS

C

The d sound

THE NLF AIMS

- Hear and identify the initial sound *d*.
- Read the letter that represents the sound *d*.

WHAT YOU NEED

RESOURCES

- *Hector Hedgehog's Big Book of Rhymes (Alphabet)* page 5
- Letter Card *d*
- Alphabet Frieze
- Cards with names of children in class whose names start with *d*

KEY LESSON POINTERS

VOCABULARY

alphabet   letter   name   sound   word
letter shape   capital   rhyme   trace
start/beginning

THE CHILDREN should throughout the lesson:

- distinguish between the letter sound *d* and the letter name *d*, pronounced "dee"
- pronounce the pure sound *d* without blurring it by adding a vowel as in *di*
- focus exclusively on the sound activity and not stray onto unrelated topics.

YOU should throughout the lesson:

- emphasise the *d* sound at all times
- emphasise the difference between the letter sound and the letter name
- ensure correct pronunciation of the pure *d* sound
- encourage the use of examples such as the words *dog* and *door* and not *dragon* or *dress* where *d* is part of the *dr* cluster
- ensure that enough time is spent looking at and talking about the book and rhyme
- emphasise starting at the correct point when tracing/writing the letter *d* and moving finger/pencil in the correct direction.

THE LESSON

STARTING THE LESSON

- Show the children *Hector Hedgehog's Big Book of Rhymes (Alphabet)*.

  Ask: "What is this book about?"

  Confirm that the book is about the letters of the alphabet.

  Ask: "How many letters are in the alphabet?"

  Confirm 26 letters.

  Ask: "Which letter comes first?"

  Confirm that *a* comes first.

TEACHING THE LESSON

- Open the book at page 5 and tell them that this will be today's activity. (*Be sure to spend some time together, looking at the page.*)

  Ask: "What can you see in the picture?"

  Discuss the content, focusing on the *d* words such as *dog* and *dinner*. (*Emphasise the* d *words. Ensure the children focus exclusively on the objectives of the activity. Don't let them stray onto unrelated topics.*)

- Read the rhyme, emphasising the *d* words.

  Reread and encourage the children to join in.

  Ask: "What did *Dexter dog* find for dinner?"

  Confirm a *dinosaur* bone, heavily emphasising the *d* at the start of *dinosaur*.

  Tell them to listen carefully and to say what sound they can hear at the beginning of *dinosaur*.

  Confirm that it is the sound *d*.

  Tell them to listen carefully and to say what sound they can hear at the beginning of *Dexter* and *dog*.

  Confirm that it is the sound *d*. (*Be sure to check that the children pronounce the* d *correctly; not as* di.)

  Ask them to listen for other *d* words while you reread the rhyme.

  Confirm other *d* words: *digs, digging, delves, deeper, dirty*.

- Tell them that the letter *d* looks like this in books (*lower case*).

  Finger trace the letter on the page.

  Say that this is the shape (*going over the letter again*). Say again that *d* is its sound.

  Ask: "Does anyone know what its name is?"

- Show Letter Card *d* and finger trace. Confirm that it is the same letter as the one in the book.

  Ask: "What is its name?"

  Ask: "What sound does it make?"

  Ask them, as appropriate, to finger trace over the lower case letter shape *d*. (*Emphasise the correct starting point and the correct formation when tracing over the letter.*)

- Ask them if anyone could be in the *d* set with a name beginning with *d*. (*For example* **David**, **Daisy**.)

  Ask identified children to select their name cards and stick them under the correct letter on the Alphabet Frieze.

  Ask: "What do you notice about the letter at the beginning of your name?"

  Confirm that it is a capital letter and explain that it makes the same sound and that it is a very important kind of letter. It always comes at the beginning of people's names.

  Ask them, as appropriate, to finger trace over the upper case letter shape.

  Ask: "Does anyone's mummy, daddy, auntie's name begin with the sound *d*?" (*This might not need to be done if there are enough children in the class with names beginning with* **d**.)

  - Tell them that *Dexter dog* likes things that begin with *d*.

  Ask them to listen carefully and tell you which things *Dexter dog* would like.

  Give examples: *daffodil* or *poppy*, *desk* or *table*, *horse* or *duck*, *dinosaur* or *lion*.

- Reread the rhyme with the class, encouraging the children to join in. You should the track words with a pointer to focus on the direction of print, return sweep and correspondence between the spoken and the written word.

FURTHER PRACTICE

DEVELOPING SKILLS

Some or all of these activities must be done to ensure progress:

- Find the letter *d* on the Alphabet Frieze.

- Find *d* letters in the alphabet rhyme.

- Find the letter *d* in books and around the classroom.

- Cut out pictures from magazines to make a book about *d*.

- *d* – where is my sound – beginning or end?

  You say a word and children answer *beginning* or *end*.

  Suggested words:

desk	bed	dig	lad
bud	dummy	said	red
dinosaur	dandelion	sad	weed
desert	day	nod	

- **Listening/memory game**

  How to play

  You: "*Dexter* went to the market and bought some *dates*."

  First child: "*Dexter* went to the market and bought some dates and *doughnuts*."

  Children in turn: "*Dexter* went to the market and bought some *dates*, *doughnuts* and (add another *d* word)."

- **Alliteration**

  Children say a name in the possessive (*Davina's*, *Donald's* or other) and add another *d* word (*Davina's desk*, *Donald's dog*, for example).

  OR

- **Paint/draw flower people**

  Name them, for example, *Dalip daffodil*, *Donna daisy*, *Deena dandelion*.

NOTE

When the children line up, ask those whose names begin with *d* to come forward first then those whose names begin with *c* to come.

ACTIVITIES AT HOME

- Look for an object starting with *d* to take to school.
- My Sounds Book.

AUDITORY DISCRIMINATION

IDENTIFYING ALPHABET SOUNDS

d

The **d** sound

THE NLF AIMS

- Hear and identify the initial sound *d*.
- Read the letter that represents the sound *d*.
- Write the letter that represents the sound *d*.

WHAT YOU NEED

RESOURCES

- *Hector Hedgehog's Big Book of Rhymes (Alphabet)* page 5
- Letter Card *d*
- Whiteboard/chalkboard/easel
- Collection of *d* pictures and other pictures
- Workbook 1 page 2
- Teacher's copy of Workbook 1 page 2
- Alphabet Frieze

KEY LESSON POINTERS

VOCABULARY

alphabet letter name sound word letter shape capital rhyme trace start/beginning middle match

THE CHILDREN should throughout the lesson:

- distinguish between the letter sound *d* and the letter name *d*, pronounced "dee"
- pronounce the pure sound *d* without blurring it by adding a vowel as in *du*
- focus exclusively on the sound activity and not stray onto unrelated topics.

YOU should throughout the lesson:

- emphasise the *d* sound at all times
- emphasise the difference between the letter sound and the letter name
- ensure correct pronunciation of the pure *d* sound
- encourage the use of examples such as the words *dog* and *dinner* and not *dragon* where *d* is part of the *dr* cluster
- ensure that enough time is spent looking at and talking about the book and rhyme
- emphasise starting at the correct point when tracing/writing the letter *d* and moving finger/pencil in the correct direction.

STARTING THE LESSON

- Read the *d* rhyme with the class.
- Review Lesson 3.

TEACHING THE LESSON

- Show the children the *d* Letter Card.
  Ask: "What sound does this letter shape make?" (*Trace letter shape with finger.*)
  Stick the *d* Letter Card on the board.

- Tell the children that they can only put pictures of objects starting with *d* on the board.
  Select a picture starting with *d*, such as **dinosaur**. (*Remember not to use pictures of words such as* **dragon**, *where* **d** *is part of the* **dr** *cluster.*)
  Ask: "Can this picture go on the board?"
  Repeat using the other *d* pictures. (*Encourage children when giving an answer to give the reason:* "**Dog** *can go in the* **d** *set because it starts with* **d**.")

- Introduce Workbook 1 page 2 to the children.
  Show the teacher's copy of Workbook 1 page 2.
  Ask: "What sound does the letter in the middle of the page make?"
  Ask them to identify the pictures on the page.
  Repeat the words emphasising the *d* in the *d* words.
  Tell them that they have to match the pictures that start with *d* to the letter *d* shape in the middle.
  Ask them to choose a *d* picture that will match to *d*.
  Demonstrate matching by drawing a line from the letter to the picture.
  Ask the children to match the *d* to the other appropriate pictures on the page.

■ Children complete Workbook 1 page 2.
(*Remember to remove teacher's copy of workbook
before children start work.*)

You may wish the children to colour one, two or
all of the pictures that start with *d*. You may wish
the children to cross out the pictures that don't
start with *d*.

Encourage the children to listen to the
instructions you give, such as:

– "Colour one *d* picture."

– "Colour two *d* pictures."

– "Colour all the *d* pictures."

– "Colour any *d* pictures that are animals."

Listening is an important skill and every
opportunity should be taken to help children
develop it.

NOW OR LATER

■ Finger trace the *d* letter shape.

Demonstrate the correct letter formation giving a
commentary as you do so: "Round and down and
round and right up and down." Remind the
children that when making *d*, it starts as if it is
going to be *c*. (*Remember to demonstrate the
letter so that the children see it from the correct
direction.*)

■ Ask the children to write the *d* letter shape on
their hand, on the desk, on the floor.

Ask the children to write the *d* letter shape on the
board.

Ask the children to write the *d* letter shape on the
sample copy of page 2.

Ask the children to write the *d* letter shapes in
Workbook 1 page 2.

FURTHER PRACTICE

DEVELOPING SKILLS

**Some or all of these activities must be done
to ensure progress:**

■ Find the letter *d* on the Alphabet Frieze.

■ Find *d* letters in the alphabet rhyme.

■ Find the letter *d* in books and around the
classroom.

■ Practise letter formation.

■ Cut out pictures from magazines to make a
book about *d*.

■ **_d_ – where is my sound – beginning or end?**
You say a word and children answer
beginning or *end*.

Suggested words:

door	mad	domino	diver
pad	glad	dance	digger
head	shed	hood	daffodil
wood	dungeon		

■ **Listening/memory game**

How to play:

You: "*Dexter* went to the market and
bought some *dates*."

First child: "*Dexter* went to the market and
bought some *dates* and *doughnuts*."

Children in turn: "*Dexter* went to the
market and bought some *dates*,
doughnuts and (add another *d* word)."

■ **Alliteration**

Children say a name in the possessive
(*Davina's, Donald's* or other) and add
another *d* word (*Davina's desk, Donald's
dog*).

OR

■ **Paint/draw flower people**

Name them, for example, *Dalip daffodil,
Donna daisy, Deena dandelion*.

NOTE

When the children line up, ask those whose
names begin with *d* to come forward first,
then those whose names begin with *c* to
come.

ACTIVITIES AT HOME

■ My Sounds Book.

d

The c and d sounds

THE NLF AIMS

- Hear and differentiate between the initial sounds *c* and *d* in words.
- Read the letters that represent the sounds *c* and *d*.

WHAT YOU NEED

RESOURCES

- *Hector Hedgehog's Big Book of Rhymes (Alphabet)*
- Letter Cards *c* and *d*
- Whiteboard/chalkboard/easel
- Collection of *c* and *d* pictures and other pictures
- Workbook 1 page 3
- Teacher's copy of Workbook 1 page 3
- Alphabet Frieze
- Quick Cards

KEY LESSON POINTERS

VOCABULARY

alphabet letter name sound word letter shape capital rhyme trace start/beginning

THE CHILDREN should throughout the lesson:

- distinguish between the letter sounds *c* and *d* and the letter names *c* (see) and *d* (dee)
- pronounce the pure sound *c* and the pure sound *d*
- focus exclusively on the sound activity and not stray onto unrelated topics.

YOU should throughout the lesson:

- emphasise the *c* and *d* sounds at all times
- emphasise the difference between the letter sound and the letter name
- ensure correct pronunciation of the pure *c* and *d* sounds
- encourage the use of examples such as the words *carrot* and *cake* and not *clown* where *c* is part of the *cl* cluster, and *dog* and *door* and not *dragon* where *d* is part of the *dr* cluster
- ensure that enough time is spent looking at and talking about the book and rhyme.

STARTING THE LESSON

- Review the sounds learned to date. Use Letter Cards *c* and *d* and revisit *Hector Hedgehog's Big Book of Rhymes (Alphabet)* if necessary.

TEACHING THE LESSON

- Show the children the *c* Letter Card.

  Ask: "What sound does this letter make?" The children may need a prompt: "Remember **Candy** the **cat**?" (*Emphasise the* c *at the beginning of* **Candy** *and* **cat**.)

  Encourage the children to listen carefully and to tell you which word begins with *c*: **candle** or **fish**, **horse** or **cauliflower**, **cake** or **button**.

- Show the children the *d* Letter Card.

  Ask: "What sound does this letter make?" The children may need a prompt: "Remember **Dexter dog**?" (*Emphasise the* d *at the beginning of* **Dexter** *and* **dog**.)

  Encourage the children to listen carefully and to tell you which word begins with *d*: **duck** or **house**, **dandelion** or **bed**, **jam** or **dinner**.

- Stick the *c* Letter Card and the *d* Letter Card on the board.

  Tell the children that they can only put pictures of objects starting with *c* on the board with the *c*, and only put pictures of objects starting with *d* on the board with the *d*.

  Give the children *c* or *d* pictures and ask them in turn to put them in the correct place.

  (*Remember not to use pictures of words such as* **clown** *where* c *is part of the* **cl** *cluster, or* **crown** *where* c *is part of the* **cr** *cluster, or* **dragon** *where* d *is part of the* **dr cluster**.)

  (*Encourage children when putting card on board to give the reason:* "**Cake** *can go in the* c *set because it starts with* **c**." "**Dinosaur** *can go in the* d *set because it starts with* **d**.")

As the children become more confident, pictures starting with other letters can be introduced. The children should be expected to say why the picture cannot go in the *c* set or the *d* set: "*House* cannot go in the *c* set or the *d* set because it doesn't begin with *c* or *d*."

■ Show the teacher's copy of Workbook 1 page 3.

Point to *c* and ask what sound the letter makes.

Point to *d* and ask what sound the letter makes.

Invite the children to point to another letter that makes the *c* sound.

Invite the children to point to another letter that makes the *d* sound.

Ask the children to identify the pictures on the page.

Repeat the words emphasising the *c* in the *c* words and the *d* in the *d* words.

Tell them that they have to choose the sound that the picture starts with and draw a circle around it.

Demonstrate the procedure for the picture of the caterpillar.

Ask the children to choose the correct sound for the other pictures, inviting the children to circle the correct letters on the teacher's copy.

■ Children complete Workbook 1 page 3.
(*Remember to remove teacher's copy of workbook before the children start work.*)

FURTHER PRACTICE

DEVELOPING SKILLS

Some or all of these activities must be done to ensure progress:

■ Practise letter formation.

■ **Quick Cards**

Children have the *c* card and the *d* card face up on the table. You call out a word: *cot, door, café* and so on, and the children point to/hold up the appropriate card.

You hold up a picture of an object starting with *c* or *d* and the children point to/hold up the appropriate card.

■ **Peek-a-Boo**

See Unit 2 Introduction.

NOTE

Quick Cards

If the children hold up the cards, ensure that all the letters are the right way up and facing in the right direction. In the early stages it might be better for the children to point to the cards.

ACTIVITIES AT HOME

■ My Sounds Book.

c&d

The a sound

THE NLF AIMS

- Hear and identify the initial sound *a*.
- Read the letter that represents the sound *a*.

WHAT YOU NEED

RESOURCES

- *Hector Hedgehog's Big Book of Rhymes (Alphabet)* page 2
- Letter Card *a*
- Alphabet Frieze
- Cards with names of children in class whose names start with *a*

KEY LESSON POINTERS

VOCABULARY

alphabet letter name sound word letter shape capital rhyme trace start/beginning

THE CHILDREN should throughout the lesson:

- distinguish between the letter sound *a* and the letter name *a*, pronounced "ai"
- pronounce the short sound *a*
- focus exclusively on the sound activity and not stray onto unrelated topics.

YOU should throughout the lesson:

- emphasise the *a* sound at all times
- emphasise the difference between the letter sound and the letter name
- ensure correct pronunciation of the short *a* sound
- encourage the use of examples such as the words *apple* and *ambulance* and not *aeroplane* which starts with the long *a* sound
- ensure that enough time is spent looking at and talking about the book and rhyme
- emphasise starting at the correct point when tracing/writing the letter *a* and moving finger/pencil in the correct direction.

THE LESSON

STARTING THE LESSON

Quick revision of *c* and *d*.

Some or all of the following should be done to ensure progression:

- Show the Letter Cards and ask what sound each letter makes.

  Confirm that the letters make the sounds *c* and *d*.

  Ask: "What are the names of the letters?"

- Stick the cards on the board.

  Ask children in turn to find the card with the letter that makes the *c*, *d* sound.

  Ask the children to find the card that the word *daffodil, caterpillar, cage, dentist* and so on starts with.

  Tell the children they have to think about the names of the letters now and ask them to find *c* (*see*) and *d* (*dee*).

TEACHING THE LESSON

- "Now let's see what today's letter is going to be."

  Show the children *Hector Hedgehog's Big Book of Rhymes (Alphabet)*.

  Ask: "How many letters are in the alphabet?"

  Ask: "What is the first letter of the alphabet?"

  Confirm *a*.

- Open the book at page 2 and tell them that today's activity will be about the first letter of the alphabet *a*. (*Be sure to spend some time together, looking at the page.*)

  Ask: "What can you see in the picture?"

  Discuss the content focusing on words such as *apples, astronauts*. (*Emphasise the* a *words. Ensure the children focus exclusively on the objectives of the activity. Don't let them stray onto unrelated topics.*)

- Read the rhyme, emphasising the *a* words.

  Reread and encourage the children to join in.

  Ask: "What things did you hear about in the rhyme?"

  Confirm *apples, astronauts* and *acrobats* heavily emphasising the *a* at the start of each word.

  Tell them to listen carefully and to say what sound they can hear at the beginning of *apples*.

  Confirm that it is the sound *a*.

  Tell them to listen carefully and to say what sound they can hear at the beginning of *astronauts* and *acrobats*.

  Confirm that it is the sound *a*.

  Ask them to listen for other *a* words while you reread the rhyme.

  Confirm other *a* words: *and, alphabet, along*.

FUN Phonics

■ Tell them that the letter *a* looks like this in books (lower case).

Finger trace the letter on the page.

Say that this is the shape (*going over the letter again*). Say again that *a* is its sound.

Ask: "Does anyone know what its name is?"

Ask them to listen carefully and tell you which things could go in an *a* book.

Give examples: *ambulance* or *car*, *anorak* or *dungarees*, *ash* or *desk*. (*Encourage children when giving an answer to give the reason: "Anorak can go in the a set because it starts with a." "Diver would have to go in the d set because it starts with d."*)

■ Show Letter Card *a* and finger trace. Confirm that it is the same letter as the one in the book.

Ask: "What is its name?"

Ask: "What sound does it make?"

Ask them, as appropriate, to finger trace over the lower case letter shape *a*. (*Emphasise the correct starting point and the correct formation when tracing over the letter.*)

■ Ask them if anyone could be in the *a* set with a name beginning with the *a* sound. (*For example*, **Alison, Ahmed**.)

Ask identified children to select their name cards and stick them under the correct letter on the Alphabet Frieze.

Ask: "What do you notice about the letter at the beginning of your name?"

Confirm that it is a capital letter and explain that it makes the same sound and that it is a very important kind of letter. It always comes at the beginning of people's names.

Ask them, as appropriate, to finger trace over the upper case letter shape.

Ask: "Does anyone's mummy, daddy, auntie's name begin with the sound *a*?" (*Emphasise names beginning with the sound* a *and not the name* a *as this could include such names as* **Amy**. *At this point you should indicate that sometimes the letter says its name in words and not its sound. Today you are looking at the sound that* a *makes.*)

■ Reread the rhyme with the class encouraging the children to join in. You should track the words with a pointer to focus on the direction of print, return sweep and correspondence between the spoken and the written word.

FURTHER PRACTICE

DEVELOPING SKILLS

Some or all of these activities must be done to ensure progress:

■ Find the letter *a* on the Alphabet Frieze.

■ Find *a* letters in the alphabet rhyme.

■ Find the letter *a* in books and around the classroom.

■ Cut out pictures from magazines to make a book about *a*.

■ **Listening/memory game**

How to play:

You: "*Alan* went to the market and bought *apples*."

First child: "*Alan* went to the market and bought *apples* and *apricots*."

Children in turn: "*Alan* went to the market and bought *apples*, *apricots* and (add another *a* word)."

■ **Alliteration**

Children say a name in the possessive (*Akbar's, Annie's, Amrit's*) and add another *a* word (*Akbar's ambulance, Annie's anorak, Amrit's anchor*).

OR

■ **Paint/draw fruit people**

Name them, for example, *Ahmed apple, Angela apricot.*

NOTE

■ When the children line up, ask those whose names begin with *a* to come forward first then those whose names begin with *d*, then *c*, to come.

■ When the children line up, ask, for example, *Alison* and *Akash* to come forward. Then ask: "Who else can come to the line?" Confirm that they can go into the line if their own name begins with *a*.

ACTIVITIES AT HOME

■ Look for an object starting with *a* to take to school.

■ My Sounds Book.

a

The **a** sound

THE NLF AIMS

- Hear and identify the initial sound *a*.
- Read the letter that represents the sound *a*.
- Write the letter that represents the sound *a*.

WHAT YOU NEED

RESOURCES

- *Hector Hedgehog's Big Book of Rhymes (Alphabet)* page 2
- Letter Card *a*
- Whiteboard/chalkboard/easel
- Collection of *a* pictures and other pictures
- Workbook 1 page 4
- Teacher's copy of Workbook 1 page 4
- Alphabet Frieze

KEY LESSON POINTERS

VOCABULARY

alphabet   letter   name   sound   word
letter shape   capital   rhyme   trace
start/beginning   middle   match

THE CHILDREN should throughout the lesson:

- distinguish between the letter sound *a* and the letter name *a*, pronounced "ai"
- pronounce the short sound *a*
- focus exclusively on the sound activity and not stray onto unrelated topics.

YOU should throughout the lesson:

- emphasise the *a* sound at all times
- emphasise the difference between the letter sound and the letter name
- ensure that enough time is spent looking at and talking about the book and rhyme
- emphasise starting at the correct point when tracing/writing the letter *a* and moving finger/pencil in the correct direction.

THE LESSON

STARTING THE LESSON

- Read the *a* rhyme with the class.
- Review Lesson 6.

TEACHING THE LESSON

- Show the children the *a* Letter Card.

  Ask: "What sound does this letter shape make?" (*Trace letter shape with finger.*)

  Stick the *a* Letter Card on the board.

- Tell the children that they can only put pictures of objects starting with *a* on the board.

  Select a picture starting with *a*, such as **alligator**.

  Ask: "Can this go in the *a* set?" (*Encourage children when giving an answer to give the reason:* "**Alligator** *can go in the* **a** *set because it starts with* **a**.")

  Repeat using the other *a* and non-*a* pictures. (*Encourage children when giving an answer for a non-***a** *picture to give the reason:* "**Nest** *cannot go in the* **a** *set because it does not start with* **a**.")

- Introduce Workbook 1 page 4 to the children.

  Show the teacher's copy of Workbook 1 page 4.

  Ask: "What sound does the letter in the middle of the page make?"

  Ask them to identify the pictures on the page.

  Repeat the words emphasising the *a* in the *a* words.

  Tell them that they have to match the pictures that start with *a* to the letter *a* shape in the middle.

  Ask them to choose a picture that will match to *a*.

  Demonstrate matching by drawing a line from the letter to the picture.

  Ask the children to match the *a* to the other appropriate pictures on the page.

- Children complete Workbook 1 page 4 (Matching). (*Remember to remove teacher's copy of workbook before children start to work.*)

  (*You may wish children to colour one, two or all of the pictures that start with* **a**. *You may wish children to cross out pictures that don't start with* **a**.)

  Remember to give clear instructions for colouring. This activity can incorporate the additional skills of listening to and following instructions.

NOW OR LATER

- Finger trace the **a** letter shape.

  Demonstrate the correct letter formation giving a commentary as you do so: "Round and down and round and up and down." Remind the children that when making **a**, it starts as if it is going to be **c**. (*Remember to demonstrate the letter so that the children see it from the correct direction.*)

Ask the children to write the **a** letter shape on their hand, on the desk, on the floor.

Ask the children to write the **a** letter shape on the board.

Ask the children to write the **a** letter shape on the sample copy of page 4.

Ask the children to write **a** letter shapes in Workbook 1 page 4.

FURTHER PRACTICE

DEVELOPING SKILLS

Some or all of these activities must be done to ensure progress:

- Find the letter *a* on the Alphabet Frieze.

- Find *a* letters in the alphabet rhyme.

- Find the letter *a* in books and around the classroom.

- Practise letter formation.

- **Listening/memory game**

  How to play:

  You: "*Alan* went to the market and bought *apples*."

  First child: "*Alan* went to the market and bought *apples* and *apricots*."

  Children in turn: "*Alan* went to the market and bought *apples, apricots* and (add another *a* word)."

- **Alliteration**

  Children say a name in the possessive (*Akbar's, Annie's, Amrit's*) and add another *a* word (*Akbar's ambulance, Annie's anorak, Amrit's anchor*).

OR

- **Paint/draw fruit people**

  Name them, for example, *Ahmed apple, Angela apricot.*

NOTE

- When the children line up, ask those whose names begin with *a* to come forward first. At this point children with names that begin with the long *a*, such as *Amy*, should be reminded that sometimes the letter *a* makes its name and not its sound.

- When the children line up, ask, for example, *Alison* and *Akash* to come forward. Then ask: "Who else can come to the line?" Confirm that they can go into the line if their own name begins with *a*.

ACTIVITIES AT HOME

- My Sounds Book.

a

The c d and a sounds

THE NLF AIMS

- Hear and differentiate between the initial sounds *c*, *d* and *a* in words.
- Read the letters that represent the sounds *c*, *d* and *a*.

WHAT YOU NEED

RESOURCES

- *Hector Hedgehog's Big Book of Rhymes (Alphabet)*
- Letter Cards *c*, *d* and *a*
- Whiteboard/chalkboard/easel
- Collection of *c*, *d* and *a* pictures and other pictures
- Workbook 1 page 5
- Teacher's copy of Workbook 1 page 5
- Alphabet Frieze
- Quick Cards

KEY LESSON POINTERS

VOCABULARY

alphabet   letter   name   sound   word
letter shape   capital   rhyme   trace
start/beginning

THE CHILDREN should throughout the lesson:

- distinguish between the letter sounds *c*, *d* and *a* and the letter names *c* (*see*), *d* (*dee*) and *a* (*ai*)
- pronounce the pure sound *c* and the pure sound *d*
- focus exclusively on the sound activity and not stray onto unrelated topics.

YOU should throughout the lesson:

- emphasise the *c*, *d* and *a* sounds at all times
- emphasise the difference between the letter sound and the letter name
- ensure correct pronunciation of the pure *c* and *d* sounds
- encourage the use of examples such as the words *carrot*, *cake* and not *clown* where *c* is part of the *cl* cluster, and *dog*, *door* and not *dragon* where *d* is part of the *dr* cluster
- ensure that enough time is spent looking at and talking about the book and rhyme.

THE LESSON

STARTING THE LESSON

- Review all sounds learned to date. Use Letter Cards *c*, *d* and *a* and revisit *Hector Hedgehog's Big Book of Rhymes (Alphabet)* if necessary.

TEACHING THE LESSON

- Show the children the *c* Letter Card.

  Ask: "What sound does this letter make?" The children may need a prompt: "Remember **Candy** the **cat**?" (*Emphasise the* **c** *at the beginning of* **Candy** *and* **cat**.)

  Encourage the children to listen carefully and to tell you which word begins with *c*: **candle** or **fish**, **horse** or **cauliflower**, **cake** or **button**.

- Show the children the *d* Letter Card.

  Ask: "What sound does this letter make?" The children may need a prompt: "Remember **Dexter dog**?" (*Emphasise the* **d** *at the beginning of* **Dexter** *and* **dog**.)

  Encourage the children to listen carefully and to tell you which word begins with *d*: **duck** or **house**, **dandelion** or **bed**, **jam** or **dinner**.

- Show the children the *a* Letter Card.

  Ask: "What sound does this letter make?" The children may need a prompt: "Remember the **astronauts**?" (*Emphasise the* **a** *at the beginning of* **astronauts**.)

  Encourage the children to listen carefully and to tell you which word begins with *a*: **apples** or **bananas**, **cabbage** or **astronauts**, **dolphin** or **alligators**.

- Stick Letter Cards *c*, *d* and *a* on the board(s).

  Explain to the children that the board with the *c* is for all the pictures that start with *c* and the board with the *d* is for all the pictures that start with *d* and that the board with the *a* is for all the pictures that start with *a*.

- Give the children *c, d* or *a* pictures and ask them in turn to put them on the correct board. (*Encourage children when putting card on the board to give the reason:* "**Ambulance** *can go in the* **a** *set because it starts with* **a**." "**Duck** *can go in the* **d** *set because it starts with* **d**.")

  As the children become more confident, pictures starting with other letters can be introduced. The children should be expected to say that mouse, for example, cannot go in the *c, d* or *a* set because it doesn't begin with *c, d* or *a*.

- Show the teacher's copy of Workbook 1 page 5.

  Point to *c* and ask what sound the letter makes.

  Point to *d* and ask what sound the letter makes.

  Point to *a* and ask what sound the letter makes.

  Invite the children to point to another letter that makes the *c* sound.

  Invite the children to point to another letter that makes the *d* sound.

  Invite the children to point to another letter that makes the *a* sound.

  Ask the children to identify the pictures on the page.

  Repeat the words emphasising the *c* in the *c* words, the *d* in the *d* words and the *a* in the *a* words.

  Tell them that they have to choose the sound that the picture starts with and draw a circle around it.

  Demonstrate the procedure for the picture of the ant.

  Ask the children to choose the correct sound for the other pictures, inviting the children to circle the correct letters on the sample copy.

- Children complete Workbook 1 page 5. (*Remember to remove teacher's copy of workbook before children start work.*)

FURTHER PRACTICE

DEVELOPING SKILLS

Some or all of these activities must be done to ensure progress:

- Practise letter formation

- Quick Cards

  Children have the *c, d* and *a* cards face up on the table. You call out a word: *cot, door, ambulance* and so on, and the children point to/hold up the appropriate card.

  You hold up a picture of an object starting with *c, d* or *a* and the children point to/hold up the appropriate card.

- Peek-a-Boo

  See Unit 2 Introduction.

NOTE

Quick Cards

- If the children hold up the cards, ensure that all the letters are the right way up and facing in the right direction. In the early stages it might be better for the children to point to the cards.

ACTIVITIES AT HOME

- My Sounds Book.

c d a

The h sound

BEFORE YOU START

THE NLF AIMS

- Hear and identify the initial sound *h*.
- Read the letter that represents the sound *h*.

WHAT YOU NEED

RESOURCES

- *Hector Hedgehog's Big Book of Rhymes (Alphabet)* page 10
- Letter Cards *c*, *d*, *a* and *h*
- Alphabet Frieze
- Cards with names of children in class whose names start with *h*
- Whiteboard/chalkboard/easel

KEY LESSON POINTERS

VOCABULARY

alphabet letter name sound word letter shape capital rhyme trace start/beginning

THE CHILDREN should throughout the lesson:

- distinguish between the letter sound *h* and the letter name *h*
- pronounce the pure sound *h*, without blurring it by adding a vowel as in *hi*
- focus exclusively on the sound activity and not stray onto unrelated topics.

YOU should throughout the lesson:

- emphasise the *h* sound at all times
- emphasise the difference between the letter sound and the letter name
- ensure correct pronunciation of the pure *h* sound
- ensure that enough time is spent looking at and talking about the book and rhyme
- emphasise starting at the correct point when tracing/writing the letter *h* and moving finger/pencil in the correct direction.

THE LESSON

STARTING THE LESSON

Quick revision of *c*, *d* and *a*, reading the letter that represents the sound and knowing the sound.

Some or all of the following should be done to ensure progression:

- Show Letter Cards and ask what sound each letter makes.

  Confirm that the letters make the sounds *c*, *d* and *a*.

  Ask: "What are the names of the letters?"

- Stick the cards on the board.

  Ask the children to find the card with the letter that makes the *c*, *d*, *a* sound.

  Ask the children to find the card that the word *camera*, *danger*, *apple* and so on starts with.

  Tell the children they have to think about the names of the letters now and ask them to find *c* (*see*) and *d* (*dee*) and *a* (*ai*).

TEACHING THE LESSON

- "Now let's see what today's letter is going to be."

- Open the book at page 10 and tell them that this will be today's activity. (*Be sure to spend some time together, looking at the page.*)

  Ask: "What can you see in the picture?"

  Discuss the content focusing on the *h* words such as **hedgehog** and **hurricane**. (*Emphasise the* **h** *words. Ensure the children focus exclusively on the objectives of the activity. Don't let them stray onto unrelated topics.*)

- Read the rhyme, emphasising the *h* words.

  Reread and encourage the children to join in.

  Ask: "What did **Hector** the **hedgehog** and **Hannah** the shrew take to **Hannah's hole** in the ground?"

  Confirm **helmets** and **hats** heavily emphasising the *h* at the start of each word.

  Tell them to listen carefully and to say what sound they can hear at the beginning of **helmets**.

  Confirm that it is the sound *h*.

  Tell them to listen carefully and to say what sound they can hear at the beginning of **hats**.

  Confirm that it is the sound **h**. (*Check that the children pronounce the* **h** *correctly; not as* **hi**.)

Ask them to listen for other *h* words while you reread the rhyme.

Confirm other *h* words: *help, here's, hurricane, Hector, hedgehog, Hannah, hurry, hole.*

■ Tell them that the letter *h* looks like this in books (lower case).

Finger trace the letter on the page.

Say that this is the shape (*going over the letter again*). Say again that *h* is its sound.

Ask: "Does anyone know what its name is?"

Show Letter Card *h* and finger trace. Confirm that it is the same letter as the one in the book.

Ask: "What is its name?"

Ask: "What sound does it make?"

Ask them to finger trace over the letter shape. (*Emphasise the correct starting point and the correct formation when tracing over the letter.*)

■ Ask them if anyone could be in the *h* set with a name beginning with the sound *h*. (*For example,* **Heather**, **Hammad**.)

Ask identified children to select their name cards and stick them under the correct letter on the Alphabet Frieze.

Ask: "What do you notice about the letter at the beginning of your name?"

Confirm that it is a capital letter and explain that it makes the same sound and that it is a very important kind of letter. It always comes at the beginning of people's names.

Ask them, as appropriate, to finger trace over the upper case letter shape.

Ask: "Does anyone's mummy, daddy, auntie's name begin with the sound *h*?" (*This may not need to be done if there are enough children in the class with names beginning with* **h**.)

■ Tell them that *Hector* and *Hannah* like things beginning with *h.*

Ask them to listen carefully and tell you which other things *Hector* and *Hannah* would like to take to the hills.

Give examples *hammer* or *nails*, *hankie* or *book*, *lion* or *hippo*.

■ Reread the rhyme with the class, encouraging the children to join in. You should track the words with a pointer to focus on the direction of print, return sweep and correspondence between the spoken and the written word.

FURTHER PRACTICE

DEVELOPING SKILLS

Some or all of these activities must be done to ensure progress:

■ Find the letter *h* on the Alphabet Frieze.

■ Find *h* letters in the alphabet rhyme.

■ Find the letter *h* in books and around the classroom.

■ Cut out pictures from magazines to make a book about *h*.

■ Practise letter formation.

■ **Listening/memory game**
   How to play:

   You: "*Hector* went to the market and bought *hankies*."

   First child: "*Hector* went to the market and bought *hankies* and *hats*."

   Children in turn: "*Hector* went to the market and bought *hankies, hats* and (add another *h* word)."

■ **Alliteration**

   Children say a name in the possessive (*Helen's, Hammad's*) and add another *h* word (*Helen's house, Hammad's horse*).

   OR

■ **Paint/draw hat people**

   Name them, for example, *Hetty hat, Henry hat*.

NOTE

■ When the children line up, ask, for example, *Henry* and *Hans* to come forward. Then ask: "Who else can come to the line?" Confirm that they can go into the line if their own name begins with *h*.

ACTIVITIES AT HOME

■ Look for an object starting with *h* to take to school.

■ My Sounds Book.

h

The h sound

THE NLF AIMS

- Hear and identify the initial sound *h*.
- Read the letter that represents the sound *h*.
- Write the letter that represents the sound *h*.

WHAT YOU NEED

RESOURCES

- *Hector Hedgehog's Big Book of Rhymes (Alphabet)* page 10
- Letter Card *h*
- Whiteboard/chalkboard/easel
- Collection of *h* pictures and other pictures
- Workbook 1 page 6
- Teacher's copy of Workbook 1 page 6
- Alphabet Frieze

KEY LESSON POINTERS

VOCABULARY

alphabet letter name sound word
letter shape capital rhyme trace
start/beginning middle match

THE CHILDREN should throughout the lesson:

- distinguish between the letter sound *h* and the letter name *h*
- pronounce the pure sound *h* without blurring it by adding a vowel as in *hi*
- focus exclusively on the sound activity and not stray onto unrelated topics.

YOU should throughout the lesson:

- emphasise the *h* sound at all times
- emphasise the difference between the letter sound and the letter name
- ensure correct pronunciation of the pure sound *h*
- ensure that enough time is spent looking at and talking about the book and rhyme
- emphasise starting at the correct point when tracing/writing the letter *h* and moving finger/pencil in the correct direction.

STARTING THE LESSON

- Read the *h* rhyme with the class.
- Review Lesson 9.

TEACHING THE LESSON

- Show the children the *h* Letter Card.
  Ask: "What sound does this letter shape make?" (*Trace letter shape with finger.*)
  Stick the *h* Letter Card on the board.

- Tell the children that they can only put pictures of objects starting with *h* on the board.
  Select a picture starting with *h*, such as *horse*.
  Ask: "Can this picture go on the board?"
  Repeat using the other *h* and non-*h* pictures. (*Encourage children when giving an answer for non-*h* pictures to give the reason: "**Violin** cannot go in the* h *set because it does not start with* h.*")

- Introduce Workbook 1 page 6 to children.
  Show the teacher's copy of Workbook 1 page 6.
  Ask: "What sound does the letter in the middle of the page make?"
  Ask them to identify the pictures on the page.
  Repeat the words emphasising the *h* in the *h* words.
  Tell them that they have to match the pictures that start with *h* to the letter *h* shape in the middle.
  Ask them to choose a picture that will match to *h*.
  Demonstrate matching by drawing a line from the letter to the picture.
  Ask the children to match the *h* to the other appropriate pictures on the page.

- Children complete Workbook 1 page 6 (Matching). (*Remember to remove teacher's copy of workbook before children start to work.*)

  (*You may wish children to colour one, two or all of the pictures that start with* **h**. *You may wish children to cross out pictures that don't start with* **h**.)

  Remember to give clear instructions for colouring. This activity can incorporate the additional skills of listening to and following instructions.

NOW OR LATER

- Finger trace the *h* letter shape.

  Demonstrate the correct letter formation giving a commentary as you do so: "Straight down and up halfway and round and down." (*Remember to demonstrate the letter so that the children see it from the correct direction.*)

- Ask the children to write the *h* letter shape on their hand, on the desk, on the floor.

  Ask the children to write the *h* letter shape on the board.

  Ask the children to write the *h* letter shape on the sample copy of Workbook page 6.

  Ask the children to write *h* letter shapes in Workbook 1 page 6.

DEVELOPING SKILLS

Some or all of these activities must be done to ensure progress:

- Find the letter *h* on the Alphabet Frieze.
- Find *h* letters in the alphabet rhyme.
- Find the letter *h* in books and around the classroom.
- Practise letter formation.

NOTE

- When the children line up, ask those whose names begin with *h* to come forward first, then those whose names begin with *a, d, c* to come.
- When the children line up, ask, for example, *Henry* and *Hans* to come forward. Then ask: "Who else can come to the line?" Confirm that they can go into the line if their own name begins with *h*.

ACTIVITIES AT HOME

- My Sounds Book.

AUDITORY DISCRIMINATION

IDENTIFYING ALPHABET SOUNDS

h

51

The c d a and h sounds

THE NLF AIMS

- Hear and differentiate between the initial sounds *c*, *d*, *a* and *h* in words.
- Read the letters that represent the sounds *c*, *d*, *a* and *h*.

WHAT YOU NEED

RESOURCES

- *Hector Hedgehog's Big Book of Rhymes (Alphabet)*
- Letter Cards *c*, *d*, *a* and *h*
- Whiteboard/chalkboard/easel
- Collection of *c*, *d*, *a* and *h* pictures and other pictures
- Workbook 1 page 7
- Teacher's copy of Workbook 1 page 7
- Alphabet Frieze
- Quick Cards

KEY LESSON POINTERS

VOCABULARY

alphabet   letter   name   sound   word
letter shape   capital   rhyme   trace
start/beginning

THE CHILDREN should throughout the lesson:

- distinguish between the letter sounds *c*, *d*, *a* and *h* and the letter names *c*, *d*, *a* and *h*
- pronounce the pure sounds *c*, *d* and *h*
- focus exclusively on the sound activity and not stray onto unrelated topics.

YOU should throughout the lesson:

- emphasise the *c*, *d*, *a* and *h* sounds at all times
- emphasise the difference between the letter sound and the letter name
- ensure correct pronunciation of the *c*, *d*, *a* and *h* sounds
- encourage the use of examples such as the words *carrot* and *cake* and not *clown* where *c* is part of the *cl* cluster, and *dog* and *door* and not *dragon* where *d* is part of the *dr* cluster
- ensure that enough time is spent looking at and talking about the book and rhyme.

STARTING THE LESSON

- Review all the sounds learned to date. Use Letter Cards *c, d, a* and *h* and revisit *Hector Hedgehog's Big Book of Rhymes (Alphabet)* if necessary.

TEACHING THE LESSON

- Show the children the *d* Letter Card.

  Ask: "What sound does this letter make?" The children may need a prompt: "Remember **Dexter dog**?" (*Emphasise the* **d** *at the beginning of* **Dexter** *and* **dog**.)

  Encourage the children to listen carefully and to tell you which word begins with **d**: **duck** or **house**, **dandelion** or **bed**, **jam** or **dinner**.

- Show the children the *a* Letter Card.

  Ask: "What sound does this letter make?" The children may need a prompt: "Remember the **astronauts**?" (*Emphasise the* **a** *at the beginning of* **astronauts**.)

  Encourage the children to listen carefully and to tell you which word begins with **a**: **apples** or **bananas**, **cabbage** or **astronauts**, **dolphin** or **alligators**.

- Show the children the *h* Letter Card.

  Ask: "What sound does this letter make?" The children may need a prompt: "Remember **Hector** the **hedgehog**?" (*Emphasise the* **h** *at the beginning of* **Hector** *and* **hedgehog**.)

  Tell the children to listen carefully and tell you which word begins with **h**: **hospital** or **elephant**, **tent** or **house**, **hose** or **garden**.

- Stick Letter Cards *d, a* and *h* on the board(s).

  Explain to the children that the board with the *d* is for all the pictures that start with *d* and the board with the *a* is for all the pictures that start with *a* and that the board with the *h* is for all the pictures that start with *h*.

■ Give the children *d, a* or *h* pictures and ask them in turn to put them on the correct the board. (*Encourage children when putting card on board to give the reason:* "**Helicopter** *can go in the* **h** *set because it starts with* **h**." "**Door** *can go in the* **d** *set because it starts with* **d**.")

As the children become more confident, pictures starting with other letters can be introduced. The children should be expected to say that *telephone*, for example, cannot go in the *d, a* or *h* set because it doesn't begin with *d, a* or *h*.

■ Show the teacher's copy of Workbook 1 page 7.

Point to *h* and ask what sound the letter makes.

Point to *d* and ask what sound the letter makes.

Point to *a* and ask what sound the letter makes.

Point to *c* and ask what sound the letter makes.

Invite the children to point to another letter that makes the *h* sound.

Invite the children to point to another letter that makes the *d* sound.

Invite the children to point to another letter that makes the *a* sound.

Invite the children to point to another letter that makes the *c* sound.

Ask the children to identify the pictures on the page.

Repeat the words emphasising the *h* in the *h* words, the *d* in the *d* words, the *a* in the *a* words and the *c* in the *c* words.

Tell them that they have to choose the sound that the picture starts with and draw a circle around it.

Demonstrate the procedure for the picture of the dog.

Ask the children to choose the correct sound for the other pictures, inviting the children to circle the correct letters on the sample copy.

■ Children complete Workbook 1 page 7. (*Remember to remove teacher's copy of workbook before children start to work.*)

FURTHER PRACTICE

DEVELOPING SKILLS

Some or all of these activities must be done to ensure progress:

■ Practise letter formation.

■ **Quick Cards**

Children have the *c, d, a* and *h* cards face up on the table. You call out a word: *cot, door, ambulance, helicopter* and so on, and the children point to/hold up appropriate card.

You hold up a picture of an object starting with *c, d, a* or *h* and the children point to/hold up the appropriate card.

■ **Peek-a-Boo**

See Unit 2 Introduction.

NOTE

Quick Cards

■ If the children hold up the cards, ensure that all the letters are the right way up and facing in the right direction. In the early stages it might be better for the children to point to the cards.

ACTIVITIES AT HOME

■ My Sounds Book.

c d a h

The **m** sound

BEFORE YOU START

THE NLF AIMS

- Hear and identify the initial sound *m*.
- Read the letter that represents the sound *m*.
- Write the letter that represents the sound *m*.

WHAT YOU NEED

RESOURCES

- *Hector Hedgehog's Big Book of Rhymes (Alphabet)* page 15
- Letter Cards *c, d, a, h* and *m*
- Alphabet Frieze
- Cards with names of children in class whose names start with *m*
- Whiteboard/chalkboard/easel
- Workbook 1 page 8
- Teacher's copy of Workbook 1 page 8

KEY LESSON POINTERS

VOCABULARY

alphabet letter name sound word
letter shape capital rhyme trace
start/beginning middle match

THE CHILDREN should throughout the lesson:

- distinguish between the letter sound *m* and the letter name *m*
- pronounce the pure sound *m*, without blurring it by adding a vowel as in *mi*
- focus exclusively on the sound activity and not stray onto unrelated topics.

YOU should throughout the lesson:

- emphasise the *m* sound at all times
- emphasise the difference between the letter sound and the letter name
- ensure correct pronunciation of the pure *m* sound
- ensure that enough time is spent looking at and talking about the book and rhyme
- emphasise starting at the correct point when tracing/writing the letter *m* and moving finger/pencil in the correct direction.

THE LESSON

STARTING THE LESSON

Quick revision of *c, d, a, h.*

Some or all of the following should be done to ensure progression:

- Show Letter Cards and ask what sound each letter makes.

  Confirm that the letters make the sounds *c, d, a,* and *h.*

  Ask: "What are the names of the letters?"

- Stick the cards on the board.

  Ask the children to find the card with the letter that makes the *c, d, a* or *h* sound.

  Ask the children to find the card that the word *cook, dog, animal, hedgehog* and so on starts with.

  Tell the children they have to think about the names of the letters now and ask them to find *c* (*see*), *d* (*dee*), *a* (*ai*) and *h.*

TEACHING THE LESSON

- "Now let's see what today's letter is going to be."

- Open the book at page 15 and tell them that this will be today's activity. (*Be sure to spend some time together, looking at the page.*)

  Ask: "What can you see in the picture?"

  Discuss the content, focusing on the *m* words such as *microwave* and *mince*. (*Emphasise the* **m** *words. Ensure the children focus exclusively on the objectives of the activity. Don't let them stray onto unrelated topics.*)

- Read the rhyme, emphasising the *m* words.

  Reread and encourage the children to join in.

  Ask: "Who made the *mince* in the *microwave*?"

  Confirm *Myrtle* and *Merlin* and *Mickey* heavily emphasising the *m* at the start of each word.

  Tell them to listen carefully and to say what sound they can hear at the beginning of *Myrtle*.

  Confirm that it is the sound *m.*

  Tell them to listen carefully and to say what sound they can hear at the beginning of *Merlin* and *Mickey*.

  Confirm that it is the sound *m.* (*Check that the children pronounce the* **m** *correctly; not as* **mi**.)

  Ask them to listen for other *m* words while you reread the rhyme.

Confirm other *m* words: *mix, mushroom, marigolds, make, mince, mouse, mix, melt, moonlight, marvellous, meal, mummy.*

- Tell them that the letter *m* looks like this in books (*lower case*).

  Finger trace the letter on the page.

  You say that this is the shape (*going over the letter again*). You say again that *m* is its sound.

  Ask: "Does anyone know what its name is?"

  Show Letter Card *m* and finger trace. Confirm that it is the same letter as the one in the book.

  Ask: "What is its name?"

  Ask: "What sound does it make?"

  Ask them, as appropriate, to finger trace over the letter shape. (*Emphasise the correct starting point and the correct formation when tracing over the letter.*)

- Ask them if anyone could be in the *m* set, with a name beginning with *m*. (*For example,* **Manjit, Morris.**)

  Ask identified children to select their name cards and stick them under the correct letter on the Alphabet Frieze.

  Ask: "What do you notice about the letter at the beginning of your name?"

  Confirm that it is a capital letter and discuss its function.

  Ask them, as appropriate, to finger trace over the upper case letter shape.

- Tell them that *Myrtle* and *Merlin* and *Mickey* like things beginning with *m*.

  Ask them to listen carefully and tell you which other things *Myrtle* and *Merlin* and *Mickey* would like.

  Give examples *mirror* or *wall, dancing* or *music, milk* or *lemonade.*

- Reread the rhyme with the class, encouraging the children to join in. You should track the words with a pointer to focus on the direction of print, return sweep and correspondence between the spoken and the written word.

NOW OR LATER

- Workbook 1 page 8. When introducing page 8, use the same method as for page 1, Lesson 2.

  Demonstrate the correct letter formation giving a commentary as you do so.

↓m

FURTHER PRACTICE

DEVELOPING SKILLS

Some or all of these activities must be done to ensure progress:

- Find the letter *m* on the Alphabet Frieze.

- Find *m* letters in the alphabet rhyme.

- Find the letter *m* in books and around the classroom.

- Cut out pictures from magazines to make a book about *m*.

- *m* – where is my sound – beginning or end?

  You say a word and children answer *beginning* or *end*.

  Suggested words:

monkey	hum	music	pram
swim	matches	metal	drum
money	magic	plum	mirror
from	ham		

NOTE

- When the children line up, ask those whose names begin with *m* to come forward first then those whose names begin with letters already taught to come.

- When the children line up, ask, for example, *Martin* and *Moya* to come forward. Then ask: "Who else can come to the line?" Confirm that they can go into the line if their own name begins with *m*.

ACTIVITIES AT HOME

- Look for an object starting with *m* to take to school.
- My Sounds Book.

m

The c d a h and m sounds

THE NLF AIMS

- Hear and differentiate between the initial sounds *c*, *d*, *a*, *h* and *m* in words.
- Read the letters that represent the sounds *c*, *d*, *a*, *h* and *m*.

WHAT YOU NEED

RESOURCES

- Letter Cards *c*, *d*, *a*, *h* and *m*
- Whiteboard/chalkboard/easel
- Collection of *c*, *d*, *a*, *h* and *m* pictures and other pictures
- Workbook 1 page 9
- Teacher's copy of Workbook 1 page 9
- Alphabet Frieze
- Quick Cards
- Additional Support 1

KEY LESSON POINTERS

VOCABULARY

alphabet   letter   name   sound   word
letter shape   capital   rhyme   trace
start/beginning

THE CHILDREN should throughout the lesson:

- distinguish between the letter sounds *c*, *d*, *a*, *h* and *m* and the letter names *c*, *d*, *a*, *h* and *m*
- pronounce the pure sounds *c*, *d*, *h* and *m*
- focus exclusively on the sound activity and not stray onto unrelated topics.

YOU should throughout the lesson:

- emphasise the *c*, *d*, *a*, *h* and *m* sounds at all times
- emphasise the difference between the letter sound and the letter name
- ensure correct pronunciation of the *c*, *d*, *a*, *h* and *m* sounds
- encourage the use of examples such as the words *carrot* and *cake* and not *clown* where *c* is part of the *cl* cluster, and *dog* and *door* and not *dragon* where *d* is part of the *dr* cluster
- ensure that enough time is spent looking at and talking about the book and rhyme.

THE LESSON

STARTING THE LESSON

- Review all the sounds learned to date. Use Letter Cards *c, d, a, h* and *m* and revisit *Hector Hedgehog's Big Book of Rhymes (Alphabet)* if necessary.

TEACHING THE LESSON

- Show the children the *m* Letter Card.

  Ask: "What sound does this letter make?" The children may need a prompt: "Remember **Myrtle** and **Merlin** and **Mickey MacMouse**?" (*Emphasise the* **m** *at the beginning of* **Myrtle, Merlin, Mickey** *and* **MacMouse**.)

  Encourage the children to listen carefully and to tell you which word begins with *m*: **money** or **sugar**, **book** or **marbles**, **music** or **van**.

- Show the children the *a* Letter Card.

  Ask: "What sound does this letter make?" the children may need a prompt: "Remember the **astronauts**?" (*Emphasise the* **a** *at the beginning of* **astronauts**.)

  Encourage the children to listen carefully and to tell you which word begins with *a*: **apples** or **desk**, **animal** or **door**, **dolphin** or **alligators**.

- Show the children the *h* Letter Card.

  Ask: "What sound does this letter make?" The children may need a prompt: "Remember **Hector** the **hedgehog**?" (*Emphasise the* **h** *at the beginning of* **Hector** *and* **hedgehog**.)

  Tell the children to listen carefully and tell you which word begins with *h*: **hospital** or **elephant**, **tent** or **house**, **hose** or **garden**.

- Stick Letter Cards *a, h* and *m* on the board(s).

  Explain to the children that the board with the *m* is for all the pictures that start with *m*, the board with the *a* is for all the pictures that start with *a* and that the board with the *h* is for all the pictures that start with *h*.

■ Give the children *m, a* or *h* pictures and ask them in turn to put them on the correct board. (*Encourage children when putting card on the board to give the reason:* "**Helicopter** *can go in the* **h** *set because it starts with* **h**; **moon** *can go in the* **m** *set because it starts with* **m**.")

As the children become more confident, pictures starting with other letters can be introduced. The children should be expected to say that *bike*, for example, cannot go in the *h* set, *m* set or *a* set because it doesn't begin with *h, a* or *m*.

■ Show the teacher's copy of Workbook 1 page 9.

Ask the children if anyone could point to the letter that makes the sound *m*.

Ask the children if someone could point to another letter that makes the sound *m*.

Repeat for all the *m* letters.

Ask the children, one at a time, to point to a letter of their choice and tell the class what sound it makes.

Repeat for all the letters.

Ask the children to identify the pictures on the page.

Repeat the words emphasising the *h* in the *h* words, the *d* in the *d* words, the *a* in the *a* words, the *c* in the *c* words and the *m* in the *m* words.

Tell them that they have to choose the sound that the picture starts with and draw a circle around it.

Demonstrate the procedure for the picture of the dinosaur.

Ask the children to choose the correct sound for the other pictures, inviting the children to circle the correct letters on the sample copy.

■ Children complete Workbook 1 page 9. (*Remember to remove teacher's copy of workbook before children start to work.*)

NOW OR LATER

■ Repeat the above lesson for further practice.

■ Children complete Additional Support 1.

DEVELOPING SKILLS

Some or all of these activities must be done to ensure progress:

■ Practise letter formation.

■ **Quick Cards**

Children have the *c, d, a, h* and *m* cards face up on the table. You call out a word: *carrot, dinner, astronaut* and so on, and the children point to/hold up the appropriate card.

You hold up a picture of an object starting with *c, d, a, h* or *m* and the children point to/hold up the appropriate card.

■ **What's my sound?**

You say a word and children say the sound that the word starts with: money – *m*.

■ **Peek-a-Boo**

See Unit 2 Introduction.

NOTE

Quick Cards

■ If the children hold up the cards, ensure that all letters are the right way up and facing in the right direction. In the early stages it might be better for the children to point to the cards.

ACTIVITIES AT HOME

■ My Sounds Book.

cdahm

The s sound

THE NLF AIMS

- Hear and identify the initial sound *s*.
- Read the letter that represents the sound *s*.
- Write the letter that represents the sound *s*.

WHAT YOU NEED

RESOURCES

- *Hector Hedgehog's Big Book of Rhymes (Alphabet)* page 24
- Letter Cards *c, d, a, h, m* and *s*
- Alphabet Frieze
- Cards with names of children in class whose names start with *s*
- Whiteboard/chalkboard/easel
- Workbook 1 page 10
- Teacher's copy of Workbook 1 page 10

KEY LESSON POINTERS

VOCABULARY

alphabet letter name sound word letter shape capital rhyme trace start/beginning middle match

THE CHILDREN should throughout the lesson:

- distinguish between the letter sound *s* and the letter name *s*
- pronounce the pure sound *s*, without blurring it by adding a vowel as in *su*
- focus exclusively on the sound activity and not stray onto unrelated topics.

YOU should throughout the lesson:

- emphasise the *s* sound at all times
- emphasise the difference between the letter sound and the letter name
- ensure correct pronunciation of the pure *s* sound
- encourage the use of examples such as the words *sock* and *sandal* and not *slipper* where *s* is part of the *sl* cluster, or *string* where *s* is part of the triple cluster *str*
- ensure that enough time is spent looking at and talking about the book and rhyme
- emphasise starting at the correct point when tracing/writing the letter *s* and moving finger/pencil in the correct direction.

STARTING THE LESSON

Quick revision of all Letter Cards to date.

Some or all of the following should be done to ensure progression:

- Show Letter Cards and ask what sound each letter makes.

  Confirm that the letters make the sounds *c, d, a, h* and *m*.

  Ask: "What are the names of the letters?"

- Stick the cards on the board.

  Ask the children to find the card with the letter that makes the *c, d, a, h* or *m* sound.

  Ask the children to find the card that the word *cup, diver, animal, happy, mask* and so on starts with.

  Tell the children they have to think about the names of the letters now and ask them to find *c, d, a, h* and *m*.

TEACHING THE LESSON

- "Now let's see what today's letter is going to be."

- Open the book at page 24 and tell them that this will be today's activity. (*Be sure to spend some time together, looking at the page.*)

  Ask: "What can you see in the picture?"

  Discuss the content focusing on the *s* words such as **seal** and **seaweed**. (*Emphasise the* s *words. Ensure the children focus exclusively on the objectives of the activity. Don't let them stray onto unrelated topics.*)

- Read the rhyme, emphasising the *s* words.

  Reread and encourage the children to join in.

  Ask: "How many **sandwiches** did **Sammy** get?"

  Confirm **seven soggy sandwiches**.

  Tell them to listen carefully and to say what sound they can hear at the beginning of **Sammy**.

  Confirm that it is the sound *s*.

  Tell them to listen carefully and to say what sound they can hear at the beginning of **seal**.

  Confirm that it is the sound *s*. (*Check that the children pronounce the* s *correctly; not as* su.)

  Ask them to listen for other **s** words while you reread the rhyme.

  Confirm other **s** words: **sea, seaweed, silly, said, sailor, sold, sardines, sand, salt, super**.

- Tell them that the letter *s* looks like this in books (*lower case*).

Finger trace the letter on the page.

You say that this is the shape (*going over the letter again*). You say again that *s* is its sound.

Ask: "Does anyone know what its name is?"

Show Letter Card *s* and finger trace. Confirm that it is the same letter as the one in the book.

Ask: "What is its name?"

Ask: "What sound does it make?"

Ask them, as appropriate, to finger trace over the letter shape. (*Emphasise the correct starting point and the correct formation when tracing over the letter.*)

■ Ask them if anyone could be in the *s* set, with a name beginning with *s*. (*For example,* **Sally**, **Samir**.)

Ask identified children to select their name card and stick it under the correct letter on the Alphabet Frieze.

Ask: "What do you notice about the letter at the beginning of your name?"

Confirm that it is a capital letter and discuss its function.

Ask them, as appropriate, to finger trace over the upper case letter shape.

Ask: "Does anyone's mummy, daddy, auntie's name begin with the sound *s*?" (*This may not need to be done if there are enough children in the class with names beginning with* **s**.)

■ Tell them that *Sammy* likes things beginning with *s*.

Ask them to listen carefully and tell you which other things *Sammy* would like.

Give examples: *sausages* or *biscuits*, *cake* or *sandwiches*, *sand* or *water*.

■ Reread the rhyme with the class encouraging the children to join in. You should track the words with a pointer to focus on the direction of print, return sweep and correspondence between the spoken and the written word.

NOW OR LATER

■ Workbook 1 page 10.

Demonstrate the correct letter formation giving a commentary as you do so: "Round and down and round." (*Draw children's attention to the fact that the down stroke is on a slant and not straight down. Remember to demonstrate the letter so that children see it from the correct direction.*)

FURTHER PRACTICE

DEVELOPING SKILLS

Some or all of these activities must be done to ensure progress:

■ Find the letter *s* on the Alphabet Frieze.

■ Find *s* letters in the alphabet rhyme.

■ Find the letter *s* in books and around the classroom.

■ Practise letter formation.

■ Cut out pictures from magazines to make a book about *s*.

■ *s* – where is my sound – beginning or end?

You say a word and children answer *beginning* or *end*.

Suggested words:

sausage	soap	kiss	silver
miss	seven	boss	song
sun	pass	mess	sand
fuss	sink		

NOTE

■ When the children line up, ask those whose names begin with *s* to come forward first then those whose names begin with letters already taught to come.

■ When the children line up, ask, for example, *Sally* and *Samir* to come forward. Then ask: "Who else can come to the line?" Confirm that they can go into the line if their own name begins with *s*.

ACTIVITIES AT HOME

■ Look for an object starting with *s* to take to school.

■ My Sounds Book.

S

The c d a h m and s sounds

THE NLF AIMS

- Hear and differentiate between the initial sounds c, d, a, h, m and s in words.
- Read the letters that represent the sounds c, d, a, h, m and s.

WHAT YOU NEED

RESOURCES

- Letter Cards c, d, a, h, m and s
- Whiteboard/chalkboard/easel
- Collection of h, m and s pictures and other pictures
- Workbook 1 page 11
- Teacher's copy of Workbook 1 page 11
- Alphabet Frieze
- Quick Cards
- Additional Support 2

KEY LESSON POINTERS

VOCABULARY

alphabet letter name sound word letter shape capital rhyme trace start/beginning match

THE CHILDREN should throughout the lesson:

- distinguish between the letter sounds c, d, a, h, m and s and the letter names c, d, a, h, m and s
- pronounce the pure sounds c, d, h, m and s
- focus exclusively on the sound activity and not stray onto unrelated topics

YOU should throughout the lesson:

- emphasise the c, d, a, h, m and s sounds at all times
- emphasise the difference between the letter sound and the letter name
- ensure correct pronunciation of the c, d, a, h, m and s sounds
- encourage the use of examples such as the words *carrot* and *cake* and not *clown* where c is part of the *cl* cluster, and *dog* and *door* and not *dragon* where d is part of the *dr* cluster, and *sun* and *sink* and not *swing* where s is part of the *sw* cluster
- ensure that enough time is spent looking at and talking about the book and rhyme.

THE LESSON

STARTING THE LESSON

- Review all the sounds learned to date. Use Letter Cards *c, d, a, h, m* and *s* and revisit *Hector Hedgehog's Big Book of Rhymes (Alphabet)* if necessary.

TEACHING THE LESSON

- Show the children the *s* Letter Card.

  Ask: "What sound does this letter make?" The children may need a prompt: "Remember *Sammy* the *seal*?" (*Emphasise the* s *at the beginning of* **Sammy** *and* **seal**.)

  Encourage the children to listen carefully and to tell you which word begins with *s*: *sack* or *ten*, *card* or *six*, *silver* or *gold*.

- Show the children the *a* Letter Card.

  Ask: "What sound does this letter make?" The children may need a prompt: "Remember the **astronauts**?" (*Emphasise the* a *at the beginning of* **astronauts**.)

  Encourage the children to listen carefully and to tell you which word begins with *a*: *apples* or *desk*, *ambulance* or *door*, *dolphin* or *alligators*.

- Show the children the *h* Letter Card.

  Ask: "What sound does this letter make?" The children may need a prompt: "Remember *Hector* the *hedgehog*?" (*Emphasise the* h *at the beginning of* **Hector** *and* **Hedgehog**.)

  Tell the children to listen carefully and tell you which word begins with *h*: *hospital* or *elephant*, *tent* or *house*, *hose* or *garden*.

- Stick Letter Cards *h, m* and *s* on the board(s).

  Explain to the children that the board with the *h* is for all the pictures that start with *h*, the board with the *m* is for all the pictures that start with *m* and that the board with the *s* is for all the pictures that start with *s*.

- Give the children *h, m* or *s* pictures and ask them in turn to put them on the correct board. (*Encourage children when putting a card on the board to give the reason:* "**Helicopter** *can go in the* **h** *set because it starts with* **h**." "**Moon** *can go in the* **m** *set because it starts with* **m**.")

  As the children become more confident, pictures starting with other letters can be introduced. The children should be expected to say that *river*, for example, cannot go in the *h* set or the *m* set or the *s* set because it doesn't begin with *h, m* or *s*.

- Show the teacher's copy of Workbook 1 page 11.

  Ask the children if anyone could point to the letter that makes the sound *s*.

  Ask the children to point to a letter of their choice and tell the class what sound it makes.

  Ask the children to identify the pictures on the page.

  Repeat the words emphasising the *h* in the *h* words, the *d* in the *d* words, the *s* in the *s* words, the *c* in the *c* words and the *m* in the *m* words.

  Tell them that they have to match the letter to the correct picture, that is, the picture starting with the sound.

  Demonstrate the procedure for *d*.

- Children complete Workbook 1 page 11. (*Remember to remove teacher's copy before children start to work.*)

NOW OR LATER

- Repeat the above lesson for further practice.
- Children complete Additional Support 2.

FURTHER PRACTICE

DEVELOPING SKILLS

Some or all of these activities must be done to ensure progress:

- Practise letter formation.

- **Quick Cards**

  Children have the *c, d, a, h, m* and *s* cards face up on the table. You call out a word: *carrot, dinner, astronaut* and so on, and the children point to/hold up the appropriate card.

  You hold up a picture of an object starting with *c, d, a, h, m* or *s* and the children point to/hold up the appropriate card.

- **What is my sound?**

  You say a word and children say the sound that the word starts with: *sock – s*.

- **Peek-a-Boo**

  See Unit 2 Introduction.

NOTE

Quick Cards

- If the children hold up the cards*-, ensure that all letters are the right way up and facing in the right direction. In the early stages it might be better for the children to the point to cards.

The focus of this unit is alphabet letters and their corresponding sounds. However, you should begin to look at raising the children's awareness of CVC words with medial *a*. Magnetic letters could be used.

Suggested words:

hat	cat	mat	Sam
ham	mad	sat	had

ACTIVITIES AT HOME

- My Sounds Book.

c d a h m s

The t sound

THE NLF AIMS

- Hear and identify the initial sound *t*.
- Read the letter that represents the sound *t*.
- Write the letter that represents the sound *t*.

WHAT YOU NEED

RESOURCES

- *Hector Hedgehog's Big Book of Rhymes (Alphabet)* page 25
- Letter Cards *c, d, a, h, m, s* and *t*
- Alphabet Frieze
- Cards with names of children in class whose names start with *t*
- Whiteboard/chalkboard/easel
- Workbook 1 page 12
- Teacher's copy of Workbook 1 page 12

KEY LESSON POINTERS

VOCABULARY

alphabet   letter   name   sound   word
letter shape   capital   rhyme   trace
start/beginning   middle   match

THE CHILDREN should throughout the lesson:

- distinguish between the letter sound *t* and the letter name *t*
- pronounce the pure sound *t*, without blurring it by adding a vowel as in *ti*
- focus exclusively on the sound activity and not stray onto unrelated topics.

YOU should throughout the lesson:

- emphasise the *t* sound at all times
- emphasise the difference between the letter sound and the letter name
- ensure correct pronunciation of the pure *t* sound
- encourage the use of examples such as the words *ten* and *tie* and not *tractor* where *t* is part of the *tr* cluster
- ensure that enough time is spent looking at and talking about the book and rhyme
- emphasise starting at the correct point when tracing/writing the letter *t* and moving finger/pencil in the correct direction.

THE LESSON

STARTING THE LESSON

Quick revision of *c, d, a, h, m* and *s*.

Some or all of the following should be done to ensure progression:

- Show Letter Cards and ask what sound each letter makes.

  Confirm that the letters make the sounds *c, d, a, h, m* and *s*.

  Ask: "What are the names of the letters?"

- Stick the cards on the board.

  Ask the children to find the card with the letter that makes the *c, d, a, h, m* or *s* sound.

  Ask the children to find the card that the word **cup, diver, animal, happy, mask, sad** and so on starts with.

  Tell the children they have to think about the names of the letters now and ask them to find *c* (*see*) and *d* (*dee*), *a* (*ai*), *h, m* and *s*.

TEACHING THE LESSON

- "Now let's see what today's letter is going to be."

- Open the book at page 25 and tell them that this will be today's activity. (*Be sure to spend some time together, looking at the page.*)

  Ask: "What can you see in the picture?"

  Discuss the content focusing on the *t* words

- Read the rhyme, emphasising the *t* words.

  Reread and encourage the children to join in.

  Ask: "Where was **Tiddle Tum Tom** going?"

  Confirm into **town**, heavily emphasising the *t* at the start of **town**.

  Tell them to listen carefully and to say what sound they can hear at the beginning of **Tiddle**.

  Confirm that it is the sound *t*.

  Tell them to listen carefully and to say what sound they can hear at the beginning of **Tum** and **Tom**.

  Confirm that it is the sound *t*. (*Check that the children pronounce the* t *correctly; not as* ti.)

  Ask them to listen for other *t* words while you reread the rhyme.

  Confirm other *t* words: **toddles, town, tumbles, taps, tiny, turns, tail** and **tips**.

- Tell them that the letter *t* looks like this in books (*lower case*).

Finger trace the letter on the page.

You say that this is the shape (*going over the letter again*). You say again that *t* is its sound.

Ask: "Does anyone know what its name is?"

Show Letter Card *t* and finger trace. Confirm that it is the same letter as the one in the book.

Ask: "What is its name?"

Ask: "What sound does it make?"

Ask them, as appropriate, to finger trace over the letter shape. (*Emphasise the correct starting point and the correct formation when tracing over the letter.*)

■ Ask them if anyone could be in the *t* set, with a name beginning with *t*. (*For example,* **Tanya, Terry**.)

Ask identified children to select their name card and stick it under the correct letter on the Alphabet Frieze.

Ask: "What do you notice about the letter at the beginning of your name?"

Confirm that it is a capital letter and discuss its function.

Ask them, as appropriate, to finger trace over the upper case letter shape.

Ask: "Does anyone's mummy, daddy, auntie's name begin with the sound *t*?" (*This may not need to be done if there are enough children in the class with names beginning with* **t**.)

■ Tell them that **Tiddle Tum Tom** likes things beginning with *t*.

Ask them to listen carefully and tell you which other things **Tiddle Tum Tom** would like.

Give examples: **tortoise** or **horse**, **piano** or **tambourine**, **tin** or **bottle**.

■ Reread the rhyme with the class, encouraging the children to join in. You should track the words with a pointer to focus on the direction of print, return sweep and correspondence between the spoken and the written word.

NOW OR LATER

■ Workbook 1 page 12.

Demonstrate the correct letter formation giving a commentary as you do so: "Straight down and round and then a little line across." (*Remember to demonstrate the letter so that children see it from the correct direction.*)

FURTHER PRACTICE

DEVELOPING SKILLS

Some or all of these activities must be done to ensure progress:

■ Find the letter *t* on the Alphabet Frieze.

■ Find *t* letters in the alphabet rhyme.

■ Find the letter *t* in books and around the classroom.

■ Practise letter formation.

■ Cut out pictures from magazines to make a book about *t*.

■ *t* – where is my sound – beginning or end?

You say a word and children answer *beginning* or *end*.

Suggested words:

telephone	tiger	hat	tin
hut	toddler	net	eat
teddy	toe	feet	touch
boot	table		

NOTE

■ When the children line up, ask those whose names begin with *t* to come forward first, then those whose names begin with letters already taught to come.

■ When the children line up, ask, for example, *Tanya* and *Terry* to come forward. Then ask: "Who else can come to the line?" Confirm that they can go into the line if their own name begins with *t*.

ACTIVITIES AT HOME

■ Look for an object starting with *t* to take to school.
■ My Sounds Book.

AUDITORY DISCRIMINATION

IDENTIFYING ALPHABET SOUNDS

Review

THE NLF AIMS

- Hear and differentiate between the initial sounds *c, d, a, h, m, s* and *t* in words.
- Read the letters that represent the sounds *c, d, a, h, m, s* and *t*.

WHAT YOU NEED

RESOURCES

- Letter Cards *c, d, a, h, m, s* and *t*
- Whiteboard/chalkboard/easel
- Collection of *m, s* and *t* pictures and other pictures
- Workbook 1 page 13
- Teacher's copy of Workbook 1 page 13
- Alphabet Frieze
- Quick Cards
- Additional Support 3
- Assessment 2.1

KEY LESSON POINTERS

VOCABULARY

alphabet letter name sound word letter shape capital rhyme trace start/beginning

THE CHILDREN should throughout the lesson:

- distinguish between the letter sounds *c, d, a, h, m, s* and *t* and the letter names *c, d, a, h, m, s* and *t*
- pronounce the pure sounds *c, d, h, m, s* and *t*
- focus exclusively on the sound activity and not stray onto unrelated topics.

YOU should throughout the lesson:

- emphasise the *c, d, a, h, m, s* and *t* sounds at all times
- emphasise the difference between the letter sound and the letter name
- ensure correct pronunciation of the *c, d, a, h, m, s* and *t* sounds
- encourage the use of examples such as the words *saw* and *salt* and not *swim* where *s* is part of the *sw* cluster, and *dog* and *door* and not *dragon* where *d* is part of the *dr* cluster, and *top* and *tent* and not *trousers* where *t* is part of the *tr* cluster
- ensure that enough time is spent looking at and talking about the book and rhyme.

STARTING THE LESSON

- Review all the sounds learned to date. Use Letter Cards *c, d, a, h, m, s* and *t* and revisit *Hector Hedgehog's Big Book of Rhymes (Alphabet)* if necessary.

TEACHING THE LESSON

- Show the children the *m* Letter Card.

  Ask: "What sound does this letter make?" The children may need a prompt: "Remember *Myrtle* and *Merlin* and *Mickey MacMouse*?" (*Emphasise the* **m** *at the beginning of* **Myrtle, Merlin, Mickey** *and* **MacMouse**.)

  Encourage the children to listen carefully and to tell you which word begins with *m*: *match* or *bed*, *money* or *sugar*, *book* or *marbles*.

- Show the children the *t* Letter Card.

  Ask: "What sound does this letter make?" The children may need a prompt: "Remember *Tiddle Tum Tom*?" (*Emphasise the* **t** *at the beginning of* **Tiddle, Tum** *and* **Tom**.)

  Encourage the children to listen carefully and to tell you which word begins with *t*: *toffee* or *chocolate*, *doll* or *teddy*, *moon* or *tank*.

- Show the children the *s* Letter Card.

  Ask: "What sound does this letter make?" The children may need a prompt: "Remember *Sammy* the *seal*?" (*Emphasise the* **s** *at the beginning of* **Sammy** *and* **seal**.)

  Tell the children to listen carefully and tell you which word begins with *s*: *sardine* or *goat*, *book* or *suit*, *banana* or *supper*.

- Stick Letter Cards *m, s* and *t* on the board(s).

  Explain to the children that the board with the *m* is for all the pictures that start with *m* and the board with the *s* is for all the pictures that start with *s* and that the board with the *t* is for all the pictures that start with *t*.

- Give the children *m*, *s* or *t* pictures and ask them in turn to put them on the correct board. (*Encourage children when putting card on the board to give the reason:* "**Teddy** *can go in the* **t** *set because it starts with* **t**." "**Moon** *can go in the* **m** *set because it starts with* **m**.")

   As the children become more confident, pictures starting with other letters can be introduced. The children should be expected to say that *wellington*, for example, cannot go in the *t* set or the *m* set or the *s* set because it doesn't begin with *t*, *m* or *s*.

- Show the teacher's copy of Workbook 1 page 15.

   Ask the children if anyone could point to the letter that makes the sound *s*.

   Ask the children to point to a letter of their choice and tell the class what sound it makes.

   Repeat for all the letters.

   Ask the children to identify the pictures on the page.

   Repeat the words emphasising the *s* in the *s* words, the *t* in the *t* words, the *m* in the *m* words, the *d* in the *d* words and the *h* in the *h* words.

   Tell them that they have to choose the sound that the picture starts with and draw a circle around it.

   Demonstrate the procedure for the picture of the sandwich.

   Ask the children to choose the correct sound for the other pictures, inviting the children to circle the correct letters on the sample copy.

- Children complete Workbook 1 page 13. (*Remember to remove teacher's copy of workbook before children start to work.*)

NOW OR LATER

- Repeat the above lesson for further practice.
- Children complete Additional Support 3.

FURTHER PRACTICE

DEVELOPING SKILLS

Some or all of these activities must be done to ensure progress:

- Practise letter formation.

- **Quick Cards**

   Children have the *c*, *d*, *a*, *h*, *m*, *s* and *t* cards face up on the table. You call out the word: *carrot*, *dinner*, *astronaut*, *house* and so on and the children point to/hold up the appropriate card.

   You hold up a picture of an object starting with *c*, *d*, *a*, *h*, *m*, *s* or *t* and the children point to/hold up the appropriate card.

- **What's my sound? (1)**

   You say a word and children say the sound that the word starts with: *teddy – t*.

   The *t* and *d* sounds are easily confused. It is often difficult for children to hear the difference between the two sounds. Give plenty of practice.

- **What's my sound? (2)**

   You say a word and the children say *t* or *d* sound that the word starts with.

   Suggested words:

tie	die	door
tin	din	ten
den	teddy	daddy
desk	tip	dip

- **Peek-a-Boo**

   See Unit 2 Introduction.

NOTE

Quick Cards

- If the children hold up the cards, ensure that all the letters are the right way up and facing in the right direction. In the early stages it might be better for the children to point to the cards.

ASSESSMENT 2.1

ACTIVITIES AT HOME

My Sounds Book.

Review and s t

The p sound

THE NLF AIMS

- Hear and identify the initial sound *p*.
- Read the letter that represents the sound *p*.
- Write the letter that represents the sound *p*.

WHAT YOU NEED

RESOURCES

- *Hector Hedgehog's Big Book of Rhymes (Alphabet)* page 18
- Letter Cards *c, d, a, h, m, s, t* and *p*
- Alphabet Frieze
- Cards with names of children in class whose names start with *p*
- Whiteboard/chalkboard/easel
- Workbook 1 page 14
- Teacher's copy of Workbook 1 page 14

KEY LESSON POINTERS

VOCABULARY

alphabet letter name sound word letter shape capital rhyme trace start/beginning middle match

THE CHILDREN should throughout the lesson:

- distinguish between the letter sound *p* and the letter name *p*
- pronounce the pure sound *p*, without blurring it by adding a vowel as in *pi*
- focus exclusively on the sound activity and not stray onto unrelated topics.

YOU should throughout the lesson:

- emphasise the *p* sound at all times
- emphasise the difference between the letter sound and the letter name
- ensure correct pronunciation of the pure *p* sound
- ensure that enough time is spent looking at and talking about the book and rhyme
- emphasise starting at the correct point when tracing/writing the letter *p* and moving finger/pencil in the correct direction.

STARTING THE LESSON

Quick revision of *c, d, a, h, m, s* and *t*.

Some or all of the following should be done to ensure progression:

- Show Letter Cards and ask what sound each letter makes.

  Confirm that the letters make the sounds *c, d, a, h, m, s* and *t*.

  Ask: "What are the names of the letters?"

- Stick the cards on the board.

  Ask the children to find the card with the letter that makes the *c, d, a, h, m, s* and *t* sound.

  Ask the children to find the card with the letter that the word *monster, song, tadpole* and so on starts with.

  Tell the children they have to think about the names of the letters now and ask them to find *c, d, a, h, m, s* and *t*.

  (*Be aware of the needs of the children in terms of the letter sounds that they are unsure of and give more practice.*)

TEACHING THE LESSON

- "Now let's see what today's letter is going to be."

- Open the book at page 18 and tell them that this will be today's activity. (*Be sure to spend some time together, looking at the page.*)

  Ask: "What can you see in the picture?"

  Discuss the content focusing on the *p* words such as *popcorn* and *Pam*.

- Read the rhyme, emphasising the *p* words.

  Reread and encourage the children to join in.

  Ask: "What did *Pam* pick at?"

  Confirm *peach, pasta* and *popcorn* heavily emphasising the *p*.

  Tell them to listen carefully and to say what sound they can hear at the beginning of *Pam*.

  Confirm that it is the sound *p*.

  Tell them to listen carefully and to say what sound they can hear at the beginning of *pickety*.

  Confirm that it is the sound *p*. (*Check that the children pronounce the* **p** *correctly; not as* **pi**.)

  Ask them to listen for other *p* words while you reread the rhyme.

  Confirm other *p* words: *perfect, pale, purple, pest, Pickety, picks, peach, pasta, popcorn, pokes, potatoes, pancakes, pies, pushes, pickles, puddings, peas, pouts, parsley, Parmesan, picky, pink, puff.*

■ Tell them that the letter *p* looks like this in books (*lower case*).

Finger trace the letter on the page.

You say that this is the shape (*going over the letter again*). You say again that *p* is its sound.

Ask: "Does anyone know what its name is?"

Show Letter Card *p* and finger trace. Confirm that it is the same letter as the one in the book.

Ask: "What is its name?"

Ask: "What sound does it make?"

Ask them, as appropriate, to finger trace over the letter shape. (*Emphasise the correct starting point and the correct formation when tracing over the letter.*)

■ Ask them if anyone could be in the *p* set, with a name beginning with *p*. (*For example,* **Paul, Paramjit.**)

Ask identified children to select their name cards and stick them under the correct letter on the Alphabet Frieze.

Ask: "What do you notice about the letter at the beginning of your name?"

Confirm that it is a capital letter and discuss its function.

Ask them, as appropriate, to finger trace over the upper case letter shape.

■ Ask: "What sound would *Pam* like things beginning with?"

Confirm that it is the sound *p*.

Ask them to tell you things that *Pam* would like.

Give examples if necessary: *pudding* or *jam*, *peaches* or *apples*, *dish* or *pot*.

■ Reread the rhyme with the class, encouraging the children to join in. You should track the words with a pointer to focus on the direction of print, return sweep and correspondence between the spoken and the written word.

NOW OR LATER

■ Workbook 1 page 14.

Demonstrate the correct letter formation giving a commentary as you do so:

"Down, back up, round and in."
(*Remember to demonstrate the letter so that children see it from the correct direction.*)

FURTHER PRACTICE

DEVELOPING SKILLS

Some or all of these activities must be done to ensure progress:

■ Find the letter *p* on the Alphabet Frieze.

■ Find *p* letters in the alphabet rhyme.

■ Find the letter *p* in books and around the classroom.

■ Practise letter formation.

■ Cut out pictures from magazines to make a book about *p*.

■ **What is my name?**

You say the sound that a letter makes and children say the corresponding letter name.

■ **What is my sound?**

You say a letter name and children say the sound that letter makes.

■ *p* – where is my sound – beginning or end?

You say a word and children answer *beginning* or *end*.

Suggested words:

cup	parrot	puddle	pick
slip	chip	hop	pie
pear	tap	peach	pink
rope	flap		

NOTE

■ When the children line up, ask those whose names begin with *p* to come forward first then those whose names begin with letters already taught to come.

■ When the children line up, ask, for example, *Paul* and *Paramjit* to come forward. Then ask: "Who else can come to the line?" Confirm that they can go into the line if their own name begins with *p*.

ACTIVITIES AT HOME

■ Look for an object starting with *p* to take to school.

■ My Sounds Book.

p

The o sound

BEFORE YOU START

THE NLF AIMS

- Hear and identify the initial sound *o*.
- Read the letter that represents the sound *o*.
- Write the letter that represents the sound *o*.

WHAT YOU NEED

RESOURCES

- *Hector Hedgehog's Big Book of Rhymes (Alphabet)* page 17
- Letter Cards *c, d, a, h, m, s, t, p* and *o*
- Alphabet Frieze
- Cards with names of children in class whose names start with *o*
- Whiteboard/chalkboard/easel
- Workbook 1 page 15
- Teacher's copy of Workbook 1 page 15

KEY LESSON POINTERS

VOCABULARY

alphabet letter name sound word
letter shape capital rhyme trace
start/beginning middle match

THE CHILDREN should throughout the lesson:

- distinguish between the letter sound *o* and the letter name *o*
- pronounce the short sound *o*
- focus exclusively on the sound activity and not stray onto unrelated topics.

YOU should throughout the lesson:

- emphasise the *o* sound at all times
- emphasise the difference between the letter sound and the letter name
- ensure that enough time is spent looking at and talking about the book and rhyme
- emphasise starting at the correct point when tracing/writing the letter *o* and moving finger/pencil in the correct direction.

THE LESSON

STARTING THE LESSON

Quick revision of *c, d, a, h, m, s, t* and *p*.

Some or all of the following should be done to ensure progression:

- Show Letter Cards and ask what sound each letter makes.

  Confirm that the letters make the sounds *c, d, a, h, m, s, t* and *p*.

  Ask: "What are the names of the letters?"

- Stick the cards on the board.

  Ask the children to find the card with the letter that makes the *c, d, a, h, m, s, t* and *p* sound.

  Ask the children to find the card that the word *man, soap, taxi, penguin* and so on starts with.

  Tell the children they have to think about the names of the letters now and ask them to find *c, d, a, h, m, s, t* and *p*.

  (*Be aware of the needs of the children in terms of the letter sounds that they are unsure of and give more practice.*)

TEACHING THE LESSON

- "Now let's see what today's letter is going to be."

- Open the book at page 17 and tell them that this will be today's activity. (*Be sure to spend some time together, looking at the page.*)

  Ask: "What can you see in the picture?"

  Discuss the content focusing on the *o* words such as *otter* and *orange*. (*Emphasise the* o *words. Ensure the children focus exclusively on the objectives of the activity. Don't let them stray onto unrelated topics.*)

- Read the rhyme, emphasising the *o* words.

  Reread and encourage the children to join in.

  Ask: "Where did *Ollie otter* go on the *orange* train?"

  Confirm to *Oxford*.

  Tell them to listen carefully and to say what sound they can hear at the beginning of *Oxford*.

  Confirm that it is the sound *o*.

  Tell them to listen carefully and to say what sound they can hear at the beginning of *Ollie* and *otter*.

  Confirm that it is the sound *o*.

Ask them to listen for other *o* words while you reread the rhyme.

Confirm other *o* words: ***October, orange, Oscar, ostrich, offers, olive, odd, oblong, on, offended***.

■ Tell them that the letter *o* looks like this in books (lower case).

Finger trace the letter on the page.

You say that this is the shape (*going over the letter again*). You say again that *o* is its sound.

Ask: "Does anyone know what its name is?"

Show Letter Card *o* and finger trace. Confirm that it is the same letter as the one in the book.

Ask: "What is its name?"

Ask: "What sound does it make?"

Ask them, as appropriate, to finger trace over the letter shape.

■ Ask them if anyone could be in the *o* set, with a name beginning with *o*. (*For example*, **Olive, Oliver**.)

Ask identified children to select their name cards and stick them under the correct letter on the Alphabet Frieze.

Ask: "What do you notice about the letter at the beginning of your name?"

Confirm that it is a capital letter and discuss its function.

Ask them, as appropriate, to finger trace over the upper case letter shape.

■ Ask: "What sound would *Ollie* like things beginning with?"

Confirm that it is the sound *o*.

Ask them to tell you things that *Ollie* would like.

Give examples if necessary: ***on*** or ***in, odd*** or ***even, penguin*** or ***ostrich***.

■ Reread the rhyme with the class, encouraging the children to join in. You should track the words with a pointer to focus on the direction of print, return sweep and correspondence between spoken and written word.

NOW OR LATER

■ Workbook 1 page 15.
Demonstrate the correct letter formation giving a commentary as you do so.

FURTHER PRACTICE

DEVELOPING SKILLS

Some or all of these activities must be done to ensure progress:

■ Find the letter *o* on the Alphabet Frieze.

■ Find as many *o* letters as you can in the alphabet rhyme.

■ Find the letter *o* in books and around the classroom.

■ Practise letter formation.

■ Cut out pictures from magazines to make a book about *o*.

■ **What's my name?**
You say the sound that a letter makes and children say the corresponding letter name.

■ **What's my sound?**
You say a letter name and the children say sound that letter makes.

NOTE

■ When the children line up, ask those whose names begin with *o* to come forward first then those whose names begin with letters already taught to come.

■ Children will not meet many words starting with the short *o* sound. While words such as *oats, oil, onion* start with the letter *o*, it is not the sound *o*. Tell the children that the *o* does not make its usual sound in these cases.

■ At this point many children may be ready to blend CVC words with the sounds taught. The skill is taught formally at a later stage but raising awareness may be appropriate now.

Suggested words:

cot	dot	hot	mop	pot
top	cod	hop	pod	

ACTIVITIES AT HOME

■ Look for an object starting with *o* to take to school.

■ My Sounds Book.

O

Review

THE NLF AIMS

- Hear and differentiate between the initial sounds *s*, *t*, *p* and *o* in words.
- Read the letters that represent the sounds *s*, *t*, *p* and *o*.

WHAT YOU NEED

RESOURCES

- Letter Cards *c*, *d*, *a*, *h*, *m*, *s*, *t*, *p* and *o*
- Whiteboard/chalkboard/easel
- Collection of *t*, *p* and *o* pictures and other pictures
- Workbook 1 page 16
- Teacher's copy of Workbook 1 page 16
- Alphabet Frieze
- Quick Cards
- Additional Support 4

KEY LESSON POINTERS

VOCABULARY

alphabet   letter   name   sound   word
letter shape   capital   rhyme   trace
start/beginning   match

THE CHILDREN should throughout the lesson:

- distinguish between the letter sounds *s*, *t*, *p* and *o* and the letter names *s*, *t*, *p* and *o*
- pronounce the pure sounds *s*, *t* and *p*
- focus exclusively on the sound activity and not stray onto unrelated topics

YOU should throughout the lesson:

- emphasise the *s*, *t*, *p* and *o* sounds at all times
- emphasise the difference between the letter sound and the letter name
- ensure correct pronunciation of the *s*, *t*, *p* and *o* sounds
- encourage the use of examples such as the words *saw* and *salt* and not *swim* where *s* is part of the *sw* cluster, and *pot* and *pudding* and not *plate* where *p* is part of the *pl* cluster, and *tap* and *teddy* and not *train* where *t* is part of the *tr* cluster
- ensure that enough time is spent looking at and talking about the book and rhyme.

STARTING THE LESSON

- Review all the sounds learned to date. Use Letter Cards *c*, *d*, *a*, *h*, *m*, *s*, *t*, *p* and *o* and revisit *Hector Hedgehog's Big Book of Rhymes (Alphabet)* if necessary.

TEACHING THE LESSON

- Show the children the *o* Letter Card.

  Ask: "What sound does this letter make?" The children may need a prompt: "Remember ***Ollie*** the ***otter***?" (*Emphasise the* o *at the beginning of* **Ollie** *and* **otter**.)

  Ask the children to tell you the words which begin with *o*. Give clues if necessary: *olive* or *pear*, *ostrich* or *band*, *book* or *orchestra*.

- Show the children the *p* Letter Card.

  Ask: "What sound does this letter make?" The children may need a prompt: "Remember ***Pickety Pam***?" (*Emphasise the* p *at the beginning of* **Pickety** *and* **Pam**.)

  Ask the children to tell you the words which begin with *p*. Give clues if necessary: *pasta* or *rice*, *pink* or *red*, *salt* or *pepper*.

- Show the children the *t* Letter Card.

  Ask: "What sound does this letter make?" The children may need a prompt: "Remember ***Tiddle Tum Tom***?" (*Emphasise the* t *at the beginning of* **Tiddle**, **Tum** *and* **Tom**.)

  Ask the children to tell you the words which begin with *t*. Give clues if necessary: *six* or *ten*, *fish* or *turtle*, *television* or *computer*.

- Stick Letter Cards *t*, *p* and *o* on the board(s).

  Explain to the children that the board with the *t* is for all the pictures that start with *t* and the board with the *p* is for all the pictures that start with *p* and that the board with the *o* is for all the pictures that start with *o*.

■ Give the children *t, p* or *o* pictures and ask them in turn to put them on the correct board. (*Encourage children when putting card on the board to give the reason:* "**Teddy** *can go in the* **t** *set because it starts with* **t**." "**Piano** *can go in the* **p** *set because it starts with* **p**.")

Pictures starting with other letters should be included. The children should be expected to say that **yo-yo**, for example, cannot go in the *t* set or the *p* set or the *o* set because it doesn't begin with *t, p* or *o*.

■ Show the teacher's copy of Workbook 1 page 16.

Ask the children to point to a letter of their choice and tell the class what sound it makes.

Ask the children to identify the pictures on the page.

Repeat the words emphasising the *t* in the *t* words, the *p* in the *p* words, the *o* in the *o* words, and the *s* in the *s* words.

Tell them that they have to match the letter to the correct picture; the picture starting with the sound.

Demonstrate the procedure for *p*.

■ Children complete Workbook 1 page 16. (*Remember to remove teacher's copy of workbook before children start to work.*)

NOW OR LATER

■ Repeat the above lesson for further practice.

■ Children complete Additional Support 4.

FURTHER PRACTICE

DEVELOPING SKILLS

Some or all of these activities must be done to ensure progress:

■ Practise letter formation.

■ **Quick Cards**

Children have the *p* and *o* cards, plus any Letter Cards that they need further practice in, face up on the table. You call out a word: *potato, octopus, orange, peach* and so on and the children point to/hold up the appropriate card.

You hold up a picture of an object starting with *p* or *o*, plus any letters that the children need further practice in, and the children hold up the appropriate card.

■ **What's my sound? (1)**

You say a word and children say the sound that the word starts with: poppy – *p*.

The *d, t* and *p* sounds are easily confused. It is often difficult for children to hear the difference between the three sounds. Give plenty of practice.

■ **What's my sound? (2)**

You say a word and the children say the *t, d* or *p* sound that the word starts with.

Suggested words:

daddy	poppy	teddy	pasta
doll	desk	tip	dip
pip	tot	dot	pot
ten	den	pen	push

■ **Peek-a-Boo**

See Unit 2 Introduction.

NOTE

Quick Cards

■ If the children hold up the cards, ensure that all the letters are the right way up and facing in the right direction. In the early stages it might be better for the children to point to the cards.

ACTIVITIES AT HOME

■ My Sounds Book.

Review

The n sound

THE NLF AIMS

- Hear and identify the initial sound *n*.
- Read the letter that represents the sound *n*.
- Write the letter that represents the sound *n*.

WHAT YOU NEED

RESOURCES

- *Hector Hedgehog's Big Book of Rhymes (Alphabet)* page 16
- Letter Cards *c, d, a, h, m, s, t, p, o* and *n*
- Alphabet Frieze
- Cards with names of children in class whose names start with *n*
- Whiteboard/chalkboard/easel
- Workbook 1 page 17
- Teacher's copy of Workbook 1 page 17

KEY LESSON POINTERS

VOCABULARY

alphabet   letter   name   sound   word
letter shape   capital   rhyme   trace
start/beginning   middle   match

THE CHILDREN should throughout the lesson:

- distinguish between the letter sound *n* and the letter name *n*
- pronounce the pure sound *n*, without blurring it by adding a vowel as in *nu*
- focus exclusively on the sound activity and not stray onto unrelated topics.

YOU should throughout the lesson:

- emphasise the *n* sound at all times
- emphasise the difference between the letter sound and the letter name
- ensure correct pronunciation of the pure *n* sound
- ensure that enough time is spent looking at and talking about the book and rhyme
- emphasise starting at the correct point when tracing/writing the letter *n* and moving finger/pencil in the correct direction.

STARTING THE LESSON

Quick revision of *c, d, a, h, m, s, t, p* and *o*.

Some or all of the following should be done to ensure progression:

- Show Letter Cards and ask what sound each letter makes.

  Confirm that the letters make the sounds *c, d, a, h, m, s, t, p* and *o*.

  Ask: "What are the names of the letters?"

- Stick the cards on the board.

  Ask the children to find the card with the letter that makes the *c, d, a, h, m, s, t, p* and *o* sound.

  Ask the children to find the card that the word *cabbage, diamond, astronaut, helmet, money, silver, toffee, piano, otter* and so on starts with.

  Tell the children they have to think about the names of the letters now and ask them to find *c, d, a, h, m, s, t, p* and *o*.

  (*Be aware of the needs of the children in terms of the letter sounds that they are unsure of and give more practice.*)

TEACHING THE LESSON

- "Now let's see what today's letter is going to be."

- Open the book at page 16 and tell them that this will be today's activity. (*Be sure to spend some time together, looking at the page.*)

  Ask: "What can you see in the picture?"

  Discuss the content focusing on the *n* words such as *neighbours* and *naughty*. (*Emphasise the* **n** *words. Ensure the children focus exclusively on the objectives of the activity. Don't let them stray onto unrelated topics.*)

- Read the rhyme, emphasising the *n* words.

  Reread and encourage the children to join in.

  Ask: "How many *nosey neighbours* are there?"

  Confirm *nine*, heavily emphasising the *n*.

  Tell them to listen carefully and to say what sound they can hear at the beginning of *nine*.

  Confirm that it is the sound *n*.

  Tell them to listen carefully and to say what sound they can hear at the beginning of *neighbours*.

  Confirm that it is the sound *n*. (*Check that the children pronounce the* **n** *correctly, not as* **nu**.)

Ask them to listen for other *n* words while you reread the rhyme.

Confirm other *n* words: *nosey, nonsense, naughty, nephews, niggle, nip, noise, neat, Nora, nanny, nags*.

■ Tell them that the letter *n* looks like this in books (*lower case*).

Finger trace the letter on the page.

You say that this is the shape (*going over the letter again*). You say again that *n* is its sound.

Ask: "Does anyone know what its name is?"

Show Letter Card *n* and finger trace. Confirm that it is the same letter as the one in the book.

Ask: "What is its name?"

Ask: "What sound does it make?"

Ask them, as appropriate, to finger trace over the letter shape. (*Emphasise the correct starting point and the correct formation when tracing over the letter.*)

■ Ask them if anyone could be in the *n* set, with a name beginning with *n*. (*For example,* **Nasir**, **Nicole**.)

Ask identified children to select their name cards and stick them under the correct letter on the Alphabet Frieze.

Ask: "What do you notice about the letter at the beginning of your name?"

Confirm that it is a capital letter and discuss its function. (*Extend as appropriate to streets, towns.*)

Ask them, as appropriate, to finger trace over the upper case letter shape.

■ Ask: "What sound would *Nora nanny* like things beginning with?"

Confirm that it is the sound *n*.

Ask them to tell you things that *Nora nanny* would like.

Give examples if necessary: *nuts* or *sweets*, *needles* or *pins*, *cage* or *nest*.

■ Reread the rhyme with the class, encouraging the children to join in. You should track the words with a pointer to focus on the direction of print, return sweep and correspondence between the spoken and the written word.

NOW OR LATER

■ Workbook 1 page 17.

Demonstrate the correct letter formation giving a commentary as you do so.

n

FURTHER PRACTICE

DEVELOPING SKILLS

Some or all of these activities must be done to ensure progress:

■ Find the letter *n* on the Alphabet Frieze.

■ Find *n* letters in the alphabet rhyme.

■ Find the letter *n* in books and around the classroom.

■ Practise letter formation.

■ Cut out pictures from magazines to make a book about *n*.

■ **What's my name?**

You say the sound that a letter makes and children say the corresponding letter name.

■ **What's my sound?**

You say a letter name and children say the sound that letter makes.

■ **n – where is my sound – beginning or end?**

You say a word and children answer *beginning* or *end*.

Suggested words:

bun	needle	news	spoon
when	nurse	nasty	gran
neck	fun	stone	nut
night	line	nest	fan

NOTE

■ When the children line up, ask those whose names begin with *n* to come forward first then those whose names begin with letters already taught to come.

■ When the children line up, ask, for example, *Nasir* and *Nicole* to come forward. Then ask: "Who else can come to the line?" Confirm that they can go into the line if their own name begins with *n*.

ACTIVITIES AT HOME

■ Look for an object starting with *n* to take to school.

■ My Sounds Book.

AUDITORY DISCRIMINATION

IDENTIFYING ALPHABET SOUNDS

n

The g sound

THE NLF AIMS

- Hear and identify the initial sound *g*.
- Read the letter that represents the sound *g*.
- Write the letter that represents the sound *g*.

WHAT YOU NEED

RESOURCES

- *Hector Hedgehog's Big Book of Rhymes (Alphabet)* page 9
- Letter Cards *c, d, a, h, m, s, t, p, o, n* and *g*
- Alphabet Frieze
- Cards with names of children in class whose names start with *g*
- Whiteboard/chalkboard/easel
- Workbook 1 page 18
- Teacher's copy of Workbook 1 page 18

KEY LESSON POINTERS

VOCABULARY

alphabet   letter   name   sound   word
letter shape   capital   rhyme   trace
start/beginning   middle   match

THE CHILDREN should throughout the lesson:

- distinguish between the letter sound *g* and the letter name *g*
- pronounce the pure sound *g* without blurring it by adding a vowel as in *gi*
- focus exclusively on the sound activity and not stray onto unrelated topics.

YOU should throughout the lesson:

- emphasise the *g* sound at all times
- emphasise the difference between the letter sound and the letter name
- ensure correct pronunciation of the pure *g* sound
- ensure that enough time is spent looking at and talking about the book and rhyme
- emphasise starting at the correct point when tracing/writing the letter *g* and moving finger/pencil in the correct direction.

STARTING THE LESSON

Quick revision of *c, d, a, h, m, s, t, p, o* and *n*.

Some or all of the following should be done to ensure progression:

- Show Letter Cards and ask what sound each letter makes.

  Confirm that the letters make the sounds *c, d, a, h, m, s, t, p, o* and *n*.

  Ask: "What are the names of the letters?"

- Stick the cards on the board.

  Ask the children to find the card with the letter that makes the *c, d, a, h, m, s, t, p, o* and *n* sound.

  Ask the children to find the card that the word **camera, donkey,** and **handle, meat, sink, time, pet, organ, nettles** and so on starts with.

  Tell the children they have to think about the names of the letters now and ask them to find *c, d, a, h, m, s, t, p, o* and *n*.

  (*Be aware of the needs of the children in terms of the letter sounds that they are unsure of and give more practice.*)

TEACHING THE LESSON

- "Now let's see what today's letter is going to be."

- Open the book at page 9 and tell them that this will be today's activity. (*Be sure to spend some time together, looking at the page.*)

  Ask: "What can you see in the picture?"

  Discuss the content, focusing on the **g** words such as **garden** and **gorilla**. (*Emphasise the* **g** *words. Ensure the children focus exclusively on the objectives of the activity. Don't let them stray onto unrelated topics.*)

- Read the rhyme, emphasising the **g** words.

  Reread and encourage the children to join in.

  Ask: "Where was **Gabby**?"

  Confirm in the **garden** by the **gate**, heavily emphasising the **g**.

  Tell them to listen carefully and to say what sound they can hear at the beginning of **garden**.

  Confirm that it is the sound **g**.

  Tell them to listen carefully and to say what sound they can hear at the beginning of **gate**.

  Confirm that it is the sound **g**.

  Ask them to listen for other **g** words while you reread the rhyme.

Confirm other *g* words: *gorilla, goat, gulps, Gabby, get, goes, garage, gosh, gasps.*

■ Tell them that the letter *g* looks like this in books (*lower case*).

Finger trace the letter on the page.

You say that this is the shape (*going over the letter again*). You say again that *g* is its sound.

Ask: "Does anyone know what its name is?"

Show Letter Card *g* and finger trace. Confirm that it is the same letter as the one in the book.

Ask: "What is its name?"

Ask: "What sound does it make?"

Ask them, as appropriate, to finger trace over the letter shape. (*Emphasise the correct starting point and the correct formation when tracing over the letter.*)

■ Ask them if anyone could be in the *g* set, with a name beginning with *g*. (*For example,* **Gareth, Gayle.**)

Ask identified children to select their name cards and stick them under the correct letter on the Alphabet Frieze.

Ask: "What do you notice about the letter at the beginning of your name?"

Confirm that it is a capital letter and discuss its function. (*Extend as appropriate to streets, towns, start of sentences.*)

Ask them, as appropriate, to finger trace over the upper case letter shape.

■ Ask: "What sound would *Gabby* like things beginning with?"

Confirm that it is the sound *g*.

Ask them to tell you things that *Gabby* would like.

Give examples if necessary: **gold** or **silver**, **ducks** or **geese**, **golf** or **football.**

■ Reread the rhyme with the class, encouraging the children to join in. You should track the words with a pointer to focus on the direction of print, return sweep and correspondence between spoken and written word.

NOW OR LATER

■ Workbook 1 page 18.

Demonstrate the correct letter formation giving a commentary as you do so.

FURTHER PRACTICE

DEVELOPING SKILLS

Some or all of these activities must be done to ensure progress:

■ Find the letter *g* on the Alphabet Frieze.

■ Find *g* letters in the alphabet rhyme.

■ Find the letter *g* in books and around the classroom.

■ Practise letter formation.

■ Cut out pictures from magazines to make a book about *g*.

■ **What's my name?**

You say the sound that a letter makes and children say the corresponding letter name.

■ **What's my sound?**

You say a letter name and children say the sound that letter makes.

■ ***g* – where is my sound – beginning or end?**

You say a word and children answer *beginning* or *end*.

Suggested words:

goat	gift	mug	gold
pig	game	plug	goal
gate	drug	dog	guess
good	flag	bag	rug

NOTE

■ When the children line up, ask those whose names begin with *g* to come forward first, then those whose names begin with letters already taught to come. At this point children with names that begin with the soft *g* (*j*) such as *Geraldine, Gillian, Giles* should be reminded that sometimes the letter makes a different sound.

ACTIVITIES AT HOME

■ Look for an object starting with *g* to take to school.

■ My Sounds Book.

g

Review

THE NLF AIMS

- Hear and differentiate between the initial sounds *p, o, n* and *g* in words.
- Read the letters that represent the sounds *p, o, n* and *g*.

WHAT YOU NEED

RESOURCES

- Letter Cards of letters learned to date
- Whiteboard/chalkboard/easel
- Collection of *p, n* and *g* pictures and other pictures
- Workbook 1 page 19
- Teacher's copy of Workbook 1 page 19
- Alphabet Frieze
- Quick Cards
- Additional Support 5

KEY LESSON POINTERS

VOCABULARY

alphabet letter name sound word letter shape capital rhyme trace start/beginning

THE CHILDREN should throughout the lesson:

- distinguish between the letter sounds *p, o, n* and *g* and the letter names *p, o, n* and *g*
- pronounce the pure sounds *p, n,* and *g*
- focus exclusively on the sound activity and not stray onto unrelated topics.

YOU should throughout the lesson:

- emphasise the *p, o, n* and *g* sounds at all times
- emphasise the difference between the letter sound and the letter name
- ensure correct pronunciation of the *p, o, n* and *g* sounds
- encourage the use of examples such as the words *gate* and *goat* and not *grass* where *g* is part of the *gr* cluster, and *pot* and *pudding* and not *plate* where *p* is part of the *pl* cluster, and *tap* and *teddy* and not *train* where *t* is part of the *tr* cluster
- ensure that enough time is spent looking at and talking about the book and rhyme.

STARTING THE LESSON

- Review all the sounds learned to date. Use Letter Cards and revisit *Hector Hedgehog's Big Book of Rhymes (Alphabet)* if necessary.

TEACHING THE LESSON

- Show the children the *n* Letter Card.

  Ask: "What sound does this letter make?" The children may need a prompt: "Remember **Nora nanny**?" (*Emphasise the* **n** *at the beginning of* **Nora** *and* **nanny**.)

  Ask the children to tell you the words which begin with *n*. Give clues if necessary: **nuts** or **apples**, **bangle** or **necklace**, **book** or **newspaper**.

- Show the children the *p* Letter Card.

  Ask: "What sound does this letter make?" The children may need a prompt: "Remember **Pickety Pam**?" (*Emphasise the* **p** *at the beginning of* **Pickety** *and* **Pam**.)

  Ask the children to tell you the words which begin with *p*. Give clues if necessary: **pasta** or **rice**, **pink** or **red**, salt or **pepper**.

- Show the children the *g* Letter Card.

  Ask: "What sound does this letter make?" The children may need a prompt: "Remember the **gorilla** in the **garage**?" (*Emphasise the* **g** *at the beginning of* **gorilla** *and* **garage**.)

  Ask the children to tell you the words which begin with *g*. Give clues if necessary: **garden** or **pond**, **gallop** or **run, goal** or **ball**.

- Stick Letter Cards *p, n* and *g* on the board(s).

  Explain to the children that the board with the *p* is for all the pictures that start with *p*, the board with the *n* is for all the pictures that start with *n* and that the board with the *g* is for all the pictures that start with *g*.

- Give the children *p*, *n* or *g* pictures and ask them in turn to put them on the correct board. (*Encourage children when putting a card on the board to give the reason: "**Gate** can go in the **g** set because it starts with **g**." "**Nail** can go in the **n** set because it starts with **n**".*)

  Pictures starting with other letters should be included. The children should be expected to say that *web*, for example, cannot go in the *n* set or the *p* set or the *g* set because it doesn't begin with *n*, *p* or *g*.

- Show the teacher's copy of Workbook 1 page 19.

  Ask the children if anyone could point to the letter that makes the sound *n*.

  Ask the children if someone could point to another letter that makes the sound *n*.

  Repeat for all the *n* letters.

  Ask the children to point to a letter of their choice and tell the class what sound it makes.

  Repeat for all the letters.

  Ask the children to identify the pictures on the page.

  Repeat the words emphasising the *n* in the *n* words, the *p* in the *p* words, the *g* in the *g* words and the *o* in the *o* words.

  Tell them that they have to choose the sound that the picture starts with and draw a circle around the letter.

  Demonstrate the procedure for the picture of the orange.

  Ask the children to choose the correct sound for the other pictures, inviting the children to circle the correct letters on the sample copy.

- Children complete Workbook 1 page 19. (*Remember to remove teacher's copy of workbook before children start to work.*)

LATER

- Repeat the above lesson for further practice.
- Children complete Additional Support 5.

DEVELOPING SKILLS

Some or all of these activities must be done to ensure progress:

- Practise letter formation.

- **Quick Cards**

  Children have the *n* and *g* cards, plus any Letter Cards that they need further practice in, face up on the table. You call out a word: *napkin, nuts, gate, necklace, garden* and the children point to/hold up the appropriate card.

  You hold up a picture of an object starting with *n* or *g*, plus any letters that the children need further practice in, and the children hold up the appropriate card.

- **What's my sound?** (1)

  You say a word and children say the sound that the word starts with: goat – g.

  The *c* and *g* sounds are easily confused. It is often difficult for children to hear the difference between the two sounds. Give plenty of practice.

- **What's my sound?** (2)

  You say a word and children say the *c* or *g* sound that the word starts with.

  Suggested words:

coat	goat
got	cot
goal	coal
cave	gave
cap	gap

- **Peek-a-Boo**

  See Unit 2 Introduction.

NOTE

Quick Cards

- If the children hold up the card, ensure that all letters are the right way up and facing in the right direction. In the early stages it might be better for the children to point to the cards.

ACTIVITIES AT HOME

- My Sounds Book.

Review

The w sound

THE NLF AIMS

- Hear and identify the initial sound *w*.
- Read the letter that represents the sound *w*.
- Write the letter that represents the sound *w*.

WHAT YOU NEED

RESOURCES

- *Hector Hedgehog's Big Book of Rhymes (Alphabet)* page 28
- Letter Cards *c, d, a, h, m, s, t, p, o, n, g* and *w*
- Alphabet Frieze
- Cards with names of children in class whose names start with *w*
- Whiteboard/chalkboard/easel
- Workbook 1 page 20
- Teacher's copy of Workbook 1 page 20

KEY LESSON POINTERS

VOCABULARY

alphabet   letter   name   sound   word
letter shape   capital   rhyme   trace
start/beginning   middle   match

THE CHILDREN should throughout the lesson:

- distinguish between the letter sound *w* and the letter name *w*
- pronounce the pure sound *w*, without blurring it by adding a vowel as in *wi*
- focus exclusively on the sound activity and not stray onto unrelated topics.

YOU should throughout the lesson:

- emphasise the *w* sound at all times
- emphasise the difference between the letter sound and the letter name
- ensure correct pronunciation of the pure *w* sound
- ensure that enough time is spent looking at and talking about the book and rhyme
- emphasise starting at the correct point when tracing/writing the letter *w* and moving finger/pencil in the correct direction.

STARTING THE LESSON

Quick revision of *c, d, a, h, m, s, t, p, o, n* and *g*.

Some or all of the following should be done to ensure progression:

- Show Letter Cards and ask what sound each letter makes.

  Confirm that the letters make the sounds *c, d, a, h, m, s, t, p, o, n* and *g*.

- Ask the children to find the card with the letter that the word *carrot, dentist, apple, horse, mouth, sun, toast, peach, octopus, nurse, gate* and so on starts with.

  Tell the children they have to think about the names of the letters now and ask them to find *c, d, a, h, m, s, t, p, o, n* and *g*.

  (*Be aware of the needs of the children in terms of the letter sounds that they are unsure of and give more practice.*)

TEACHING THE LESSON

- "Now let's see what today's letter is going to be."

- Open the book at page 28 and tell them that this will be today's activity. (*Be sure to spend some time together, looking at the page.*)

  Ask: "What can you see in the picture?"

  Discuss the content, focusing on the *w* words such as *witch* and *wok*. (*Emphasise the* **w** *words. Ensure the children focus on the objective of the activity. Don't let them stray onto unrelated topics.*)

- Read the rhyme, emphasising the *w* words.

  Reread and encourage the children to join in.

  Ask: "What did *Wanda* put in the *wok*?"

  Confirm *wasps, weeds, wet, woolly* sock, heavily emphasising the *w*.

  Tell them to listen carefully and to say what sound they can hear at the beginning of *weeds*.

  Confirm that it is the sound *w*.

  Tell them to listen carefully and to say what sound they can hear at the beginning of *wasps*.

  Confirm that it is the sound *w*. (*Check that the children pronounce the* **w** *correctly; not as* **wi**.)

  Ask them to listen for other *w* words while you reread the rhyme.

  Confirm other *w* words: *wave, wand, works, weaves, witch, Wanda, wok, with, wet, woolly, worm.*

- Tell them that the letter **w** looks like this in books (*lower case*).

  Finger trace the letter on the page.

  You say that this is the shape (*going over the letter again*). You say again that **w** is its sound.

  Ask: "Does anyone know what its name is?"

  Show Letter Card **w** and finger trace. Confirm that it is the same letter as the one in the book.

  Ask: "What is its name?"

  Ask: "What sound does it make?"

  Ask them, as appropriate, to finger trace over the letter shape. (*Emphasise the correct starting point and the correct formation when tracing over the letter.*)

- Ask them if anyone could be in the **w** set, with a name beginning with **w**. (*For example,* **Wilma**, **William**.)

  Ask identified children to select their name cards and stick them under the correct letter on the Alphabet Frieze.

  Ask: "What do you notice about the letter at the beginning of your name?"

  Confirm that it is a capital letter and discuss its function. (*Extend as appropriate to streets, towns, start of sentences.*)

  Ask them, as appropriate, to finger trace over the upper case letter shape.

- Ask: "What sound would *Wanda* like things beginning with?"

  Confirm that it is the sound **w**.

  Ask them to tell you things that *Wanda* would like.

  Give examples if necessary: *wool* or *tie*, *watch* or *bangle*, *door* or *window*.

- Reread the rhyme with the class, encouraging the children to join in. You should track the words with a pointer to focus on the direction of print, return sweep and correspondence between the spoken and the written word.

NOW OR LATER

- Workbook 1 page 20.

  Demonstrate the correct letter formation giving a commentary as you do so.

FURTHER PRACTICE

DEVELOPING SKILLS

Some or all of these activities must be done to ensure progress:

- Find the letter *w* on the Alphabet Frieze.

- Find *w* letters in the alphabet rhyme.

- Find the letter *w* in books and around the classroom.

- Practise letter formation.

- Cut out pictures from magazines to make a book about *w*.

- **What's my name?**

  You say the sound that a letter makes and children say the corresponding letter name.

- **What's my sound?**

  You say a letter name and children say the sound that letter makes.

NOTE

- When the children line up, ask those whose names begin with *w* to come forward first then those whose names begin with letters already taught.

- When the children line up, ask, for example, *Wilma* and *William* to come forward. Then ask: "Who else can come to the line?" Confirm that they can go into the line if their own name begins with *w*.

ACTIVITIES AT HOME

- Look for an object starting with *w* to take to school.
- My Sounds Book.

The **f** sound

BEFORE YOU START

THE NLF AIMS

- Hear and identify the initial sound *f*.
- Read the letter that represents the sound *f*.
- Write the letter that represents the sound *f*.

WHAT YOU NEED

RESOURCES

- *Hector Hedgehog's Big Book of Rhymes (Alphabet)* page 8
- Letter Cards *c, d, a, h, m, s, t, p, o, n, g, w,* and *f*
- Alphabet Frieze
- Cards with names of children in class whose names start with *f*
- Whiteboard/chalkboard/easel
- Workbook 1 page 21
- Teacher's copy of Workbook 1 page 21

KEY LESSON POINTERS

VOCABULARY

alphabet   letter   name   sound   word
letter shape   capital   rhyme   trace
start/beginning   middle   match

THE CHILDREN should throughout the lesson:

- distinguish between the letter sound *f* and the letter name *f*
- pronounce the pure sound *f* without blurring it by adding a vowel as in *fi*
- focus exclusively on the sound activity and not stray onto unrelated topics.

YOU should throughout the lesson:

- emphasise the *f* sound at all times
- emphasise the difference between the letter sound and the letter name
- ensure correct pronunciation of the pure *f* sound
- ensure that enough time is spent looking at and talking about the book and rhyme
- emphasise starting at the correct point when tracing/writing the letter *f* and moving finger/pencil in the correct direction.

THE LESSON

STARTING THE LESSON

Quick revision of *c, d, a, h, m, s, t, p, o, n, g* and *w*.

Some or all of the following should be done to ensure progression:

- Show Letter Cards and ask what sound each letter makes.

  Confirm that the letters make the sounds *c, d, a, h, m, s, t, p, o, n, g* and *w*.

  Ask: "What are the names of the letters?"

- Stick cards on the board.

  Ask the children to find the card with the letter that makes the *c, d, a, h, m, s, t, p, o, n, g* and *w* sound.

  Ask the children to find the card with the letter that the word *camera, donkey, and, handle, meat, sink, time, pet, organ, nettles, garden, gooseberry, watch* and so on starts with.

  Tell the children they have to think about the names of the letters now and ask them to find *c, d, a, h, m, s, t, p, o, n, g* and *w*.

  (*Be aware of the needs of the children in terms of the letter sounds that they are unsure of and give more practice.*)

TEACHING THE LESSON

- "Now let's see what today's letter is going to be."

- Open the book at page 8 and tell them that this will be today's activity. (*Be sure to spend some time together, looking at the page.*)

  Ask: "What can you see in the picture?"

  Discuss the content, focusing on the *f* words such as *fish* and *fins*. (*Emphasise the* **f** *words. Ensure the children focus exclusively on the objectives of the activity. Don't let them stray onto unrelated topics.*)

- Read the rhyme, emphasising the *f* words.

  Reread and encourage the children to join in.

  Ask: "How many *fins* did the *fine feathered fish* have?"

  Confirm *five furry fins*, heavily emphasising the *f*.

  Tell them to listen carefully and to say what sound they can hear at the beginning of *five*.

  Confirm that it is the sound *f*.

  Tell them to listen carefully and to say what sound they can hear at the beginning of *furry*.

  Confirm that it is the sound *f*. (*Check that the children pronounce the* **f** *correctly; not as* **fi**.)

Ask them to listen for other *f* words while you reread the rhyme.

Confirm other *f* words: ***four, falls, fish, fins, fishy, fine, feathered.***

■ Tell them that the letter *f* looks like this in books (*lower case*).

Finger trace the letter on the page.

You say that this is the shape (*going over the letter again*). You say again that *f* is its sound.

Ask: "Does anyone know what its name is?"

Show Letter Card *f* and finger trace. Confirm that it is the same letter as the one in the book.

Ask: "What is its name?"

Ask: "What sound does it make?"

Ask them, as appropriate, to finger trace over the letter shape. (*Emphasise the correct starting point and the correct formation when tracing over the letter.*)

■ Ask them if anyone could be in the *f* set, with a name beginning with *f*. (*For example,* **Fay, Fabio**.)

Ask identified children to select their name cards and stick them under the correct letter on the Alphabet Frieze.

Ask: "What do you notice about the letter at the beginning of your name?"

Confirm that it is a capital letter and discuss its function.(*Extend as appropriate to streets, towns, start of sentences.*)

Ask them, as appropriate, to finger trace over the upper case letter shape.

■ Ask: "What sound would the ***fish*** like things beginning with?"

Confirm that it is the sound *f*.

Ask them to tell you things that the ***fish*** would like.

Give examples if necessary: ***fox*** or ***duck, fire*** or ***wasps, hand*** or ***foot.***

■ Reread the rhyme with the class, encouraging the children to join in. You should track the words with a pointer to focus on the direction of print, return sweep and correspondence between the spoken and the written word.

NOW OR LATER

■ Workbook 1 page 21.

Demonstrate the correct letter formation giving a commentary as you do so.

FURTHER PRACTICE

DEVELOPING SKILLS

Some or all of these activities must be done to ensure progress:

■ Find the letter *f* on the Alphabet Frieze.

■ Find *f* letters in the alphabet rhyme.

■ Find the letter *f* in books and around the classroom.

■ Practise letter formation.

■ Cut out pictures from magazines to make a book about *f*.

■ **What's my name?**

You say the sound that a letter makes and children say the corresponding letter name.

■ **What's my sound?**

You say the letter name and children say the sound that letter makes.

NOTE

■ When the children line up, ask those whose names begin with *f* to come forward first, then those whose names begin with letters already taught.

■ When the children line up, ask, for example, *Fay* and *Fabio* to come forward. Then ask: "Who else can come to the line?" Confirm that they can go into the line if their own name begins with *f*.

■ Some children have difficulty producing the *f* sound. Encourage them to put their top teeth on their bottom lip to make the sound. (*Watch out for those children who make the* th *sound.*)

ACTIVITIES AT HOME

■ Look for an object starting with *f* to take to school.

■ My Sounds Book.

f

Review

THE NLF AIMS

- Hear and differentiate between the initial sounds *c, d, a, h, m, s, t, p, o, n, g, w* and *f* in words.
- Read the letters that represent the sounds *c, d, a, h, m, s, t, p, o, n, g, w* and *f*.

WHAT YOU NEED

RESOURCES

- Letter Cards *c, d, a, h, m, s, t, p, o, n, g, w* and *f*
- Whiteboard/chalkboard/easel
- Workbook 1 page 22
- Teacher's copy of Workbook 1 page 22
- Alphabet Frieze
- Headbands with slits
- Quick Cards
- Additional Support 6, 7, 8
- Assessment 2.2

KEY LESSON POINTERS

VOCABULARY

alphabet letter name sound word letter shape capital rhyme trace start/beginning match

THE CHILDREN should throughout the lesson:

- distinguish between the letter sounds and the letter names *c, d, a, h, m, s, t, p, o, n, g, w* and *f*
- pronounce the pure sounds *c, d, h, m, s, t, p, n, g, w* and *f*
- focus exclusively on the sound activity and not stray onto unrelated topics.

YOU should throughout the lesson:

- emphasise the *c, d, a, h, m, s, t, p, o, n, g, w* and *f* sounds at all times
- emphasise the difference between the letter sound and the letter name
- ensure correct pronunciation of the *c, d, a, h, m, s, t, p, o, n, g, w* and *f* sounds
- encourage the use of examples such as the words *gate* and *goose* and not *grapes* or *green* where *g* is part of the *gr* cluster, and *fish* and *fan* and not *flowers* where the *f* is part of the *fl* cluster, and *tap* and *teddy* and not *train* where *t* is part of the *tr* cluster
- ensure that enough time is spent looking at and talking about the book and rhyme.

STARTING THE LESSON

- Review all the sounds learned to date. Use Letter Cards and revisit *Hector Hedgehog's Big Book of Rhymes (Alphabet)* if necessary.

TEACHING THE LESSON

- Show the children the *f* Letter Card.

  Ask: "What sound does this letter make?" The children may need a prompt: "Remember the **fine feathered fish**?" (*Emphasise the* **f** *at the beginning of* **fine, feathered** *and* **fish**.)

  Ask the children to tell you the words which begin with *f*. Give clues if necessary: **four** or **eight, folder** or **box, car** or **fiddle**.

- Show the children the *w* Letter Card.

  Ask: "What sound does this letter make?" The children may need a prompt: "Remember **Wanda** the **witch**?" (*Emphasise the* **w** *at the beginning of* **Wanda** *and* **witch**.)

  Ask the children to tell you which words begin with *w*. Give clues if necessary: **windmill** or **pencil, wasp** or **bee, fairy** or **wand**.

- Show the children the *g* Letter Card.

  Ask: "What sound does this letter make?" The children may need a prompt: "Remember the **gorilla** in the **garage**?" (*Emphasise the* **g** *at the beginning of* **gorilla** *and* **garage**.)

  Tell the children to listen carefully and tell you which words begin with *g*. Give clues if necessary: **ducks** or **geese, give** or **take, go** or **stop**.

- Give three children headbands with *g, w* and *f* to wear.

Invite them to stand in three separate places at the front of the group/class.

Explain to the children that the child (*name*) with the *g* headband likes words beginning with *g*, the child (*name*) with the *w* headband likes words beginning with *w*, and the child (*name*) with the *f* headband likes words beginning with *f*. (*If possible, match the children's names to the* **g**, **w** *and* **f** *headbands, for example,* **Gordon**, **Wendy**, **Farida**.)

Invite the children to stand in the correct place, **Gordon's** set, **Wendy's** set or **Farida's** set, by calling out words. The children determine which set they go to by the initial sound of the word.

Suggested words:

goose	funny	window
garden	fish	watch
go	fox	wasp
gate	feather	wellington
guitar	face	water
garage	field	web
game	family	waves
ghost	fan	weather
gas	fast	witch
gather	five	well

Ask all the children in **Farida's** set (*f*) to say their word: *funny*, *fish*, *fox* and so on. (*Children begin to put emphasis on the* **f** *sound.*)

Ask: "Why are you in the *f* set?"

Confirm that all the words start with *f*.

Ask all the children in **Gordon's** set (*g*) to say their word: *goose*, *garden* and so on. (*Children begin to put emphasis on the* **g** *sound.*)

Ask: "Why are you in the *g* set?"

Confirm that all the words start with **g**.

Ask all the children in **Wendy's** set (*w*) to say their word: *window*, *watch*, *wasp* and so on. (*Children begin to put emphasis on the* **w** *sound.*)

Ask: "Why are you in the *w* set?"

Confirm that all the words start with *w*.

■ Children complete Workbook 1 page 22.

LATER

■ Repeat the above lesson for further practice.

■ Children complete Additional Support 6, 7, 8.

FURTHER PRACTICE

DEVELOPING SKILLS

Some or all of these activities must be done to ensure progress:

■ Practise letter formation.

■ **Quick Cards**

Children have the *g*, *w* and *f* cards, plus any Letter Cards that they need further practice in, face up on the table. You call out a word: *gate, watch, feather* and the children point to/hold up the appropriate card.

You hold up a picture of an object starting with *g, w* or *f*, plus any letters that the children need further practice in, and the children hold up the appropriate card.

■ **What's my sound? (1)**

You say a word and children say the sound that the word starts with: web – *w*.

The *g* and *c* sounds are easily confused. It is often difficult for children to hear the difference between the two sounds. Give plenty of practice.

■ **What's my sound? (2)**

You say a word and children say the *c* or *g* sound that the word starts with.

Suggested words:

cot	got
game	came
cap	gap
coal	goal
coat	goat

■ **Peek-a-Boo**

See Unit 2 Introduction.

NOTE

Quick Cards

■ If the children hold up the cards, ensure that all letters are the right way up and facing in the right direction. In the early stages it might be better for the children to point to the cards.

ASSESSMENT 2.2

ACTIVITIES AT HOME

■ My Sounds Book.

Review

The b sound

THE NLF AIMS

- Hear and identify the initial sound *b*.
- Read the letter that represents the sound *b*.
- Write the letter that represents the sound *b*.

WHAT YOU NEED

RESOURCES

- *Hector Hedgehog's Big Book of Rhymes (Alphabet)* page 3
- Letter Cards *c, d, a, h, m, s, t, p, o, n, g, w, f,* and *b*
- Alphabet Frieze
- Cards with names of children in class whose names start with *b*
- Whiteboard/chalkboard/easel
- Workbook 2 page 1
- Teacher's copy of Workbook 2 page 1

KEY LESSON POINTERS

VOCABULARY

alphabet letter name sound word
letter shape capital rhyme trace
start/beginning middle match

THE CHILDREN should throughout the lesson:

- distinguish between the letter sound *b* and the letter name *b*
- pronounce the pure sound *b* without blurring it by adding a vowel as in *bi*
- focus exclusively on the sound activity and not stray onto unrelated topics.

YOU should throughout the lesson:

- emphasise the *b* sound at all times
- emphasise the difference between the letter sound and the letter name
- ensure correct pronunciation of the pure *b* sound
- ensure that enough time is spent looking at and talking about the book and rhyme
- emphasise starting at the correct point when tracing/writing the letter *b* and moving finger/pencil in the correct direction.

THE LESSON

STARTING THE LESSON

Quick revision of Letter Cards learned to date.

Some or all of the following should be done to ensure progression:

- Show Letter Cards and ask what sound each letter makes.

  Confirm that the letters make the sounds *c, d, a, h, m, s, t, p, o, n, g, w* and *f.*

  Ask: "What are the names of the letters?"

- Stick the cards on the board.

  Ask the children to find the card with the letter that makes the *c, d, a, h, m, s, t, p, o, n, g, w* and *f* sound.

  Ask the children to find the card that the word *cup, and, door, hutch, music, sew, tin, purse, orange, nurse, geese, web, feet* and so on starts with.

  Tell the children they have to think about the names of the letters now and ask them to find *c, d, a, h, m, s, t, p, o, n, g, w* and *f.*

  (*Be aware of the needs of the children in terms of the letter sounds that they are unsure of and give more practice.*)

TEACHING THE LESSON

- "Now let's see what today's letter is going to be."

- Open the book at page 3 and tell them that this will be today's activity. (*Be sure to spend some time together, looking at the page.*)

  Ask: "What can you see in the picture?"

  Discuss the content, focusing on the *b* words such as *bee* and *busy*. (*Emphasise the* **b** *words. Ensure the children focus exclusively on the objectives of the activity. Don't let them stray onto unrelated topics.*)

- Read the rhyme, emphasising the *b* words.

  Reread and encourage the children to join in.

  Ask: "Who was very busy?"

  Confirm *Becky Bee*, heavily emphasising the *b*.

  Tell them to listen carefully and to say what sound they can hear at the beginning of *Becky*.

  Confirm that it is the sound *b*.

  Tell them to listen carefully and to say what sound they can hear at the beginning of *bee*.

  Confirm that it is the sound *b*. (*Check that the children pronounce the* **b** *correctly; not as* **bi**.)

  Ask them to listen for other *b* words while you reread the rhyme.

Confirm other **b** words: *buzzes, bushes, bumps, be, busy, bangs, Boris, beetle, bounces, back, beneath, beetles.*

■ Tell them that the letter **b** looks like this in books, magazines, signs (*lower case*).

Finger trace the letter on the page.

You say that this is the shape (*going over the letter again*). You say again that **b** is its sound.

Ask: "Does anyone know what its name is?"

Show Letter Card **b** and finger trace. Confirm that it is the same letter as the one in the book.

Ask: "What is its name?"

Ask: "What sound does it make?"

Ask them, as appropriate, to finger trace over the letter shape. (*Emphasise the correct starting point and the correct formation when tracing over the letter.*)

■ Ask them if anyone could be in the **b** set, with a name beginning with **b**. (*For example,* **Bob, Balveen.**)

Ask identified children to select their name cards and stick them under the correct letter on the Alphabet Frieze.

Ask: "What do you notice about the letter at the beginning of your name?"

Confirm that it is a capital letter and discuss its function. It always comes at the beginning of people's names. (*Extend as appropriate to streets, towns, start of sentences.*)

Ask them, as appropriate, to finger trace over the upper case letter shape.

■ Ask: "What sound would *Becky bee* like things beginning with?"

Confirm that it is the sound **b**.

Ask them to tell you things that *Becky bee* would like.

Give examples if necessary: **bat** or **car**, **apple** or **banana**, **video** or **book**.

■ Reread the rhyme with the class, encouraging the children to join in. You should track the words with a pointer to focus on the direction of print, return sweep and correspondence between the spoken and the written word.

NOW OR LATER

■ Workbook 2 page 1.

Demonstrate the correct letter formation giving a commentary as you do so.

FURTHER PRACTICE

DEVELOPING SKILLS

Some or all of these activities must be done to ensure progress:

■ Find the letter *b* on the Alphabet Frieze.

■ Find *b* letters in the alphabet rhyme.

■ Find the letter *b* in books and around the classroom.

■ Practise letter formation.

■ Cut out pictures from magazines to make a book about *b*.

■ **What's my name?**

You say the sound that a letter makes and children say the corresponding letter name.

■ **What's my sound?**

You say a letter name and children say the sound that letter makes.

■ **b – where is my sound – beginning or end?**

You say a word and children answer *beginning* or *end*.

Suggested words:

bundle	back	rob
web	book	tub
big	banana	bottle
crab	cub	slab
bunny	biscuit	rub

NOTE

■ When the children line up, ask those whose names begin with *b* to come forward first, then those whose names begin with letters already taught to come.

■ When the children line up, ask, for example, *Bob* and *Balveen*, to come forward. Then ask: "Who else can come to the line?" Confirm that they can go into the line if their own name begins with *b*.

ACTIVITIES AT HOME

■ Look for an object starting with *b* to take to school.

■ My Sounds Book.

b

The e sound

THE NLF AIMS

- Hear and identify the initial sound *e*.
- Read the letter that represents the sound *e*.
- Write the letter that represents the sound *e*.

WHAT YOU NEED

RESOURCES

- *Hector Hedgehog's Big Book of Rhymes (Alphabet)* pages 6 and 7
- Letter Cards *c, d, a, h, m, s, t, p, o, n, g, w, f, b* and *e*
- Alphabet Frieze
- Cards with names of children in class whose names start with *e*
- Whiteboard/chalkboard/easel
- Workbook 2 page 2
- Teacher's copy of Workbook 2 page 2

KEY LESSON POINTERS

VOCABULARY

alphabet letter name sound word
letter shape capital rhyme trace
start/beginning middle match

THE CHILDREN should throughout the lesson:

- distinguish between the letter sound *e* and the letter name *e*
- pronounce the short vowel sound *e*
- focus exclusively on the sound activity and not stray onto unrelated topics.

YOU should throughout the lesson:

- emphasise the *e* sound at all times
- ensure that enough time is spent looking at and talking about the book and rhyme
- emphasise starting at the correct point when tracing/writing the letter *e* and moving finger/pencil in the correct direction.

STARTING THE LESSON

Quick revision of Letter Cards learned to date. Some or all of the following should be done to ensure progression:

■ Show Letter Cards and ask what sound each letter makes.

Confirm that the letters make the sounds *c, d, a, h, m, s, t, p, o, n, g, w, f,* and *b*.

Ask: "What are the names of the letters?"

■ Stick the cards on the board.

Ask the children to find the card with the letter that makes the *c, d, a, h, m, s, t, p, o, n, g, w, f,* and *b* sound.

Ask the children to find the card that the word *cot, digger, animal, hip, muscle* and so on starts with.

Tell the children they have to think about the names of the letters now and ask them to find *c, d, a, h, m, s, t, p, o, n, g, w, f,* and *b*. (*Be aware of the needs of the children in terms of the letter sounds that they are unsure of and give more practice.*)

TEACHING THE LESSON

■ "Now let's see what today's letter is going to be."

■ Open the book at page 6 and tell them that this will be today's activity. (*Be sure to spend some time together, looking at the page.*)

Ask: "What can you see in the picture?"

Discuss the content, focusing on the *e* words such as *elephants* and *eggs*. (*Emphasise the* e *words. Ensure the children focus exclusively on the objectives of the activity. Don't let them stray onto unrelated topics.*)

■ Read the rhyme, emphasising the *e* words.

Reread and encourage the children to join in.

Ask: "What did *Ella* the *elephant* put in the teapot?"

Confirm *eggs*, heavily emphasising the *e*.

Tell them to listen carefully and to say what sound they can hear at the beginning of *Ella*.

Confirm that it is the sound *e*.

Tell them to listen carefully and to say what sound they can hear at the beginning of *elephant*.

Confirm that it is the sound *e*.

Ask them to listen for other *e* words while you reread the rhyme.

Confirm other *e* words: *everyone, eggs, envelopes, Egbert, endlessly, every, everything.*

- Tell them that the letter *e* looks like this in books, magazines, signs (*lower case*).

  Finger trace the letter on the page.

  You say that this is the shape (*going over the letter again*). You say again that *e* is its sound.

  Ask: "Does anyone know what its name is?"

  Show Letter Card *e* and finger trace. Confirm that it is the same letter as the one in the book.

  Ask: "What is its name?"

  Ask: "What sound does it make?"

  Ask them, as appropriate, to finger trace over the letter shape. (*Emphasise the correct starting point and the correct formation when tracing over the letter.*)

- Ask them if anyone could be in the *e* set, with a name beginning with *e*. (*For example*, **Eleanor**, **Edward**.)

  Ask identified children to select their name cards and stick them under the correct letter on the Alphabet Frieze.

  Ask: "What do you notice about the letter at the beginning of your name?"

  Confirm that it is a capital letter and discuss its function. It always comes at the beginning of people's names.(*Extend as appropriate to streets, towns, start of sentences.*)

  Ask them, as appropriate, to finger trace over the upper case letter shape.

- Ask: "What sound would *Ella* like things beginning with?"

  Confirm that it is the sound *e*.

  Ask them to tell you things that *Ella* would like.

  Give examples if necessary: **eggs** or **rolls**, **begin** or **end**, **exit** or **open**.

- Reread the rhyme with the class, encouraging the children to join in. You should track the words with a pointer to focus on the direction of print, return sweep and correspondence between the spoken and the written word.

NOW OR LATER

- Workbook 2 page 2.

  Demonstrate the correct letter formation giving a commentary as you do so.

DEVELOPING SKILLS

Some or all of these activities must be done to ensure progress:

- Find the letter *e* on the Alphabet Frieze.

- Find *e* letters in the alphabet rhyme.

- Find the letter *e* in books and around the classroom.

- Practise letter formation.

- Cut out pictures from magazines to make a book about *e*.

- **What's my name?**

  You say the sound that a letter makes and children say the corresponding letter name.

- **What's my sound?**

  You say a letter name and children say the sound that letter makes.

NOTE

- When the children line up, ask those whose names begin with *e* to come forward first then those whose names begin with letters already taught.

- There are some names where the letter does not make the sound *e* such as *Eileen*. Tell the children that the *e* is making a different sound.

- At this point many children may be ready to blend CVC words with the sounds taught. The skill is taught formally at a later stage but raising awareness may be appropriate now.

  Suggested words:

den	hen	men	set
ten	pen	net	get
wet	bed	hem	met
Ted	pet	web	bet
peg	wed	beg	fed

ACTIVITIES AT HOME

- Look for an object starting with *e* to take to school.
- My Sounds Book.

e

The r sound

BEFORE YOU START

THE NLF AIMS

- Hear and identify the initial sound *r*.
- Read the letter that represents the sound *r*.
- Write the letter that represents the sound *r*.

WHAT YOU NEED

RESOURCES

- *Hector Hedgehog's Big Book of Rhymes (Alphabet)* pages 22 and 23
- Letter Cards *c, d, a, h, m, s, t, p, o, n, g, w, f, b, e* and *r*
- Alphabet Frieze
- Cards with names of children in class whose names start with *r*
- Whiteboard/chalkboard/easel
- Workbook 2 page 3
- Teacher's copy of Workbook 2 page 3

KEY LESSON POINTERS

VOCABULARY

alphabet   letter   name   sound   word
letter shape   capital   rhyme   trace
start/beginning   middle   match

THE CHILDREN should throughout the lesson:

- distinguish between the letter sound *r* and the letter name *r*
- pronounce the pure sound *r* without blurring it by adding a vowel as in *ri*
- focus exclusively on the sound activity and not stray onto unrelated topics.

YOU should throughout the lesson:

- emphasise the *r* sound at all times
- emphasise the difference between the letter sound and the letter name
- ensure correct pronunciation of the pure *r* sound
- ensure that enough time is spent looking at and talking about the book and rhyme
- emphasise starting at the correct point when tracing/writing the letter *r* and moving finger/pencil in the correct direction.

THE LESSON

STARTING THE LESSON

Quick revision of Letter Cards learned to date.
Some or all of the following should be done to ensure progression:

- Show Letter Cards and ask what sound each letter makes.
  Confirm that the letters make the sounds *c, d, a, h, m, s, t, p, o, n, g, w, f, b* and *e*.
  Ask: "What are the names of the letters?"

- Stick the cards on the board.
  Ask the children to find the card with the letter that makes the *c, d, a, h, m, s, t, p, o, n, g, w, f, b* and *e* sound.
  Ask the children to find the card that the word *caravan, dive, alligator, head, money, sausages, tent, piano, off, needle, gooseberry, watch, fish, beetle, egg* and so on starts with.
  Tell the children they have to think about the names of the letters now and ask them to find *c, d, a, h, m, s, t, p, o, n, g, w, f, b* and *e*.
  (*Be aware of the needs of the children in terms of the letter sounds that they are unsure of and give more practice.*)

TEACHING THE LESSON

- "Now let's see what today's letter is going to be."

- Open the book at pages 22 and 23 and tell them that this will be today's activity. (*Be sure to spend some time together, looking at the page.*)
  Ask: "What can you see in the picture?"
  Discuss the content, focusing on the *r* words such as **rat** and **rook**. (*Emphasise the* **r** *words. Ensure the children focus exclusively on the objectives of the activity. Don't let them stray onto unrelated topics.*)

- Read the rhyme, emphasising the *r* words.
  Reread and encourage the children to join in.
  Ask: "What colour was the book?"
  Confirm **ruby red**, heavily emphasising the **r**.
  Tell them to listen carefully and to say what sound they can hear at the beginning of **ruby**.
  Confirm that it is the sound *r*.
  Tell them to listen carefully and to say what sound they can hear at the beginning of **red**.
  Confirm that it is the sound *r*.
  Ask them to listen for other *r* words while you reread the rhyme.

Confirm other *r* words: ***Racketty rat, Raggedy rook, read, rousing, roll, raincoats, rainforests, rainbows, ranches, river, row, raft, railway, roam.***

■ Tell them that the letter *r* looks like this in books, magazines, signs (*lower case*).
Finger trace the letter on the page.
You say that this is the shape (*going over the letter again*). You say again that *r* is its sound.
Ask: "Does anyone know what its name is?"
Show Letter Card *r* and finger trace. Confirm that it is the same letter as the one in the book.
Ask: "What is its name?"
Ask: "What sound does it make?"
Ask them, as appropriate, to finger trace over the letter shape. (*Emphasise the correct starting point and the correct formation when tracing over the letter.*)

■ Ask them if anyone could be in the *r* set, with a name beginning with *r*. (*For example,* **Ravi, Rose**.)
Ask identified children to select their name cards and stick them under the correct letter on the Alphabet Frieze.
Ask: "What do you notice about the letter at the beginning of your name?"
Confirm that it is a capital letter and discuss its function. It always comes at the beginning of people's names. (*Extend as appropriate to streets, towns, start of sentences.*)
Ask them, as appropriate, to finger trace over the upper case letter shape.

■ Ask: "What sound would *Racketty rat* like things beginning with?"
Confirm that it is the sound **r**.
Ask them to tell you things that *Racketty rat* would like.
Give examples if necessary: ***ribbon*** or ***bow, custard*** or ***rice, path*** or ***road***.

■ Reread the rhyme with the class, encouraging the children to join in. You should track the words with a pointer to focus on the direction of print, return sweep and correspondence between the spoken and the written word.

NOW OR LATER

■ Workbook 2 page 3.
Demonstrate the correct letter formation giving a commentary as you do so.

FURTHER PRACTICE

DEVELOPING SKILLS

Some or all of these activities must be done to ensure progress:

■ Find the letter *r* on the Alphabet Frieze.

■ Find *r* letters in the alphabet rhyme.

■ Find the letter *r* in books and around the classroom.

■ Practise letter formation.

■ Cut out pictures from magazines to make a book about *r*.

■ **What's my name?**
You say the sound that a letter makes and children say the corresponding letter name.

■ **What's my sound?**
You say a letter name and children say the sound that letter makes.

NOTE

■ When the children line up, ask those whose names begin with *r* to come forward first then those whose names begin with letters already taught.

■ When the children line up, ask, for example, *Rose* and *Ravi* to come forward. Then ask: "Who else can come to the line?" Confirm that they can go into the line if their own name begins with *r*.

ACTIVITIES AT HOME

■ Look for an object starting with *r* to take to school.
■ My Sounds Book.

AUDITORY DISCRIMINATION

IDENTIFYING ALPHABET SOUNDS

r

Review

THE NLF AIMS

- Hear and differentiate between initial sounds *b*, *e* and *r*.
- Read the letters that represent the sounds *b*, *e* and *r*.

WHAT YOU NEED

RESOURCES

- Letter Cards *b*, *e* and *r*
- Alphabet Frieze
- Whiteboard/chalkboard/easel
- Workbook 2 page 4
- Teacher's copy of Workbook 2 page 4
- Headbands with slits
- Quick Cards
- Additional Support 9

KEY LESSON POINTERS

VOCABULARY

alphabet letter name sound word
letter shape capital rhyme trace
start/beginning

THE CHILDREN should throughout the lesson:

- distinguish between the letter sounds *b*, *e* and *r* and the letter names *b*, *e* and *r*
- pronounce the pure sounds *b* and *r*
- focus exclusively on the sound activity and not stray onto unrelated topics.

YOU should throughout the lesson:

- emphasise the *b*, *e* and *r* sounds at all times
- emphasise the difference between the letter sound and the letter name
- ensure correct pronunciation of the pure *b* and *r* sounds
- encourage the use of examples such as the words *bus* and *book* and not *brush* where *b* is part of the *br* cluster
- ensure that enough time is spent looking at and talking about the book and rhyme.

THE LESSON

STARTING THE LESSON

- Quick revision of all the sounds learned to date.
  Use Letter Cards and revisit *Hector Hedgehog's Big Book of Rhymes (Alphabet)* if necessary.

TEACHING THE LESSON

- Show the children the *b* Letter Card.
  Ask: "What sound does this letter make?" The children may need a prompt: "Remember **Becky bee**?" (*Emphasise the* **b** *at the beginning of* **Becky** *and* **bee**.)
  Ask the children to tell you the words which begin with *b*. Give clues if necessary: **box** or **piano**, **bed** or **chair**, **man** or **baby**.

- Show the children the *e* Letter Card.
  Ask: "What sound does this letter make?" The children may need a prompt: "Remember **Ella elephant**?" (*Emphasise the* **e** *at the beginning of* **Ella** *and* **elephant**.)
  Ask the children to tell you the words which begin with *e*. Give clues if necessary: **egg** or **cake**, **end** or **beginning**, **full** or **empty**.

- Show the children the *r* Letter Card.
  Ask: "What sound does this letter make?" The children may need a prompt: "Remember **Racketty rat**?" (*Emphasise the* **r** *at the beginning of* **Racketty** *and* **rat**.)
  Ask the children to tell you the words which begin with *r*. Give clues if necessary: **rubber** or **pencil**, **roll** or **cake**, **pasta** or **rice**.

- Give three children headbands with *b*, *e* and *r* to wear.

Invite them to stand in three separate places at the front of the group/class.

Explain to the children that the child (*name*) with the *b* headband likes words beginning with *b*, the child (*name*) with the *e* headband likes words beginning with *e*, and the child (*name*) with the *r* headband likes words beginning with *r*. (*If possible, match the children's names to the* **b**, **e** *and* **r** *headbands, for example,* **Billy, Emily, Roshan.**)

Invite the children to stand in the correct place, **Billy's** set, **Emily's** set, **Roshan's** set, by calling out words. The children determine which set they go to by the initial sound of the word.

Suggested words:

book	egg	ribbon
bus	elephant	red
bed	exit	rabbit
bundle	empty	ring
basket	exercise	rubber
book	end	river
baby	Edward	road
bird	enter	rock
bag	eggcup	raspberry
bangle	Ellen	ruler

Ask all the children in **Billy's** set (*b*) to say their word: **book, bus, bed** and so on. (*Children begin to put emphasis on the* **b** *sound.*)

Ask: "Why are you in the *b* set?"

Confirm that all the words start with *b*.

Ask all the children in **Emily's** set (*e*) to say their word: **egg, elephant, exit** and so on. (*Children begin to put emphasis on the* **e** *sound.*)

Ask: "Why are you in the *e* set?"

Confirm that all the words start with *e*.

Ask all the children in **Roshan's** set (*r*) to say their word: **ribbon, red, rabbit** and so on. (*Children begin to put emphasis on the* **r** *sound.*)

Ask: "Why are you in the *r* set?"

Confirm that all the words start with *r*.

■ Children complete Workbook 2 page 4.

LATER

■ Repeat the above lesson for further practice.

■ Children complete Additional Support 9.

FURTHER PRACTICE

DEVELOPING SKILLS

Some or all of these activities must be done to ensure progress:

■ Practise letter formation.

■ **Quick Cards**

Children have the *b*, *e* and *r* cards, plus any Letter Cards that they need further practice in, face up on the table. You call out a word: *box, egg, ring* and the children point to/hold up the appropriate card.

You hold up a picture of the object starting with *b*, *e* or *r*, plus any letters that the children need further practice in, and children hold up the appropriate card.

■ **What's my sound? (1)**

You say a word and children say sound that the word starts with: ribbon – *r*.

The *p*, *b* and *d* sounds are easily confused. It is often difficult for children to differentiate the fine auditory discrimination between the three sounds. Give plenty of practice.

■ **What's my sound? (2)**

You say a word and children say the *b*, *d* or *p* sound that the word starts with.

Suggested words:

bought	bid	dig	bed	dead
bad	dad	bin	din	bun
done	Ben	pen	bat	pat
bear	pear	pin	pig	den
pot	dot	pad		

■ *b*, *d* and *p* are visually easily confused. Give plenty of practice.

■ **Quick Cards**

Children have the *b*, *d* and *p* cards face up on the table. You call out a word: *doughnut, dentist, dash, bed, busy, dinner, big, daisy, pot, push, pink, potato, building* and children point to/hold up the appropriate card. (*It may be best to start with a combination of 2 sounds.*)

■ **Peek-a-Boo**

See Unit 2 Introduction.

ACTIVITIES AT HOME

■ My Sounds Book.

Review

The l sound

THE NLF AIMS

- Hear and identify the initial sound *l*.
- Read the letter that represents the sound *l*.
- Write the letter that represents the sound *l*.

WHAT YOU NEED

RESOURCES

- *Hector Hedgehog's Big Book of Rhymes (Alphabet)* page 14
- Letter Cards *c, d, a, h, m, s, t, p, o, n, g, w, f, b, e, r,* and *l*
- Alphabet Frieze
- Cards with names of children in class whose names start with *l*
- Whiteboard/chalkboard/easel
- Workbook 2 page 5
- Teacher's copy of Workbook 2 page 5

KEY LESSON POINTERS

VOCABULARY

alphabet letter name sound word
letter shape capital rhyme trace
start/beginning middle match

THE CHILDREN should throughout the lesson:

- distinguish between the letter sound *l* and the letter name *l*
- pronounce the pure sound *l* without blurring it by adding a vowel as in *li*
- focus exclusively on the sound activity and not stray onto unrelated topics.

YOU should throughout the lesson:

- emphasise the *l* sound at all times
- emphasise the difference between the letter sound and the letter name
- ensure correct pronunciation of the pure *l* sound
- ensure that enough time is spent looking at and talking about the book and rhyme
- emphasise starting at the correct point when tracing/writing the letter *l* and moving finger/pencil in the correct direction.

THE LESSON

STARTING THE LESSON

Quick revision of Letter Cards learned to date.

Some or all of the following should be done to ensure progression:

- Show Letter Cards and ask what sound each letter makes.

  Confirm that the letters make the sounds *c, d, a, h, m, s, t, p, o, n, g, w, f, b, e* and *r*.

  Ask: "What are the names of the letters?"

- Stick the cards on the board.

  Ask the children to find the card with the letter that makes the *c, d, a, h, m, s, t, p, o, n, g, w, f, b, e* and *r* sound.

  Ask the children to find the card that the word **cabbage, doctor, anorak, house, man, sink, time, pet, organ, nettles, goose, garden, window, feather, bee, elephant, rose, egg, book** and so on starts with.

  Tell the children they have to think about the names of the letters now and ask them to find *c, d, a, h, m, s, t, p, o, n, g, w, f, b, e* and *r*.

  (*Be aware of the needs of the children in terms of the letter sounds that they are unsure of and give more practice.*)

TEACHING THE LESSON

- "Now let's see what today's letter is going to be."
- Open the book at page 14 and tell them that this will be today's activity. (*Be sure to spend some time together, looking at the page.*)

  Ask: "What can you see in the picture?"

  Discuss the content, focusing on the *l* words such as **leaves** and **look**. (*Emphasise the* l *words. Ensure the children focus exclusively on the objectives of the activity. Don't let them stray onto unrelated topics.*)

- Read the rhyme, emphasising the *l* words.

  Reread and encourage the children to join in.

  Ask: "Who has lost her **ladybird**?"

  Confirm **Lucy**, heavily emphasising the *l*.

  Tell them to listen carefully and to say what sound they can hear at the beginning of **Lucy**.

  Confirm that it is the sound *l*.

  Tell them to listen carefully and to say what sound they can hear at the beginning of **ladybird**.

  Confirm that it is the sound *l*.

  Ask them to listen for other *l* words while you reread the rhyme.

Confirm other *l* words: ***look, ladders, lettuces, lawn, logs, lost, leaves.***

■ Tell them that the letter *l* looks like this in books, magazines, signs (*lower case*).

Finger trace the letter on the page.

You say that this is the shape (*going over the letter again*). You say again that *l* is its sound.

Ask: "Does anyone know what its name is?"

Show Letter Card *l* and finger trace. Confirm that it is the same letter as the one in the book.

Ask: "What is its name?"

Ask: "What sound does it make?"

Ask them, as appropriate, to finger trace over the letter shape. (*Emphasise the correct starting point and the correct formation when tracing over the letter.*)

■ Ask them if anyone could be in the *l* set, with a name beginning with *l*. (*For example,* **Louise, Liam.**)

Ask identified children to select their name cards and stick them under the correct letter on the Alphabet Frieze.

Ask: "What do you notice about the letter at the beginning of your name?"

Confirm that it is a capital letter and discuss its function. It always comes at the beginning of people's names.(*Extend as appropriate to streets, towns, start of sentences.*)

Ask them, as appropriate, to finger trace over the upper case letter shape.

■ Ask: "What sound would *Lucy* like things beginning with?"

Confirm that it is the sound *l*.

Ask them to tell you things that *Lucy* would like.

Give examples if necessary: ***liquorice*** or ***toffee***, ***tiger*** or ***lion***, ***big*** or ***little***.

■ Reread the rhyme with the class, encouraging the children to join in. You should track the words with a pointer to focus on the direction of print, return sweep and correspondence between the spoken and the written word.

NOW OR LATER

■ Workbook 2 page 5.

Demonstrate the correct letter formation giving a commentary as you do so.

FURTHER PRACTICE

DEVELOPING SKILLS

Some or all of these activities must be done to ensure progress:

■ Find the letter *l* on the Alphabet Frieze.

■ Find *l* letters in the alphabet rhyme.

■ Find the letter *l* in books and around the classroom.

■ Practise letter formation.

■ Cut out pictures from magazines to make a book about *l*.

■ **What's my name?**

You say the sound that a letter makes and children say the corresponding letter name.

■ **What's my sound?**

You say a letter name and children say the sound that letter makes.

■ *l* – **where is my sound – beginning or end?**

You say a word and children answer *beginning* or *end*.

Suggested words:

ladder	loft	fall
bell	stool	hill
lid	ball	line
look	goal	lift
hole	lady	lamp

NOTE

■ When the children line up, ask those whose names begin with *l* to come forward first then those whose names begin with letters already taught.

■ When the children line up, ask, for example, *Lewis* and *Laura* to come forward. Then ask: "Who else can come to the line?" Confirm that they can go into the line if their own name begins with *l*.

ACTIVITIES AT HOME

■ Look for an object starting with *l* to take to school.

■ My Sounds Book.

l

The k sound

BEFORE YOU START

THE NLF AIMS

- Hear and identify the initial sound *k*.
- Read the letter that represents the sound *k*.
- Write the letter that represents the sound *k*.

WHAT YOU NEED

RESOURCES

- *Hector Hedgehog's Big Book of Rhymes (Alphabet)* page 13
- Letter Cards *c, d, a, h, m, s, t, p, o, n, g, w, f, b, e, r, l* and *k*
- Alphabet Frieze
- Cards with names of children in class whose names start with *k*
- Whiteboard/chalkboard/easel
- Workbook 2 page 6
- Teacher's copy of Workbook 2 page 6

KEY LESSON POINTERS

VOCABULARY

alphabet   letter   name   sound   word
letter shape   capital   rhyme   trace
start/beginning   middle   match

THE CHILDREN should throughout the lesson:

- distinguish between the letter sound *k* and the letter name *k*
- pronounce the pure sound *k* without blurring it by adding a vowel as in *ki*
- focus exclusively on the sound activity and not stray onto unrelated topics.

YOU should throughout the lesson:

- emphasise the *k* sound at all times
- emphasise the difference between the letter sound and the letter name
- ensure correct pronunciation of the pure *k* sound
- ensure that enough time is spent looking at and talking about the book and rhyme
- emphasise starting at the correct point when tracing/writing the letter *k* and moving finger/pencil in the correct direction.

THE LESSON

STARTING THE LESSON

Quick revision of Letter Cards learned to date.
Some or all of the following should be done to ensure progression:

- Show Letter Cards and ask what sound each letter makes.
  Confirm that the letters make the sounds *c, d, a, h, m, s, t, p, o, n, g, w, f, b, e, r* and *l*.
  Ask: "What are the names of the letters?"

- Stick the cards on the board.
  Ask the children to find the card with the letter that makes the *c, d, a, h, m, s, t, p, o, n, g, w, f, b, e, r* and *l* sound.
  Ask the children to find the card that the word *cake, duck, ambulance, hedgehog, mouth, soap, towel, pear, otter, nose, garage, wall, field, butter, exit, rice, empty, book, lorry* and so on starts with.
  Tell the children they have to think about the names of the letters now and ask them to find *c, d, a, h, m, s, t, p, o, n, g, w, f, b, e, r* and *l*.
  (*Be aware of the needs of the children in terms of the letter sounds that they are unsure of and give more practice.*)

TEACHING THE LESSON

- "Now let's see what today's letter is going to be."

- Open the book at page 13 and tell them that this will be today's activity. (*Be sure to spend some time together, looking at the page.*)
  Ask: "What can you see in the picture?"
  Discuss the content focusing on the *k* words such as *kippers* and *koalas*. (*Emphasise the* k *words. Ensure the children focus exclusively on the objectives of the activity. Don't let them stray onto unrelated topics.*)

- Read the rhyme, emphasising the *k* words.
  Reread and encourage the children to join in.
  Ask: "What did *Kurt* want to see?"
  Confirm a *kicking kangaroo*, heavily emphasising the *k*.
  Tell them to listen carefully and to say what sound they can hear at the beginning of *kicking*.
  Confirm that it is the sound *k*.
  Tell them to listen carefully and to say what sound they can hear at the beginning of *kangaroo*.
  Confirm that it is the sound *k*.
  Ask them to listen for other *k* words while you reread the rhyme.

Confirm other *k* words: ***Kurt, keen, keeper, Karlos, kippers, koalas, kiosk.***

■ Tell them that the letter *k* looks like this in books, magazines, signs (*lower case*).

Finger trace the letter on the page.

You say that this is the shape (*going over the letter again*). You say again that *k* is its sound.

Ask: "Does anyone know what its name is?"

Show Letter Card *k* and finger trace. Confirm that it is the same letter as the one in the book.

Ask: "What is its name?"

Ask: "What sound does it make?"

Ask them, as appropriate, to finger trace over the letter shape. (*Emphasise the correct starting point and the correct formation when tracing over the letter.*)

■ Ask them if anyone could be in the *k* set with a name beginning with the sound *k*. (*For example,* **Kim, Kieran**.)

Ask identified children to select their name cards and stick them under the correct letter on the Alphabet Frieze.

Ask: "What do you notice about the letter at the beginning of your name?"

Confirm that it is a capital letter and discuss its function. (*Extend as appropriate to streets, towns, start of sentences.*)

Ask them, as appropriate, to finger trace over the upper case letter shape.

Ask: "Does anyone's mummy, daddy, auntie's name begin with the sound *k*?" (*This may not need to be done if there are enough children in the class with names beginning with* **k**.)

■ Ask: "What sound would the ***kicking kangaroo*** like things beginning with?"

Confirm that it is the sound *k*.

Ask them to tell you things that the ***kicking kangaroo*** would like.

Give examples if necessary: ***key*** or ***door***, ***kettle*** or ***pot***, ***elephant*** or ***kangaroo***.

■ Reread the rhyme with the class, encouraging the children to join in. You should track the words with a pointer to focus on the direction of print, return sweep and correspondence between the spoken and the written word.

NOW OR LATER

■ Workbook 2 page 6.

Demonstrate the correct letter formation giving a commentary as you do so.

FURTHER PRACTICE

DEVELOPING SKILLS

Some or all of these activities must be done to ensure progress:

■ Find the letter *k* on the Alphabet Frieze.

■ Find *k* letters in the alphabet rhyme.

■ Find the letter *k* in books and around the classroom.

■ Practise letter formation.

■ Cut out pictures from magazines to make a book about *k*.

■ **What's my name?**

You say the sound that a letter makes and children say the corresponding letter name.

■ **What's my sound?**

You say a letter name and children say the sound that letter makes.

NOTE

■ When the children line up, ask those whose names begin with *k* to come forward first then those whose names begin with letters already taught.

■ When the children line up, ask, for example, *Kim* and *Kieran* to come forward. Then ask: "Who else can come to the line?" Confirm that they can go into the line if their own name begins with *k*.

■ At this point you should draw the children's attention to the fact that *c* and *k* can both make the same sound.

ACTIVITIES AT HOME

■ Look for an object starting with *k* to take to school.

■ My Sounds Book.

AUDITORY DISCRIMINATION

IDENTIFYING ALPHABET SOUNDS

k

Review

THE NLF AIMS

- Hear and differentiate between initial sounds *b*, *e*, *r*, *l* and *k*.
- Read the letters that represent the sounds *b*, *e*, *r*, *l* and *k*.

WHAT YOU NEED

RESOURCES

- Letter Cards *b*, *e*, *r*, *l* and *k*
- Alphabet Frieze
- Whiteboard/chalkboard/easel
- Workbook 2 page 7
- Teacher's copy of Workbook 2 page 7
- Headbands with slits
- Quick Cards
- Additional Support 10

KEY LESSON POINTERS

VOCABULARY

alphabet   letter   name   sound   word   letter shape   capital   rhyme   trace   start/beginning   match

THE CHILDREN should throughout the lesson:

- distinguish between the letter sounds *b*, *e*, *r*, *l* and *k* and the letter names *b*, *e*, *r*, *l* and *k*
- pronounce the pure sounds *b*, *r*, *l* and *k*
- focus exclusively on the sound activity and not stray onto unrelated topics.

YOU should throughout the lesson:

- emphasise the *b*, *e*, *r*, *l* and *k* sounds at all times
- emphasise the difference between the letter sound and the letter name
- ensure correct pronunciation of the pure *b*, *r*, *l* and *k* sounds
- encourage the use of examples such as the words *bus* and *book* and not *brush* where *b* is part of the *br* cluster
- ensure that enough time is spent looking at and talking about the book and rhyme.

STARTING THE LESSON

- Quick revision of all the sounds learned to date.

  Use Letter Cards and revisit *Hector Hedgehog's Big Book of Rhymes (Alphabet)* if necessary.

TEACHING THE LESSON

- Show the children the *l* Letter Card.

  Ask: "What sound does this letter make?" The children may need a prompt: "Remember the **lost ladybird**?" (*Emphasise the* **l** *at the beginning of* **lost** *and* **ladybird**.)

  Ask the children to tell you the words which begin with *l*. Give clues if necessary: **lock** or **key**, **ladder** or **pole**, **rock** or **lollipop**.

- Show the children the *k* Letter Card.

  Ask: "What sound does this letter make?" The children may need a prompt: "Remember the **kicking kangaroo**?" (*Emphasise the* **k** *at the beginning of* **kicking** *and* **kangaroo**.)

  Ask the children to tell you the words which begin with *k*. Give clues if necessary: **key** or **door**, **kitten** or **puppy**, **trousers** or **kilt**.

- Show the children the *r* Letter Card.

  Ask: "What sound does this letter make?" The children may need a prompt: "Remember **Racketty rat**? (*Emphasise the* **r** *at the beginning of* **Racketty** *and* **rat**.)

  Ask the children to tell you the words which begin with *r*. Give clues if necessary: **rubber** or **pencil**, **roll** or **cake**, **pasta** or **rice**.

- Give three children headbands with *r*, *l* and *k* to wear.

Invite them to stand in three separate places at the front of the group/class.

Explain to the children that the child (*name*) with the *r* headband likes words beginning with *r*, the child (*name*) with the *l* headband likes words beginning with *l*, and the child (*name*) with the **k** headband likes words beginning with **k**. (*If possible, the children's names who have the headbands should start with the letter being focused:* **Ravi, Lizzy, Katy**.)

Invite the children to stand in the correct place, **Ravi's** set, **Lizzy's** set, **Katy's** set, by calling out words. The children determine which set they go to by the initial sound of the word.

Suggested words:

rice	kite	lemon
roll	kitten	lunch
rocket	key	log
race	kettle	lolly
rubber	kilt	ladder
ruler	kiwi	lock
rug	king	little
red	kick	lid
rabbit	kerb	lion
robot	kangaroo	light

Ask all the children in **Ravi's** set (*r*) to say their word: ***rice, roll, rocket***. (*Children begin to put emphasis on the* **r** *sound*.)

Ask: "Why are you in the **r** set?"

Confirm that all the words start with **r**.

Ask all the children in **Katy's** set (*k*) to say their word: ***kite, kitten, key***. (*Children begin to put emphasis on the* **k** *sound*.)

Ask: "Why are you in the **k** set?"

Confirm that all the words start with **k**.

Ask all the children in **Lizzy's** set (*l*) to say their word: ***lemon, lunch, log***. (*Children begin to put emphasis on the* **l** *sound*.)

Ask: "Why are you in the *l* set?"

Confirm that all the words start with *l*.

■ Children complete Workbook 2 page 7.

NOW OR LATER

■ Repeat the above lesson for further practice.

■ Children complete Additional Support 10.

FURTHER PRACTICE

DEVELOPING SKILLS

Some or all of these activities must be done to ensure progress:

■ Practise letter formation.

■ **Quick Cards**

Children have the *r*, *l* and *k* cards, plus any Letter Cards that they need further practice in, face up on the table. You call out a word: *road, lolly, king* and so on and the children point to/hold up the appropriate card.

You hold up a picture of an object starting with *r*, *l* or *k* plus any letters that the children need further practice in, and children hold up the appropriate card

■ **What's my sound?**

You say a word and children say sound that the word starts with: lamp – *l*.

■ **Peek-a-Boo**

See Unit 2 Introduction.

NOTE

Quick Cards

■ If the children hold up the cards, ensure that all letters are the right way up and facing in the right direction. In the early stages it might be better for the children to point to the cards.

ACTIVITIES AT HOME

■ My Sounds Book.

Review

The j sound

THE NLF AIMS

- Hear and identify the initial sound *j*.
- Read the letter that represents the sound *j*.
- Write the letter that represents the sound *j*.

WHAT YOU NEED

RESOURCES

- *Hector Hedgehog's Big Book of Rhymes (Alphabet)* page 12
- Letter Cards *c, d, a, h, m, s, t, p, o, n, g, w, f, b, e, r, l, k* and *j*
- Alphabet Frieze
- Cards with names of children in class whose names start with *j*
- Whiteboard/chalkboard/easel
- Workbook 2 page 8
- Teacher's copy of Workbook 2 page 8

KEY LESSON POINTERS

VOCABULARY

alphabet letter name sound word
letter shape capital rhyme trace
start/beginning middle match

THE CHILDREN should throughout the lesson:

- distinguish between the letter sound *j* and the letter name *j*
- pronounce the pure sound *j* without blurring it by adding a vowel as in *ji*
- focus exclusively on the sound activity and not stray onto unrelated topics.

YOU should throughout the lesson:

- emphasise the *j* sound at all times
- emphasise the difference between the letter sound and the letter name
- ensure correct pronunciation of the pure *j* sound
- ensure that enough time is spent looking at and talking about the book and rhyme
- emphasise starting at the correct point when tracing/writing the letter *j* and moving finger/pencil in the correct direction.

STARTING THE LESSON

Quick revision of Letter Cards learned to date. Some or all of the following should be done to ensure progression:

- Show Letter Cards and ask what sound each letter makes.
  Confirm that the letters make the sounds *c, d, a, h, m, s, t, p, o, n, g, w, f, b, e, r, l* and *k*.
  Ask: "What are the names of the letters?"

- Stick the cards on the board.
  Ask the children to find the card with the letter that makes the *c, d, a, h, m, s, t, p, o, n, g, w, f, b, e, r, l* and *k* sound.
  Ask the children to find the card that the word *candle, kite, lamp, ring* and so on starts with.
  Tell the children they have to think about the names of the letters now and ask them to find *c, d, a, h, m, s, t, p, o, n, g, w, f, b, e, r, l* and *k*.
  (*Be aware of the needs of the children in terms of the letter sounds that they are unsure of and give more practice.*)

TEACHING THE LESSON

- "Now let's see what today's letter is going to be."

- Open the book at page 12 and tell them that this will be today's activity. (*Be sure to spend some time together, looking at the page.*)
  Ask: "What can you see in the picture?"
  Discuss the content, focusing on the *j* words such as *juggler* and *jackets*. (*Emphasise the* **j** *words. Ensure they focus exclusively on the objectives of the activity. Don't let them stray onto unrelated topics.*)

- Read the rhyme, emphasising the *j* words.
  Reread and encourage the children to join in.
  Ask: "What is *Jason*?"
  Confirm a *juggler*, heavily emphasising the *j*.
  Tell them to listen carefully and to say what sound they can hear at the beginning of *Jason*.
  Confirm that it is the sound *j*.
  Tell them to listen carefully and to say what sound they can hear at the beginning of *juggler*.
  Confirm that it is the sound *j*.
  Ask them to listen for other *j* words while you reread the rhyme.

Confirm other *j* words: *jackets, jangled, juggled, jumpers, jeans, jam, jars, jelly, jiggled, jingled, jewels.*

■ Tell them that the letter *j* looks like this in books, magazines, signs (*lower case*).

Finger trace the letter on the page.

You say that this is the shape (*going over the letter again*). You say again that *j* is its sound.

Ask: "Does anyone know what its name is?"

Show Letter Card *j* and finger trace. Confirm that it is the same letter as the one in the book.

Ask: "What is its name?"

Ask: "What sound does it make?"

Ask them, as appropriate, to finger trace over the letter shape. (*Emphasise the correct starting point and the correct formation when tracing over the letter.*)

■ Ask them if anyone could be in the *j* set with a name beginning with the sound *j*. (*For example,* **Jamal**, **Joyce**.)

Ask identified children to select their name cards and stick them under the correct letter on the Alphabet Frieze.

Ask: "What do you notice about the letter at the beginning of your name?"

Confirm that it is a capital letter and discuss its function. (*Extend as appropriate to streets, towns, start of sentences.*)

Ask them, as appropriate, to finger trace over the upper case letter shape.

■ Ask: "What sound would **Jason** like things beginning with?"

Confirm that it is the sound *j*.

Ask them to tell you things that **Jason** would like.

Give examples if necessary: *jam* or *butter, jump* or *run, custard* or *jelly*.

■ Reread the rhyme with the class, encouraging the children to join in. You should track the words with a pointer to focus on the direction of print, return sweep and correspondence between the spoken and the written word.

NOW OR LATER

■ Workbook 2 page 8.

Demonstrate the correct letter formation giving a commentary as you do so.

FURTHER PRACTICE

DEVELOPING SKILLS

Some or all of these activities must be done to ensure progress:

■ Find the letter *j* on the Alphabet Frieze.

■ Find *j* letters in the alphabet rhyme.

■ Find the letter *j* in books and around the classroom.

■ Practise letter formation.

■ Cut out pictures from magazines to make a book about *j*.

■ **What's my name?**

You say the sound that a letter makes and children say the corresponding letter name.

■ **What's my sound?**

You say a letter name and children say the sound that letter makes.

NOTE

■ When the children line up, ask those whose names begin with *j* to come forward first, then those whose names begin with letters already taught.

■ When the children line up, ask, for example, *Jamal* and *Joyce* to come forward. Then ask: "Who else can come to the line?" Confirm that they can go into the line if their own name begins with *j*.

ACTIVITIES AT HOME

■ Look for an object starting with *j* to take to school.

■ My Sounds Book.

j

The **v** sound

THE NLF AIMS

- Hear and identify the initial sound *v*.
- Read the letter that represents the sound *v*.
- Write the letter that represents the sound *v*.

WHAT YOU NEED

RESOURCES

- *Hector Hedgehog's Big Book of Rhymes (Alphabet)* page 27
- Letter Cards *c, d, a, h, m, s, t, p, o, n, g, w, f, b, e, r, l, k, j* and *v*
- Alphabet Frieze
- Cards with names of children in class whose names start with *v*
- Whiteboard/chalkboard/easel
- Workbook 2 page 9
- Teacher's copy of Workbook 2 page 9

KEY LESSON POINTERS

VOCABULARY

alphabet letter name sound word
letter shape capital rhyme trace
start/beginning middle match

THE CHILDREN should throughout the lesson:

- distinguish between the letter sound *v* and the letter name *v*
- pronounce the pure sound *v* without blurring it by adding a vowel as in *vi*
- focus exclusively on the sound activity and not stray onto unrelated topics.

YOU should throughout the lesson:

- emphasise the *v* sound at all times
- emphasise the difference between the letter sound and the letter name
- ensure correct pronunciation of the pure *v* sound
- ensure that enough time is spent looking at and talking about the book and rhyme
- emphasise starting at the correct point when tracing/writing the letter *v* and moving finger/pencil in the correct direction.

STARTING THE LESSON

- Quick revision of Letter Cards learned to date. Some or all of the following should be done to ensure progression:

- Show Letter Cards and ask what sound each letter makes.

  Confirm that the letters make the sounds *c, d, a, h, m, s, t, p, o, n, g, w, f, b, e, r, l, k* and *j*.

  Ask: "What are the names of the letters?"

- Stick the cards on the board.

  Ask the children to find the card with the letter that makes the *c, d, a, h, m, s, t, p, o, n, g, w, f, b, e, r, l, k* and *j* sound.

  Ask the children to find the card that the word *cake, juice, kitten, ladder* and so on starts with.

  Tell the children they have to think about the names of the letters now and ask them to find *c, d, a, h, m, s, t, p, o, n, g, w, f, b, e, r, l, k* and *j*.

  (*Be aware of the needs of the children in terms of the letter sounds that they are unsure of and give more practice.*)

TEACHING THE LESSON

- "Now let's see what today's letter is going to be."

- Open the book at page 27 and tell them that this will be today's activity. (*Be sure to spend some time together, looking at the page.*)

  Ask: "What can you see in the picture?"

  Discuss the content, focusing on the *v* words such as *vet* and *village*. (*Emphasise the* **v** *words. Ensure the children focus exclusively on the objectives of the activity. Don't let them stray onto unrelated topics.*)

- Read the rhyme, emphasising the *v* words.

  Reread and encourage the children to join in.

  Ask: "What colour was *Victor's van*?"

  Repeat *violet*, heavily emphasising the *v*.

  Tell them to listen carefully and to say what sound they can hear at the beginning of *violet*.

  Confirm that it is the sound *v*.

  Tell them to listen carefully and to say what sound they can hear at the beginning of *van*.

  Confirm that it is the sound *v*.

  Ask them to listen for other *v* words while you reread the rhyme.

Confirm other *v* words: ***Victor, vegetables, vicar, vitamin, vet, very, vague, village.***

■ Tell them that the letter *v* looks like this in books, magazines, signs (*lower case*).

Finger trace the letter on the page.

You say that this is the shape (*going over the letter again*). You say again that *v* is its sound.

Ask: "Does anyone know what its name is?"

Show Letter Card *v* and finger trace. Confirm that it is the same letter as the one in the book.

Ask: "What is its name?"

Ask: "What sound does it make?"

Ask them, as appropriate, to finger trace over the letter shape. (*Emphasise the correct starting point and the correct formation when tracing over the letter.*)

■ Ask them if anyone could be in the *v* set with a name beginning with the sound *v*. (*For example,* **Vicky, Vikram**.)

Ask identified children to select their name cards and stick them under the correct letter on the Alphabet Frieze.

Ask: "What do you notice about the letter at the beginning of your name?"

Confirm that it is a capital letter and discuss its function. (*Extend as appropriate to streets, towns, start of sentences.*)

Ask them, as appropriate, to finger trace over the upper case letter shape.

■ Ask: "What sound would *Victor* like things beginning with?"

Confirm that it is the sound *v*.

Ask them to tell you things that *Victor* would like.

Give examples if necessary: ***violet*** or ***pansy, violin*** or ***piano, camera*** or ***video***.

■ Reread the rhyme with the class, encouraging the children to join in. You should track the words with a pointer to focus on the direction of print, return sweep and correspondence between the spoken and the written word.

NOW OR LATER

■ Workbook 2 page 9.

Demonstrate the correct letter formation giving a commentary as you do so.

FURTHER PRACTICE

DEVELOPING SKILLS

Some or all of these activities must be done to ensure progress:

■ Find the letter *v* on the Alphabet Frieze.

■ Find *v* letters in the alphabet rhyme.

■ Find the letter *v* in books and around the classroom.

■ Practise letter formation.

■ Cut out pictures from magazines to make a book about *v*.

■ **What's my name?**

You say the sound that a letter makes and children say the corresponding letter name.

■ **What's my sound?**

You say a letter name and children say the sound that letter makes.

■ ***v* – where is my sound – beginning or end?**

You say a word and children answer *beginning* or *end*.

Suggested words:

glove	have	violin	van
vet	give	vest	vase
dove	voice	live	victory
video	save	love	brave

(*You may wish to explain that* v *is always followed by* e *at the end of words.*)

NOTE

■ When the children line up, ask those whose names begin with *v* to come forward first then those whose names begin with letters already taught.

■ When the children line up, ask, for example, *Vicky* and *Vikram* to come forward. Then ask: "Who else can come to the line?" Confirm that they can go into the line if their own name begins with *v*.

ACTIVITIES AT HOME

■ Look for an object starting with *v* to take to school.

■ My Sounds Book.

The **u** sound

BEFORE YOU START

THE NLF AIMS

- Hear and identify the initial sound *u*.
- Read the letter that represents the sound *u*.
- Write the letter that represents the sound *u*.

WHAT YOU NEED

RESOURCES

- *Hector Hedgehog's Big Book of Rhymes (Alphabet)* page 26
- Letter Cards *c, d, a, h, m, s, t, p, o, n, g, w, f, b, e, r, l, k, j, v* and *u*
- Alphabet Frieze
- Cards with names of children in class whose names start with *u*
- Whiteboard/chalkboard/easel
- Workbook 2 page 10
- Teacher's copy of Workbook 2 page 10

KEY LESSON POINTERS

VOCABULARY

alphabet   letter   name   sound   word
letter shape   capital   rhyme   trace
start/beginning   middle

THE CHILDREN should throughout the lesson:

- distinguish between the letter sound *u* and the letter name *u*
- pronounce the short sound *u*
- focus exclusively on the sound activity and not stray onto unrelated topics.

YOU should throughout the lesson:

- emphasise the *u* sound at all times
- emphasise the difference between the letter sound and the letter name
- ensure correct pronunciation of the *u* sound
- ensure that enough time is spent looking at and talking about the book and rhyme
- emphasise starting at the correct point when tracing/writing the letter *u* and moving finger/pencil in the correct direction.

THE LESSON

STARTING THE LESSON

Quick revision of *c, d, a, h, m, s, t, p, o, n, g, w, f, b, e, r, l, k, j* and *v*.

Some or all of the following should be done to ensure progression:

- Show Letter Cards and ask what sound each letter makes.

  Confirm that the letters make the sounds *c, d, a, h, m, s, t, p, o, n, g, w, f, b, e, r, l, k, j* and *v*.

  Ask: "What are the names of the sounds?"

- Stick the cards on the board.

  Ask the children to find the card with the letter that makes the *c, d, a, h, m, s, t, p, o, n, g, w, f, b, e, r, l, k, j* and *v* sound.

  Ask the children to find the card that the word *van, jelly, key* starts with. Give practice with other words as appropriate.

  Tell the children they have to think about the names of the letters now and ask them to find *c, d, a, h, m, s, t, p, o, n, g, w, f, b, e, r, l, k, j* and *v*.

  (*Be aware of the needs of the children in terms of the letter sounds that they are unsure of and give more practice.*)

TEACHING THE LESSON

- "Now let's see what today's letter is going to be."

- Open the book at page 26 and tell them that this will be today's activity. (*Be sure to spend some time together, looking at the page.*)

  Ask: "What can you see in the picture?"

  Discuss the content, focusing on the *u* words such as *umbrella* and *untidy*. (*Emphasise the* **u** *words. Ensure the children focus exclusively on the objectives of the activity. Don't let them stray onto unrelated topics.*)

- Read the rhyme, emphasising the *u* words.

  Reread and encourage the children to join in.

  Ask: "What did *uppity uncle* unfold?"

  Confirm *umbrella*, heavily emphasising the *u*.

  Tell them to listen carefully and to say what sound they can hear at the beginning of *uncle*.

  Confirm that it is the sound *u*.

  Tell them to listen carefully and to say what sound they can hear at the beginning of *uppity*.

  Confirm that it is the sound *u*.

Ask them to listen for other **u** words while you reread the rhyme.

Confirm other **u** words: ***umbrella, upside down, unfolds, untidy***.

■ Tell them that the letter **u** looks like this in books, magazines, signs (*lower case*).

Finger trace the letter on the page.

You say that this is the shape (*going over the letter again*). You say again that **u** is its sound.

Ask: "Does anyone know what its name is?"

Show Letter Card **u** and finger trace. Confirm that it is the same letter as the one in the book.

Ask: "What is its name?"

Ask: "What sound does it make?"

Ask them, as appropriate, to finger trace over the letter shape. (*Emphasise the correct starting point and the correct formation when tracing over the letter.*)

■ Ask them if anyone could be in the **u** set with a name beginning with the sound **u**. (*For example,* **Ursula, Umberto.**)

Ask identified children to select their name card and stick it under the correct letter on the Alphabet Frieze.

Ask: "What do you notice about the letter at the beginning of your name?"

Confirm that it is a capital letter and discuss its function. (*Extend as appropriate to streets, towns, start of sentences.*)

Ask them, as appropriate, to finger trace over the upper case letter shape.

■ Ask: "What sound would ***uppity uncle*** like things beginning with?"

Confirm that it is the sound **u**.

Ask them to tell you things that ***uppity uncle*** would like.

Give examples if necessary: ***umbrella*** or ***bag, up*** or ***down, over*** or ***under***.

■ Reread the rhyme with the class, encouraging the children to join in. You should track the words with a pointer to focus on the direction of print, return sweep and correspondence between the spoken and the written word.

NOW OR LATER

■ Workbook 2 page 10.

■ Demonstrate the correct letter formation giving a commentary as you do so.

DEVELOPING SKILLS

Some or all of these activities must be done to ensure progress:

■ Find the letter *u* on the Alphabet Frieze.

■ Find *u* letters in the alphabet rhyme.

■ Find the letter *u* in books and around the classroom.

■ Practise letter formation.

■ Cut out pictures from magazines to make a book about *u*.

■ **What's my name?**

You say the sound that a letter makes and children say the corresponding letter name.

■ **What's my sound?**

You say a letter name and children say the sound that letter makes.

NOTE

■ When the children line up, ask those whose names begin with *u* to come forward first then those whose names begin with letters already taught.

■ When the children line up, ask, for example, *Ursula* and *Umberto* to come forward. Then ask: "Who else can come to the line?" Confirm that they can go into the line if their own name begins with *u*.

■ At this point many children may be ready to blend CVC words with the sounds taught. The skill is taught formally at a later stage but raising awareness may be appropriate now.

Suggested words:

cub	dug	hut	mum	sum
cut		hum	mud	sun
cup	fun	hub	mug	
		hug		
pup	nut	rug	rub	jug
pub	nun	rut	run	jut

ACTIVITIES AT HOME

■ Look for an object starting with *u* to take to school.

■ My Sounds Book.

u

Review

THE NLF AIMS

- Hear and differentiate between initial sounds *c, d, a, h, m, s, t, p, o, n, g, w, f, b, e, r, l, k, j, v* and *u*.
- Read the letters that represent the sounds *c, d, a, h, m, s, t, p, o, n, g, w, f, b, e, r, l, k, j, v* and *u*.

WHAT YOU NEED

RESOURCES

- Letter Cards *c, d, a, h, m, s, t, p, o, n, g, w, f, b, e, r, l, k, j, v* and *u*
- Alphabet Frieze
- Whiteboard/chalkboard/easel
- Workbook 2 page 11
- Teacher's copy of Workbook 2 page 11
- Headbands with slits
- Quick Cards
- Additional Support 11
- Assessment 2.3

KEY LESSON POINTERS

VOCABULARY

alphabet letter name sound word
letter shape capital rhyme trace
start/beginning

THE CHILDREN should throughout the lesson:

- distinguish between the letter sounds and letter names *c, d, a, h, m, s, t, p, o, n, g, w, f, b, e, r, l, k, j, v* and *u*
- pronounce the pure sounds *c, d, h, m, s, t, p, n, g, w, f, b, r, l, k, j, v* and *u*
- focus exclusively on the sound activity and not stray onto unrelated topics.

YOU should throughout the lesson:

- emphasise the *c, d, a, h, m, s, t, p, o, n, g, w, f, b, e, r, l, k, j, v* and *u* sounds at all times
- emphasise the difference between the letter sound and the letter name
- ensure correct pronunciation of the *c, d, a, h, m, s, t, p, o, n, g, w, f, b, e, r, l, k, j, v* and *u* sounds
- encourage the use of examples such as the words *gate* and *goose* and not *grapes* or *green* where *g* is part of the *gr* cluster, and *fish* and *fan* and not *flowers* where *f* is part of the *fl* cluster, and *bus* and *book* and not *brush* where *b* is part of the *br* cluster
- ensure that enough time is spent looking at and talking about the book and rhyme.

STARTING THE LESSON

- Quick revision of all the sounds learned to date.
  Use Letter Cards and revisit *Hector Hedgehog's Big Book of Rhymes (Alphabet)* if necessary

TEACHING THE LESSON

- Show the children the *j* Letter Card.
  Ask: "What sound does this letter make?" The children may need a prompt: "Remember *Jason* the *juggler*?" (*Emphasise the* **j** *at the beginning of* **Jason** *and* **juggler**.)
  Ask the children to tell you the words which begin with *j*. Give clues if necessary: *jug* or *mug*, *jumper* or *cardigan*, *run* or *jump*.

- Show the children the *v* Letter Card.
  Ask: "What sound does this letter make?" The children may need a prompt: "Remember *Victor* the *vet*?" (*Emphasise the* **v** *at the beginning of* **Victor** *and* **vet**.)
  Ask the children to tell you the words which begin with *v*. Give clues if necessary: *violin* or *guitar*, *vest* or *teeshirt*, *car* or *van*.

- Show the children the *u* Letter Card.
  Ask: "What sound does this letter make?" The children may need a prompt: "Remember *uppity uncle*?" (*Emphasise the* **u** *at the beginning of* **uppity** *and* **uncle**.)
  Ask the children to tell you the words which begin with *u*. Give clues if necessary: *up* or *down*, *over* or *under*, *uncle* or *aunt*.

- Give three children headbands with *j*, *v* and *u* to wear.

Invite them to stand in three separate places at the front of the group/class.

Explain to the children that the child (*name*) with the *j* headband likes words beginning with *j*, the child (*name*) with the *v* headband likes words beginning with *v*, and the child (*name*) with the *u* headband likes words beginning with *u*. (*If possible, match the children's names to the* **j**, **v** *and* **u** *headbands, for example,* **Jawaad, Valerie, Ursula**.)

Invite the children to stand in the correct place, **Jawaad's** set, **Valerie's** set, **Ursula's** set, by calling out words. The children determine which set they go to by the initial sound of the word.

Suggested words:

jelly	van	up
juice	violin	under
jug	visit	ugly
jacket	vase	umbrella
jumper	vet	underwear
janitor	vinegar	upstairs
jam	vegetables	upset
jigsaw	velcro	unfold
jog	volcano	undress

Ask all the children in **Jawaad's** set (*j*) to say their word: **jelly, juice, jug** and so on. (*Children begin to put emphasis on the* **j** *sound*.)

Ask: "Why are you in the *j* set?"

Confirm that the words all start with *j*.

Ask all the children in **Valerie's** set (*v*) to say their word: **van, violin, visit** and so on. (*Children begin to put emphasis on the* **v** *sound*.)

Ask: "Why are you in the *v* set?"

Confirm that the words all start with *v*.

Ask all the children in **Ursula's** set (*u*) to say their word: **up, under, ugly** and so on. (*Children begin to put emphasis on the* **u** *sound*.)

Ask: "Why are you in the *u* set?"

Confirm that the words all start with *u*.

■ Children complete Workbook 2 page 11.

LATER

■ Repeat the above lesson for further practice.

■ Children complete Additional Support 11.

FURTHER PRACTICE

DEVELOPING SKILLS

Some or all of these activities must be done to ensure progress:

■ Practise letter formation.

■ **Quick Cards**

Children have the *j*, *v* and *u* cards, plus any Letter Cards that they need further practice in, face up on the table. You call out a word: *jug, vase, under* and so on and the children point to/hold up the appropriate card.

You hold up a picture of an object starting with *j*, *v* or *u*, plus any letters that the children need further practice in, and children hold up the appropriate card.

■ **What's my sound? (1)**

You say a word and children say the sound that the word starts with: violin – *v*.

The *v* and *f* sounds are easily confused. It is often difficult for children to hear the difference between the two sounds. Give plenty of practice.

■ **What's my sound? (2)**

You say a word and children say the *v* or *f* sound that the word starts with.

Suggested words:

| fan | van | fete | vet | fish |
| vase | fun | visit | velcro | funny |

■ **Peek-a-Boo**

See Unit 2 Introduction.

NOTE

Quick Cards

■ If the children hold up the cards, ensure that all the letters are the right way up and facing in the right direction. In the early stages it might be better for the children to point to the cards.

ASSESSMENT 2.3

ACTIVITIES AT HOME

■ My Sounds Book.

Review

The z sound

THE NLF AIMS

- Hear and identify the initial sound *z*.
- Read the letter that represents the sound *z*.
- Write the letter that represents the sound *z*.

WHAT YOU NEED

RESOURCES

- *Hector Hedgehog's Big Book of Rhymes (Alphabet)* page 31
- Letter Cards *c, d, a, h, m, s, t, p, o, n, g, w, f, b, e, r, l, k, j, v, u* and *z*
- Alphabet Frieze
- Cards with names of children in class whose names start with *z*
- Whiteboard/chalkboard/easel
- Workbook 2 page 12
- Teacher's copy of Workbook 2 page 12

KEY LESSON POINTERS

VOCABULARY

alphabet   letter   name   sound   word
letter shape   capital   rhyme   trace
start/beginning   middle   match

THE CHILDREN should throughout the lesson:

- distinguish between the letter sound *z* and the letter name *z*
- pronounce the pure sound *z* without blurring it by adding a vowel as in *zi*
- focus exclusively on the sound activity and not stray onto unrelated topics.

YOU should throughout the lesson:

- emphasise the *z* sound at all times
- emphasise the difference between the letter sound and the letter name
- ensure correct pronunciation of the pure *z* sound
- ensure that enough time is spent looking at and talking about the book and rhyme
- emphasise starting at the correct point when tracing/writing the letter *z* and moving finger/pencil in the correct direction.

THE LESSON

STARTING THE LESSON

- Quick revision of *c, d, a, h, m, s, t, p, o, n, g, w, f, b, e, r, l, k, j, v* and *u*.

  Some or all of the following should be done to ensure progression:

- Show Letter Cards and ask what sound each letter makes.

  Confirm that the letters make the sounds *c, d, a, h, m, s, t, p, o, n, g, w, f, b, e, r, l, k, j, v* and *u*.

  Ask: "What are the names of the letters?"

- Stick the cards on the board.

  Ask the children to find the card with the letter that makes *c, d, a, h, m, s, t, p, o, n, g, w, f, b, e, r, l, k, j, v* and *u* sound.

  Ask the children to find the card that the word *under, visitor, jump* and so on starts with.

  Tell the children they have to think about the names of the letters now and ask them to find *c, d, a, h, m, s, t, p, o, n, g, w, f, b, e, r, l, k, j, v* and *u*.

  (*Be aware of the needs of the children in terms of the letter sounds that they are unsure of and give more practice.*)

TEACHING THE LESSON

- "Now let's see what today's letter is going to be."

- Open the book at page 31 and tell them that this will be today's activity. (*Be sure to spend some time together, looking at the page.*)

  Ask: "What can you see in the picture?"

  Discuss the content, focusing on the *z* words such as *zoo* and *zebra*. (*Emphasise the z words. Ensure the children focus exclusively on the objectives of the activity. Don't let them stray onto unrelated topics.*)

- Read the rhyme, emphasising the *z* words.

  Reread and encourage the children to join in.

  Ask: "Who lived in a zoo?"

  Confirm *Zoe* and *Ziggy*, heavily emphasising the *z*.

  Tell them to listen carefully and to say what sound they can hear at the beginning of *Zoe*.

  Confirm that it is the sound *z*.

  Tell them to listen carefully and to say what sound they can hear at the beginning of *Ziggy*.

  Confirm that it is the sound *z*.

  Ask them to listen for other *z* words while you reread the rhyme.

Confirm other *z* words: ***zebra, zoo, zany, Zippity, Zee, zip***.

■ Tell them that the letter **z** looks like this in books, magazines, signs (*lower case*).

Finger trace the letter on the page.

You say that this is the shape (*going over the letter again*). You say again that **z** is its sound.

Ask: "Does anyone know what its name is?"

Show Letter Card **z** and finger trace. Confirm that it is the same letter as the one in the book.

Ask: "What is its name?"

Ask: "What sound does it make?"

Ask them, as appropriate, to finger trace over the letter shape. (*Emphasise the correct starting point and the correct formation when tracing over the letter.*)

■ Ask them if anyone could be in the **z** set with a name beginning with the sound **z**. (*For example,* **Zara, Zak**.)

Ask identified children to select their name cards and stick them under the correct letter on the Alphabet Frieze.

Ask: "What do you notice about the letter at the beginning of your name?"

Confirm that it is a capital letter and discuss its function. (*Extend as appropriate to streets, towns, start of sentences.*)

Ask them, as appropriate, to finger trace over the upper case letter shape.

■ Ask: "What sound would **Zoe** and **Ziggy** like things beginning with?"

Confirm that it is the sound **z**.

Ask them to tell you things that **Zoe** and **Ziggy** would like.

Give examples if necessary: **zig-zag** or **curly**, **zip** or **buttons**, **fly** or **zoom**.

■ Reread the rhyme with the class, encouraging the children to join in. You should the track words with a pointer to focus on the direction of print, return sweep and correspondence between the spoken and the written word.

NOW OR LATER

■ Workbook 2 page 12.

Demonstrate the correct letter formation giving a commentary as you do so.

FURTHER PRACTICE

DEVELOPING SKILLS

Some or all of these activities must be done to ensure progress:

■ Find the letter *z* on the Alphabet Frieze.

■ Find *z* letters in the alphabet rhyme.

■ Find the letter *z* in books and around the classroom.

■ Practise letter formation.

■ Cut out pictures from magazines to make a book about *z*.

■ **What's my name?**

You say the sound that a letter makes and children say the corresponding letter name.

■ **What's my sound?**

You say a letter name and children say the sound that letter makes.

NOTE

■ When the children line up, ask those whose names begin with *z* to come forward first then those whose names begin with letters already taught.

■ When the children line up, ask, for example, *Zara* and *Zak* to come forward. Then ask: "Who else can come to the line?" Confirm that they can go into the line if their own name begins with *z*.

ACTIVITIES AT HOME

■ Look for an object starting with *z* to take to school.

■ My Sounds Book.

AUDITORY DISCRIMINATION

IDENTIFYING ALPHABET SOUNDS

Z

The y sound

THE NLF AIMS

- Hear and identify the initial sound *y*.
- Read the letter that represents the sound *y*.
- Write the letter that represents the sound *y*.

WHAT YOU NEED

RESOURCES

- *Hector Hedgehog's Big Book of Rhymes (Alphabet)* page 30
- Letter Cards *c, d, a, h, m, s, t, p, o, n, g, w, f, b, e, r, l, k, j, v, u, z* and *y*
- Alphabet Frieze
- Cards with names of children in class whose names start with *y*
- Whiteboard/chalkboard/easel
- Workbook 2 page 13
- Teacher's copy of Workbook 2 page 13

KEY LESSON POINTERS

VOCABULARY

alphabet letter name sound word letter shape capital rhyme trace start/beginning middle

THE CHILDREN should throughout the lesson:

- distinguish between the letter sound *y* and the letter name *y*
- pronounce the pure sound *y* without blurring it by adding a vowel as in *yi*
- focus exclusively on the sound activity and not stray onto unrelated topics.

YOU should throughout the lesson:

- emphasise the *y* sound at all times
- emphasise the difference between the letter sound and the letter name
- ensure correct pronunciation of the pure *y* sound
- ensure that enough time is spent looking at and talking about the book and rhyme
- emphasise starting at the correct point when tracing/writing the letter *y* and moving finger/pencil in the correct direction.

THE LESSON

STARTING THE LESSON

Quick revision of *c, d, a, h, m, s, t, p, o, n, g, w, f, b, e, r, l, k, j, v, u* and *z*.

Some or all of the following should be done to ensure progression:

- Show Letter Cards and ask what sound each letter makes.

  Confirm that the letters make the sounds *c, d, a, h, m, s, t, p, o, n, g, w, f, b, e, r, l, k, j, v, u* and *z*.

  Ask: "What are the names of the letters?"

- Stick the cards on the board.

  Ask the children to find the card with the letter that makes *c, d, a, h, m, s, t, p, o, n, g, w, f, b, e, r, l, k, j, v, u* and *z* sound.

  Ask the children to find the card that the word *voice, jumper, zoo* and so on starts with.

  Tell the children they have to think about the names of the letters now and ask them to find *c, d, a, h, m, s, t, p, o, n, g, w, f, b, e, r, l, k, j, v, u* and *z*.

  (*Be aware of the needs of the children in terms of the letter sounds that they are unsure of and give more practice.*)

TEACHING THE LESSON

- "Now let's see what today's letter is going to be."
- Open the book at page 30 and tell them that this will be today's activity. (*Be sure to spend some time together, looking at the page.*)

  Ask: "What can you see in the picture?"

  Discuss the content, focusing on the *y* words such as *yacht* and *yanked*. (*Emphasise the* y *words. Ensure the children focus exclusively on the objectives of the activity. Don't let them stray onto unrelated topics.*)

- Read the rhyme, emphasising the *y* words.

  Reread and encourage the children to join in.

  Ask: "What did *Yasmin* have for tea yesterday?"

  Repeat *yoghurt*, heavily emphasising the *y*.

  Tell them to listen carefully and to say what sound they can hear at the beginning of *Yasmin*.

  Confirm that it is the sound *y*.

  Tell them to listen carefully and to say what sound they can hear at the beginning of *yoghurt*.

  Confirm that it is the sound *y*.

  Ask them to listen for other *y* words while you reread the rhyme.

Confirm other *y* words: *yesterday, yo-yo, yacht, yodelled, yelled, yanked, yellow, yawned, yelp*.

■ Tell them that the letter *y* looks like this in books, magazines, signs (*lower case*).

Finger trace the letter on the page.

You say that this is the shape (*going over the letter again*). You say again that *y* is its sound.

Ask: "Does anyone know what its name is?"

Show Letter Card *y* and finger trace. Confirm that it is the same letter as the one in the book.

Ask: "What is its name?"

Ask: "What sound does it make?"

Ask them, as appropriate, to finger trace over the letter shape. (*Emphasise the correct starting point and the correct formation when tracing over the letter.*)

■ Ask them if anyone could be in the *y* set with a name beginning with the sound *y*. (*For example,* **Yolanda**, **Yasmin**.)

Ask identified children to select their name cards and stick them under the correct letter on the Alphabet Frieze.

Ask: "What do you notice about the letter at the beginning of your name?"

Confirm that it is a capital letter and discuss its function. (*Extend as appropriate to streets, towns, start of sentences.*)

Ask them, as appropriate, to finger trace over the upper case letter shape.

■ Ask: "What sound would *Yasmin* like things beginning with?"

Confirm that it is the sound *y*.

Ask them to tell you things that *Yasmin* would like.

Give examples if necessary: *yacht* or *bus*, *yes* or *no*, *dog* or *yak*.

■ Reread the rhyme with the class, encouraging the children to join in. You should track the words with a pointer to focus on the direction of print, return sweep and correspondence between the spoken and the written word.

NOW OR LATER

■ Workbook 2 page 13.

Demonstrate the correct letter formation giving a commentary as you do so.

FURTHER PRACTICE

DEVELOPING SKILLS

Some or all of these activities must be done to ensure progress:

■ Find the letter *y* on the Alphabet Frieze.

■ Find *y* letters in the alphabet rhyme.

■ Find the letter *y* in books and around the classroom.

■ Practise letter formation.

■ Cut out pictures from magazines to make a book about *y*.

■ **What's my name?**

You say the sound that a letter makes and children say the corresponding letter name.

■ **What's my sound?**

You say a letter name and children say the sound that letter makes.

NOTE

■ When the children line up, ask those whose names begin with *y* to come forward first then those whose names begin with letters already taught in turn.

ACTIVITIES AT HOME

■ Look for an object starting with *y* to take to school.

■ My Sounds Book.

y

Review

BEFORE YOU START

THE NLF AIMS

- Hear and differentiate between initial sounds *c, a, d, h, m, s, t, p, o, n, g, w, f, b, e, r, l, k, j, v, u, y* and *z* in words.
- Read the letters that represent the sounds *c, a, d, h, m, s, t, p, o, n, g, w, f, b, e, r, l, k, j, v, u, y* and *z*.

WHAT YOU NEED

RESOURCES

- Letter Cards *c, a, d, h, m, s, t, p, o, n, g, w, f, b, e, r, l, k, j, v, u, y* and *z*
- Alphabet Frieze
- Whiteboard/chalkboard/easel
- Workbook 2 page 14
- Teacher's copy of Workbook 2 page 14
- Headbands with slits
- Quick Cards
- Additional Support 12

KEY LESSON POINTERS

VOCABULARY

alphabet letter name sound word letter shape capital rhyme trace start/beginning match

THE CHILDREN should throughout the lesson:

- distinguish between the letter sounds and the letter names *c, d, h, m, s, t, p, o, n, g, w, f, b, e, r, l, k, j, v, u, y* and *z*
- pronounce the pure sounds *c, d, h, m, s, t, p, n, g, w, f, b, r, l, k, j, v, y* and *z*
- focus exclusively on the sound activity and not stray onto unrelated topics.

YOU should throughout the lesson:

- emphasise the *c, a, d, h, m, s, t, p, o, n, g, w, f, b, e, r, l, k, j, v, u, y* and *z* sounds at all times
- emphasise the difference between the letter sound and the letter name
- ensure correct pronunciation of the *c, a, d, h, m, s, t, p, o, n, g, w, f, b, e, r, l, k, j, v, u, y* and *z* sounds
- encourage the use of examples such as the words *gate* and *goose* and not *grapes* or *green* where *g* is part of the *gr* cluster, and *fish* and *fan* and not *flowers* where *f* is part of the *fl* cluster, and *bus* and *book* and not *brush* where *b* is part of the *br* cluster.

THE LESSON

STARTING THE LESSON

- Quick revision of all the sounds learned to date.

  Use Letter Cards and revisit *Hector Hedgehog's Big Book of Rhymes (Alphabet)* if necessary.

TEACHING THE LESSON

- Show the children the *z* Letter Card.

  Ask: "What sound does this letter make?" The children may need a prompt: "Remember *Zoe* and *Ziggy*?" (*Emphasise the* **z** *at the beginning of* **Zoe** *and* **Ziggy**.)

  Ask the children to tell you the words which begin with *z*. Give clues if necessary: *zip* or *button, zoo* or *park, horse* or *zebra*.

- Show the children the *y* Letter Card.

  Ask: "What sound does this letter make?" The children may need a prompt: "Remember *Yasmin* and her *yacht*?" (*Emphasise the* **y** *at the beginning of* **Yasmin** *and* **yacht**.)

  Ask the children to tell you the words which begin with *y*. Give clues if necessary: *yoghurt* or *pudding, red* or *yellow, horse* or *yak*.

- Show the children the *v* Letter Card.

  Ask: "What sound does this letter make?" The children may need a prompt: "Remember *Victor* the *vet*?" (*Emphasise the* **v** *at the beginning of* **Victor** *and* **vet**.)

  Ask the children to tell you the words which begin with *v*. Give clues if necessary: *vest* or *cardigan, pot* or *vase, bus* or *van*.

- Give three children headbands with *z, y* and *v* to wear.

Invite them to stand in three separate places at the front of the group/class.

Explain to the children that the child (*name*) with the *z* headband likes words beginning with *z*, the child (*name*) with the *y* headband likes words beginning with **y**, and the child (*name*) with the *v* headband likes words beginning with **v**. (*If possible, match the children's names to the* **z, y** *and* **v** *headbands, for example,* **Zara, Yasmin, Vicky**.)

Invite the children to stand in the correct place, **Zara's** set, **Yasmin's** set, **Vicky's** set, by calling out words. The children determine which set they go to by the initial sound of the word.

Suggested words:

zoo	yellow	van
zip	yacht	violet
zigzag	yo-yo	vase
zebra	yoghurt	vest
zero	yolk	video

Ask all the children in **Zara's** set (z) to say their word: **zoo, zip, zigzag** and so on. (*Children begin to put emphasis on the* **z** *sound*.)

Ask: "Why are you in the **z** set?"

Confirm that the words all start with **z**.

Ask all the children in **Yasmin's** set (y) to say their word: **yellow, yacht, yo-yo** and so on. (*Children begin to put emphasis on the* **y** *sound*.)

Ask: "Why are you in the **y** set?"

Confirm that the words all start with **y**.

Ask all the children in **Vicky's** set (v) to say their word: **van, violet, vase** and so on. (*Children begin to put emphasis on the* **v** *sound*.)

Ask: "Why are you in the **v** set?"

Confirm that the words all start with **v**.

■ Children complete Workbook 2 page 14.

LATER

■ Repeat the above lesson for further practice.

■ Children complete Additional Support 12.

FURTHER PRACTICE

DEVELOPING SKILLS

Some or all of these activities must be done to ensure progress:

■ Practise letter formation.

■ **Quick Cards**

Children have the *z, y* and *v* cards, plus any Letter Cards that they need further practice in, face up on the table. You call out a word: *zigzag, yacht, Velcro* and so on and children point to/hold up the appropriate card.

You hold up a picture of an object starting with *z, y* or *v*, plus any Letter Cards that the children need further practice in, and children hold up the appropriate card.

■ **What's my sound?**

You say a word and children say the sound that the word starts with: yo-yo – *y*.

■ **Peek-a-Boo**

See Unit 2 Introduction.

NOTE

Quick Cards

■ If the children hold up the cards, ensure that all letters are the right way up and facing in the right direction. In the early stages it might be better for the children to point to the cards.

ACTIVITIES AT HOME

■ My Sounds Book.

AUDITORY DISCRIMINATION

IDENTIFYING ALPHABET SOUNDS

Review

111

The i sound

BEFORE YOU START

THE NLF AIMS

- Hear and identify the initial sound *i*.
- Read the letter that represents the sound *i*.
- Write the letter that represents the sound *i*.

WHAT YOU NEED

RESOURCES

- *Hector Hedgehog's Big Book of Rhymes (Alphabet)* page 11
- Letter Cards *c, d, a, h, m, s, t, p, o, n, g, w, f, b, e, r, l, k, j, v, u, z, y* and *i*
- Alphabet Frieze
- Cards with names of children in class whose names start with *i*
- Whiteboard/chalkboard/easel
- Workbook 2 page 15
- Teacher's copy of Workbook 2 page 15

KEY LESSON POINTERS

VOCABULARY

alphabet letter name sound word
letter shape capital rhyme trace
start/beginning middle match

THE CHILDREN should throughout the lesson:

- distinguish between the letter sound *i* and the letter name *i*
- pronounce the short sound *i*
- focus exclusively on the sound activity and not stray onto unrelated topics.

YOU should throughout the lesson:

- emphasise the *i* sound at all times
- emphasise the difference between the letter sound and the letter name
- ensure that enough time is spent looking at and talking about the book and rhyme
- emphasise starting at the correct point when tracing/writing the letter *i* and moving finger/pencil in the correct direction.

THE LESSON

STARTING THE LESSON

Quick revision of *c, d, a, h, m, s, t, p, o, n, g, w, f, b, e, r, l, k, j, v, u, z* and *y*.

Some or all of the following should be done to ensure progression:

- Show Letter Cards and ask what sound each letter makes.

  Confirm that the letters make the sounds *c, d, a, h, m, s, t, p, o, n, g, w, f, b, e, r, l, k, j, v, u, z* and *y*.

  Ask: "What are the names of the letters?"

- Stick the cards on the board.

  Ask the children to find the card with the letter that makes *c, d, a, h, m, s, t, p, o, n, g, w, f, b, e, r, l, k, j, v, u, z* and *y* sound.

  Ask the children to find the card that the word *yoyo, zip, ugly* and so on starts with.

  Tell the children they have to think about the names of the letters now and ask them to find *c, d, a, h, m, s, t, p, o, n, g, w, f, b, e, r, l, k, j, v, u, z* and *y*.

  (*Be aware of the needs of the children in terms of the letter sounds that they are unsure of and give more practice.*)

TEACHING THE LESSON

- "Now let's see what today's letter is going to be."

- Open the book at page 11 and tell them that this will be today's activity. (*Be sure to spend some time together, looking at the page.*)

  Ask: "What can you see in the picture?"

  Discuss the content, focusing on *i* words such as **iguana** and **ichthyosaur**. (*Emphasise the i words. Ensure the children focus exclusively on the objectives of the activity. Don't let them stray onto unrelated topics.*)

- Read the rhyme, emphasising the the *i* words.

  Reread and encourage the children to join in.

  Ask: "What is the name of **Imogen's** friend?"

  Confirm **Izzy**, heavily emphasising the *i*.

  Tell them to listen carefully and to say what sound they can hear at the beginning of **Izzy**.

  Confirm that it is the sound *i*.

  Tell them to listen carefully and to say what sound they can hear at the beginning of **Imogen**.

  Confirm that it is the sound *i*.

  Ask them to listen for other *i* words while you reread the rhyme.

Confirm other *i* words: ***iguana, invited, in, Icabod, ichthyosaur, ink, indigo, insisted.***

■ Tell them that the letter *i* looks like this in books, magazines, signs (*lower case*).

Finger trace the letter on the page.

You say that this is the shape (*going over the letter again*). You say again that *i* is its sound.

Ask: "Does anyone know what its name is?"

Show Letter Card *i* and finger trace. Confirm that it is the same letter as the one in the book.

Ask: "What is its name?"

Ask: "What sound does it make?"

Ask them, as appropriate, to finger trace over the letter shape. (*Emphasise the correct starting point and the correct formation when tracing over the letter.*)

■ Ask them if anyone could be in the *i* set with a name beginning with the sound *i*. (*For example,* **Idris, Indira.**)

Ask identified children to select their name cards and stick them under the correct letter on the Alphabet Frieze.

Ask: "What do you notice about the letter at the beginning of your name?"

Confirm that it is a capital letter and discuss its function. (*Extend as appropriate to streets, towns, start of sentences.*)

Ask them, as appropriate, to finger trace over the upper case letter shape.

■ Ask: "What sound would *Imogen* like things beginning with?"

Confirm that it is the sound *i*.

Ask them to tell you things that *Imogen* would like.

Give examples if necessary: ***ink*** or ***paint***, ***inside*** or ***outside***, ***animals*** or ***insects***.

■ Reread the rhyme with the class, encouraging the children to join in. You should track the words with a pointer to focus on the direction of print, return sweep and correspondence between the spoken and the written word.

NOW OR LATER

■ Workbook 2 page 15.

■ Demonstrate the correct letter formation giving a commentary as you do so.

FURTHER PRACTICE

DEVELOPING SKILLS

Some or all of these activities must be done to ensure progress:

■ Find the letter *i* on the Alphabet Frieze.

■ Find *i* letters in the alphabet rhyme.

■ Find the letter *i* in books and around the classroom.

■ Practise letter formation.

■ Cut out pictures from magazines to make a book about *i*.

■ **What's my name?**

You say the sound that a letter makes and children say the corresponding letter name.

■ **What's my sound?**

You say a letter name and children say the sound that letter makes.

NOTE

■ When the children line up, ask those whose names begin with *i* to come forward first then those whose names begin with letters already taught in turn.

■ At this point many children may be ready to blend CVC words with the sounds taught. The skill is taught formally at a later stage but raising awareness may be appropriate now.

Suggested words:

sit	tin	did	pig	him
sip	tip	dig	pin	hid
Sid	Tim	din	pit	hit
		dim	pip	hip

fit	bin	nib	rib	wig
fin	bit	nip	rip	win
fig	big		rid	
	bib		rig	
			rim	

kit	jig	lip
kid	Jim	lid
		lit

ACTIVITIES AT HOME

■ Look for an object starting with *i* to take to school.

■ My Sounds Book.

The q sound

THE NLF AIMS

- Hear and identify the initial sound q.
- Read the letter that represents the sound q.
- Write the letter that represents the sound q.

WHAT YOU NEED

RESOURCES

- *Hector Hedgehog's Big Book of Rhymes (Alphabet)* page 20
- Letter Cards *c, d, a, h, m, s, t, p, o, n, g, w, f, b, e, r, l, k, j, v, u, z, y, i* and *q*
- Alphabet Frieze
- Cards with names of children in class whose names start with *y*
- Whiteboard/chalkboard/easel
- Workbook 2 page 16
- Teacher's copy of Workbook 2 page 16

KEY LESSON POINTERS

VOCABULARY

alphabet   letter   name   sound   word
letter shape   capital   rhyme   trace
start/beginning   middle   match

THE CHILDREN should throughout the lesson:

- distinguish between the letter sound *q* and the letter name *q*
- focus exclusively on the sound activity and not stray onto unrelated topics.

YOU should throughout the lesson:

- emphasise the *q* sound at all times
- emphasise the difference between the letter sound and the letter name
- ensure that the children know that *q* is followed by *u* in the English language
- ensure that enough time is spent looking at and talking about the book and rhyme
- emphasise starting at the correct point when tracing/writing the letter *q* and moving finger/pencil in the correct direction.

STARTING THE LESSON

Quick revision of *c, d, a, h, m, s, t, p, o, n, g, w, f, b, e, r, l, k, j, v, u, z, y* and *i*.

Some or all of the following should be done to ensure progression:

- Show Letter Cards and ask what sound each letter makes.

  Confirm that the letters make the sounds *c, d, a, h, m, s, t, p, o, n, g, w, f, b, e, r, l, k, j, v, u, z, y* and *i*.

  Ask: "What are the names of the letters?"

- Stick the cards on the board.

  Ask the children to find the card with the letter that makes the *c, d, a, h, m, s, t, p, o, n, g, w, f, b, e, r, l, k, j, v, u, z, y* and *i* sound.

  Ask the children to find the card that the word *infant, yellow, zip* and so on starts with.

  Tell the children they have to think about the names of the letters now and ask them to find *c, d, a, h, m, s, t, p, o, n, g, w, f, b, e, r, l, k, j, v, u, z, y* and *i*.

  (*Be aware of the needs of the children in terms of the letter sounds that they are unsure of and give more practice.*)

TEACHING THE LESSON

- "Now let's see what today's letter is going to be."

- Open the book at page 20 and tell them that this will be today's activity. (*Be sure to spend some time together, looking at the page.*)

  Ask: "What can you see in the picture?"

  Discuss the content, focusing on the *q* words such as *Queenie* and *quads*. (*Emphasise the* q *words. Ensure the children focus exclusively on the objectives of the activity. Don't let them stray onto unrelated topics.*)

- Read the rhyme, emphasising the *q* words.

  Reread and encourage the children to join in.

  Ask: "What is the duck's name?"

  Confirm *Queenie*, heavily emphasising the *q*.

  Tell them to listen carefully and to say what sound they can hear at the beginning of *Queenie*.

  Confirm that it is the sound *q*.

  Tell them to listen carefully and to say what sound they can hear at the beginning of *quads*.

Confirm that it is the sound *q*.

Ask them to listen for other *q* words while you reread the rhyme.

Confirm other *q* words: **quick, quackers, quibble, quarrel, quiet, quite, quarter**.

■ Tell them that the letter *q* looks like this in books, magazines, signs (*lower case*).

Finger trace the letter on the page.

You say that this is the shape (*going over the letter again*). You say again that *q* is its sound.

Tell the children that in the English language, *q* is always followed by *u*.

Ask the children to find the *qu* words in the rhyme such as **quibble** and **quite**.

Show Letter Card *q* and finger trace. Confirm that it is the same letter as the one in the book.

Reinforce that in print, the *q* is always followed by *u*.

Ask: "What is its name?"

Ask: "What sound does it make?"

Ask them, as appropriate, to finger trace over the letter shape. (*Emphasise the correct starting point and the correct formation when tracing over the letter.*)

■ Few names start with *q* in the English language.

■ Ask "What sound would **Queenie** like things to begin with?"

Confirm that it is the sound *q*.

Ask them to tell you things that **Queenie** would like.

Give examples if necessary: **quilt** or **blanket**, **run** or **quiver**, **quack** or **bark**.

■ Reread the rhyme with the class encouraging the children to join in. You should track the words with a pointer to focus on the direction of print, return sweep and correspondence between the spoken and the written word.

NOW OR LATER

■ Workbook 2 page 16.

Demonstrate the correct letter formation giving a commentary as you do so.

FURTHER PRACTICE

DEVELOPING SKILLS

Some or all of these activities must be done to ensure progress:

■ Find the letter *q* on the Alphabet Frieze.

■ Find *q* letters in the alphabet rhyme.

■ Find the letter *q* in books and around the classroom.

■ Practise letter formation.

■ Cut out pictures from magazines to make a book about *q*.

■ **What's my name?**

You say the sound that a letter makes and children say the corresponding letter name.

■ **What's my sound?**

You say a letter name and children say the sound that letter makes.

NOTE

■ There are few words that children at this stage will meet beginning with *q*: queen, *quilt, quick, quack, quads, quarter, quarrel*. If any *q* words are met regularly in reading/writing material, focus on the *qu* at the beginning. In writing, some children may represent *qu* as *cw* (*which is aurally similar*). This should be addressed before a habit is established.

ACTIVITIES AT HOME

■ Look for an object starting with *q* to take to school.

■ My Sounds Book.

AUDITORY DISCRIMINATION

IDENTIFYING ALPHABET SOUNDS

q

The x sound

THE NLF AIMS

- Hear and identify the sound *x* at the end of words.
- Read the letter that represents the sound *x*.
- Write the letter that represents the sound *x*.

WHAT YOU NEED

RESOURCES

- *Hector Hedgehog's Big Book of Rhymes (Alphabet)* page 29
- Letter Cards *c, d, a, h, m, s, t, p, o, n, g, w, f, b, e, r, l, k, j, v, u, z, y, i, q* and *x*
- Alphabet Frieze
- Whiteboard/chalkboard/easel
- Workbook 2 page 17
- Teacher's copy of Workbook 2 page 17
- Homework Sheet 2A
- Assessments 2.4, 2.5

KEY LESSON POINTERS

VOCABULARY

alphabet   letter   name   sound   word
letter shape   capital   rhyme   trace
start/beginning/end   match

THE CHILDREN should throughout the lesson:

- distinguish between the letter sound *x* and the letter name *x*
- focus exclusively on the sound activity and not stray onto unrelated topics.

YOU should throughout the lesson:

- emphasise the *x* sound at all times
- emphasise the difference between the letter sound and the letter name
- ensure that enough time is spent looking at and talking about the book and rhyme
- emphasise starting at the correct point when tracing/writing the letter *x* and moving finger/pencil in the correct direction.

THE LESSON

STARTING THE LESSON

Quick revision of *c, d, a, h, m, s, t, p, o, n, g, w, f, b, e, r, l, k, j, v, u, z, y, i* and *q*.

Some or all of the following should be done to ensure progression:

- Show Letter Cards and ask what sound each letter makes.

  Confirm that the letters make the sounds *c, d, a, h, m, s, t, p, o, n, g, w, f, b, e, r, l, k, j, v, u, z, y, i* and *q*.

  Ask: "What are the names of the letters?"

- Stick the cards on the board.

  Ask the children to find the card with the letter that makes the *c, d, a, h, m, s, t, p, o, n, g, w, f, b, e, r, l, k, j, v, u, z, y, i* and *q* sound.

  Ask the children to find the card that the word **quilt, in, yummy** and so on starts with.

  Tell the children they have to think about the names of the letters now and ask them to find *c, d, a, h, m, s, t, p, o, n, g, w, f, b, e, r, l, k, j, v, u, z, y, i* and *q*.

  (*Be aware of the needs of the children in terms of the letter sounds that they are unsure of and give more practice.*)

TEACHING THE LESSON

- "Now let's see what today's letter is going to be."

- Open the book at page 29 and tell them that this will be today's activity. (*Be sure to spend some time together, looking at the page.*)

  Ask: "What can you see in the picture?"

  Discuss the content, focusing on the words with *x* at the end, such as *ox* and *fox*. (*Emphasise the* **x** *at the end of the words. Ensure the children focus exclusively on the objectives of the activity. Don't let them stray onto unrelated topics.*)

- Read the rhyme, emphasising the words with *x* at the end.

  Reread and encourage the children to join in.

  Ask: "Who said 'stand on that **box**'?"

  Confirm the *fox, fox, fox*, heavily emphasising the *x* at the end.

  Tell them to listen carefully and to say what sound they can hear at the end of *fox*.

  Confirm that it is the sound *x*.

Tell them to listen carefully and to say what sound they can hear at the end of *box*.

Confirm that it is the sound *x*.

Discuss with the children that *x* is not often found in words. A few words start with *x*, such as *xylophone* and *x-ray*, but in these words the letter *x* does not make the sound *x*. The *x* sound is usually found at the end of words.

Ask them to listen for other words with *x* at the end while you reread the rhyme.

Confirm other *x* words: *six, mix, fix*.

■ Tell them that the letter *x* looks like this in books, magazines, signs (*lower case*).

Finger trace the letter on the page.

You say that this is the shape (*going over the letter again*). You say again that *x* is its sound.

Ask: "Does anyone know what its name is?"

Show Letter Card *x* and finger trace. Confirm that it is the same letter as the one in the book.

Ask: "What is its name?"

Ask: "What sound does it make?"

Ask them, as appropriate, to finger trace over the letter shape. (*Emphasise the correct starting point and the correct formation when tracing over the letter.*)

■ Few names start with *x* in the English language.

■ Ask "What sound would the *fox* like things to end with?"

Confirm that it is the sound *x*.

Ask them to tell you things that the *fox* would like.

Give examples if necessary: *fix* or *bend, seven* or *six, cat* or *fox*.

■ Reread the rhyme with the class, encouraging the children to join in. You should track the words with a pointer to focus on the direction of print, return sweep and correspondence between the spoken and the written word.

NOW OR LATER

■ Workbook 2 page 17.

Demonstrate the correct letter formation giving a commentary as you do so.

DEVELOPING SKILLS

Some or all of these activities must be done to ensure progress:

■ Find the letter *x* on the Alphabet Frieze.

■ Find *x* letters in the alphabet rhyme.

■ Find the letter *x* in books and around the classroom.

■ Practise letter formation.

■ Cut out pictures from magazines to make a book about *x*.

■ **What's my name?**

You say the sound that a letter makes and children say the corresponding letter name.

■ **What's my sound?**

You say a letter name and children say the sound that letter makes.

ASSESSMENTS 2.4, 2.5

ACTIVITIES AT HOME

■ My Sounds Book.
■ Homework Sheet 2.1.

AUDITORY DISCRIMINATION

IDENTIFYING ALPHABET SOUNDS

X

The a e i o u sounds

THE NLF AIMS

- Know that *a, e, i, o,* and *u* are special letters called vowels.
- Know that there are five vowels in the alphabet.

WHAT YOU NEED

RESOURCES

- Letter Cards *a, e, i, o* and *u*
- Alphabet Frieze
- Whiteboard/chalkboard/easel
- Workbook 2 page 18
- Teacher's copy of Workbook 2 page 18
- Additional Support 13

KEY LESSON POINTERS

VOCABULARY

alphabet   letter   name   sound
word   letter shape   capital   rhyme
trace   start/beginning   middle
alphabetical order   vowel   match

THE CHILDREN should throughout the lesson:

- distinguish between the sounds of the vowels and the names of the vowels
- focus exclusively on the sound activity and not stray onto unrelated topics.

YOU should throughout the lesson:

- emphasise the sound of the vowels and the names of the vowels.

STARTING THE LESSON

Quick revision of *a, e, i, o* and *u.*

Some or all of the following should be done to ensure progression:

- Show Letter Cards and ask what sound each letter makes.

  Ask: "Does anyone know the names of the letters *a, e, i, o* and *u*?"

- Stick the cards on the board.

  Ask the children to find the card with the letter that makes the *a, e, i, o* and *u* sound.

  Ask the children to find the card that the word *apple, exit, ink* and so on starts with.

  Tell the children they have to think about the names of the letters now and ask them to find *a, e, i, o* and *u.*

TEACHING THE LESSON

- Stick the selection of *a, e, i, o* and *u* pictures on the board.

  Discuss the pictures. Emphasise the initial sounds.

  Ask the children to sort the pictures into sets.

  Ask: "Which pictures could go together?"

  After discussion confirm that some would go in the *a* set, some in the *e* set, some in the *i* set, some in the *o* set and some in the *u* set.

  Ask: "Why do some go in the *a* set, *e* set, *i* set, *o* set and *u* set?"

  Confirm that the pictures all start with *a, e, i, o* and *u.*

Ask the children to put the correct Letter Card with the corresponding set.

Ask: "How many Letter Cards are there?"

Confirm there are five.

Ask: "What are they?"

Confirm *a*, *e*, *i*, *o* and *u*.

Ask: "What are these letters called?"

Confirm that they are vowels.

Tell the children that we always say them in that order: *a*, *e*, *i*, *o* and *u*.

Ask the children if they know why. (*Refer to Alphabet Frieze.*)

Tell the children that we say the vowels in the order that they come in the alphabet.

Tell the children a rhyme that helps them to remember the order: *Angry elephants in orange underwear.*

Highlight *a* in *angry*, *e* in *elephants*, *i* in *in*, *o* in *orange*, *u* in *underwear*.

Ask the children to say the vowels (*sounds*) to memorise.

Ask the children to say the vowels (*names*) to memorise.

A good strategy to use:

> You say *a*, *e*, *i*, *o* . . . children fill in *u*.
> You say *a*, *e*, *i* . . . children fill in *o* and *u*.
> You say *a*, *e* . . . children fill in *i*, *o* and *u*.

The children say the vowels and clap to the rhythm.

■ Workbook 2 page 18.

NOW OR LATER

■ Repeat the above and children complete Additional Support 13.

DEVELOPING SKILLS

■ **Peek-a-Boo**

See Unit 2 Introduction.

NOTE

■ The focus of this unit is alphabet letters and their corresponding sounds. However, you should begin to look at raising the children's awareness of CVC words with middle *a*, *e*, *i*, *o* and *u* (*see Word List for all CVC words*).

a e i o u

The **sh** sound

THE NLF AIMS

- Hear and identify the digraph *sh*.
- Read the letters that represent the sound *sh*.
- Write the letters that represent the sound *sh*.

WHAT YOU NEED

RESOURCES

- Letter Cards *s*, *h* and *sh*
- Whiteboard/chalkboard/easel
- Workbook 2 page 19
- Teacher's copy of Workbook 2 page 19

KEY LESSON POINTERS

VOCABULARY

alphabet letter name sound word letter shape capital rhyme trace start/beginning/end middle join match

THE CHILDREN should throughout the lesson:

- know that two letters can join to make one sound
- focus exclusively on the sound activity and not stray onto unrelated topics.

YOU should throughout the lesson:

- emphasise the *sh* sound at all times
- ensure the children know that two letters can make one sound.

STARTING THE LESSON

- Quick revision of *s* and *h*, reading the letter that represents the sound and knowing the sound.

  Show Letter Cards and ask what sound each letter makes.

  Ask: "What are the names of the letters?"

TEACHING THE LESSON

- Tell the children that sometimes two letters join together to make one sound.

- Tell the children that when *s* and *h* join together they make the sound *sh*.

  Tell the children that it is a quiet sound – it's the sound that you would say if you wanted someone to be quiet.

  Ask the children to say *sh*.

  Ask: "Which two letters make the *sh* sound?"

  Confirm *s* and *h* (*sounds and names*).

  Ask the children to tell you words that start with *sh*. Give clues, if necessary, *shoe* or *boot*, *boat* or *ship*, *shop* or *house*.

- Tell the children that they have to listen very carefully this time because the sounds at the beginning can sound alike.

  Ask the children to tell you which words start with *sh*. Give clues: *shoe* or *sock*, *soup* or *shop*, *shell* or *sell*.

- Tell the children that *sh* is not always at the beginning.

  Say *fish*, *dish*, *wish*.

  Ask: "Where is the *sh* sound in *fish*? in *dish*? in *wish*?"

  Confirm that it is at the end.

- Ask: "Which two letters make the *sh* sound?"

  Ask a child to write the two letters that make the *sh* sound on the board.

NOW OR LATER

- Workbook 2 page 19.

  Ensure that the children can identify the pictures before asking them to complete the page.

DEVELOPING SKILLS

Some or all of these activities must be done to ensure progress:

- *sh* – where is my sound – beginning or end?

  You say a word and children answer *beginning* or *end*.

  Suggested words:

shop	fish	shed	wish
wash	shelf	shadow	shift
dish	rush		

- What is my sound?

  You say a word and children say *s* or *sh*.

  Suggested words:

sock	shock	sad	shed
shoe	sew	ship	safe
bus	bush	toss	rash
mash	mess	mesh	lass
grass	brush	rush	sun

  (*This is an auditory activity, so only one s is heard at the end of words ending in double s.*)

sh

The **ch** sound

(BEFORE YOU START)

THE NLF AIMS

- Hear and identify the digraph *ch*.
- Read the letters that represent the sound *ch*.
- Write the letters that represent the sound *ch*.

WHAT YOU NEED

RESOURCES

- Letter Cards *c*, *h*, *ch*, *s* and *sh*
- White board/chalk board/easel
- Workbook 2 page 20
- Teacher's copy of Workbook 2 page 20
- Quick Cards

KEY LESSON POINTERS

VOCABULARY

alphabet   letter   name   sound   word
letter shape   capital   rhyme   trace
start/beginning/end   middle   join   match

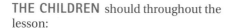

THE CHILDREN should throughout the lesson:

- know that two letters can join to make one sound
- focus exclusively on the sound activity and not stray onto unrelated topics.

YOU should throughout the lesson:

- emphasise the *ch* sound at all times
- ensure the children know that two letters can make one sound.

THE LESSON

STARTING THE LESSON

- Quick revision of *s* and *h*, reading the letter that represents the sound and knowing the sound.

  Ask: "What sound do *s* and *h* make when they join together?"

  Confirm that the sound is *sh*.

  Ask the children to tell you words beginning with *sh*.

  Ask the children to tell you words ending with *sh*.

TEACHING THE LESSON

- Show the children the *c* Letter Card.

  Ask: "What sound does this make?"

  Confirm that it makes the *c* sound.

  Show the children the *h* Letter Card.

  Ask: "What sound does this make?"

  Confirm that it makes the *h* sound.

- Tell the children that when *c* and *h* join together they make the sound *ch*.

  Tell the children that it is the sound that they can hear in a sneeze.

  Demonstrate.

  Ask the children to say *ch*.

  Ask: "Which two letters make the *ch* sound?"

  Confirm *c* and *h* (*sounds and names*).

  Ask the children to tell you words that start with *ch*. Give clues, if necessary, *chick* or *house*, *bread* or *cheese*, *chin* or *pin*.

■ Tell the children that they have to listen very carefully this time because the sounds at the beginning can sound alike.

Ask the children to tell you which words start with *ch*. Give clues: *chop* or *shop*, *ship* or *chip*, *chin* or *shin*, *chalk* or *shock*.

■ Tell the children that *ch* is not always at the beginning.

Say *much, such, rich*.

Ask: "Where is the *ch* sound in *much*? in *such*? in *rich*?"

Confirm that it is at the end.

Say the word *church*.

Ask: "Where can you hear the *ch* sound in *church*?"

Confirm at the beginning and at the end.

■ Ask: "Which two letters make the *ch* sound?"

Ask a child to write the two letters that make the *ch* sound on the board.

NOW OR LATER

■ Workbook 2 page 20.

Ensure that the children can identify the pictures before asking them to complete the page.

FURTHER PRACTICE

DEVELOPING SKILLS

Some or all of these activities must be done to ensure progress:

■ *ch* – where is my sound – beginning or end?

You say a word and children answer *beginning* or *end*.

Suggested words:

rich	chop	much	such
chin	cheese	touch	cheek

■ What is my sound?

You say a word and children say *sh* or *ch*.

Suggested words:

chip	ship	chin	shin
chop	shop	mash	much
rich	rush	cheep	sheep

■ Quick Cards

Children have the *sh* and *ch* cards face up on the table. You call out a word starting with *sh* or *ch* and children point to the *ch* or *sh* card.

Suggested words:

short	shed	shirt	shell
chap	chest	chick	chip

Do the same for words with *ch* or *sh* at the end.

Suggested words:

much	touch	rich	such
fish	wash	dish	brush

ch

The wh sound

THE NLF AIMS

- Hear and identify the digraph *wh*.
- Read the letters that represent the sound *wh*.
- Write the letters that represent the sound *wh*.

WHAT YOU NEED

RESOURCES

- Letter Cards *s*, *c*, *w*, *h*, *sh*, *ch*, and *wh*
- Whiteboard/chalkboard/easel
- Workbook 2 page 21
- Teacher's copy of Workbook 2 page 21
- Quick Cards

KEY LESSON POINTERS

VOCABULARY

alphabet letter name sound word
letter shape capital rhyme trace
start/beginning/end middle join match

THE CHILDREN should throughout the lesson:

- know that two letters can join to make one sound
- focus exclusively on the sound activity and not stray onto unrelated topics.

YOU should throughout the lesson:

- emphasise the *wh* sound at all times
- ensure the children know that two letters can make one sound.

THE LESSON

STARTING THE LESSON

- Quick revision of *s*, *c* and *h*, reading the letter that represents the sound and knowing the sound.

  Ask: "What sound do *s* and *h* make when they join together?"

  Confirm that the sound is *sh*.

  Ask the children to tell you words beginning with *sh*.

  Ask the children to tell you words ending with *sh*.

  Ask: "What sound do *c* and *h* make when they join together?"

  Confirm that the sound is *ch*.

  Ask the children to tell you words beginning with *ch*.

  Ask the children to tell you words ending with *ch*.

TEACHING THE LESSON

- Show the children the *w* card.

  Ask: "What sound does this make?"

  Confirm that it makes the *w* sound.

  Show the children the *h* card.

  Ask: "What sound does this make?"

  Confirm that it makes the *h* sound.

■ Tell the children that when **w** and **h** join together they make the sound **wh**.

Tell children that it is a quiet sound – it's a **wh**ispering sound.

Ask the children to say **wh**.

Ask: "Which two letters make the **wh** sound?"

Confirm **w** and **h** (*sounds and names*).

Ask the children to tell you words that start with **wh**. Give clues, if necessary, **whistle** or **bell**, **wheel** or **tyre**, **whip** or **iron**.

Ask: "Where is the **wh** sound in **wheel**? in **whip**? in **whistle**?"

Confirm that it is at the beginning.

■ Ask: "Which two letters make the **wh** sound?"

Ask a child to write the two letters that make the **wh** sound on the board.

NOW OR LATER

■ Workbook 2 page 21.

Ensure that the children can identify the pictures before asking them to complete the page.

FURTHER PRACTICE

DEVELOPING SKILLS

Some or all of these activities must be done to ensure progress:

The *w* and *wh* sounds are easily confused. It is often difficult for children to hear the difference between the two sounds. Give plenty of practice.

■ **What is my sound?**

You say a word and children say *w* or *wh* or point to/hold up a card with *w* or *wh*.

Suggested words:

| wool | wheel | watch | whip |
| web | when | weed | whistle |

■ **Quick Cards**

Children have the *sh*, *ch* and *wh* cards face up on the table. You call out a word and children point to the *sh*, *ch* or *wh* card.

Suggested words:

wheel	shed	cheese	where
shadow	where	shoe	shop
chin	chalk	sheep	why

NOTE

■ The authors acknowledge that *wh* does not appear in the NLF until Year 2 but feel that it is appropriate to include it here.

BLENDING AND SEGMENTING

IDENTIFYING SOUNDS (CONSONANT DIGRAPHS)

wh

The **th** sound

(BEFORE YOU START)

THE NLF AIMS

- Hear and identify the digraph *th*.
- Read the letters that represent the sound *th*.
- Write the letters that represent the sound *th*.

WHAT YOU NEED

RESOURCES

- Letter Cards *s, c, w , t , h* and *sh, ch, wh, th*
- Whiteboard/chalkboard/easel
- Workbook 2 page 22
- Teacher's copy of Workbook 2 page 22
- Quick Cards
- Assessment 2.6

KEY LESSON POINTERS

VOCABULARY

alphabet letter name sound word
letter shape capital rhyme trace
start/beginning/end middle join match

THE CHILDREN should throughout the lesson:

- know that two letters can join to make one sound
- focus exclusively on the sound activity and not stray onto unrelated topics.

YOU should throughout the lesson:

- emphasise the *th* sound at all times
- ensure children know that two letters can make one sound.

THE LESSON

STARTING THE LESSON

- Quick revision of *s, c, w* and *h*, reading the letter that represents the sound and knowing the sound.

  Ask: "What sound do *s* and *h* make when they join together?"

  Confirm that the sound is *sh*.

  Ask the children to tell you words beginning with *sh*.

  Ask the children to tell you words ending with *sh*.

  Ask: "What sound do *c* and *h* make when they join together?"

  Confirm that the sound is *ch*.

  Ask the children to tell you words beginning with *ch*.

  Ask the children to tell you words ending with *ch*.

  Ask: "What sound do *w* and *h* make when they join together?"

  Confirm that the sound is *wh*.

  Ask the children to tell you words beginning with *wh*.

  Ask the children to tell you words ending with *wh*.

TEACHING THE LESSON

- Show the children the *t* Letter Card.

  Ask: "What sound does this letter make?"

  Confirm that it makes the *t* sound.

  Show the children the *h* Letter Card.

  Ask: "What sound does this letter make?"

  Confirm that it makes the *h* sound.

■ Tell the children that when *t* and *h* join together they make the sound *th*.

Tell the children that the *th* sound can be quiet or loud (*voiced*).

Ask the children to say the quiet *th*.

Tell the children that the quiet *th* is in words like *thimble*, *think*.

Tell the children that sometimes it is a loud (*voiced*) *th* in words like *the*, *they*, *that*.

Ask: "Which two letters make the *th* sound?"

Confirm *t* and *h* (*sounds and names*).

Ask the children to tell you words that start with the quiet *th*. Give clues, if necessary, *thimble* or *needle*, *thank* or *letter*, *write* or *think*.

■ Ask: "Where is the *th* sound in *thumb*? in *thermometer*? in *thistle*?"

Confirm that it is at the beginning.

■ Tell the children that *th* is not always at the beginning.

Say *bath*, *with*, *path*.

Ask: "Where is the *th* sound in *bath*? in *with*? in *path*?"

Confirm that it is at the end.

■ Ask: "Which two letters make the *th* sound?"

Ask a child to write the two letters that make the *th* sound on the board.

NOW OR LATER

■ Workbook 2 page 22.

Ensure that the children can identify the pictures before asking them to complete the page.

DEVELOPING SKILLS

Some or all of these activities must be done to ensure progress:

■ *th* – where is my sound – beginning or end?

You say a word and children answer *beginning* or *end*.

Suggested words:

thistle	bath	think	with
path	thunder	thank	cloth
moth	thud		

The *f* and *th* sounds are easily confused. It is often difficult for children to hear the difference between the two sounds. Children are more likely to substitute *f* for *th* rather than *th* for *f*. Give plenty of practice.

■ **What is my sound?**

You say a word and children say *f* or *th* or point to/hold up the card with *f* or *th*.

Suggested words:

fought	thought	thumb	funny
think	finger	path	Biff
bath	with	puff	huff

■ **Quick Cards**

Children have the *sh*, *ch*, *wh* and *th* cards face up on the table. You call out a word and children point to the *sh*, *ch*, *wh* or *th* card.

Suggested words:

whip	shiver	chin	thimble
shelf	why	shoe	think

NOTE

■ Some children may have difficulty pronouncing the *th* sound. Encourage them to put their tongue out between their teeth to make the sound.

■ The voiced *th* comes in some words such as *the*, *they*, *this*, which are in the list of High Frequency Words. The voiced *th* should be emphasised and practised when dealing with these words.

ASSESSMENT 2.6

th

UNIT 3

BLENDING AND SEGMENTING

The main reason for studying phonics is to give children strategies for reading and spelling. Encourage children at all times to use the strategies for reading and spelling. **It is important for children to know the strategies. It is more important for them to use the strategies when reading text.**

INTRODUCTION

Unit 3 of *Fun Phonics* covers the NLF word level work required for Reception Year and Year 1 Term 1, in which pupils should be taught:

- alphabetical and phonic knowledge
- links between sound and spelling patterns.

The Unit is divided into four main sections:

- Onset and rime
- Consonant vowel blends at the beginning of words
- Medial vowels
- Rhyming

The lessons follow the same patterns throughout, making them easy and reassuring to use. You may wish to spend more time on some lessons than others, depending on the needs of your pupils. You may also choose to teach the lessons to the whole class or a group, depending on the class structure and organisation.

The term **sound** is used generally rather than the clumsier phrase "letter that represents the sound".

USING THE WORKBOOK, LESSONS 7–15

There is a great deal of help and guidance suggested for teaching the neccessary skills for Workbook 3 pages 6 to 10 in lessons 7–15. You can decide if your class requires this level of support and modify your approach if they do not. Remember that many skills are required to complete these pages including: knowledge of onset and rime; handwriting; spatial awareness; following instructions and sequence of procedures. Your pupils' development in these areas will, of course, vary and should determine how much help and guidance you give.

Writing initial sounds

BEFORE YOU START

THE NLF AIMS

- Identify and write the letters that represent the initial sounds in spoken words, *m, k, b, a, h, l, j, d.*

WHAT YOU NEED

RESOURCES

- Letter Cards *m, k, b, a, h, l, j, d*
- Alphabet Frieze
- Chalkboard/whiteboard
- Workbook 3 page 1

KEY LESSON POINTERS

VOCABULARY

alphabet   letter   name   sound   word
difference   first/beginning

THE CHILDREN should throughout the lesson:

- distinguish between the letter sound and the letter name
- pronounce the pure sounds
- focus on the correct letter formation.

YOU should throughout the lesson:

- emphasise the difference between the letter sound and the letter name
- ensure correct pronunciation of the pure *m, k, b, h, l, j, d* sounds
- ensure correct letter formation.

THE LESSON

STARTING THE LESSON

SKILLS REVIEW

- Quick revision of Letter Cards in Resources: sounds and names.

TEACHING THE LESSON

- Ask children, in turn, to write the letters that represent the sounds ***m, k, b, a, h, l, j, d*** on the board.

  Ask: "Which way does the pen/chalk go first if you are going to write the letter ***m***?"

  Ask: "Then which way does it go?" (*Encourage the child to describe aloud the formation of the letter as she or he writes, for example, "Down, up, round and down, up, round and down."*)

  Ask the child to stand back and look carefully at what they have done. Give praise, even if not exactly right: "That's good but you didn't make it exactly the right way."

  Ask if they know what they did wrong. (*Encourage children to self correct: "I forgot to go down first". Repeat: "You forgot to go down first".*)

  If the child doesn't know how to correct it, ask if anyone could help.

- Repeat this procedure for the other letters.

■ Tell the children that you are going to say a word and they have to write the sound that the word starts with.

Ask children in turn to write the letters (initial sounds) on the board. (*Remember to emphasise the initial sound.*)

Suggest words such as: ***moon, kettle, bus, anorak, hat, lemon, jelly, dance, microwave, key, balloon, and, hill, lift, jolly, digger.***

Encourage the children to tell you the sound before they write it. The children should describe aloud the movement as they write.

■ Children complete Workbook 3 page 1. Some children may need an Alphabet Strip as a model for the letters. (*Ensure that children can identify pictures and that they know to write the initial sound for each picture.*)

FURTHER PRACTICE

DEVELOPING SKILLS

Some or all of these activities must be done to ensure progress:

■ **Practise writing letters to dictation**

You say the sound of the letter, children write the letter.

You say a word, children write the letter sound that it begins with.

■ **Common mistakes that must be addressed**

Forming *a* or *d* by doing the downstroke first

Forming *a* by going in a clockwise direction

Forming *b* like a number 6.

It is important to establish good handwriting skills at this early stage. As handwriting is a motor skill, poor habits once established are difficult to change. Time needs to be spent on this.

■ **What is my sound?**

Trace a letter in the air and describe its formation. (*Remember to demonstrate the letter so that children can see it from the correct direction.*)

Children say what sound it is.

■ **Touch-to-tell letters**

Children close their eyes and feel a letter to work out what it is. (*Any cut out letter, such as magnetic letters or letters made from sandpaper, will do.*)

■ **I Spy**

NOTE

■ If using sandpaper letters, an identifying mark such as a smooth sticker could be put at the starting point.

■ If using magnetic letters, there could be confusion between *d* and *p* and between *n* and *u*. Children should recognise that they would have to look before making the final decision. Encourage them to say it could be an *n* or a *u* depending on which way up it is.

m k b a h l j d

Writing initial sounds

BEFORE YOU START

THE NLF AIMS

- Identify and write the letters that represent the initial sounds in spoken words, *e, y, c, z, w, u, p, t*.

WHAT YOU NEED

RESOURCES

- Letter Cards *e, y, c, z, w, u, p, t*
- Alphabet Frieze
- Chalkboard/whiteboard
- Workbook 3 page 2

KEY LESSON POINTERS

VOCABULARY

alphabet   letter   name   sound   word
difference   first/beginning

THE CHILDREN should throughout the lesson:

- distinguish between the letter sound and the letter name
- pronounce the pure sounds
- focus on the correct letter formation.

YOU should throughout the lesson:

- emphasise the difference between the letter sound and the letter name
- ensure correct pronunciation of the pure *y, c, z, w, p, t* sounds
- ensure correct letter formation.

THE LESSON

STARTING THE LESSON

SKILLS REVIEW

- Quick revision of Letter Cards in Resources: sounds and names.

TEACHING THE LESSON

- Ask children, in turn, to write the letters that represent the sounds *e, y, c, z, w, u, p, t* on the board.

  Ask: "Which way does the pen/chalk go first if you are going to write the letter *c*?"

  Ask: "Then which way does it go?" (*Encourage the child to describe aloud the formation of the letter as she or he writes.*)

  Ask the child to stand back and look carefully at what they have done. Give praise, even if not exactly right: "That's good but you didn't make it exactly the right way."

  A child may have reversed the letter, as ɔ.

  Ask if they know what they did wrong. (*Encourage children to self correct: "I went round the wrong way". Repeat: "You went round the wrong way".*)

  If the child doesn't know how to correct it, ask if anyone could help.

- Repeat this procedure for the other letters.

■ Tell the children that you are going to say a word and they have to write the sound that the word starts with.

Ask children in turn to write the letters (initial sounds) on the board. (*Remember to emphasise the initial sound.*)

Suggest words such as: *elephant, yellow, camera, zip, window, under, potato, telephone, egg, tortoise, up, yo-yo, carrot, web, zoo, pink.*

Encourage the children to tell you the sound before they write it. The children should describe aloud the movement as they write.

■ Children complete Workbook 3 page 2. Some children may need an Alphabet Strip as a model for the letters. (*Ensure that children can identify pictures and that they know to write the initial sound for each picture.*)

FURTHER PRACTICE

DEVELOPING SKILLS

Some or all of these activities must be done to ensure progress:

■ **Practise writing letters to dictation**

You say the sound of a letter, children write the letter.

You say a word, children write the letter sound that it begins with.

■ **Common mistakes that must be addressed**

Forming *u* without a downstroke at the end

Forming *p* starting at the bottom and going up and round.

It is important to establish good handwriting skills at this early stage. As handwriting is a motor skill, poor habits once established are difficult to change. Time needs to be spent on this.

■ **What is my sound?**

Trace a letter in the air and describe its formation. (*Remember to demonstrate the letter so that children can see it from the correct direction.*)
Children say what sound it is.

■ **Touch-to-tell letters**

Children close their eyes and feel a letter to work out what it is. (*Any cut out letter, such as magnetic letters or letters made from sandpaper, will do.*)

■ **I Spy**

NOTE

■ If using sandpaper letters, an identifying mark such as a smooth sticker could be put at the starting point.

■ If using magnetic letters, there could be confusion between *d* and *p* and between *n* and *u*. Children should recognise that they would have to look before making the final decision. Encourage them to say it could be an *n* or a *u* depending on which way up it is.

e y c z w u p t

Writing initial sounds

THE NLF AIMS

- Identify and write the letters that represent the initial sounds in spoken words, *o, f, g, i, r, s, v, n.*

WHAT YOU NEED

RESOURCES

- Letter Cards *o, f, g, i, r, s, v, n*
- Alphabet Frieze
- Chalkboard/whiteboard
- Workbook 3 page 3
- Assessment 3.1

KEY LESSON POINTERS

VOCABULARY

alphabet   letter   name   sound   word
difference   first/beginning

THE CHILDREN should throughout the lesson:

- distinguish between the letter sound and the letter name
- pronounce the pure sounds
- focus on the correct letter formation.

YOU should throughout the lesson:

- emphasise the difference between the letter sound and the letter name
- ensure correct pronunciation of the pure *f, g, r, s, v, n* sounds
- ensure correct letter formation.

THE LESSON

STARTING THE LESSON

SKILLS REVIEW

- Quick revision of Letter Cards in Resources: sounds and names.

TEACHING THE LESSON

- Ask children, in turn, to write the letters that represent the sounds *o, f, g, i, r, s, v, n* on the board.

  Ask: "Which way does the pen/chalk go first if you are going to write the letter *g*?"

  Ask: "Then which way does it go?" (*Encourage the child to describe aloud the formation of the letter as she or he writes.*)

  Ask the child to stand back and look carefully at what they have done. Give praise, even if not exactly right: "That's good but you didn't make it exactly the right way."

  Ask if they know what they did wrong. (*Encourage children to self correct: "I forgot to go round first". Repeat: "You forgot to go round first."*)

  Say: "Remember, it starts as if it were going to be *c*, then it thinks its going to be *a* but it goes straight down and round."

  If the child doesn't know how to correct it, ask if anyone could help.

- Repeat this procedure for the other letters.

- Tell the children that you are going to say a word and they have to write the sound that the word starts with.

  Ask children in turn to write the letters (initial sounds) on the board. (*Remember to emphasise the initial sound.*)

  Suggest words such as: ***octopus, goat, ring, van, fox, insects, Saturday, newspaper, off, go, vest, fish, in, sad, nuts.***

  Encourage the children to tell you the sound before they write it. The children should describe aloud the movement as they write.

- Children complete Workbook 3 page 3. Some children may need an Alphabet Strip as a model for the letters. (*Ensure that children can identify pictures and that they know to write the initial sound for each picture.*)

FURTHER PRACTICE

DEVELOPING SKILLS

Some or all of these activities must be done to ensure progress:

- **Practise writing letters to dictation**

  You say the sound of a letter, children write the letter.

  You say a word, children write the letter sound that it begins with.

- **Common mistakes that must be addressed**

  Forming *a* by doing the downstroke first

  Forming *o* by going in the wrong direction: forming the circle in a clockwise direction

  Forming *n* by going up and round.

- **What is my sound?**

  Trace a letter in the air and describe its formation. (*Remember to demonstrate the letter so that children can see it from the correct direction.*)
  Children say what sound it is.

- **Touch-to-tell letters**

  Children close their eyes and feel a letter to work out what it is. (*Any cut out letter, such as magnetic letters or letters made from sandpaper, will do.*)

- **I Spy**

ASSESSMENT 3.1

NOTE

- If using sandpaper letters, an identifying mark such as a smooth sticker could be put at the starting point.

- If using magnetic letters, there could be confusion between *d* and *p* and between *n* and *u*. Children should recognise that they would have to look before making the final decision. Encourage them to say it could be an *n* or a *u* depending on which way up it is.

o f g i r s v n

Writing consonant digraphs

THE NLF AIMS

- Identify and write the letters that represent the digraphs, *sh, ch, wh, th*.

WHAT YOU NEED

RESOURCES

- Letter Cards *sh, ch, wh, th*
- Chalkboard/whiteboard
- Workbook 3 pages 4 and 5
- Headbands with slits
- Assessment 3.2

KEY LESSON POINTERS

VOCABULARY

alphabet   letter   name   sound   word
difference   first/beginning

THE CHILDREN should throughout the lesson:

- distinguish between the letter sound and the letter name
- pronounce the pure sounds.

YOU should throughout the lesson:

- emphasise the difference between the letter sound and the letter name
- ensure correct pronunciation of the pure *s, c, w, t, h* sounds
- ensure the children know that two letters can make one sound.

STARTING THE LESSON

SKILLS REVIEW

- Quick revision of Letter Cards in Resources.
  Ask: "Which two letters join together to make *sh*?"
  Confirm *s* and *h*.
  Write *sh* on the board.
  Ask: "Which two letters join together to make *ch*?"
  Confirm *c* and *h*.
  Write *ch* on the board.
  Ask: "Which two letters join together to make *wh*?"
  Confirm *w* and *h*.
  Write *wh* on the board.
  Ask: "Which two letters join together to make *th*?"
  Confirm *t* and *h*.
  Write *th* on the board.
  (*Remember to encourage the children to form the letters in the correct way.*)

TEACHING THE LESSON

- Give four children headbands to wear with *sh, ch, wh, th* cards in the slits.

Ask them to stand in four separate places in front of the group/class.

Explain that those with *sh* headbands like words beginning with *sh*, those with *ch* headbands like words beginning with *ch*, those with *wh* headbands like words beginning with *wh* and those with *th* headbands like words beginning with *th*.

- Tell the children you will call out words beginning or ending with *sh, ch, wh* and *th*. Ask them to stand beside/behind the child wearing the headband with the sound that their word begins or ends with.

Suggested words (digraph at beginning):

shop	shell	sheep	children
chin	whistle	chicken	thimble
whisk	shed	chilly	shoe
when	where	thank	chimp
think	thunder	chimney	shadow

Suggested words (digraph at end):

bath	much	fish	brush
wish	with	cloth	such
moth	dish	touch	rich
rush	teeth	hush	Beth

- Tell the children that you are going to say a word and they should listen for the *sh, ch, wh* and *th* sounds in the words.

Say a word, for example, *shop*.

Ask: "Do you hear the *sh, ch, wh* or *th* sound?"

Confirm that it is *sh*.

Ask: "Is it at the beginning or the end of the word?"

Confirm that it is at the beginning.

Ask a child to write *sh* on the board.

Encourage the children to tell you the two letters (names or sounds) that make the sound.

Repeat the procedure for the others words:

shout	much	whip	church
fish	think	sharp	shed
whisper	chocolate	whistle	thin
chips	with	mouth	thunder
wash	chin	shelf	why

Monitor correct letter formation as the children write.

- Children complete Workbook 3 page 4. (*Ensure that children can identify pictures and that they know to write the two letters that make the initial sound for each word.*)

LATER

- Repeat the lesson, as appropriate, then children complete Workbook 3 page 5.

DEVELOPING SKILLS

Some or all of these activities must be done to ensure progress:

- Practise writing digraphs to dictation

  You say a digraph, children write the letters that represent it.

  You say a word, children write the letters that represent the digraph at the beginning/end of the word.

- Children sort pictures of objects into sets of *sh, ch, wh, th*.

ASSESSMENT 3.2

sh ch wh th

Onset and rime

THE NLF AIMS

- Identify onset and rime in spoken words.
- Write the letter that represents the onset (initial sound) in the written word.
- Read words with emphasis on the rime.

WHAT YOU NEED

RESOURCES

- Letter Cards *c, m, s, f, h, b, p, r*
- Rhyme Picture Cards
- Onset and Rime Cards *c, m, s, f, h, b, p, r, -at*
- Chalkboard/whiteboard

KEY LESSON POINTERS

VOCABULARY

alphabet letter name sound
letter name letter sound word vowel
same/different first/beginning/in front
rime/rhyme (see Note)

THE CHILDREN should throughout the lesson:

- distinguish between the letter sound and the letter name
- pronounce the pure sounds.

YOU should throughout the lesson:

- emphasise the difference between the letter sound and the letter name
- ensure correct pronunciation of sounds
- emphasise the rime in words
- ensure correct letter formation.

STARTING THE LESSON

SKILLS REVIEW

- Quick revision of Letter Cards in Resources.

TEACHING THE LESSON

- Tell the children that you want to write some words but they have to help with the first sound.

  Write *-at* on the board.

  Tell the children that you want the word to be *cat*.

  Ask: "What sound is missing at the beginning?"

  Confirm that it is *c*.

  Write *c* to complete the word.

  Ask: "What does the word say?"

  Confirm *cat*.

  Write *-at* on the board again.

  Tell the children that you want the word to be *mat*.

  Ask: "What sound is missing at the beginning?"

  Confirm that it is *m*.

  Write *m* to complete the word.

  Ask: "What does the word say?"

  Confirm *mat*.

  Write *-at* on the board again.

  Tell the children that you want the word to be *sat*.

  Ask: "What sound is missing at the beginning?"

  Confirm that it is *s*.

  Write *s* to complete the word.

  Ask: "What does the word say?"

  Confirm *sat*.

- Ask the children to look at and read *cat, mat* and *sat*. Emphasise the rime *-at* in all the words.

  Ask: "What do you notice about *cat, mat, sat*?"

  After discussion, confirm that they all have the same two letters at the end: *a* and *t*, which make the *-at* rime.

  Ask: "What is different about the words?"

  Confirm that the sounds at the beginning are different.

- ■ Write **-at** on the board.

  Tell the children that you want the word to be **fat**.

  Ask: "What sound is missing at the beginning?"

  Ask a child to come to the board and write the missing sound in the correct place.

  Ask: "What does the word say?"

  Confirm **fat**.

  Repeat the above procedure with individual children for **hat, bat, pat, rat**.

  A child may write the wrong letter, for example, **v** instead of **f** in fat, writing **vat**.

  Ask: "What is the word you were asked for?"

  Confirm **fat**.

  Ask: "What does **fat** start with?"

  Confirm **f**.

  Ask the child to write **f** on board. (*This will establish if she or he knows how to write the letter* **f**.)

  Ask: "What word did you write when asked to write **fat**?"

  Confirm **vat**.

  Ask the child to correct the word. (*Encourage children to self correct.*)

  Write **-at** on the board again.

  Tell the children that you want the word to be **chat**.

  Ask: "What sound is missing at the beginning?"

  Confirm that it is **ch**.

  Ask: "Which letters make **ch**?"

  Confirm **c** and **h**.

  Ask a child to write the missing sound **ch** in the correct place.

  Ask: "What does the word say?"

  Confirm **chat**.

- ■ Ask the children to look at and read **cat, mat, sat, fat, hat, bat, pat, rat, chat**. Emphasise the rime in the words.

  Confirm that the words start with different sounds and that the words rhyme.

  Ask "What is the rime?"

  Confirm that it is **-at**.

FURTHER PRACTICE

DEVELOPING SKILLS

Some or all of these activities must be done to ensure progress:

- ■ Onset and Rime Cards

  Children have the *c, m, s, f, h, b, p, r* cards and *-at* Rime Cards. Ask the children to make the words *cat, mat, sat, fat, hat, bat, pat* and *rat*. (Eight *-at* cards would be necessary to make and display all the words.)

- ■ Rhyme Picture Cards

  Children sort a selection of Rhyme Picture Cards (*-at* Rime Picture Cards and other picture cards) into those that can go in the *-at* set and those that cannot.

NOTE

Rhymes and rimes are not identical. Rhymes have word endings which sound the same but are not necessarily spelled in the same way, such as *socks* and *fox*. Rimes are word endings which always retain the same spelling pattern, such as *box* and *fox*.

-at

Onset and rime

THE NLF AIMS

- Identify onset and rime in spoken words.
- Write the letter that represents the onset (initial sound) in the written word.
- Read words with emphasis on rime.

WHAT YOU NEED

RESOURCES

- Letter Cards *c, m, s, f, h, b, p, r, t, v*
- Rhyme Picture Cards
- Onset and Rime Cards *b, s, c, f, m, p, h, r, t, v, -an, -at*
- Chalkboard/whiteboard

KEY LESSON POINTERS

VOCABULARY

alphabet   letter   name   sound
letter name   letter sound   word
same/different   first/beginning/in front
rime/rhyme (see Note)

THE CHILDREN should throughout the lesson:

- distinguish between the letter sound and the letter name
- pronounce the pure sounds.

YOU should throughout the lesson:

- emphasise the difference between the letter sound and the letter name
- emphasise the rime in words
- ensure correct pronunciation of sounds
- ensure correct letter formation.

THE LESSON

STARTING THE LESSON

SKILLS REVIEW

- Quick revision of Letter Cards.

TEACHING THE LESSON

- Write *c, m, s, f, h, b, p, r* on the board.
  Write *-at* on the board.
  Ask a child to choose a sound and write it on the line in front of *-at*.
  Ask: "What word has been written?"
  Repeat using the other letters.

- Ask the children to look at and read the words *cat, mat, sat, fat, hat, bat, pat* and *rat*. Emphasise the rime *-at* in all the words.

- Tell the children that you want to write some words with a different rime and they have to help with the first sound.
  Write *-an* on the board.
  Tell the children that you want the word to be *van*.
  Ask: "What sound is missing at the beginning?"
  Confirm that it is *v*.
  Write *v* to complete the word.
  Ask: "What does the word say?"
  Confirm *van*.
  Write *-an* on the board again.
  Tell the children that you want the word to be *can*.
  Ask: "What sound is missing at the beginning?"
  Confirm that it is *c*.
  Write *c* to complete the word.
  Ask: "What does the word say?"
  Confirm *can*.
  Write *-an* on the board again.
  Tell the children that you want the word to be *man*.
  Ask: "What sound is missing at the beginning?"
  Confirm that it is *m*.
  Write *m* to complete the word.
  Ask: "What does the word say?"
  Confirm *man*.

- Ask the children to look at and read *van, can* and *man*. Emphasise the rime *-an* in the words.

  Ask: "What do you notice about *van, can, man*?"

  After discussion, confirm that they all have the same two letters at the end: *a* and *n*, which is the *-an* rime.

  Ask: "What is different about the words?"

  Confirm that the sounds at the beginning are different.

- Write *-an* on the board.

  Tell the children that you want the word to be *pan*.

  Ask: "What sound is missing at the beginning?"

  Confirm *p*.

  Ask a child to come to the board and write the missing sound in the correct place.

  Ask: "What does the word say?"

  Confirm *pan*.

  Repeat the above procedure with *ran, tan, fan, ban*.

  A child may write the wrong letter, for example, *p* instead of *b* in *ban*.

  Ask the child: "What word was asked for?"

  Confirm *ban*.

  Ask: "What does *ban* start with?"

  Confirm *b*.

  Ask the child to write *b* on board. (*This will establish if she or he knows how to write the letter* b.)

  Ask: "What did you write when you were asked to write *ban*?"

  Confirm *pan*.

  Ask the child to correct the word. (*Always encourage children to self correct.*)

- Ask the children to look at and read *van, can, man, pan, ran, tan, fan, ban*. Emphasise the rime in the words.

  Ask: "What is the rime?"

  Confirm that it is *-an*.

FURTHER PRACTICE

DEVELOPING SKILLS

Some or all of these activities must be done to ensure progress:

- **Onset and Rime Cards**

  Children have *b, c, f, m, p, r, t, v* cards and *-an* Rime Cards. Ask the children to make the words *ban, can, man, pan, ran, tan, fan* and *van*. (Eight *-an* cards would be necessary to make and display all the words.)

- **Rhyme Picture Cards**

  Children sort a selection of Rhyme Picture Cards (*-an* Rime Picture Cards and other picture cards) into those that can go in the *-an* set and those that cannot.

NOTE

Rhymes and rimes are not identical. Rhymes have word endings which sound the same but are not necessarily spelled in the same way, such as *socks* and *fox*. Rimes are word endings which always retain the same spelling pattern, such as *box* and *fox*.

-an

Onset and rime

THE NLF AIMS

- Identify onset and rime in spoken words.
- Write the letters that represent the initial sound (onset) in the written word.
- Read words with emphasis on rime.
- Write CVC words (with a model).

WHAT YOU NEED

RESOURCES

- Letter Cards *c, m, s, f, h, b, p, r, t, v*
- Rhyme Picture Cards
- Onset and Rime Cards *b, s, c, f, m, p, h, r, t, v, -an, -at*
- Chalkboard/whiteboard
- Workbook 3 page 6
- Teacher's copy of Workbook 3 page 6
- Headbands with slits

KEY LESSON POINTERS

VOCABULARY

alphabet letter name
sound vowel word
same/different first/beginning/in front
rime/rhyme (see Note) circle
cross out dotted line underneath

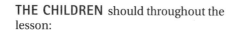 **THE CHILDREN** should throughout the lesson:

- distinguish between the letter sound and the letter name
- pronounce the pure sounds.

YOU should throughout the lesson:

- emphasise the difference between the letter sound and the letter name
- emphasise the rime in words
- ensure correct pronunciation of sounds
- ensure correct letter formation.

THE LESSON

STARTING THE LESSON

SKILLS REVIEW

- Quick revision of Letter Cards.

TEACHING THE LESSON

- Write *b, c, f, m, p, r, t, v* on the board.
  Write *-an* on the board.
  Ask a child to choose a sound and write it on the line in front of *-an*.
  Ask: "What word has been written?"
  Repeat using the other letters.
  Ask the children to look at and read the words *ban, can, fan, man, pan, ran, tan, van*.
  Emphasise the rime *-an* in all the words.

- Write *c, m, s, f, h, b, p, r* on the board.
  Write *-at* on the board.
  Ask a child to choose a sound and write it on the line in front of *-at*.
  Ask: "What word has been written?"
  Repeat using the other letters.
  Ask the children to look at and read the words *cat, mat, sat, fat, hat, bat, pat* and *rat*.
  Emphasise the rime *-at* in all the words. (*Include* **chat** *if appropriate for your pupils*.)

- Show the teacher's copy of Workbook 3 page 6.
  Ask the children to identify the first picture. (*cat*)
  Ask: "What sound does *cat* start with?"
  Confirm that it is *c*.
  Ask a child to point to the *c* on the teacher's copy.
  Ask: "What is the other sound?"
  Confirm *d*.

- Tell the children that they should circle *c* because it is the correct sound and cross out *d* because it is the wrong sound.
  Demonstrate.

- Tell the children that they have to write the correct sound on the line.

  Ask: "What is the correct sound?"

  Confirm *c* and write it on the line.

  Ask: "What word is it?"

  Confirm *cat.*

- Tell the children that they now should write the whole word *cat* on the dotted line underneath.

  Ask: "How many sounds can you hear in the word *cat?*"

  Confirm that there are three sounds.

  Ask: "What is the first sound?"

  Confirm *c* and write it on the dotted line.

  Ask: "What is the next sound?"

  Confirm *a* and write it.

  Ask: "What is the last sound?"

  Confirm *t* and write it.

  Ask: "What does the word say?"

  Confirm *cat.*

  Repeat the procedure for *mat, van* and *fan.*

  Ask the children which words rhyme.

  Confirm *mat* and *cat, van* and *fan.*

- Children complete Workbook 3 page 6. (*Remember to remove teacher's copy before children complete page.*)

FURTHER PRACTICE

DEVELOPING SKILLS

Some or all of these activities must be done to ensure progress:

- **Onset and Rime Cards**

  Children have a selection of *b, s, c, f, m, p, h, r, t, v* cards and *-an* and *-at* Rime Cards. Ask the children to make the words *van, can, man, pan, ran, tan, fan, ban, bat, sat, cat, fat, mat, pat, hat, rat.* (More of each card would be necessary to make and display all words.)

- **Picture Rhyme Cards**

  Children sort a selection of Picture Rhyme Cards (*-an* and *-at* rime) into those that can go in the *-an* set and those that can go in the *-at* set.

- **Headbands with rimes**

  Give two children headbands, one with the *-at* rime and one with the *-an* rime.

Invite them to stand in two separate places in front of the group. Explain that the child with the *-at* headband likes words with the *-at* rime and the child with the *-an* headband likes words with the *-an* rime. Tell the children you will call out words with the *-an* or *-at* rime. Ask them in turn to take their place behind the child with the matching headband.

Suggested words:

flan	gran	plan	fan	ban
flat	pat	sat	man	can
bat	cat	fat	hat	mat
van	tan	rat	ran	pan
chat				

NOTE

A variety of word wheels and pull throughs can be used to practise onset and rime skills.

-an -at

Onset and rime

BEFORE YOU START

THE NLF AIMS

- Identify onset and rime in spoken words.
- Write the letters that represent the initial sound (onset) in the written word.
- Read words with emphasis on rime.

WHAT YOU NEED

RESOURCES

- Letter Cards *c, m, s, f, h, b, p, r, t, v*
- Rhyme Picture Cards
- Onset and Rime Cards *c, m, s, f, h, b, p, r, t, v, d, l, f, j, m, t, h, p, -og, -op*
- Chalkboard/whiteboard

KEY LESSON POINTERS

VOCABULARY

alphabet   letter   name   sound
letter name   letter sound   word   vowel
same/different   first/beginning/in front
rime/rhyme (see Note)

THE CHILDREN should throughout the lesson:

- distinguish between the letter sound and the letter name
- pronounce the pure sounds.

YOU should throughout the lesson:

- emphasise the difference between the letter sound and the letter name
- emphasise the rime in words
- ensure correct pronunciation of sounds
- ensure correct letter formation.

THE LESSON

STARTING THE LESSON

SKILLS REVIEW

- Quick revision of Letter Cards.

TEACHING THE LESSON

- Write *c, m, s, f, h, b, p, r, t, v* on the board.
  Write *-at* on the board.
  Ask a child to choose a sound and write it on the line in front of *-at* to make a word.
  Ask: "What word has been written?"
  Repeat using the other letters.
  Ask the children to look at and read the words.
  Emphasise the rime *-at* in the words.
  Write *-an* on the board.
  Ask a child to choose a sound and write it on the line in front of *-an* to make a word.
  Ask: "What word has been written?"
  (*There is now a choice as some letters don't make real words, for example,* **san**. *If the children write a nonsense word, you should say that the word does rime but is not a real word.*)
  Repeat using the other letters.
  Ask the children to look at and read the words.
  Emphasise the rime *-an* in the words.

- Tell the children that you want to write some words with a different rime and they have to help with the first sound.
  Write *-og* on the board.
  Ask: "What do you notice about the vowel sound?"
  Confirm that it is *o* and that last time it was *a*.
  Tell the children that you want the word to be *dog*.
  Ask: "What sound is missing from the beginning?"
  Confirm that it is *d*.
  Ask a child to write in the missing sound in the correct place.
  Ask: "What does the word say?"
  Confirm *dog*.
  Write *-og* again on the board.
  Tell the children that you want the word to be *log*.
  Ask: "What sound is missing from the beginning?"
  Confirm that it is *l*.

Ask a child to write in the missing sound in the correct place.

Ask: "What does the word say?"

Confirm **log**.

Write **-og** on the board again.

Tell the children that you want the word to be **fog**.

Ask: "What sound is missing from the beginning?"

Confirm that it is **f**.

Ask a child to write in the missing sound in the correct place.

Ask: "What does the word say?"

Confirm **fog**.

Ask the children to look at and read **dog, log, fog**. Emphasise the rime **-og** in the words.

Ask: "What do you notice about **dog, log, fog**?"

After discussion, confirm that they all have the same two letters at the end: **o** and **g**, which is the **-og** rime.

Ask: "What is different about the words?"

Confirm that the sounds at the beginning are different.

Write **-og** on the board.

Tell the children that you want the word to be **jog**.

Ask: "What sound is missing from the beginning?"

Confirm that it is **j**.

Ask a child to write in the missing sound in the correct place.

Ask: "What does the word say?"

Confirm **jog**.

Ask the children to look at and read **dog, log, fog, jog**. Emphasise the rime in the words.

Ask: "What is the rime?"

Confirm that it is **-og**.

Confirm that the words all start with different letters and that they rhyme.

■ Repeat the procedure for words with the **-op** rime.

Suggested words:

hop   mop   top   pop   shop   chop

FURTHER PRACTICE

DEVELOPING SKILLS

Some or all of these activities must be done to ensure progress:

■ **Onset and Rime Cards**

Children have a selection of *d, l, f, j, m, t, h, p* cards and *-og, -op* Rime Cards. Ask the children to make the words *dog, log, fog, jog, mop, top, hop, pop*. (More of each card would be necessary to make and display all words.)

■ **Picture Rhyme Cards**

Children sort a selection of Picture Rhyme Cards (*-og* and *-op* rime) into those that can go in the *-og* set and those that can go in the *-op* set.

NOTE

Rhymes and rimes are not identical. Rhymes have word endings which sound the same but are not necessarily spelled in the same way, such as *socks* and *fox*. Rimes are word endings which always retain the same spelling pattern, such as *box* and *fox*.

BLENDING AND SEGMENTING

ONSET AND RIME

-og -op

Onset and rime

THE NLF AIMS

- Identify onset and rime in spoken words.
- Write the letters that represent the initial sound (onset) in the written word.
- Read words with emphasis on rime.
- Write CVC words (with a model).

WHAT YOU NEED

RESOURCES

- Letter Cards *d, l, f, j, m, t, h, p*
- Rhyme Picture Cards
- Onset and Rime Cards *d, l, f, j, m, t, h, p, -og, -op*
- Chalkboard/whiteboard
- Workbook 3 page 7
- Teacher's copy of Workbook 3 page 7
- Headbands with slits

KEY LESSON POINTERS

VOCABULARY

alphabet   letter   name
sound   word   vowel
same/different   first/beginning/in front
rime/rhyme (see Note)   circle   cross
dotted line   underneath   middle

THE CHILDREN should throughout the lesson:

- distinguish between the letter sound and the letter name
- pronounce the pure sounds.

YOU should throughout the lesson:

- emphasise the difference between the letter sound and the letter name
- emphasise the rime in words
- ensure correct pronunciation of sounds
- ensure correct letter formation.

STARTING THE LESSON

SKILLS REVIEW

- Quick revision of Letter Cards.

TEACHING THE LESSON

- Write *d, l, f, j* on the board.
  Write *-og* on the board.
  Ask a child to choose a sound and write it on the line in front of *-og*.
  Ask: "What word has been written?"
  Repeat using the other letters.
  Ask the children to look at and read the words *dog, log, fog, jog*. Emphasise the rime *-og* in all the words.

- Write *m, t, h, p* on the board.
  Write *-op* on the board.
  Ask a child to choose a sound and write it on the line in front of *-op*.
  Ask: "What word has been written?"
  Repeat using the other letters.

- Ask the children to look at and read the words *mop, top, hop, pop*. Emphasise the rime *-op* in all the words. (*Include* **shop** *and* **chop** *if appropriate for your pupils.*)

- Show the teacher's copy of Workbook 3 page 7.
  Ask the children to identify the first picture. (*dog*)
  Ask: "What sound does *dog* start with?"
  Confirm that it is *d*.
  Ask a child to point to the *d* on the teacher's copy.
  Ask: "What is the other sound?"
  Confirm *b*.

- Tell the children that they should circle *d* because it is the correct sound and cross out *b* because it is the wrong sound.
  Demonstrate.

- Tell the children that they have to write the correct sound on the line.

  Ask: "What is the correct sound?"

  Confirm *d* and write it on the line.

  Ask: "What word is it?"

  Confirm *dog*.

- Tell the children that they should now write the whole word *dog* on the dotted line underneath.

  Ask: "How many sounds can you hear in the word *dog*?"

  Confirm that there are three sounds.

  Ask: "What is the first sound?"

  Confirm *d* and write it on the dotted line.

  Ask: "What is the next sound?"

  Confirm *o* and write it.

  Ask: "What is the last sound?"

  Confirm *g* and write it. (*Ensure the correct letter formation when children are writing.*)

  Ask: "What does the word say?"

  Confirm *dog*.

  Repeat the procedure for *log*, *hop* and *mop*, asking the children to write the letters/words as and when appropriate.

  Ask the children which words rhyme.

  Confirm *dog* and *log*, *hop* and *mop*.

  Ask: "Which vowel is in the middle of *log, dog, hop, mop*?"

  Confirm *o*.

- Children complete Workbook 3 page 7. (*Remember to remove teacher's copy before children complete page.*)

FURTHER PRACTICE

DEVELOPING SKILLS

Some or all of these activities must be done to ensure progress:

- **Onset and Rime Cards**

  Children have a selection of *d, l, f, j, m, t, h, p* cards and *-og* and *-op* Rime Cards. Ask the children to make the words *dog, log, fog, jog, mop, top, hop, pop*. (More of each card would be necessary to make and display all words.)

- **Rhyme Picture Cards**

  Children sort a selection of Rhyme Picture Cards (*-og* and *-op* rime) into those that can go in the *-og* set and those that can go in the *-op* set.

- **Headbands with rimes**

  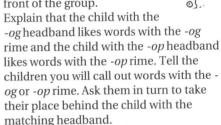

  Give two children headbands, one with *-og* rime and one with *-op* rime. Invite them to stand in two separate places in front of the group. Explain that the child with the *-og* headband likes words with the *-og* rime and the child with the *-op* headband likes words with the *-op* rime. Tell the children you will call out words with the *-og* or *-op* rime. Ask them in turn to take their place behind the child with the matching headband.

  Suggested words:

frog	dog	stop	Mog
flop	fog	clog	chop
drop	shop	log	jog
plop	hop	mop	top

- **Odd One Out**

  Show 3 or 4 picture cards like *dog, mop, log, frog*. The child chooses the one which has a different rime and explains choice.

NOTE

Rhymes and rimes are not identical. Rhymes have word endings which sound the same but are not necessarily spelled in the same way, such as *socks* and *fox*. In contrast, rimes are word endings which always retain the same spelling pattern, such as *box* and *fox*.

-og -op

Onset and rime

THE NLF AIMS

- Identify onset and rime in spoken words.
- Write the letters that represent the initial sound (onset) in the written word.
- Read words with emphasis on rime.

WHAT YOU NEED

RESOURCES

- Letter Cards *d, l, f, j, h, m, p, t*
- Rhyme Picture Cards
- Onset and Rime Cards *d, l, f, j, h, m, p, t, h, p, t, d, n, v, w, s, -en, -et*
- Chalkboard/whiteboard
- Headbands with slits

KEY LESSON POINTERS

VOCABULARY

alphabet   letter   name
sound   letter name   letter sound
word   vowel   same/different
first/beginning/in front
rime/rhyme (see Note)

THE CHILDREN should throughout the lesson:

- distinguish between the letter sound and the letter name
- pronounce the pure sounds.

YOU should throughout the lesson:

- emphasise the difference between the letter sound and the letter name
- emphasise the rime in words
- ensure correct pronunciation of sounds
- ensure correct letter formation.

THE LESSON

STARTING THE LESSON

SKILLS REVIEW

- Quick revision of Letter Cards.

STARTING THE LESSON

- Write *d, l, f, j* on the board.
  Write *-og* on the board.
  Ask a child to choose a sound and write it on the line in front of *-og* to make a real word.
  Ask: "What word has been written?"
  Repeat using the other letters.
  Ask the children to look at and read the words written. Emphasise the rime *-og* in the words.

- Write *h, m, p, t* on the board.
  Write *-op* on the board.
  Ask a child to choose a sound and write it on the line in front of *-op* to make a word.
  Ask: "What word has been written?"
  Repeat using the other letters.
  Ask the children to look at and read the words written. Emphasise the rime *-op* in all the words.

- Tell the children that you want to write some words with a different rime and they have to help with the first sound.
  Write *-en* on the board.
  Ask: "What do you notice about the vowel sound?"
  Confirm that it is *e* and that last time it was *o*.
  Tell the children that you want the word to be *hen*.
  Ask: "What sound is missing from the beginning?"
  Confirm that it is *h*.
  Ask a child to write in the missing sound in the correct place.
  Ask: "What does the word say?"
  Confirm *hen*.
  Write *-en* on the board again.
  Tell the children that you want the word to be *pen*.
  Ask: "What sound is missing from the beginning?"
  Confirm that it is *p*.
  Ask a child to write in the missing sound in the correct place.
  Ask: "What does the word say?"
  Confirm *pen*.

Write *-en* on the board again.

Tell the children that you want the word to be **ten**.

Ask: "What sound is missing from the beginning?"

Confirm that it is **t**.

Ask a child to write in the missing sound in the correct place.

Ask: "What does the word say?"

Confirm **ten**.

Ask the children to look at and read **hen, pen, ten**. Emphasise the rime *-en* in the words.

Ask: "What do you notice about **hen, pen, ten**?"

After discussion, confirm that they all have the same two letters at the end: **e** and **n**, which make the **-en** rime.

Ask: "What is different about the words?"

Confirm that the sounds at the beginning are different.

Write *-en* on the board.

Tell the children that you want the word to be **den**.

Ask: "What sound is missing from the beginning?"

Confirm that it is **d**.

■ Ask a child to write in the missing sound in the correct place.

Ask: "What does the word say?"

Confirm **den**.

Ask the children to look at and read **hen, pen, ten, den**. Emphasise the rime in the words.

Ask: "What is the rime?"

Confirm that it is **-en**.

■ Repeat the procedure for **when**. (*Ensure children know that two letters make the sound* **wh**.)

■ Repeat the procedure for words with the **-et** rime.

Suggested words:

net   wet   vet   set   get   jet   let
met   pet

FURTHER PRACTICE

DEVELOPING SKILLS

Some or all of these activities must be done to ensure progress:

■ **Onset and Rime Cards**

Children have a selection of *h, p, t, d, n, v, w, s* cards and *-en* and *-et* Rime Cards. Ask the children to make the words *hen, pen, ten, den, net, vet, wet, set*. (More of each card would be necessary to make and display all words.)

■ **Rhyme Picture Cards**

Children sort a selection of Rhyme Picture Cards (*-en* and *-et* rime) into those that can go in the *-en* set and those that can go in the *-et* set.

■ **Headbands with rimes**

Give two children headbands, one with the *-et* rime and one with the *-en* rime. Invite them to stand in two separate places in front of the group. Explain that the child with the *-et* headband likes words with the *-et* rime and the child with the *-en* headband likes words with the *-en* rime. Tell the children you will call out words with the *-en* or *-et* rime. Ask them in turn to take their place behind the child with the matching headband.

Suggested words:

pet	wet	get	set
pen	hen	Ben	vet
jet	den	men	bet
met	let	ten	when

NOTE

Rhymes and rimes are not identical. Rhymes have word endings which sound the same but are not necessarily spelled in the same way, such as *socks* and *fox*. In contrast, rimes are word endings which always retain the same spelling pattern, such as *box* and *fox*.

-en -et

Onset and rime

BEFORE YOU START

THE NLF AIMS

- Identify onset and rime in spoken words.
- Write the letters that represent the initial sound (onset) in the written word.
- Read words with emphasis on rime.
- Write CVC words (with a model).

WHAT YOU NEED

RESOURCES

- Letter Cards *h, p, t, d, n, v, w, s*
- Rhyme Picture Cards
- Onset and Rime Cards *h, p, t, d, n, v, w, s, -en, -et*
- Chalkboard/whiteboard
- Workbook 3 page 8
- Teacher's copy of Workbook 3 page 8
- Headbands with slits

KEY LESSON POINTERS

VOCABULARY

alphabet   letter   name
sound   word   vowel
same/different   first/beginning/in front
rime/rhyme (see Note)   circle   cross out
dotted line   underneath   middle

THE CHILDREN should throughout the lesson:

- distinguish between the letter sound and the letter name
- pronounce the pure sounds.

YOU should throughout the lesson:

- emphasise the difference between the letter sound and the letter name
- emphasise the rime in words
- ensure correct pronunciation of sounds
- ensure correct letter formation.

THE LESSON

STARTING THE LESSON

SKILLS REVIEW
- Quick revision of Letter Cards.

TEACHING THE LESSON

- Write *h, p, t, d* on the board.
  Write *-en* on the board.
  Ask a child to choose a sound and write it on the line in front of *-en*.
  Ask: "What word has been written?"
  Repeat using the other letters.
  Ask the children to look at and read the words *hen, pen, ten, den*. Emphasise the rime *-en* in all the words. (*Include* **when** *if it is appropriate for your pupils.*)

- Write *n, v, w, s* on the board.
  Write *-et* on the board.
  Ask a child to choose a sound and write it on the line in front of *-et*.
  Ask: "What word has been written?"
  Repeat using the other letters.

- Ask the children to look at and read the words *net, vet, wet, set*. Emphasise the rime *-et* in all the words.

- Show the teacher's copy of Workbook 3 page 8.

  Ask the children to identify the first picture. (*hen*)

  Ask: "What sound does *hen* start with?"

  Confirm that it is *h*.

  Ask a child to point to the *h* on the teacher's copy.

  Ask: "What is the other sound?"

  Confirm *r*.

  Confirm the procedure: to circle *h* and to cross out *r* because it is the wrong sound.

  Ask a child to complete the procedure.

  Ask: "What do you have to do next?"

  Confirm: "Write the correct letter *h* on the line."

  Ask a child to complete the procedure.

  Ask: "What do you have to do next?"

  Confirm: "Write the whole word on the dotted line."

  Ask a child to complete procedure. (*Ensure the correct letter formation when children are writing.*)

  Ask: "What sounds make the word?"

  Confirm *h, e, n*.

  Ask: "What does the word say?"

  Repeat the procedure for *men*, *net* and *vet*.

  Ask: "Which words rime?"

  Confirm *hen* and *men*, *net* and *vet*.

  Ask: "Which vowel is in the middle of *hen*, *men*, *net*, *vet*?"

  Confirm *e*.

- Children complete Workbook 3 page 8. (*Remember to remove teacher's copy before children complete page.*)

FURTHER PRACTICE

DEVELOPING SKILLS

Some or all of these activities must be done to ensure progress:

- **Onset and Rime Cards**

  Children have a selection of *h, p, t, d, n, v, w, s, g, m* cards and *-en* and *-et* Rime Cards. Ask the children to make the words *hen, pen, ten, den, men, net, vet, wet, set, get, met, pet*. (More of each card would be necessary to make and display all words.)

- **Rhyme Picture Cards**

  Children sort a selection of Rhyme Picture Cards (*-en* and *-et* rime) into those that can go in the *-en* set and those that can go in the *-et* set.

- **Headbands with rimes**

  Give two children headbands, one with the *-en* rime and one with the *-et* rime. Invite them to stand in two separate places in front of the group. Explain that the child with the *-en* headband likes words with the *-en* rime and the child with the *-et* headband likes words with the *-et* rime. Tell the children you will call out words with the *-en* or *-et* rime. Ask them in turn to take their place behind the child with the matching headband.

  Suggested words:

pet	wet	get	set
pen	hen	Ben	vet
jet	den	men	bet
met	let	ten	when

NOTE

Rhymes and rimes are not identical. Rhymes have word endings which sound the same but are not necessarily spelled in the same way, such as *socks* and *fox*. In contrast, rimes are word endings which always retain the same spelling pattern, such as *box* and *fox*.

-en -et

Onset and rime

BEFORE YOU START

THE NLF AIMS

- Identify onset and rime in spoken words.
- Write the letters that represent the initial sound (onset) in the written word.
- Read words with emphasis on rime.

WHAT YOU NEED

RESOURCES

- Letter Cards *h, p, t, d, n, v, w, s*
- Rhyme Picture Cards
- Onset and Rime Cards *h, p, t, d, n, v, w, s, f, s, b, j, m, r, -ug, -un*
- Chalkboard/whiteboard

KEY LESSON POINTERS

VOCABULARY

alphabet letter name
sound letter name letter sound
word vowel same/different
first/beginning/in front
rime/rhyme (see Note)

THE CHILDREN should throughout the lesson:

- distinguish between the letter sound and the letter name
- pronounce the pure sounds.

YOU should throughout the lesson:

- emphasise the difference between the letter sound and the letter name
- emphasise the rime in words
- ensure correct pronunciation of sounds
- ensure correct letter formation.

THE LESSON

STARTING THE LESSON

SKILLS REVIEW

- Quick revision of Letter Cards.

TEACHING THE LESSON

- Write *h, p, t, d, n, v, w, s* on the board.

  Write *-en* on the board.

  Ask a child to choose a sound and write it on the line in front of *-en* to make a word.

  Ask: "What word has been written?"

  Repeat using the other letters.

  Ask the children to look at and read the words written. Emphasise the rime *-en* in the words.

- Write *-et* on the board.

  Ask a child to choose a sound and write it on the line in front of *-et* to make a word.

  Ask: "What word has been written?" (*Remember, if the children write a nonsense word you should say that it does rime but is not a real word.*)

  Repeat using the other letters.

  Ask the children to look at and read the words written. Emphasise the rime *-et* in all the words.

- Tell the children that you want to write some words with a different rime and they have to help with the first sound.

  Write *-ug* on the board.

  Ask: "What do you notice about the vowel sound?"

  Confirm that it is *u* and that last time it was *e*.

  Tell the children that you want the word to be *jug*.

  Ask: "What sound is missing from the beginning?"

  Confirm that it is *j*.

  Ask a child to write in the missing sound in the correct place.

  Ask: "What does the word say?"

  Confirm *jug*.

  Write *-ug* on the board again.

  Tell the children that you want the word to be *mug*.

  Ask: "What sound is missing from the beginning?"

  Confirm that it is *m*.

Ask a child to write in the missing sound in the correct place.

Ask: "What does the word say?"

Confirm *mug*.

Write *-ug* on the board again.

Tell the children that you want the word to be *rug*.

Ask: "What sound is missing from the beginning?"

Confirm that it is *r*.

Ask a child to write in the missing sound in the correct place.

Ask: "What does the word say?"

Confirm *rug*.

Ask the children to look at and read *jug, mug, rug*. Emphasise the rime *-ug* in the words.

Ask: "What do you notice about *jug, mug, rug*?"

After discussion, confirm that they all have the same two letters at the end: *u* and *g*, which is the *-ug* rime.

Ask: "What is different about the words?"

Confirm that the sounds at the beginning are different.

■ Write *-un* on the board.

Tell the children that you want the word to be *sun*.

Ask: "What sound is missing from the beginning?"

Confirm that it is *s*.

Ask a child to write in the missing sound in the correct place.

Ask: "What does the word say?"

Confirm *sun*.

Write *-un* on the board again and repeat the procedure for the words *bun, fun, run*. (*Encourage children to self correct if they make mistakes.*)

Ask the children to look at and read *sun, bun, fun, run*. Emphasise the rime in the words.

Ask: "What is the rime?"

Confirm that it is *-un*.

Confirm that the words start with different sounds and that they rhyme.

FURTHER PRACTICE

DEVELOPING SKILLS

Some or all of these activities must be done to ensure progress:

■ **Onset and Rime Cards**

Children have a selection of *f, s, b, j, m, r, t* cards and *-ug* and *-un* Rime Cards. Ask the children to make the words *run, fun, sun, bun, jug, mug, rug, tug*. (More of each card would be necessary to make and display all words.)

■ **Rhyme Picture Cards**

Children sort a selection of Rhyme Picture Cards (*-ug* and *-un* rime) into those that can go in the *-ug* set and those that can go in the *-un* set.

NOTE

Rhymes and rimes are not identical. Rhymes have word endings which sound the same but are not necessarily spelled in the same way, such as *socks* and *fox*. In contrast, rimes are word endings which always retain the same spelling pattern, such as *box* and *fox*.

-ug -un

Onset and rime

THE NLF AIMS

- Identify onset and rime in spoken words.
- Write the letters that represent the initial sound (onset) in the written word.
- Read words with emphasis on rime.
- Write CVC words (with a model).

WHAT YOU NEED

RESOURCES

- Letter Cards *f, s, b, j, m, r*
- Rhyme Picture Cards
- Onset and Rime Cards *f, s, b, j, m, r, -ug, -un*
- Chalkboard/whiteboard
- Workbook 3 page 9
- Teacher's copy of Workbook 3 page 9
- Headbands with slits

KEY LESSON POINTERS

VOCABULARY

alphabet   letter   name
sound   word   vowel
same/different   first/beginning/in front
rime/rhyme (see Note)   circle   cross out
dotted line   underneath   middle

THE CHILDREN should throughout the lesson:

- distinguish between the letter sound and the letter name
- pronounce the pure sounds.

YOU should throughout the lesson:

- emphasise the difference between the letter sound and the letter name
- emphasise the rime in words
- ensure correct pronunciation of sounds
- ensure correct letter formation.

THE LESSON

STARTING THE LESSON

SKILLS REVIEW

■ Quick revision of Letter Cards.

TEACHING THE LESSON

■ Write *f, s, b, j, m, r* on the board.
Write *-ug* on the board.
Ask a child to choose a sound and write it on the line in front of *-ug* to make a word.
Ask: "What word has been written?"
Repeat using the other letters. (*Remember, if the children write a nonsense word you should say that it does rime but is not a real word.*)
Ask the children to look at and read the words *bug, jug, mug, rug*. Emphasise the rime *-ug* in all the words.

■ Write *-un* on the board.
Ask a child to choose a sound and write it on the line in front of *-un* to make a word.
Ask: "What word has been written?"
Repeat using the other letters. (*Remember, if the children write a nonsense word you should say that it does rime but is not a real word.*)
Ask the children to look at and read the words *fun, sun, bun, run*. Emphasise the rime *-un* in all the words.

■ Show the teacher's copy of Workbook 3 page 9.

Ask the children to identify the first picture. (*jug*)

Ask: "What sound does *jug* start with?"

Confirm that it is *j*.

Ask a child to point to the *j* on the teacher's copy.

Ask: "What is the other sound?"

Confirm *t*.

Confirm the procedure: to circle *j* and to cross out *t* because it is the wrong sound.

Ask a child to complete the procedure.

Ask: "What do you have to do next?"

Confirm: "Write the correct letter *j* on the line."

Ask a child to complete the procedure.

Ask: "What do you have to do next?"

Confirm: "Write the whole word *jug* on the dotted line."

Ask a child to complete the procedure. (*Ensure the correct letter formation when children are writing.*)

Ask: "What sounds make the word?"

Confirm *j, u, g*.

Ask: "What does the word say?"

Confirm *jug*

Repeat the procedure for *mug, sun* and *bun*.

Ask: "Which words rime?"

Confirm *jug* and *mug, sun* and *bun*.

Ask: "Which vowel is in the middle of *jug, mug, sun, bun*?"

Confirm *u*.

■ Children complete Workbook 3 page 9. (*Remember to remove teacher's copy before children complete page.*)

FURTHER PRACTICE

DEVELOPING SKILLS

Some or all of these activities must be done to ensure progress:

■ **Onset and Rime Cards**

Children have a selection of *f, s, b, j, m, r, t* cards and *-ug* and *-un* Rime Cards. Ask the children to make the words *run, fun, sun, bun, jug, mug, rug, tug*. (More of each card would be necessary to make and display all words.)

Give the children two sets of *f, s, b, j, m, r, t* Letter Cards and 4 *-un/ -ug* Rime Cards and ask them to make as many real words as they can in one minute.

■ **Rhyme Picture Cards**

Children sort a selection of Rhyme Picture Cards (*-ug* and *-un* rime) into those that can go in the *-ug* set and those that can go in the *-un* set.

■ **Headbands with rimes**

Give two children headbands, one with the *-ug* rime and one with the *-un* rime. Invite them to stand in two separate places in front of the group. Explain that the child with the *-ug* headband likes words with the *-ug* rime and the child with the *-un* headband likes words with the *-un* rime. Tell the children you will call out words with the *-ug* or *-un* rime. Ask them in turn to take their place behind the child with the matching headband.

Suggested words:

run	jug	dug	stun
mug	fun	nun	drug
sun	rug	slug	bun
bug	plug	hug	tug

NOTE

Rhymes and rimes are not identical. Rhymes have word endings which sound the same but are not necessarily spelled in the same way, such as *socks* and *fox*. In contrast, rimes are word endings which always retain the same spelling pattern, such as *box* and *fox*.

-ug -un

Onset and rime

BEFORE YOU START

THE NLF AIMS

- Identify onset and rime in spoken words.
- Write the letters that represent the initial sound (onset) in the written word.
- Read words with emphasis on rime.

WHAT YOU NEED

RESOURCES

- Letter Cards *f, s, b, j, m, r*
- Rhyme Picture Cards
- Onset and Rime Cards *b, d, f, j, p, t, w, r, -ig, -in*
- Chalkboard/whiteboard

KEY LESSON POINTERS

VOCABULARY

alphabet letter name
sound letter name letter sound
word vowel same/different
first/beginning/in front
rime/rhyme (see Note)

THE CHILDREN should throughout the lesson:

- distinguish between the letter sound and the letter name
- pronounce the pure sounds.

YOU should throughout the lesson:

- emphasise the difference between the letter sound and the letter name
- emphasise the rime in words
- ensure correct pronunciation of sounds
- ensure correct letter formation.

THE LESSON

STARTING THE LESSON

SKILLS REVIEW

■ Quick revision of Letter Cards.

TEACHING THE LESSON

■ Write *f, s, b, j, m, r* on the board.

Write *-un* on the board.

Ask a child to choose a sound and write it on the line in front of *-un* to make a word.

Ask: "What word has been written?"

Repeat using the other letters.

Ask the children to look at and read the words written. Emphasise the rime *-un* in the words.

■ Write *-ug* on the board.

Ask a child to choose a sound and write it on the line in front of *-ug* to make a word.

Ask: "What word has been written?" (*Remember, if the children write a nonsense word you should say that it does rime but is not a real word.*)

Repeat using the other letters.

■ Ask the children to look at and read the words written. Emphasise the rime *-ug* in all the words.

■ Tell the children that you want to write some words with a different rime and they have to help with the first sound.

Write *-ig* on the board.

Ask: "What do you notice about the vowel sound?"

Confirm that it is *i*.

Tell the children that you want the word to be *pig*.

Ask: "What sound is missing from the beginning?"

Confirm that it is *p*.

Ask a child to write in the missing sound in the correct place.

Ask: "What does the word say?"

Confirm *pig*.

Write *-ig* on the board again.

Tell the children that you want the word to be *wig*.

Ask: "What sound is missing from the beginning?"

Confirm that it is *w*.

Ask a child to write in the missing sound in the correct place.

Ask: "What does the word say?"

Confirm **wig**.

Write **-ig** on the board again.

Tell the children that you want the word to be **dig**.

Ask: "What sound is missing from the beginning?"

Confirm that it is **d**.

Ask a child to write in the missing sound in the correct place.

Ask: "What does the word say?"

Confirm **dig**.

Ask the children to look at and read **pig, wig, dig**. Emphasise the rime **-ig** in the words.

Ask: "What do you notice about **pig, wig, dig**?"

After discussion, confirm that they all have the same two letters at the end: **i** and **g**, which make the **-ig** rime.

Ask: "What is different about the words?"

Confirm that the sounds at the beginning are different.

Write **-ig** on the board and repeat the procedure for **big, fig, jig, rig**. (*Encourage the children to self correct if they make mistakes.*)

Ask the children to look at and read **big, dig, fig, jig, pig, wig, rig**. Emphasise the rime in the words.

Ask: "What is the rime?"

Confirm that it is **-ig**.

Confirm that the words all start with different letters and that they rhyme.

■ Write **-in** on the board.

Tell the children that you want the word to be **bin**.

Ask: "What sound is missing from the beginning?"

Confirm that it is **b**.

Ask the children to write in the missing sound in the correct place.

Ask: "What does the word say?"

Confirm **bin**.

■ Repeat the procedure for **din, fin, pin**.

■ Repeat the procedure for **chin, shin** and **thin** if appropriate for your pupils. (*Ensure they know which two letters make the sounds **ch**, **sh** and **th**.*)

FURTHER PRACTICE

DEVELOPING SKILLS

Some or all of these activities must be done to ensure progress:

■ **Onset and Rime Cards**

Children have a selection of *b, d, f, j, p, t, w, r* cards and *-ig* and *-in* Rime Cards. Ask the children to make the words *big, dig, fig, jig, pig, wig, rig, bin, tin, win, din, fin, pin*. (More of each card would be necessary to make and display all words.)

■ **Rhyme Picture Cards**

Children sort a selection of Rhyme Picture Cards (*-ig* and *-in* rime) into those that can go in the *-ig* set and those that can go in the *-in* set.

NOTE

Rhymes and rimes are not identical. Rhymes have word endings which sound the same but are not necessarily spelled in the same way, such as *socks* and *fox*. In contrast, rimes are word endings which always retain the same spelling pattern, such as *box* and *fox*.

BLENDING AND SEGMENTING

ONSET AND RIME

-ig -in

157

Onset and rime

BEFORE YOU START

THE NLF AIMS

- Identify onset and rime in spoken words.
- Write the letters that represent the initial sound (onset) in the written word.
- Read words with emphasis on rime.
- Write CVC words (with a model).

WHAT YOU NEED

RESOURCES

- Letter Cards *b, d, f, j, p, t, w, r*
- Rhyme Picture Cards
- Onset and Rime Cards *b, d, f, j, p, t, w, r, -ig, -in*
- Chalkboard/whiteboard
- Workbook 3 page 10
- Teacher's copy of Workbook 3 page 10
- Headbands with slits

KEY LESSON POINTERS

VOCABULARY

alphabet   letter   name
sound   word   vowel
same/different   first/beginning/in front
rime/rhyme (see Note)   circle   cross
dotted line   underneath   middle

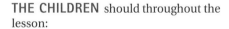

THE CHILDREN should throughout the lesson:

- distinguish between the letter sound and the letter name
- pronounce the pure sounds.

YOU should throughout the lesson:

- emphasise the difference between the letter sound and the letter name
- emphasise the rime in words
- ensure correct pronunciation of sounds
- ensure correct letter formation.

THE LESSON

STARTING THE LESSON

SKILLS REVIEW

- Quick revision of Letter Cards.

TEACHING THE LESSON

- Write *b, d, f, j, p, t, w, r* on the board.
  Write *-ig* on the board.
  Ask a child to choose a sound and write it on the line in front of *-ig*.
  Ask: "What word has been written?"
  Repeat using the other letters.
  Ask the children to look at and read the words *big, dig, fig, jig, pig, wig, rig*. Emphasise the rime *-ig* in all the words.

- Write *-in* on the board.
  Ask a child to choose a sound and write it on the line in front of *-in* to make a word.
  Ask: "What word has been written?"
  Repeat using the other letters. (*Remember, if the children write a nonsense word you should say that it does rime but is not a real word.*)
  Ask the children to look at and read the words *bin, tin, win, din, fin, pin*. Emphasise the rime -*in* in all the words.
  Include *chin, shin, thin*, if appropriate for your pupils.

- Show the teacher's copy of Workbook 3 page 10.

  Ask the children to identify the first picture. (*pig*)

  Ask: "What sound does *pig* start with?"

  Confirm that it is *p*.

  Ask a child to point to the *p* on the teacher's copy.

  Ask: "What is the other sound?"

  Confirm *g*.

  Confirm the procedure: to circle *p* and to cross out *g* because it is the wrong sound.

  Ask a child to complete the procedure.

  Ask: "What do you have to do next?"

  Confirm: "Write the correct letter *p* on the line."

  Ask a child to complete the procedure.

  Ask: "What do you have to do next?"

  Confirm: "Write the whole word *pig* on the dotted line."

  Ask a child to complete the procedure. (*Ensure the correct letter formation when children are writing.*)

  Ask: "What sounds make the word?"

  Confirm *p, i, g*.

  Ask: "What does the word say?"

  Confirm *pig*.

  Repeat the procedure for *wig*, *bin* and *tin*.

  Ask: "Which words rhyme?"

  Confirm *pig* and *wig*, *bin* and *tin*.

  Ask: "Which vowel is in the middle of *pig, wig, bin, tin*?"

  Confirm *i*.

- Children complete Workbook 3 page 10. (*Remember to remove teacher's copy before children complete page.*)

FURTHER PRACTICE

DEVELOPING SKILLS

Some or all of these activities must be done to ensure progress:

- **Onset and Rime Cards**

  Children have a selection of *b, d, f, j, p, t, w, r* cards and *-ig* and *-in* Rime Cards. Ask the children to make the words *big, dig, fig, jig, pig, wig, rig, bin, tin, win, din, fin, pin*. (More of each card would be necessary to make and display all words.)

- **Rhyme Picture Cards**

  Children sort a selection of Rhyme Picture Cards (-ig *and* -in *rime*) into those that can go in the *-ig* set and those that can go in the *-in* set.

- **Headbands with rimes**

Give two children headbands, one with the *-ig* rime and one with the *-in* rime. Invite them to stand in two separate places in front of the group. Explain that the child with the *-ig* headband likes words with the *-ig* rime and the child with the *-in* headband likes words with the *-in* rime. Tell the children you will call out words with the *-ig* or *-in* rime. Ask them in turn to take their place behind the child with the matching headband.

Suggested words:

chin	wig	pin	twin
big	thin	pig	shin
twig	fin	rig	big
fig	dig	skin	spin

NOTE

Rhymes and rimes are not identical. Rhymes have word endings which sound the same but are not necessarily spelled in the same way, such as *socks* and *fox*. In contrast, rimes are word endings which always retain the same spelling pattern, such as *box* and *fox*.

-ig -in

Consonant-vowel blends where the vowel is **a**

THE NLF AIMS

- Blend a consonant and a vowel.
- Read consonant-vowel blends.

WHAT YOU NEED

RESOURCES

- The Alphabet Letter Cards
- Flash Cards – CV blends: *a*
- Chalkboard/whiteboard

KEY LESSON POINTERS

VOCABULARY

alphabet   letter   name   sound
word   vowel   second   join (blend)

THE CHILDREN should throughout the lesson:

- distinguish between the letter sound and the letter name
- pronounce the pure sounds
- focus on blending the sounds, not sounding each letter.

YOU should throughout the lesson:

- emphasise the difference between the letter sound and the letter name
- ensure correct pronunciation of sounds
- ensure the blending of two sounds.

THE LESSON

STARTING THE LESSON

- Tell the children that letters join together to make words and that they need to be able to join letters together quickly to read well.

- Tell them that they are going to practise joining two letters together and the second letter is always going to be a vowel.
  (*Revise vowels:* **a, e, i, o, u.**)

TEACHING THE LESSON

- Show the children the **b** Letter Card.
  Confirm that the sound is **b**.
  Show the children the **a** Letter Card.
  Confirm that the sound is **a**.
  Place the **b** card and the **a** card close together.
  Ask: "What do the two letters say when they are close together?" (*This may take a lot of guidance.*)
  Confirm that it is **ba**.
  Show the children the **h** Letter Card.
  Confirm that the sound is **h**.
  Show the children the **a** Letter Card.
  Confirm that the sound is **a**.
  Place the **h** card and the **a** card close together.
  Ask: "What do the two letters say when they are close together?"
  Confirm that it is **ha**.

- Ask a child to come to the front of the class.

  Give the child the *h* and *a* cards to make *ha*. (*Ensure that the child holds the cards close together and faces the class/group holding the cards so that everyone can see them.*)

  Ask: "What sound do the two letters make when they come close together?"

  Confirm *ha*.

- Repeat the procedure by giving other children in turn *c* and *a* to make *ca*; *f* and *a* to make *fa*; *s* and *a* to make *sa*; *m* and *a* to make *ma*; *t* and *a* to make *ta*.

- Ask children in turn to name or change places with the child who is holding the *ha* cards, then *ca*, *fa*, and so on.

- Ask the child who is holding the cards that say *ca* to give them to you and sit down.

- Repeat for the other cards.

NOW OR LATER

- Repeat the procedure for *da, ga, pa, ra, na, ja, la, va*. (*Remember that this is a new skill and may require much practice and repetition.*)

DEVELOPING SKILLS

- Flash Cards

  CV blends with the vowel *a*.

Every opportunity should be taken to practise the consonant-vowel blends to gain speed and accuracy.

161

vowel-a

Consonant-vowel blends where the vowel is **a**

THE NLF AIMS

- Blend a consonant and a vowel.
- Read consonant-vowel blends.

WHAT YOU NEED

RESOURCES

- The Alphabet Letter Cards
- Flash Cards – CV blends: *a*
- Homework Sheet 3A
- Chalkboard/whiteboard

KEY LESSON POINTERS

VOCABULARY

alphabet   letter   name   sound
word   vowel   second   join (blend)

THE CHILDREN should throughout the lesson:

- distinguish between the letter sound and the letter name
- pronounce the pure sounds
- focus on blending the sounds, not sounding each letter.

YOU should throughout the lesson:

- emphasise the difference between the letter sound and the letter name
- ensure correct pronunciation of sounds
- ensure the blending of two sounds.

THE LESSON

STARTING THE LESSON

- Review Lesson 16.

TEACHING THE LESSON

- Tell the children that you are going to write some letters and they will say the letter sound.

  Write **b** on the board.

  Ask: "What sound is this?"

  Write **a** on the board.

  Ask: "What sound is this?"

  Ask: "What sound do **b** and **a** make when they join together?" (*It may be helpful to draw a line under* <u>**ba**</u> *to act as a join.*)

  Confirm **ba**.

  Write **r** on the board.

  Ask: "What sound is this?"

  Write **a** on the board.

  Ask: "What sound is this?"

  Ask: "What sound do **r** and **a** make when they join together?" (*It may be helpful to draw a line under* <u>**ra**</u> *to act as a join.*)

  Confirm **ra**.

  Repeat the procedure using some or all of the consonants *c, d, f, g, h, j, k, l, m, n, p, s, t, v, w*.

- Ask children in turn to find on the board the two letters that say **ha**, **sa** and so on, as you call out each blend.

- Ask the children to read consonant-vowel blends working towards speed and accuracy.

- Write **ma** on the board.
  Ask the children to read it.
  Confirm that it says **ma**.
  Tell the children that you want to change it to **sa**.
  Ask: "What would I have to do?"
  Confirm the change of **m** to **s**.
  Write **sa** on the board.
  Ask the children to read it.
  Confirm that it says **sa**.
  Tell the children that you want to change it to **fa**.
  Ask: "What would I have to do?"
  Confirm the change of **s** to **f**.
  Write **fa** on the board.
  Repeat as necessary for other CV blends with **a**.

- Ask children in turn to write consonant-vowel blends on the board.

FURTHER PRACTICE

DEVELOPING SKILLS

- **Flash Cards**
  CV blends with the vowel *a*.

Every opportunity should be taken to practise the consonant-vowel blends to gain speed and accuracy.

Suggested activities
Distribute 3 to 5 Flash Cards to a group of children and ask them to arrange their cards face up before starting these activities:

– **Show/give**
  The child who has the *ca* card shows or gives it to you. Repeat for other blends.

– **Choose/say**
  Children in turn choose a card and tell you what it says.

– **Choose/ask**
  One child chooses a card from the child next to him or her and asks what it says. The questioner must confirm whether or not the answer is correct.

ACTIVITIES AT HOME

- Homework Sheet 3A.

vowel – a

Consonant-vowel blends where the vowel is o

THE NLF AIMS

- Blend a consonant and a vowel.
- Read consonant-vowel blends.

WHAT YOU NEED

RESOURCES

- The Alphabet Letter Cards
- Flash Cards – CV blends: *a, o*
- Chalkboard/whiteboard

KEY LESSON POINTERS

VOCABULARY

alphabet   letter   name   sound
word   vowel   second   join (blend)

THE CHILDREN should throughout the lesson:

- distinguish between the letter sound and the letter name
- pronounce the pure sounds
- focus on blending the sounds, not sounding each letter.

YOU should throughout the lesson:

- emphasise the difference between the letter sound and the letter name
- ensure correct pronunciation of sounds
- ensure the blending of two sounds.

THE LESSON

STARTING THE LESSON

- Review Lessons 16 and 17: CV blends where the vowel is *a.*

- Ask: "Which vowel is in each of the blends?" Confirm *a.*

- Tell the children that they are going to join two letters together but the vowel will be different; it won't be *a.*

TEACHING THE LESSON

- Show the children the *j* Letter Card.
  Confirm that the sound is *j.*
  Show the children the *o* Letter Card.
  Confirm that the sound is *o.*
  Place the *j* card and the *o* card close together.
  Ask: "What do the two letters say when they are close together?"
  Confirm that it is *jo.*
  Show the children the *l* Letter Card.
  Confirm that the sound is *l.*
  Show the children the *o* Letter Card.
  Confirm that the sound is *o.*
  Place the *l* card and the *o* card close together.
  Ask: "What do the two letters say when they are close together?"
  Confirm that it is *lo.*

- Repeat the procedure for other letters *b, c, d, f, g, h, m, n, p, r, s, t, v.* Watch out for *do, go, no, so, to,* which are words in their own right as well as blends in words such as *dog, got, not, sob, top.* The children's attention should be drawn to this. (*Remember that this is a new skill and may require much practice and repetition.*)

- Ask a child to come to the front of the class.

  Give the child the **h** and **o** cards to make **ho**.

  Ask the children what the two sounds say when they come together.

  Confirm **ho**.

- Repeat the procedure by giving other children in turn **c** and **o** to make **co**; **f** and **o** to make **fo**; **s** and **o** to make **so**; **m** and **o** to make **mo**; **t** and **o** to make **to** and **b** and **o** to make **bo**.

  Ensure that the children hold the cards close together and face the class/group, holding the cards so that everyone can see them.

- Ask children in turn to name or change places with the child who is holding the **ho** cards, then **co**, **fo**, and so on.

- Ask the child who is holding the cards that say **ho** to give them to you and sit down. Repeat for the other cards.

- Repeat the activity for **do, go, po, ro, no, jo**. (*Remember that this is a new skill and may require much practice and repetition.*)

FURTHER PRACTICE

DEVELOPING SKILLS

- **Flash Cards**

  CV blends with the vowels *a* or *o*.

  Every opportunity should be taken to practise the consonant-vowel blends to gain speed and accuracy.

  ---

vowel – o

Consonant-vowel blends where the vowel is o

THE NLF AIMS

- Blend a consonant and a vowel.
- Read consonant-vowel blends.

WHAT YOU NEED

RESOURCES

- The Alphabet Letter Cards
- Flash Cards – CV blends: *a, o*
- Homework Sheets 3B and 3C
- Workbook 3 page 11
- Teacher's copy of Workbook 3 page 11
- Chalkboard/whiteboard

KEY LESSON POINTERS

VOCABULARY

alphabet   letter   name   sound
word   vowel   second   join (blend)

THE CHILDREN should throughout the lesson:

- distinguish between the letter sound and the letter name
- pronounce the pure sounds
- focus on blending the sounds, not sounding each letter.

YOU should throughout the lesson:

- emphasise the difference between the letter sound and the letter name
- ensure correct pronunciation of sounds
- ensure the blending of two sounds.

THE LESSON

STARTING THE LESSON

- Review Lesson 18: vowel is *o*.

TEACHING THE LESSON

- Tell the children that you are going to write some letters on the board.

  Write *m* on the board.

  Ask: "What sound is this?"

  Write *o* on the board.

  Ask: "What sound is this?"

  Ask: "What sound do *m* and *o* make when they join together?" (*It may be helpful to draw a line under* <u>*mo*</u> *to act as a join.*)

  Confirm *mo*.

  Write *f* on the board.

  Ask: "What sound is this?"

  Write *o* on the board.

  Ask: "What sound is this?"

  Ask: "What sound do *f* and *o* make when they join together?" (*It may be helpful to draw a line under* <u>*fo*</u> *to act as a join.*)

  Confirm *fo*.

- Repeat the procedure using some or all of the consonants *b, c, d, g, h, j, l, n, p, r, s, t, v*.

- Ask children in turn to find on the board the two letters that say *bo, co, do*, and so on as you call each blend out.

- Ask the children to read CV blends working towards speed and accuracy.

166

- Write **lo** on the board.

  Ask the children to read it.

  Confirm that it says **lo**.

  Tell the children that you want to change it to **po**.

  Ask: "What would I have to do?"

  Confirm the change of **l** to **p**.

  Write **po** on the board.

  Ask the children to read it.

  Confirm that it says **po**.

  Tell the children that you want to change it to **ro**.

  Ask: "What would I have to do?"

  Confirm the change of **p** to **r**.

  Write **ro** on the board.

  Repeat as necessary for other CV blends with **o**.

- Ask children in turn to write consonant-vowel blends on the board, with **o** as the vowel.

- Repeat the above for consonant-vowel blends where **a** is the vowel.

- Show the children the teacher's copy of Workbook 3 page 11 and ensure that they can identify the pictures and understand how to complete the page.

- Children complete Workbook 3 page 11.

  Give instructions as appropriate.

FURTHER PRACTICE

DEVELOPING SKILLS

- **Flash Cards**

  ha, sa, ca, ro, to, go and so on.

  Suggested activities

  Distribute 3 to 5 Flash Cards (CV blends with the vowel *o*) to a group of children and ask them to arrange their cards face up before starting these activities:

  – **Show/give**

  The child who has the *ro* card shows or gives it to you. Repeat for other blends.

  – **Choose/say**

  Children in turn choose a card and tell you what it says.

  – **Choose/ask**

  One child chooses a card from the child next to him or her and asks what it says. The questioner must confirm whether or not the answer is correct.

Every opportunity should be taken to practise the consonant-vowel blends to gain speed and accuracy.

ACTIVITIES AT HOME

- Homework Sheets 3B and 3C.

vowel – o

Consonant-vowel blends where the vowel is e

THE NLF AIMS

- Blend a consonant and a vowel.
- Read consonant-vowel blends.

WHAT YOU NEED

RESOURCES

- The Alphabet Letter Cards
- Flash Cards – CV blends: *a, o, e*
- Chalkboard/whiteboard

KEY LESSON POINTERS

VOCABULARY

alphabet   letter   name   sound
word   vowel   second   join (blend)

THE CHILDREN should throughout the lesson:

- distinguish between the letter sound and the letter name
- pronounce the pure sounds
- focus on blending the sounds, not sounding each letter.

YOU should throughout the lesson:

- emphasise the difference between the letter sound and the letter name
- ensure correct pronunciation of sounds
- ensure the blending of two sounds.

STARTING THE LESSON

- Quick Revision: Flash Cards for consonant-vowel blends with *a* or *o* as the vowels.
- Tell the children that the vowel for today's activity is going to be different.

TEACHING THE LESSON

- Show the children the *n* Letter Card.
  Confirm that the sound is *n*.
  Show the children the *e* Letter Card.
  Confirm that the sound is *e*.
  Place the *n* card and the *e* card close together.
  Ask: "What do the two letters say when they are close together?"
  Confirm that it is *ne*.
  Show the children the *d* Letter Card.
  Confirm that the sound is *d*.
  Show the children the *e* Letter Card.
  Confirm that the sound is *e*.
  Place the *d* card and the *e* card close together.
  Ask: "What do the two letters say when they are close together?"
  Confirm that it is *de*.

- Repeat the procedure for other letters *b, f, g, h, j, k, l, m, p, r, s, t, v, w, z*. Watch out for *be, he, me, we*, which are words in their own right as well as blends in words such as *bed, hem, met, web*. The children's attention should be drawn to this.

- Ask a child to come to the front of the class.

  Give the child the *m* and *e* cards to make *me*. Ask the children what the two sounds say when they come together.

  Confirm *me*.

- Repeat the procedure by giving other children in turn *r* and *e* to make *re*; *t* and *e* to make *te*; *k* and *e* to make *ke*; *j* and *e* to make *je*; *f* and *e* to make *fe*.

  Ensure that the children hold the cards close together and face the class/group, holding the cards so that everyone can see them.

- Ask children in turn to name or change places with the child who is holding the *me* cards, then *re*, *te*, and so on.

- Ask the child who is holding the cards that say *re* to give them to you and sit down. Repeat for the other cards.

- Repeat the activity for *be, ge, he, le, ne, pe, se, we, de*.

DEVELOPING SKILLS

- **Flash Cards**

  te, le, re, ro, to, go, ha, sa, ra and so on.

Every opportunity should be taken to practise the consonant-vowel blends to gain speed and accuracy.

vowel – e

Consonant-vowel blends where the vowel is e

BEFORE YOU START

THE NLF AIMS

- Blend a consonant and a vowel.
- Read consonant-vowel blends.

WHAT YOU NEED

RESOURCES

- The Alphabet Letter Cards
- Flash Cards – CV blends: *a, o, e*
- Homework Sheets 3D and 3E
- Chalkboard/whiteboard

KEY LESSON POINTERS

VOCABULARY

alphabet   letter   name   sound
word   vowel   second   join (blend)

THE CHILDREN should throughout the lesson:

- distinguish between the letter sound and the letter name
- pronounce the pure sounds
- focus on blending the sounds, not sounding each letter.

YOU should throughout the lesson:

- emphasise the difference between the letter sound and the letter name
- ensure correct pronunciation of sounds
- ensure the blending of two sounds.

THE LESSON

STARTING THE LESSON

- Review Lesson 20.

TEACHING THE LESSON

- Tell the children that you are going to write some letters on the board.

  Write *r* on the board.

  Ask: "What sound is this?"

  Write *e* on the board.

  Ask: "What sound is this?"

  Ask: "What sound do *r* and *e* make when they join together?" (*It may be helpful to draw a line under* <u>re</u> *to act as a join.*)

  Confirm *re*.

  Write *v* on the board.

  Ask: "What sound is this?"

  Write *e* on the board.

  Ask: "What sound is this?"

  Ask: "What sound do *v* and *e* make when they join together?" (*It may be helpful to draw a line under* <u>ve</u> *to act as a join.*)

  Confirm *ve*.

- Repeat the procedure using some or all of the consonants *b, d, f, g, h, j, k, l, m, n, p, s, t, w, z.*

- Ask children in turn to find on the board the two letters that say *de*, *ge*, *le* and so on as you call out each blend.

  Ask the children to read CV blends working towards speed and accuracy.

  Write *se* on the board.

  Ask the children to read it.

  Confirm that it says *se*.

  Tell the children that you want to change it to *we*.

  Ask: "What would I have to do?"

  Confirm the change of *s* to *w*.

  Write *we* on the board.

  Ask the children to read it.

  Confirm that it says *we*.

  Tell the children that you want to change it to *fe*.

  Ask: "What would I have to do?"

  Confirm the change of *w* to *f.*

  Write *fe* on the board.

  Repeat as necessary for other CV blends with *e*.

  Ask the children to write *re*, *pe*, *ne* and so on on the board.

- Repeat the above for consonant-vowel blends where *a* or *o* is the vowel.

FURTHER PRACTICE

DEVELOPING SKILLS

- Flash Cards

  ha, sa, ca, ro, to, go, me, re, se

  Suggested activities

  Distribute 3 to 5 Flash Cards (CV blends with the vowel *e*) to a group of children and ask them to arrange their cards face up before starting these activities:

  – **Show/give**

    The child who has the *se* card shows or gives it to you. Repeat for other blends.

  – **Choose/say**

    Children in turn choose a card and tell you what it says.

  – **Choose/ask**

    One child chooses a card from the child next to him or her and asks what it says. The questioner must confirm whether or not the answer is correct.

Every opportunity should be taken to practise the consonant-vowel blends to gain speed and accuracy.

ACTIVITIES AT HOME

- Homework Sheets 3D and 3E.

BLENDING AND SEGMENTING

CONSONANT-VOWEL BLENDS

vowel – e

Consonant-vowel blends where the vowel is u

BEFORE YOU START

THE NLF AIMS

- Blend a consonant and a vowel.
- Read consonant-vowel blends.

WHAT YOU NEED

RESOURCES

- The Alphabet Letter Cards
- Flash Cards – CV blends: *a, o, e, u*
- Chalkboard/whiteboard

KEY LESSON POINTERS

VOCABULARY

alphabet letter name sound vowel
word join (blend) different/difference
letter sound letter name

THE CHILDREN should throughout the lesson:

- distinguish between the letter sound and the letter name
- pronounce the pure sounds
- focus on blending the sounds, not sounding each letter.

YOU should throughout the lesson:

- emphasise the difference between the letter sound and the letter name
- ensure correct pronunciation of sounds
- ensure the blending of two sounds.

THE LESSON

STARTING THE LESSON

- Quick Revision: Flash Cards for consonant-vowel blends with *a, o* or *e* as the vowel.
- Tell the children that the vowel for today's activity is going to be different.

TEACHING THE LESSON

- Show the children the *d* Letter Card.
  Confirm that the sound is *d*.
  Show the children the *u* Letter Card.
  Confirm that the sound is *u*.
  Place the *d* card and the *u* card close together.
  Ask: "What do the two letters say when they are close together?"
  Confirm that it is *du*.
  Show the children the *s* Letter Card.
  Confirm that the sound is *s*.
  Show the children the *u* Letter Card.
  Confirm that the sound is *u*.
  Place the *s* card and the *u* card close together.
  Ask: "What do the two letters say when they are close together?"
  Confirm that it is *su*.

- Repeat the procedure for other letters *b, c, f, g, h, j, l, m, n, p, r, t, v.*

- Ask a child to come to the front of the class.

  Give the child the **b** and **u** cards to make **bu**.

  Ask the children what the two sounds say when they come together.

  Confirm **bu**.

- Repeat the procedure by giving other children in turn **h** and **u** to make **hu**; **j** and **u** to make **ju**; **g** and **u** to make **gu**; **m** and **u** to make **mu**; **n** and **u** to make **nu**.

  Ensure that the children hold the cards close together and face the class/group, holding the cards so that everyone can see them.

- Ask children in turn to name or change places with the child who is holding the **bu** cards, then **hu**, **ju**, and so on.

- Ask the child who is holding the cards that say **bu** to give them to you and sit down. Repeat for the other cards.

- Repeat the activity for **cu**, **fu**, **tu**, **lu**, **pu**, **ru**.

FURTHER PRACTICE

DEVELOPING SKILLS

- Flash Cards

  CV blends with vowels *a*, *e*, *o* or *u*.

Every opportunity should be taken to practise the consonant-vowel blends to gain speed and accuracy.

---

vowel – u

Consonant-vowel blends where the vowel is **u**

BEFORE YOU START

THE NLF AIMS

- Blend a consonant and a vowel.
- Read consonant-vowel blends.

WHAT YOU NEED

RESOURCES

- The Alphabet Letter Cards
- Flash Cards – CV blends: *a, o, e, u*
- Homework Sheets 3F and 3G
- Workbook 3 page 12
- Teacher's copy of Workbook 3 page 12
- Chalkboard/whiteboard

KEY LESSON POINTERS

VOCABULARY

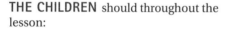

alphabet letter name sound vowel word join (blend) different/difference letter sound letter name

THE CHILDREN should throughout the lesson:

- distinguish between the letter sound and the letter name
- pronounce the pure sounds
- focus on blending the sounds, not sounding each letter.

YOU should throughout the lesson:

- emphasise the difference between the letter sound and the letter name
- ensure correct pronunciation of sounds
- ensure the blending of two sounds.

THE LESSON

SKILLS REVIEW

- Review Lesson 22.

TEACHING THE LESSON

- Tell the children that you are going to write some letters on the board.

  Write *b* on the board.

  Ask: "What sound is this?"

  Write *u* on the board.

  Ask: "What sound is this?"

  Ask: "What sound do *b* and *u* make when they join together?" (*It may be helpful to draw a line under **bu** to act as a join.*)

  Confirm *bu*.

  Write *r* on the board.

  Ask: "What sound is this?"

  Write *u* on the board.

  Ask: "What sound is this?"

  Ask: "What sound do *r* and *u* make when they join together?" (*It may be helpful to draw a line under **ru** to act as a join.*)

  Confirm *ru*.

- Repeat the procedure using some or all of the consonants *c, d, f, g, h, j, l, m, n, p, s, t, v.*

- Ask children in turn to find on the board the two letters that say *su, tu, ju* and so on as you call out each blend.

  Ask the children to read CV blends working towards speed and accuracy.

  Write *gu* on the board.

  Ask the children to read it.

  Confirm that it says *gu.*

  Tell the children that you want to change it to *lu.*

  Ask: "What would I have to do?"

  Confirm the change of *g* to *l.*

  Write *lu* on the board.

  Ask the children to read it.

  Confirm that it says *lu.*

  Tell the children that you want to change it to *pu.*

  Ask: "What would I have to do?"

  Confirm the change of *l* to *p.*

  Write *pu* on the board.

- Repeat as necessary for other CV blends with *u.*

- Ask children in turn to write *bu, ru, su* and so on on the board.

- Repeat the above for consonant-vowel blends with *e* as the vowel.

- Show the children the teacher's copy of Workbook 3 page 12 and ensure that they can identify the pictures and understand the procedure to complete the page.

- Children complete Workbook 3 page 12.

  Give instructions as appropriate.

FURTHER PRACTICE

DEVELOPING SKILLS

- **Flash Cards**

  Use *ce, le, me, gu, su, mu* and so on.

  Suggested activities

  Distribute 3 to 5 Flash Cards (CV blends with the vowel *u*) to a group of children and ask them to arrange their cards face up before starting these activities:

  – **Show/give**

  The child who has the *su* card shows or gives it to you. Repeat for other blends.

  – **Choose/say**

  Children in turn choose a card and tell you what it says.

  – **Choose/ask**

  One child chooses a card from the child next to him or her and asks what it says. The questioner must confirm whether or not the answer is correct.

  Every opportunity should be taken to practise the consonant-vowel blends to gain speed and accuracy.

ACTIVITIES AT HOME

- Homework Sheets 3F and 3G.

vowel – u

Consonant-vowel blends where the vowel is i

THE NLF AIMS

- Blend a consonant and a vowel.
- Read consonant-vowel blends.

WHAT YOU NEED

RESOURCES

- The Alphabet Letter Cards
- Flash Cards – CV blends: *a, o, e, u, i*
- Chalkboard/whiteboard

KEY LESSON POINTERS

VOCABULARY

alphabet   letter   name   sound   vowel
word   join (blend)   different/difference
letter sound   letter name

THE CHILDREN should throughout the lesson:

- distinguish between the letter sound and the letter name
- pronounce the pure sounds
- focus on blending the sounds, not sounding each letter.

YOU should throughout the lesson:

- emphasise the difference between the letter sound and the letter name
- ensure correct pronunciation of sounds
- ensure the blending of two sounds.

STARTING THE LESSON

- Quick Revision: Flash Cards for consonant-vowel blends with *a, o, e* or *u* as the vowels.

TEACHING THE LESSON

- Show the children the *p* Letter Card.
  Confirm that the sound is *p*.
  Show the children the *i* Letter Card.
  Confirm that the sound is *i*.
  Place the *p* card and the *i* card close together.
  Ask: "What do the two letters say when they are close together?"
  Confirm that it is *pi*.
  Show the children the *h* Letter Card.
  Confirm that the sound is *h*.
  Show the children the *i* Letter Card.
  Confirm that the sound is *i*.
  Place the *h* card and the *i* card close together.
  Ask: "What do the two letters say when they are close together?"
  Confirm that it is *hi*.
  Repeat the procedure for other letters *b, d, f, j, k, l, m, n, r, s, t, v, w, z*.

- Ask a child to come to the front of the class.
  Give the child the *p* and *i* cards to make *pi*.
  Ask the children what the two sounds say when they come together.
  Confirm *pi*.

- Repeat the procedure by giving other children in turn *s* and *i* to make *si*; *r* and *i* to make *ri*; *t* and *i* to make *ti*; *z* and *i* to make *zi*; *w* and *i* to make *wi*.
  Ensure that the children hold the cards close together and face the class/group, holding the cards so that everyone can see them.

- Ask children in turn to name or change places with the child who is holding the *pi* cards, then *si*, *ri* and so on.

- Ask the child who is holding the cards that say *pi* to give them to you and sit down. Repeat for the other cards.

- Repeat the activity for *bi*, *di*, *fi*, *hi*, *ji*, *li* and so on.

FURTHER PRACTICE

DEVELOPING SKILLS

- Flash Cards
  CV blends where the vowels are *a, e, i, o* or *u*.

Every opportunity should be taken to practise the consonant-vowel blends to gain speed and accuracy.

vowel – i

Consonant-vowel blends where the vowel is i

BEFORE YOU START

THE NLF AIMS

- Blend a consonant and a vowel.
- Read consonant-vowel blends.

WHAT YOU NEED

RESOURCES

- The Alphabet Letter Cards
- Flash Cards – CV blends: *a, e, o, u, i*
- Homework Sheets 3H and 3I
- Workbook 3 pages 13 and 14
- Teacher's copy of Workbook 3 pages 13 and 14
- Chalkboard/whiteboard
- Assessment 3.3

KEY LESSON POINTERS

VOCABULARY

alphabet   letter   name   sound   vowel
word   join (blend)   different/difference
letter sound   letter name

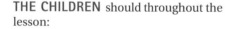

THE CHILDREN should throughout the lesson:

- distinguish between the letter sound and the letter name
- pronounce the pure sounds
- focus on blending the sounds, not sounding each letter.

YOU should throughout the lesson:

- emphasise the difference between the letter sound and the letter name
- ensure correct pronunciation of sounds
- ensure the blending of two sounds.

THE LESSON

STARTING THE LESSON

- Review Lesson 24.

TEACHING THE LESSON

- Tell the children that you are going to write some letters on the board.

  Write *n* on the board.

  Ask: "What sound is this?"

  Write *i* on the board.

  Ask: "What sound is this?"

  Ask: "What sound do *n* and *i* make when they join together?" (*It may be helpful to draw a line under* **ni** *to act as a join.*)

  Confirm *ni*.

  Write *r* on the board.

  Ask: "What sound is this?"

  Write *i* on the board.

  Ask: "What sound is this?"

  Ask: "What sound do *r* and *i* make when they join together?" (*It may be helpful to draw a line under* **ri** *to act as a join.*)

  Confirm *ri*.

- Repeat the procedure using some or all of the consonants *b, d, f, h, j, k, l, m, p, s, t, v, w, z.*

- Ask children in turn to find on the board the two letters that say *zi, hi, mi,* and so on as you call out each blend.

- Ask the children to read CV blends working towards speed and accuracy.

- Write **pi** on the board.
  Ask the children to read it.
  Confirm that it says **pi**.
  Tell the children that you want to change it to **si**.
  Ask: "What would I have to do?"
  Confirm the change of **p** to **s**.
  Write **si** on the board.
  Ask the children to read it.
  Confirm that it says **si**.
  Tell the children that you want to change it to **di**.
  Ask: "What would I have to do?"
  Confirm the change of **s** to **d**.
  Write **di** on the board.
  Repeat as necessary for other CV blends with **i**.

- Ask children in turn to write **pi**, **ji**, **li** and so on on the board.

- Repeat the above for consonant-vowel blends with **e** as the vowel.

- Show the children the teacher's copy of Workbook 3 page 13 and ensure that they can identify the pictures and understand the procedure to complete the page.

- Children complete Workbook 3 page 13.
  Give instructions as appropriate.

LATER

- Revision of all consonant-vowel blends.
  Children complete Workbook 3 page 14.

FURTHER PRACTICE

DEVELOPING SKILLS

- **Flash Cards**

  pi, ti, hi, ru, su, bu, te, le, re, ro, to, go, ha, ba, ra.

  Suggested activities
  Distribute 3 to 5 Flash Cards (CV blends with the vowel *i*) to a group of children and ask them to arrange their cards face up before starting these activities:

  – **Show/give**
    The child who has the *ti* card shows or gives it to you. Repeat for other blends.

  – **Choose/say**
    Children in turn choose a card and tell you what it says.

  – **Choose/ask**
    One child chooses a card from the child next to him or her and asks what it says. The questioner must confirm whether or not the answer is correct.

Every opportunity should be taken to practise the consonant-vowel blends to gain speed and accuracy.

ASSESSMENT 3.3

ACTIVITIES AT HOME

- Homework Sheets 3H and 3I.

vowel – i

Consonant-vowel blends and final sounds

BEFORE YOU START

THE NLF AIMS

- Identify final sounds in spoken words.
- Read CVC words with emphasis on CV blend and final sound.

WHAT YOU NEED

RESOURCES

- The Alphabet Letter Cards
- Magnetic letters
- Flash Cards: *hat, had, ham, cat, can, cap*
- Chalkboard/whiteboard

KEY LESSON POINTERS

VOCABULARY

alphabet letter name sound word vowel join (blend) different beginning end/final sound

THE CHILDREN should throughout the lesson:

- identify the final sound in words
- distinguish between the blend and the final sound in CVC words.

YOU should throughout the lesson:

- ensure clear pronunciation of the final sound in words
- ensure blending of consonant and vowel at the beginning of words
- ensure attention to the change of final consonant in words.

THE LESSON

STARTING THE LESSON

- Tell the children that they have to listen carefully for the sound at the end of words.

TEACHING THE LESSON

- Ask the children to identify the sounds at the end of words.

  Suggested words:

bus	pot	bed	web	buzz
sun	bag	lip	puff	hum
fuss	fit	lid	rub	him
men	dog	cup	huff	fuzz

  (*Emphasise strongly the sound at the end of words. In everyday speech the end sound is often inaudible or even dropped.*)

- Write **ha** on the board.

  Ask the children to read what has been written.

  Confirm that it says **ha**.

  Tell the children that you want to make it into **hat**.

  Ask: "What sound goes at the end?"

  Confirm **t** and write **t** at the end.

  Read the word **ha_ t, hat**. (*Pause before final sound.*)

  Ask the children to read the word **ha_ t, hat**.

  Write **ha** on the board.

  Confirm that the children know it says **ha**.

  Tell the children that you want to make it into **ham**.

  Ask: "What sound goes at the end?"

  Confirm **m** and write **m** at the end.

  Read the word **ha_ m, ham**. (*Pause before final sound.*)

  Ask the children to read the word **ha_ m, ham**.

  Write **ha** on the board.

  Confirm that the children know it says **ha**.

  Tell the children that you want to make it into **had**.

  Ask: "What sound goes at the end?"

  Confirm **d** and write **d** at the end.

  Read the word **ha_ d, had**. (*Pause before final sound.*)

  Ask the children to read the word **ha_ d, had**.

Read *ha_ t, hat, ha_ m, ham, ha_ d, had.*
(*Emphasise the* **ha** *blend and then the consonant at the end in each word.*)

Ask: "What do you notice about the words *hat, ham, had*?"

Confirm that they all have **ha** at the beginning and a different sound at the end.

■ Write **ca** on the board.

Ask the children to read what has been written.

Confirm that it says **ca**.

Tell the children that you want to make it into **cat**.

Ask: "What sound goes at the end?"

Confirm *t* and write *t* at the end.

Read the word **ca_ t, cat**. (*Pause before final sound.*)

Ask the children to read the word **ca_ t, cat.**

Write **ca** on the board.

Confirm that it says **ca**.

Tell the children that you want to make it into **can**.

Ask: "What sound goes at the end?"

Confirm *n* and write *n* at the end.

Read the word **ca_ n, can**. (*Pause before final sound.*)

Ask the children to read the word **ca_ n, can.**

Write **ca** on the board.

Tell the children that you want to make it into **cap**.

Ask: "What sound goes at the end?"

Confirm *p* and write *p* at the end.

Read the word **ca_ p, cap**. (*Pause before final sound.*)

Ask the children to read the word **ca_ p, cap.**

Read **ca_ t, cat, ca_ n, can, ca_ p, cap**. (*Emphasise the* **ca** *blend and then the consonant at the end in each word.*)

Ask: "What do you notice about the words **cat, can, cap**?"

Confirm that they all have **ca** at the beginning and a different sound at the end.

■ Use Flash Cards: *hat, had, ham, cat, can, cap.*

FURTHER PRACTICE

DEVELOPING SKILLS

■ **Magnetic Letters**

Children make the words *hat, had, ham, cat, can, cap.*

■ **Flash Cards**

Every opportunity should be taken to practise CVC words taught.

■ *b, d, p* and *t* are easily confused. It is often difficult for children to differentiate the fine auditory discrimination between the four sounds. Give plenty of practice.

■ **What's my sound?**

You say a word and children say the sound at the end of the word: *b, d, p* or *t*.

Suggested words:

bid	rip	cup	sip	dip	pop
bib	rid	cub	sit	did	pod
bit	rib	cut			pot
hop	hip	lid	map	sad	web
hot	hit	lip	mad	sat	wed
hob	hid	lit	mat		wet

BLENDING AND SEGMENTING

CVC WORDS

ha_t, ca_p etc.

Consonant-vowel blends and final sounds

THE NLF AIMS

- Identify final sounds in spoken words.
- Read CVC words with emphasis on CV blend and final sound.
- Write the letters that represent the final sound in words.
- Write CVC words (with a model).

WHAT YOU NEED

RESOURCES

- The Alphabet Letter Cards
- Flash Cards: *hat, had, ham, cat, can, cap, mat, man, map, sad, sat, Sam*
- Magnetic letters
- Workbook 3 page 15
- Teacher's copy of Workbook 3 page 15
- Chalkboard/whiteboard

KEY LESSON POINTERS

VOCABULARY

alphabet letter name sound word vowel join (blend) end/final sound circle cross dotted line underneath

THE CHILDREN should throughout the lesson:

- identify the final sound in words
- distinguish between the blend and the final sound in CVC words.

YOU should throughout the lesson:

- ensure clear pronunciation of the final sound in words
- ensure blending of consonant and vowel at the beginning of words
- ensure attention to the change of final consonant in words.

STARTING THE LESSON

■ Ask the children to identify the sounds at the end of the words.

Suggested words:

bus	pot	bed	web	buzz
sun	bag	lip	puff	hum
fuss	fit	lid	rub	him
men	dog	cup	huff	fuzz

TEACHING THE LESSON

■ Write **hat** on the board. (*It may be helpful to draw a line under* **ha** *to act as a join for the blend.*)

Ask the children to read the word **hat**.

(*Help children to read words by emphasising the* **ha** *blend then* **t**.)

Repeat the above for **ham, had, cat, can, cap**.

■ Write **ma** on the board.

Ask the children to read what has been written.

Confirm that it says **ma**.

Tell the children that you want to make it into **map**.

Ask: "What sound goes at the end?"

Confirm **p** and write **p** at the end.

Read the word **ma_ p, map**. (*Pause before final sound.*)

Ask the children to read the word **ma_ p, map**.

Write **ma** on the board and repeat the procedure for **man** and **mat**.

■ Write **sa** on the board.

Ask the children to read what has been written.

Confirm that it says **sa**.

Tell the children that you want to make it into **sad**.

Ask: "What sound goes at the end?"

Confirm **d** and write **d** at the end.

Read the word **sa_ d, sad**.

Ask the children to read the word **sa_ d, sad**.

Write **sa** on the board and repeat the procedure for **sat** and **Sam**.

■ Use Flash Cards: **hat, had, ham, cat, can, cap, map, man, mat, sad, sat, Sam**.

LATER

■ This skill should be further practised with the following words as well as the words already used.

bad	Jan	pan	tan	ran
bag	jam	pat	tap	rat
bat	jab	pad	tag	rag

■ Show the children the teacher's copy of Workbook 3 page 15.

Ask the children to identify the first picture. (*fan*)

Ask: "What sound can be heard at the end of *fan*?"

Confirm *n*.

Ask a child to point to *n*.

Ask: "What is the other sound?"

Confirm *m*.

Confirm the procedure: put a circle around the correct sound *n* and a cross on the wrong sound *m*.

Ask a child to complete the procedure.

Ask: "What do you have to do next?"

Confirm: "Write the correct letter on the line at the end of the word."

Ask a child to complete the procedure.

Ask: "What do you have to do next?"

Confirm: "Write the whole word *fan* on the dotted line."

Ask a child to complete the procedure.

(*Ensure the correct letter formation when children are writing.*)

Ask: "What is the word you have written?"

Confirm *fan*.

Repeat the procedure with *cap*, *mat* and *bag* as appropriate.

(*It may only be necessary to talk about the missing final sounds, words or even the procedure before children complete page.*)

■ Children complete Workbook 3 page 15.

FURTHER PRACTICE

DEVELOPING SKILLS

■ **Magnetic Letters**

Children make CVC words with medial *a*.

■ **Flash Cards**

Suggested activities

Distribute 3 to 5 Flash Cards to a group of children and ask them to arrange their cards face up before starting these activities:

– **Show/give**

The child who has the word *cat* shows or gives it to you. Repeat for other words.

– **Choose/say**

Children in turn choose a card and tell you what it says.

– **Choose/ask**

One child chooses a card from the child next to him or her and asks what it says. The questioner must confirm whether or not the answer is correct.

Every opportunity should be taken to practise CVC words taught.

■ *b*, *d*, *p* and *t* are easily confused. It is often difficult for children to differentiate the fine auditory discrimination between the four sounds. Give plenty of practice.

■ **What's my sound?**

You say a word and children say the sound at the end of the word: *b*, *d*, *p* or *t*.

Suggested words:

bid	rip	cup	sip	dip	pop
bib	rid	cub	sit	did	pod
bit	rib	cut			pot

hop	hip	lid	map	sad	web
hot	hit	lip	mad	sat	wed
hob	hid	lit	mat		wet

ha_t, ca_p etc.

Consonant-vowel blends and final sounds

THE NLF AIMS

- Identify final sounds in spoken words
- Read CVC words with emphasis on CV blend and final sound.

WHAT YOU NEED

RESOURCES

- The Alphabet Letter Cards
- Flash Cards: *cot, cod, cop, pot, pop, pod*
- Magnetic letters
- Chalkboard/whiteboard

KEY LESSON POINTERS

VOCABULARY

alphabet letter name sound word vowel join (blend) different beginning end/final sound

THE CHILDREN should throughout the lesson:

- identify the final sound in words
- distinguish between the blend and the final sound in CVC words.

YOU should throughout the lesson:

- ensure clear pronunciation of the final sound in words
- ensure blending of consonant and vowel at the beginning of words
- ensure attention to the change of final consonant in words.

THE LESSON

STARTING THE LESSON

■ Ask the children to identify the sounds at the end of the words.

Suggested words:

kiss	hat	bad	tub	buzz
pin	mug	zip	cuff	mum
mess	get	red	job	Tom
run	wig	tap	muff	fuzz

(Emphasise carefully the sound at the end of words. In everyday speech the end sound is often inaudible or even dropped.)

TEACHING THE LESSON

■ Write *co* on the board.

Ask the children to read what has been written.

Confirm that it says *co*.

Tell the children that you want to make it into *cot*.

Ask: "What sound goes at the end?"

Confirm *t* and write *t* at the end.

Read the word *co_ t, cot*.

Ask the children to read the word *co_ t, cot*.

Write *co* on the board.

Confirm that the children know that it says *co*.

Tell the children that you want to make it into *cop*.

Ask: "What sound goes at the end?"

Confirm *p* and write *p* at the end.

Read the word *co_ p, cop*.

Ask the children to read the word *co_ p, cop*.

Write *co* on the board.

Confirm that the children know that it says *co*.

Tell the children that you want to make it into *cod*.

Ask: "What sound goes at the end?"

Confirm *d* and write *d* at the end.

Read the word *co_ d, cod*.

Ask the children to read the word *co_ d, cod*.

Read *co_ t, cot, co_ p, cop, o_ d, cod*. (*Emphasise the* **co** *blend and then the consonant at the end in each word.*)

Ask: "What do you notice about the words *cot, cop, cod*?"

Confirm that they all have *co* at the beginning and a different sound at the end.

- Write *po* on the board.

  Ask the children to read what has been written.

  Confirm that it says *po*.

  Tell the children that you want to make it into *pot*.

  Ask: "What sound goes at the end?"

  Confirm *t* and write *t* at the end.

  Read the word *po_ t, pot*.

  Ask the children to read the word *po_ t, pot*.

  Write *po* on the board.

  Confirm that the children know that it says *po*.

  Tell the children that you want to make it into *pop*.

  Ask: "What sound goes at the end?"

  Confirm *p* and write *p* at the end.

  Read the word *po_ p, pop*.

  Ask the children to read the word *po_ p, pop*.

  Write *po* on the board.

  Tell the children that you want to make it into *pod*.

  Ask: "What sound goes at the end?"

  Confirm *d* and write *d* at the end.

  Read the word *po_ d, pod*.

  Ask the children to read the word *po_ d, pod*.

  Read *po_ t, pot, po_ p, pop, po_ d, pod*. (*Emphasise the* po *blend and then the consonant at the end in each word*.)

  Ask: "What do you notice about the words *pot, pop, pod*?"

  Confirm that they all have *po* at the beginning and a different sound at the end.

- Use Flash Cards: *cop, cod, cot, pot, pop, pod*.

FURTHER PRACTICE

DEVELOPING SKILLS

- **Magnetic Letters**

  Children make the words *cob, cod, cot, pot, pop, pod*.

- **Flash Cards**

  Every opportunity should be taken to practise CVC words taught.

- *b, d, p* and *t* are easily confused. It is often difficult for children to differentiate the fine auditory discrimination between the four sounds. Give plenty of practice.

- **What's my sound?**

  You say a word and children say the sound at the end of the word: *b, d, p* or *t*.

  Suggested words:

bid	rip	cup	sip	dip	pop
bib	rid	cub	sit	did	pod
bit	rib	cut			pot
hop	hip	lid	map	sad	web
hot	hit	lip	mad	sat	wed
hob	hid	lit	mat		wet

co_t, po_d etc.

Consonant-vowel blends and final sounds

BEFORE YOU START

THE NLF AIMS

- Identify final sounds in spoken words.
- Read CVC words with emphasis on CV blend and final sound.
- Write the letters that represent the final sounds in words.
- Write CVC words (with a model).

WHAT YOU NEED

RESOURCES

- The Alphabet Letter Cards
- Flash Cards: *cop, cod, cot, pot, pop, pod, rob, rod, rot, mob, mop, Mog*
- Magnetic letters
- Workbook 3 page 16
- Teacher's copy of Workbook 3 page 16
- Chalkboard/whiteboard

KEY LESSON POINTERS

VOCABULARY

alphabet   letter   name   sound   word
vowel   join (blend)   end/final sound
circle   cross   dotted line   underneath

THE CHILDREN should throughout the lesson:

- identify the final sound in words
- distinguish between the blend and the final sound in CVC words.

YOU should throughout the lesson:

- ensure clear pronunciation of the final sound in words
- ensure blending of consonant and vowel at the beginning of words
- ensure attention to the change of final consonant in words.

THE LESSON

STARTING THE LESSON

■ Ask the children to identify the sounds at the end of the words.

Suggested words:

kiss	hat	bad	tub	buzz
pin	mug	zip	cuff	mum
mess	get	red	job	Tom
run	wig	tap	muff	fuzz

(*Emphasise carefully the sound at the end of words. In everyday speech the end sound is often inaudible or even dropped.*)

TEACHING THE LESSON

■ Write **cop** on the board. (*It may be helpful to draw a line under* <u>co</u> *to act as a join for the blend.*)

Ask the children to read the word **cop**. (*Help children to read words by emphasising the* **co** *blend then* **p**.)

Repeat the above for **cod, cot, pot, pop, pod**.

■ Write **ro** on the board.

Ask the children to read what has been written.

Confirm that it says **ro**.

Tell the children that you want to make it into **rob**.

Ask: "What sound goes at the end?"

Confirm **b** and write **b** at the end.

Read the word **ro_ b, rob**.

Ask the children to read the word **ro_ b, rob**.

Write **ro** on the board and repeat the procedure for **rod, rot**.

■ Write **mo** on the board.

Ask the children to read what has been written.

Confirm that it says **mo**.

Tell the children that you want to make it into **mop**.

Ask: "What sound goes at the end?"

Confirm **p** and write **p** at the end.

Read the word **mo_p, mop**.

Ask the children to read the word **mo_p, mop**.

Write **mo** on the board and repeat the procedure for **mob, Mog**.

■ Use Flash Cards: *cop, cod, cot, pot, pop, pod, rod, rob, rot, mob, mop, Mog*.

NOW OR LATER

■ This skill should be further practised with the following words as well as the words already used:

hop	log	Tom
hot	lot	top

■ Show the children the teacher's copy of Workbook 3 page 16.

Ask the children to identify the first picture. (*cot*)

Ask: "What sound can be heard at the end of *cot*?"

Confirm *t*.

Ask a child to point to *t*.

Ask: "What is the other sound?"

Confirm *p*.

Confirm the procedure: put a circle around the correct sound *t* and a cross on the wrong sound *p*.

Ask a child to complete the procedure.

Ask: "What do you have to do next?"

Confirm: "Write the correct letter on the line at the end of the word."

Ask a child to complete the procedure.

Ask: "What do you have to do next?"

Confirm: "Write the whole word *cot* on the dotted line."

Ask a child to complete the procedure.

(*Ensure the correct letter formation when children are writing.*)

Ask: "What is the word you have written?"

Confirm *cot*.

■ Repeat the procedure with *log*, *mop* and *fox* as appropriate.

(*It may only be necessary to talk about the missing final sounds, words or even the procedure before children complete page.*)

■ Children complete Workbook 3 page 16.

FURTHER PRACTICE

DEVELOPING SKILLS

■ **Magnetic Letters**

Children make CVC words with medial *o*.

■ **Flash Cards**

Suggested activities

Distribute 3 to 5 Flash Cards to a group of children and ask them to arrange their cards face up before starting these activities:

– **Show/give**

The child who has the word *rot* shows or gives it to you. Repeat for other words.

– **Choose/say**

Children in turn choose a card and tell you what it says.

– **Choose/ask**

One child chooses a card from the child next to him or her and asks what it says. The questioner must confirm whether or not the answer is correct.

Every opportunity should be taken to practise CVC words taught.

■ *b*, *d*, *p* and *t* are easily confused. It is often difficult for children to differentiate the fine auditory discrimination between the four sounds. Give plenty of practice.

■ **What's my sound?**

You say a word and children say the sound at the end of the word: *b*, *d*, *p* or *t*.

Suggested words:

bid	rip	cup	sip	dip	pop
bib	rid	cub	sit	did	pod
bit	rib	cut			pot

hop	hip	lid	map	sad	web
hot	hit	lip	mad	sat	wed
hob	hid	lit	mat		wet

ro_b, mo_p etc.

Consonant–vowel blends and final sounds

THE NLF AIMS

- Identify final sounds in spoken words.
- Read CVC words with emphasis on CV blend and final sound.

WHAT YOU NEED

RESOURCES

- The Alphabet Letter Cards
- Flash Cards: *had, hat, ham, cat, can, cap, cot, cod, cop, pot, pop, pod, rob, rod, rot, mob, mop, Mog, peg, pet, pen, bed, beg, Ben*
- Magnetic letters
- Chalkboard/whiteboard

KEY LESSON POINTERS

VOCABULARY

alphabet letter name sound word vowel join (blend) different beginning end/final sound

THE CHILDREN should throughout the lesson:

- identify the final sound in words
- distinguish between the blend and the final sound in CVC words.

YOU should throughout the lesson:

- ensure clear pronunciation of the final sound in words
- ensure blending of consonant and vowel at the beginning of words
- ensure attention to the change of vowel in words
- ensure attention to the change of final consonant in words.

STARTING THE LESSON

■ Flash Cards – practise CVC words with medial *a* or *o*.

Draw the children's attention to the fact that a change in the end sound/letter changes the word. Show *dog* and *dot* as examples. A change in the vowel also changes the word. Show *cat* and *cot* as examples.

TEACHING THE LESSON

■ Write *pe* on the board.

Ask the children to read what has been written.

Confirm *pe*.

Tell the children that you want to make it into *pet*.

Ask: "What sound goes at the end?"

Confirm *t* and write *t* at the end.

Read the word *pe_ t, pet*.

Ask the children to read the word *pe_ t, pet*.

Write *pe* on the board.

Confirm that the children know that it says *pe*.

Tell the children that you want to make it into *peg*.

Ask: "What sound goes at the end?"

Confirm *g* and write *g* at the end.

Read the word *pe_g, peg*.

Ask the children to read the word *pe_g, peg*.

Write *pe* on the board.

Confirm that the children know that it says *pe*.

Tell the children that you want to make it into *pen*.

Ask: "What sound goes at the end?"

Confirm *n* and write *n* at the end.

Read the word *pe_n, pen*.

Ask the children to read the word *pe_n, pen*.

Read *pe_ t, pet, pe_g, peg, pe_n, pen*. (*Emphasise the* **pe** *blend and then the consonant at the end in each word.*)

Ask: "What do you notice about the words *pet, peg, pen*?"

Confirm that they all have *pe* at the beginning and a different sound at the end.

■ Write **be** on the board.

Ask the children to read what has been written.

Confirm **be**.

Tell the children that you want to make it into **bed**.

Ask: "What sound goes at the end?"

Confirm **d** and write **d** at the end.

Read the word **be_d, bed**.

Ask the children to read the word **be_d, bed**.

Write **be** on the board.

Confirm that the children know that it says **be**.

Tell the children that you want to make it into **beg**.

Ask: "What sound goes at the end?"

Confirm **g** and write **g** at the end.

Read the word **be_g, beg**.

Ask the children to read the word **be_g, beg**.

Write **Be** on the board.

Tell the children that you want to make it into **Ben**.

Ask: "What sound goes at the end?"

Confirm **n** and write **n** at the end.

(*Remember when writing the word* **Ben** *to ask children about the first letter, eliciting it should be a capital because it is a proper name.*)

Read the word **Be_n, Ben**.

Ask the children to read the word **Be_n, Ben**.

Read **be_d, bed, be_g, beg, Be_n, Ben**. (*Emphasise the* **be** *blend and then the consonant at the end in each word.*)

Ask: "What do you notice about the words **bed, beg, Ben**?"

Confirm that they all have **be** at the beginning and a different sound at the end.

■ Use Flash Cards: **pet, peg, pen, bed, beg, Ben**.

FURTHER PRACTICE

DEVELOPING SKILLS

■ **Magnetic Letters**

Children make words *pet, peg, pen, bed, beg, Ben*.

■ **Flash Cards**

Every opportunity should be taken to practise CVC words taught.

■ *b, d, p* and *t* are easily confused. It is often difficult for children to differentiate the fine auditory discrimination between the four sounds. Give plenty of practice.

■ **What's my sound?**

You say a word and children say the sound at the end of the word: *b, d, p* or *t*.

Suggested words:

bid	rip	cup	sip	dip	pop
bib	rid	cub	sit	did	pod
bit	rib	cut			pot

hop	hip	lid	map	sad	web
hot	hit	lip	mad	sat	wed
hob	hid	lit	mat		wet

BLENDING AND SEGMENTING

CVC WORDS

pe_n, be_d etc.

Consonant-vowel blends and final sounds

BEFORE YOU START

THE NLF AIMS

- Identify final sounds in spoken words.
- Read CVC words with emphasis on CV blend and final sound.
- Write the letters that represent the final sounds in words.
- Write CVC words (with a model).

WHAT YOU NEED

RESOURCES

- The Alphabet Letter Cards
- Flash Cards: *pet, peg, pen, beg, bed, Ben, leg, led, let, web, wet, wed, men, met, Meg, hem, hen, Ted, ten*
- Magnetic letters
- Workbook 3 page 17
- Teacher's copy of Workbook 3 page 17
- Chalkboard/whiteboard

KEY LESSON POINTERS

VOCABULARY

alphabet   letter   name   sound   word
vowel   join (blend)   end/final sound
circle   cross   dotted line   underneath

THE CHILDREN should throughout the lesson:

- identify the final sound in words
- distinguish between the blend and the final sound in CVC words.

YOU should throughout the lesson:

- ensure clear pronunciation of the final sound in words
- ensure blending of consonant and vowel at the beginning of words
- ensure attention to the change of final consonant in words.

THE LESSON

STARTING THE LESSON

- Write *peg* on the board. (*It may be useful to draw a line under* **pe** *to act as a join for the blend.*)

  Ask the children to read the word *peg*. (*Help children to read words by emphasising* **pe** *blend and then the* **g**.)

  Repeat the above for *pen, pet, beg, bed, Ben*.

  Remember to ensure that the children's attention is drawn to the fact that a change in the final sound/letter changes the word. Show *peg, pen* and *pet* as examples.

TEACHING THE LESSON

- Write *le* on the board.

  Ask the children to read what has been written. Confirm *le*.

  Tell the children that you want to make it into *leg*.

  Ask: "What sound goes at the end?"

  Confirm *g* and write *g* at the end.

  Read the word *le_g, leg*.

  Ask the children to read the word *le_g, leg*.

  Write *le* on the board and repeat the procedure for *led, let*.

- Write *we* on the board.

  Ask the children to read what has been written. Confirm that it says *we*.

  Tell the children that you want to make it into *web*.

  Ask: "What sound goes at the end?"

  Confirm *b* and write *b* at the end.

  Read the word *we_b, web*.

  Ask the children to read the word *we_b, web*.

  Write *we* on the board and repeat the procedure for *wet, wed*.

- Use Flash Cards: *leg, led, let, web, wet, wed*.

NOW OR LATER

■ This skill should be further practised with the following words as well as the words already used:

men	hem	Ted
met	hen	ten
Meg		

■ Show the children the teacher's copy of Workbook 3 page 17.

Ask a child to identify the first picture. (*hut*)

Ask: "What sound can be heard at the end of *hut*?"

Confirm *t*.

Ask a child to point to *t*.

Ask: "What is the other sound?"

Confirm *d*.

Confirm the procedure: put a circle around the correct sound *t* and a cross on the wrong sound *d*.

Ask a child to complete the procedure.

Ask: "What do you have to do next?"

Confirm: "Write the correct letter on the line at the end of the word."

Ask a child to complete the procedure.

Ask: "What do you have to do next?"

Confirm: "Write the whole word *hut* on the dotted line."

Ask a child to complete the procedure.

(*Ensure letter formation is correct when children are writing.*)

Ask: "What is the word you have written?"

Confirm *hut*.

■ Repeat the procedure with *ten, rug, net* as appropriate.

(*It may only be necessary to talk about the missing final sounds, words or even the procedure before children complete page.*)

■ Children complete Workbook 3 page 17.

DEVELOPING SKILLS

■ **Magnetic Letters**

Children make CVC words with medial *e*.

■ **Flash Cards**

Suggested activities

Distribute 3 to 5 Flash Cards to a group of children and ask them to arrange their cards face up before starting these activities:

– **Show/give**

The child who has the word *bed* shows or gives it to you. Repeat for other words.

– **Choose/say**

Children in turn choose a card and tell you what it says.

– **Choose/ask**

One child chooses a card from the child next to him or her and asks what it says. The questioner must confirm whether or not the answer is correct.

Every opportunity should be taken to practise CVC words taught.

■ *b*, *d*, *p* and *t* are easily confused. It is often difficult for children to differentiate the fine auditory discrimination between the four sounds. Give plenty of practice.

■ **What's my sound?**

You say a word and children say the sound at the end of the word: *b*, *d*, *p* or *t*.

Suggested words:

bid	rip	cup	sip	dip	pop
bib	rid	cub	sit	did	pod
bit	rib	cut			pot

hop	hip	lid	map	sad	web
hot	hit	lip	mad	sat	wed
hob	hid	lit	mat		wet

le_g, we_b etc.

Consonant-vowel blends and final sounds

BEFORE YOU START

THE NLF AIMS

- Identify final sounds in spoken words.
- Read CVC words with emphasis on CV blend and final sound.

WHAT YOU NEED

RESOURCES

- The Alphabet Letter Cards
- Flash Cards: *had, hat, ham, cat, can, cap, cop, cod, cot, pot, pop, pod, rob, rod, rot, mob, mop, Mog, pet, peg, pen, beg, bed, Ben, hut, hum, hug, mud, mug, mum*
- Magnetic letters
- Chalkboard/whiteboard

KEY LESSON POINTERS

VOCABULARY

alphabet letter name sound word vowel join (blend) different beginning end/final sound

THE CHILDREN should throughout the lesson:

- identify the final sound in words
- distinguish between the blend and the final sound in CVC words.

YOU should throughout the lesson:

- ensure clear pronunciation of the final sound in words
- ensure blending of consonant and vowel at the beginning of words
- ensure attention to the change of vowel/final consonant in words.

THE LESSON

STARTING THE LESSON

- Flash Cards – practise CVC words with medial *a, e* or *o.*

  Draw the children's attention to the fact that a change in the end sound/letter changes the word. Show *pop* and *pod* as examples. A change in the vowel also changes the word. Show *log* and *leg* as examples.

TEACHING THE LESSON

- Write *hu* on the board.

  Ask the children to read what has been written.

  Confirm that it says *hu.*

  Tell the children that you want to make it into *hut.*

  Ask: "What sound goes at the end?"

  Confirm *t* and write *t* at the end.

  Read the word *hu_ t, hut.*

  Ask the children to read the word *hu_ t, hut.*

  Write *hu* on the board.

  Confirm that the children know that it says *hu.*

  Tell the children that you want to make it into *hum.*

  Ask: "What sound goes at the end?"

  Confirm *m* and write *m* at the end.

  Read the word *hu_m, hum.*

  Ask the children to read the word *hu_m, hum.*

  Write *hu* on the board.

  Confirm that the children know that it says *hu.*

  Tell the children that you want to make it into *hug.*

  Ask: "What sound goes at the end?"

  Confirm *g* and write *g* at the end.

  Read the word *hu_ g, hug.*

  Ask the children to read the word *hu_ g, hug.*

  Read *hu_ t, hut, hu_m, hum, hu_ g, hug.* (*Emphasise the* **hu** *blend and then the consonant at the end in each word.*)

  Ask: "What do you notice about the words *hut, hum, hug*?"

  Confirm that they all have *hu* at the beginning and a different sound at the end.

- Write *mu* on the board.

  Ask the children to read what has been written.

  Confirm that it says *mu*.

  Tell the children that you want to make it into *mud*.

  Ask: "What sound goes at the end?"

  Confirm *d* and write *d* at the end.

  Read the word *mu_d, mud*.

  Ask the children to read the word *mu_d, mud*.

  Write *mu* on the board.

  Confirm that the children know that it says *mu*.

  Tell the children that you want to make it into *mug*.

  Ask: "What sound goes at the end?"

  Confirm *g* and write *g* at the end.

  Read the word *mu_ g, mug*.

  Ask the children to read the word *mu_ g, mug*.

  Write *mu* on the board.

  Tell the children that you want to make it into *mum*.

  Ask: "What sound goes at the end?"

  Confirm *m* and write *m* at the end.

  Read the word *mu_m, mum*.

  Ask the children to read the word *mu_m, mum*.

  Read *mu_d, mud, mu_ g, mug, mu_m, mum*. (*Emphasise the* **mu** *blend and then the consonant at the end in each word.*)

  Ask: "What do you notice about the words *mud, mug, mum*?"

  Confirm that they all have *mu* at the beginning and a different sound at the end.

- Use Flash Cards: *hut, hum, hug, mud, mug, mum*.

FURTHER PRACTICE

DEVELOPING SKILLS

- **Magnetic Letters**

  Children make the words *hut, hum, hug, mud, mug, mum*.

- **Flash Cards**

  Every opportunity should be taken to practise CVC words taught.

- *b, d, p* and *t* are easily confused. It is often difficult for children to differentiate the fine auditory discrimination between the four sounds. Give plenty of practice.

- **What's my sound?**

  You say a word and children say the sound at the end of the word: *b, d, p* or *t*.

  Suggested words:

bid	rip	cup	sip	dip	pop
bib	rid	cub	sit	did	pod
bit	rib	cut			pot

hop	hip	lid	map	sad	web
hot	hit	lip	mad	sat	wed
hob	hid	lit	mat		wet

hu_t, mu_g etc.

Consonant-vowel blends and final sounds

BEFORE YOU START

THE NLF AIMS

- Identify final sounds in spoken words.
- Read CVC words with emphasis on CV blend and final sound.
- Write the letters that represent the final sounds in words.
- Write CVC words (with a model).

WHAT YOU NEED

RESOURCES

- The Alphabet Letter Cards
- Flash Cards: *hut, hum, hug, mud, mug, mum, rug, run, rub, bud, bug, bun, bus, but, cup, cub, cut, sum, sun, tub, tug, pup, pub*
- Magnetic letters
- Workbook 3 page 18
- Teacher's copy of Workbook 3 page 18
- Chalkboard/whiteboard

KEY LESSON POINTERS

VOCABULARY

alphabet letter name sound word
vowel join (blend) end/final sound
circle cross dotted line underneath

THE CHILDREN should throughout the lesson:

- identify the final sound in words
- distinguish between the blend and the final sound in CVC words.

YOU should throughout the lesson:

- ensure clear pronunciation of the final sound in words
- ensure blending of consonant and vowel at the beginning of words
- ensure attention to the change of final consonant in words.

THE LESSON

STARTING THE LESSON

- Write **hut** on the board. (*It may be helpful to draw a line under* **hu** *to act as a join for the blend.*)

  Ask the children to read the word **hut**. (*Help children to read words by emphasising the* **hu** *blend and then the* **t**.)

  Repeat the above for **hum, hug, mud, mug, mum**.

  Remember to ensure that the children's attention is drawn to the fact that a change in the final sound changes the word. Show **hut, hum** and **hug** as examples.

TEACHING THE LESSON

- Write **ru** on the board.

  Ask the children to read what has been written. Confirm **ru**.

  Tell the children that you want to make it into **rug**.

  Ask: "What sound goes at the end?"

  Confirm **g** and write **g** at the end.

  Read the word **ru_g, rug**.

  Ask the children to read the word **ru_g, rug**.

  Write **ru** on the board and repeat the procedure for **run, rub**.

- Write **bu** on the board.

  Ask the children to read what has been written. Confirm **bu**.

  Tell the children that you want to make it into **bug**.

  Ask: "What sound goes at the end?"

  Confirm **g** and write **g** at the end.

  Read the word **bu_g, bug**.

  Ask the children to read the word **bu_g, bug**.

  Write **bu** on the board and repeat the procedure for **bun, bus**.

- Use Flash Cards: **rug, run, rub, bud, bug, bun, but, bus**.

NOW OR LATER

■ This skill should be further practised with the following words as well as the words already used:

cup	sum	tub	pup
cub	sun	tug	pub
cut			

■ Show the children the teacher's copy of Workbook 3 page 18.

Ask the children to identify the first picture. (*web*)

Ask: "What sound can be heard at the end of *web*?"

Confirm *b*.

Ask a child to point to *b*.

Ask: "What is the other sound?"

Confirm *p*.

Confirm the procedure: put a circle around the correct sound *b* and a cross on the wrong sound *p*.

Ask a child to complete the procedure.

Ask: "What do you have to do next?"

Confirm: "Write the correct letter on the line at the end of the word."

Ask a child to complete the procedure.

Ask: "What do you have to do next?"

Confirm: "Write the whole word *web* on the dotted line."

Ask a child to complete the procedure.

(*Ensure the correct letter formation when children are writing.*)

Ask: "What is the word you have written?"

Confirm *web*.

■ Repeat the procedure with *bus, peg* and *sun* as appropriate. (*It may only be necessary to talk about the missing final sounds, words or even the procedure before children complete page.*)

■ Children complete Workbook 3 page 18.

DEVELOPING SKILLS

■ **Magnetic Letters**

Children make CVC words with medial *u*.

■ **Flash Cards**

Suggested activities

Distribute 3 to 5 Flash Cards to a group of children and ask them to arrange their cards face up before starting these activities:

– **Show/give**

The child who has the word *rug* shows or gives it to you. Repeat for other words.

– **Choose/say**

Children in turn choose a card and tell you what it says.

– **Choose/ask**

One child chooses a card from the child next to him or her and asks what it says. The questioner must confirm whether or not the answer is correct.

Every opportunity should be taken to practise CVC words taught.

■ *b, d, p* and *t* are easily confused. It is often difficult for children to differentiate the fine auditory discrimination between the four sounds. Give plenty of practice.

■ **What's my sound?**

You say a word and children say the sound at the end of the word: *b, d, p* or *t*.

Suggested words:

bid	rip	cup	sip	dip	pop
bib	rid	cub	sit	did	pod
bit	rib	cut			pot

hop	hip	lid	map	sad	web
hot	hit	lip	mad	sat	wed
hob	hid	lit	mat		wet

BLENDING AND SEGMENTING

CVC WORDS

ru_g, bu_g etc.

Consonant-vowel blends and final sounds

BEFORE YOU START

THE NLF AIMS

- Identify final sounds in spoken words.
- Read CVC words with emphasis on CV blend and final sound.

WHAT YOU NEED

RESOURCES

- The Alphabet Letter Cards
- Flash Cards: *had, hat, ham, cat, can, cap, cop, cod, cot, pot, pop, pod, rob, rod, rot, mob, mop, Mog, pet, peg, pen, beg, bed, Ben, hut, hum, hug, mum, mug, mud, dig, did, dip, him, hid, hit*
- Magnetic letters
- Chalkboard/whiteboard

KEY LESSON POINTERS

VOCABULARY

alphabet letter name sound word vowel join (blend) different beginning end/final sound

THE CHILDREN should throughout the lesson:

- identify the final sound in words
- distinguish between the blend and the final sound in CVC words.

YOU should throughout the lesson:

- ensure clear pronunciation of the final sound in words
- ensure blending of consonant and vowel at the beginning of words
- ensure attention to the change of vowel/final consonant in words.

THE LESSON

STARTING THE LESSON

- Flash Cards – practise CVC words with medial *a, o, e* or *u*.

  Always draw the children's attention to the fact that a change in the final sound changes the word. Show *cup, cub* and *cut* as examples. A change in the vowel also changes the word. Show *log* and *leg* as examples.

TEACHING THE LESSON

- Write *di* on the board.

  Ask the children to read what has been written.

  Confirm that it says *di*.

  Tell the children that you want to make it into *dig*.

  Ask: "What sound goes at the end?"

  Confirm *g* and write *g* at the end.

  Read the word *di_ g, dig*.

  Ask the children to read the word *di_ g, dig*.

  Write *di* on the board.

  Confirm that the children know that it says *di*.

  Tell the children that you want to make it into *did*.

  Ask: "What sound goes at the end?"

  Confirm *d* and write *d* at the end.

  Read the word *di_ d, did*.

  Ask the children to read the word *di_ d, did*.

  Write *di* on the board.

  Confirm that the children know that it says *di*.

  Tell the children that you want to make it into *dip*.

  Ask: "What sound goes at the end?"

  Confirm *p* and write *p* at the end.

  Read the word *di_ p, dip*.

  Ask the children to read the word *di_ p, dip*.

  Read *di_ g, dig, di_ d, did, di_ p, dip*. (*Emphasise the* **di** *blend and then the consonant at the end in each word.*)

  Ask: "What do you notice about the words *dig, did, dip*?"

  Confirm that they all have *di* at the beginning and a different sound at the end.

- Write **hi** on the board.

  Ask the children to read what has been written.

  Confirm that it says **hi**.

  Tell the children that you want to make it into **him**.

  Ask: "What sound goes at the end?"

  Confirm **m** and write **m** at the end.

  Read the word **hi_ m, him**.

  Ask the children to read the word **hi_ m, him**.

  Write **hi** on the board.

  Confirm that the children know that it says **hi**.

  Tell the children that you want to make it into **hid**.

  Ask: "What sound goes at the end?"

  Confirm **d** and write **d** at the end.

  Read the word **hi_ d, hid**.

  Ask the children to read the word **hi_ d, hid**.

  Write **hi** on the board.

  Tell the children that you want to make it into **hit**.

  Ask: "What sound goes at the end?"

  Confirm **t** and write **t** at the end.

  Read the word **hi_ t, hit**.

  Ask the children to read the word **hi_ t, hit**.

  Read **hi_ m, him, hi_ d, hid, hi_ t, hit**. (*Emphasise the **hi** blend and then the consonant at the end in each word.*)

  Ask: "What do you notice about the words **him, hid, hit**?"

  Confirm that they all have **hi** at the beginning and a different sound at the end.

- Use Flash Cards: ***dig, did, dip, him, hid, hit***.

FURTHER PRACTICE

DEVELOPING SKILLS

- **Magnetic Letters**

  Children make the words *dig, did, dip, him, hid, hit*.

- **Flash Cards**

  Every opportunity should be taken to practise CVC words taught.

- *b, d, p* and *t* are easily confused. It is often difficult for children to differentiate the fine auditory discrimination between the four sounds. Give plenty of practice.

- **What's my sound?**

  You say a word and children say the sound at the end of the word: *b, d, p* or *t*.

  Suggested words:

bid	rip	cup	sip	dip	pop
bib	rid	cub	sit	did	pod
bit	rib	cut			pot

hop	hip	lid	map	sad	web
hot	hit	lip	mad	sat	wed
hob	hid	lit	mat		wet

BLENDING AND SEGMENTING

CVC WORDS

di_g, hi_m etc.

Consonant-vowel blends and final sounds

BEFORE YOU START

THE NLF AIMS

- Identify final sounds in spoken words.
- Read CVC words with emphasis on CV blend and final sound.
- Write the letters that represent the final sound in words.
- Write CVC words (with a model).

WHAT YOU NEED

RESOURCES

- The Alphabet Letter Cards
- Flash Cards: *dig, did, dip, him, hid, hit, lid, lip, lit, bin, big, bit, fig, fit, fin, dig, din, dip, pig, pin, pip, rib, rim, rip, tig, tin, tip, wig, win*
- Magnetic letters
- Workbook 3 page 19
- Teacher's copy of Workbook 3 page 19
- Chalkboard/whiteboard

KEY LESSON POINTERS

VOCABULARY

alphabet   letter   name   sound   word
vowel   join (blend)   end/final sound
circle   cross   dotted line   underneath

THE CHILDREN should throughout the lesson:

- identify the final sound in words
- distinguish between the blend and the final sound in CVC words.

YOU should throughout the lesson:

- ensure clear pronunciation of the final sound in words
- ensure blending of consonant and vowel at the beginning of words
- ensure attention to the change of final consonant in words.

THE LESSON

STARTING THE LESSON

- Write **hit** on the board. (*It may be helpful to draw a line under* <u>hi</u> *to act as a join for the blend.*)

  Ask the children to read the word **hit**. (*Help children to read words by emphasising the* **hi** *blend and then the* **t***.*)

  Repeat the above for **hid, him, dig, did, dip**.

  Remember to ensure that the children's attention is drawn to the fact that a change in the final sound changes the word. Show **fig, fin** and **fit** as examples. The final sound is different.

TEACHING THE LESSON

- Write **li** on the board.

  Ask the children to read what has been written.

  Confirm that it says **li**.

  Tell the children that you want to make it into **lid**.

  Ask: "What sound goes at the end?"

  Confirm **d** and write **d** at the end.

  Read the word **li_ d, lid**.

  Ask the children to read the word **li_ d, lid**.

  Write **li** on the board and repeat the procedure for **lip, lit**.

- Write **bi** on the board.

  Ask the children to read what has been written.

  Confirm that it says **bi**.

  Tell the children that you want to make it into **bin**.

  Ask: "What sound goes at the end?"

  Confirm **n** and write **n** at the end.

  Read the word **bi_n, bin**.

  Ask the children to read the word **bi_n, bin**.

  Write **bi** on the board and repeat the procedure for **big, bib, bit**.

- Use Flash Cards: **lid, lip, lit, bin, big, bib, bit**.

NOW OR LATER

■ This skill should be further practised with the following words as well as the words already used:

fig	dig	pig	rib	tin	wig
fin	din	pin	rim	tip	win
fit	dip	pip	rip		

■ Show the children the teacher's copy of Workbook 3 page 19.

Ask the children to identify the first picture. (*bib*)

Ask: "What sound can be heard at the end of *bib*?"

Confirm *b*.

Ask a child to point to *b*.

Ask: "What is the other sound?"

Confirm *d*.

Confirm the procedure, i.e. put a circle around the correct sound *b* and a cross on the wrong sound *d*.

Ask a child to complete the procedure.

Ask: "What do you have to do next?"

Confirm: "Write the correct letter on the line at the end of the word."

Ask a child to complete the procedure.

Ask: "What do you have to do next?"

Confirm: "Write the whole word *bib* on the dotted line."

Ask a child to complete the procedure.

(*Ensure the correct letter formation when children are writing.*)

Ask: "What is the word you have written?"

Confirm *bib*.

■ Repeat the procedure with *lid, six* and *pin* as appropriate. (*It may only be necessary to talk about the missing final sounds, words or even the procedure before children complete page.*)

■ Children complete Workbook 3 page 19.

FURTHER PRACTICE

DEVELOPING SKILLS

■ **Magnetic Letters**
Children make CVC words with medial *i*.

■ **Flash Cards**
Suggested activities
Distribute 3 to 5 Flash Cards to a group of children and ask them to arrange their cards face up before starting these activities:

– **Show/give**
The child who has the word *fit* shows or gives it to you. Repeat for other words.

– **Choose/say**
Children in turn choose a card and tell you what it says.

– **Choose/ask**
One child chooses a card from the child next to him or her and asks what it says. The questioner must confirm whether or not the answer is correct.

Every opportunity should be taken to practise CVC words taught.

■ *b, d, p* and *t* are easily confused. It is often difficult for children to differentiate the fine auditory discrimination between the four sounds. Give plenty of practice.

■ **What's my sound?**
You say a word and children say the sound at the end of the word: *b, d, p* or *t*.

Suggested words:

bid	rip	cup	sip	dip	pop
bib	rid	cub	sit	did	pod
bit	rib	cut			pot

hop	hip	lid	map	sad	web
hot	hit	lip	mad	sat	wed
hob	hid	lit	mat		wet

li_d, bi_n etc.

Medial vowels in cvc words

BEFORE YOU START

THE NLF AIMS

- Identify the medial vowel in spoken words.
- Understand that changing the medial vowel changes the word.
- Read CVC words.

WHAT YOU NEED

RESOURCES

- Vowel Detectives
- Chalkboard/whiteboard
- Magnetic letters/Letter Cards
- Flash Cards

KEY LESSON POINTERS

VOCABULARY

alphabet   letter   name   sound   word
vowel   join (blend)   first/beginning
middle   last/final

THE CHILDREN should throughout the lesson:

- distinguish between the letter sound and the letter name
- focus on the medial vowel
- focus on blending the sounds not sounding each letter.

YOU should throughout the lesson:

- emphasise the difference between the letter sound and the letter name
- ensure focus on medial vowel
- ensure blending of sounds.

THE LESSON

STARTING THE LESSON

- Ask: "What are the five vowels?"

  Confirm **a, e, i, o, u.** (*Remind children of* "**angry elephants in orange underwear**" *and give practice to ensure they know the vowels.*)

TEACHING THE LESSON

- Tell the children that they must listen carefully to the sound in the middle of the words.

  Ask the children what sound is in the middle of a number of words such as *cat, dog, tin, peg, bus, red, bat, sun, lot, lid, bag, wig, ten, rub.*

- Say the word *sat*.

  Ask: "What sound is in the middle?"

  Confirm *a*.

  Tell the children that you want to write *sat*.

  Ask: "What letter comes first?"

  Confirm *s*, and write it on the board.

  Ask: "What sound is in the middle?"

  Confirm *a*, and write it on the board.

  Ask: "What sound is at the end?"

  Confirm *t*, and write it on the board.

  Ask the children to read the word *sat*.

  Tell the children that you want to change the word to *set*.

  Ask: "What do I have to do?"

  Confirm: "Change the sound in the middle. Change *a* to *e*."

Write *set* on the board.

Ask the children to read the word *set*.

Tell the children that you want to change the word to *sit*.

Ask: "What do I have to do?"

Confirm: "Change the *e* to *i*."

Write *sit* on the board, asking the children to tell you the letters to write.

Ask the children to read the word *sit*.

Ask the children to read the words *sat, set, sit*.

Repeat the procedure with the following words:

bit, but, bet   cap, cop, cup

top, tap, tip   pin, pen, pan

Ask: "How many letters are in each word?"

Confirm three.

Ask: "What does the middle letter always have to be?"

Confirm a vowel.

(*Draw children's attention to the fact that a change in vowel changes the word.*)

Ask: "What are the vowels?"

Confirm *a, e, i, o, u.*

FURTHER PRACTICE

DEVELOPING SKILLS

■ **Magnetic Letters/Letter Cards**

Children make CVC words.

■ **Vowel Detectives**

Depending on their progress, children have three, six or nine words on their table, such as:

top	cap	tin
tap	cop	ten
tip	cup	tan

Ask the children to point to the word that says *tip*, *cop*, *ten* and so on.

■ **Flash Cards**

Every opportunity should be taken to practise CVC words taught.

medial vowels

201

Medial vowels in cvc words

BEFORE YOU START

THE NLF AIMS

- Identify the medial vowel in spoken words.
- Understand that changing the medial vowel changes the word.
- Read CVC words.
- Write CVC words.

WHAT YOU NEED

RESOURCES

- Workbook 3, pages 20 and 21
- Teacher's copy of Workbook 3, pages 20 and 21
- Vowel Detectives
- Chalkboard/whiteboard
- Magnetic letters/Letter Cards
- Flash Cards

KEY LESSON POINTERS

VOCABULARY

alphabet   letter   name   sound   word
vowel   join (blend)   first/beginning
middle   last/final

THE CHILDREN should throughout the lesson:

- distinguish between the letter sound and the letter name
- focus on the medial vowel
- focus on blending the sounds not sounding each letter.

YOU should throughout the lesson:

- emphasise the difference between the letter sound and the letter name
- ensure focus on medial vowel
- ensure blending of sounds.

THE LESSON

STARTING THE LESSON

- Ask: "What are the five vowels?"

  Confirm *a, e, i, o, u.* (*Remind children of* "**angry elephants in orange underwear**" *and give practice to ensure they know the vowels.*)

TEACHING THE LESSON

- Tell the children that they must listen carefully to the sound in the middle of the words.

  Ask the children what sound is in the middle of a number of words such as *cap, mop, fix, red, mug, rug, bin, man, rod, men, sad, wig, dot, jet, bun.*

- Say the word *fun.*

  Ask: "What sound is in the middle?"

  Confirm *u.*

  Tell the children that you want to write *fun.*

  Ask: "What letter comes first?"

  Confirm *f,* and write it on the board.

  Ask: "What sound is in the middle?"

  Confirm *u,* and write it on the board.

  Ask: "What sound is at the end?"

  Confirm *n* and write it on the board.

  Ask the children to read the word *fun.*

  Tell the children that you want to change the word to *fin.*

  Ask: "What do I have to do?"

  Confirm: "Change the sound in the middle. Change *u* to *i.*"

  Ask a child to write *fin* on the board.

  Ask the children to read the word *fin.*

Tell the children that you want to change the word to *fan*.

Ask: "What do I have to do?"

Confirm: "Change the sound in the middle. Change *i* to *a*."

Ask a child to write *fan* on the board.

Ask the children to read the word *fan*.

Ask the children to read the words *fun, fin, fan*.

Repeat the procedure with the following words:

jig, jug, jog   tag, tug
rib, rub, rob   pen, pin, pan

■ Further words to use now or later:

rid, red, rod   hat, hot, hit
hem, ham, him   lid, lad, led
not, net, nut

■ Show the teacher's copy of Workbook 3 page 20.

Ask a child what the first picture is. (*cat*)

Ask the children to read the words *cat, cot, cut*.

Ask: "Which word goes with the picture?"

Tell the children that they have to put a circle around the word that is correct. (*cat*)

Ask a child to complete the procedure.

Tell the children that they have to write the word *cat* on the dotted line.

Ask a child to write the word.

■ Children complete Workbook 2 page 20.

LATER

■ Review Lessons 36 and 37 as appropriate and children complete Workbook 3 page 21.

FURTHER PRACTICE

DEVELOPING SKILLS

■ **Magnetic Letters/Letter Cards**

Children make CVC words.

■ **Vowel Detectives**

Depending on their progress, children have three, six or nine words on their table, such as:

top	cap	tin
tap	cop	ten
tip	cup	tan

Ask them to point to the word that says *tip*, *cop*, *ten* and so on.

■ **Flash Cards**

Every opportunity should be taken to practise CVC words taught.

medial vowels

Rhyming

THE NLF AIMS

- Recognise when words rhyme.
- Identify words that rhyme.

WHAT YOU NEED

RESOURCES

- *Hector Hedgehog's Big Book of Rhymes* (Alphabet) page 15
- Rhyme Picture Cards
- Workbook 3 pages 22 and 23
- Teacher's copy of Workbook 3 pages 22 and 23

KEY LESSON POINTERS

VOCABULARY

end   rhyme   rhyming   same/different word

THE CHILDREN should throughout the lesson:

- listen for the rhyme at the end of words.

YOU should throughout the lesson:

- ensure emphasis on the rhyme at the end of words.

THE LESSON

STARTING THE LESSON

- Revisit *Hector Hedgehog's Big Book of Rhymes (Alphabet)* and read page 15, emphasising the rhyming words.

  Ask the children to tell you any words that rhyme in the poem.

  Confirm *mouse* and *house*, *too* and *stew*, *mice* and *nice*.

TEACHING THE LESSON

- Tell the children to think about words that rhyme.

  Ask: "What does rhyme mean?"

  Confirm that words that sound the same at the end are said to rhyme.

- Tell the children that you are going to say three words and two of them rhyme.

  Ask: "Which two words sound the same at the end?"

  Suggested words:

flag	bag	box
three	flower	bee
goat	clock	sock
big	dig	path
fire	tyre	book
jug	book	cook
meat	seat	bench
car	house	jar
house	mouse	rat
go	tent	went
candle	handle	light

  (*Repeat the correct rhyme when children answer.*)

- Show the teacher's copy of Workbook 3 page 22.

  Ask the children to identify all eight pictures.

  Ask: "What is the first picture?"

  Confirm *men*.

  Ask: "Which large picture rhymes with *men*: *hen* or *mug*?"

  Confirm *hen* rhymes with *men*.

Demonstrate matching the small picture (*men*) to the large picture (*hen*).

Ask: "What is the second picture?"

Confirm *jug*.

Ask: "Which large picture rhymes with *jug*: *hen* or *mug*?"

Confirm *mug* rhymes with *jug*.

Ask a child to match the small picture(*jug*) to the appropriate large picture.

■ Ask a child to choose a small picture and match it to the correct large picture by drawing a line between them.

Ask the child to say the two rhyming words that they have chosen.

Repeat the procedure for the other small pictures.

■ Children complete Workbook 3 page 22. (*Remember to remove teacher's copy before children complete page.*)

NOW OR LATER

■ Repeat the above lesson before children complete Workbook 3 page 23.

Suggested words:

shop	hop	run
ring	fast	sing
tent	go	went
help	big	wig
ball	hat	bat
jug	mug	water
carry	walk	marry
rest	best	sing
show	slow	fast

FURTHER PRACTICE

DEVELOPING SKILLS

Some or all of these activities must be done to ensure progress:

■ **Rhyme Picture Cards**

Children sort a selection of Picture Cards into sets according to rhyme.

■ Commercial rhyming games could be used if available.

NOTE

Rhymes and rimes are not identical. Rhymes have word endings which sound the same but are not necessarily spelled in the same way, such as *socks* and *fox*. Rimes are word endings which always retain the same spelling pattern, such as *box* and *fox*.

BLENDING AND SEGMENTING

RHYMING CVC WORDS

rhyming

Rhyming

THE NLF AIMS

- Recognise when words rhyme.
- Identify words that rhyme.
- Read CVC words that rhyme.
- Write CVC words that rhyme.

WHAT YOU NEED

RESOURCES

- *Hector Hedgehog's Big Book of Rhymes (Alphabet)* page 5
- Flash Cards – rhyming words with medial *a*
- Workbook 3 page 24
- Teacher's copy of Workbook 3 page 24
- Rhyme Picture Cards

KEY LESSON POINTERS

VOCABULARY

below/underneath   end   rhyme   rhyming
same   word

THE CHILDREN should throughout the lesson:

- listen for the rhyme at the end of words.

YOU should throughout the lesson:

- ensure emphasis on the rhyme at the end of words.

THE LESSON

STARTING THE LESSON

- Revisit *Hector Hedgehog's Big Book of Rhymes (Alphabet)* page 5.

  Read the rhyme and put emphasis on the rhyming words.

  Ask the children to tell you any words that rhyme in the poem: *dinner* and *thinner*, *be* and *tea*.

- Tell the children that you are going to say three words and they have to tell you which two of the words rhyme.

  Suggested words:

bus	fuss	train
go	stop	slow
water	fish	wish
bag	rag	duster
pain	train	bus
cool	thread	pool
bee	tea	ant
fox	lid	box

  (*Repeat the correct rhyme when children answer.*)

TEACHING THE LESSON

- Tell the children that you are going to say a word and they have to think of a word that rhymes with it.

  Say *hat*.

  Ask the children for words that rhyme with *hat*. Possible rhymes: *cat, fat, rat, pat, mat, bat, sat, chat, flat*.

  If the children have difficulty suggesting words that rhyme, give a clue: "A word that rhymes with *hat* and starts with *s*."

  Say *tag*.

  Ask the children for words that rhyme with *tag*. Possible rhymes: *bag, rag, sag, tag, wag, flag*.

  Say *tan*.

  Ask the children for words that rhyme with *tan*. Possible rhymes: *ban, can, fan, man, pan, ran, van, flan, gran, plan*.

  Say *map*.

  Ask the children for words that rhyme with *map*. Possible rhymes: *gap, lap, tap, wrap, flap, snap*.

- Write *cat* on the board.

  Ask the children to read *cat*.

  Ask: "What word rhymes with *cat*?"

Ask a child to write the chosen word, *mat*, for example.

Ask the children to write the words in a list to show the rhyming pattern.

Say the words *cat*, *mat*.

Ask: "What other word rhymes with *cat* and *mat*?"

Ask a child to write the chosen word, *bat*, for example.

Say the words *cat*, *mat*, *bat*.

■ Repeat the procedure for other rhyming words: *fat*, *rat*, *pat*, *sat*.

■ Repeat the procedure for the *-an*, *-ag* and *-ap* rimes.

NOW OR LATER

■ Repeat the above activities.

■ Show the teacher's copy of Workbook 3 page 24.

Discuss the picture.

Point to the first rime *-at*.

Ask the children to read the rime.

Confirm *-at*.

Ask: "What is the first word?"

Confirm *cat*.

Tell the children to look in the picture for something that rhymes with *cat*.

Confirm *hat*.

Ask a child to write *hat* on the first dotted line underneath *cat*.

Confirm that *hat* rhymes with *cat* and can go with the *-at* rime.

■ Repeat the procedure for the *-an*, *-ag* and *-ap* rimes.

EXTENSION

■ Say: "Think of another word that rhymes with *cat* and *hat*."

Ask the children to put the chosen word into a rap. For example, "*Cat* and *hat*, they rhyme with *sat*."

Ask a child to write the chosen word (*sat*) on the second line below *cat* and *hat*.

■ Repeat for *pan* and *fan*, *rag* and *bag*, *lap* and *tap*.

■ Children complete Workbook 3 page 24.
(*Remember to remove teacher's copy before children complete page.*)

FURTHER PRACTICE

DEVELOPING SKILLS

Some or all of these activities must be done to ensure progress:

■ **Rhyme Picture Cards**

Children sort a selection of Picture Cards into sets according to rhyme.

■ Commercial rhyming games could be used if available.

■ **Flash Cards**

Rhyming words with medial *a*.

BLENDING AND SEGMENTING

RHYMING CVC WORDS

rhyming

Rhyming

BEFORE YOU START

THE NLF AIMS

- Recognise when words rhyme.
- Identify words that rhyme.
- Read CVC words that rhyme.
- Write CVC words that rhyme.

WHAT YOU NEED

RESOURCES

- *Hector Hedgehog's Big Book of Rhymes (Alphabet)* page 9
- Flash Cards – rhyming: CVC words with medial *o*
- Workbook 3 page 25
- Teacher's copy of Workbook 3 page 25
- Rhyme Picture Cards

KEY LESSON POINTERS

VOCABULARY

below/underneath   end   rhyme   rhyming
same/different   word

THE CHILDREN should throughout the lesson:

- listen for the rhyme at the end of words.

YOU should throughout the lesson:

- ensure emphasis on the rhyme at the end of words.

THE LESSON

STARTING THE LESSON

- Revisit *Hector Hedgehog's Big Book of Rhymes (Alphabet)* and read page 9.

  Read the rhyme and put emphasis on the rhyming words.

  Ask the children to tell you any words that rhyme in the poem: *gate* and *plate*, *hear* and *ear*.

- Tell the children that you are going to say three words and they have to tell you which two of the words rhyme.

  Suggested words:

rust	must	walk
run	name	came
goal	foal	field
cake	apple	bake
brown	town	blue
flat	sound	round
bow	toe	foot
hand	water	sand

  (*Repeat the correct rhyme when children answer.*)

TEACHING THE LESSON

- Tell the children that you are going to say a word and they have to think of a word that rhymes with it.

  Say *lot*.

  Ask the children for words that rhyme with *lot*. Possible rhymes: *dot, hot, jot, got, not, pot, rot, tot, trot, blot, slot, spot*.

  If the children have difficulty suggesting words that rhyme, give a clue: a word that rhymes with *lot* and it starts with *p*.

  Say *nod*.

  Ask the children for words that rhyme with *nod*. Possible rhymes: *cod, pod, rod, trod, plod*.

  Say *fog*.

  Ask the children for words that rhyme with *fog*. Possible rhymes: *dog, jog, log, frog, clog*.

  Say *hop*.

  Ask the children for words that rhyme with *hop*. Possible rhymes: *mop, pop, top, flop, drop, prop*.

- Write *cot* on the board.

  Ask the children to read *cot*.

  Ask: "What word rhymes with *cot*?"

  Ask a child to write the chosen word, *dot*, for example.

Ask the children to write the words in a list to show the rhyming pattern.

Say the words *cot, dot*.

Ask: "What other word rhymes with *cot* and *dot*?"

Ask a child to write the chosen word, *got*, for example.

Say the words *cot, dot, got*.

Repeat procedure for other rhyming words: *jot, lot, not, pot, rot, shot*.

■ Repeat the procedure for the *-od*, *-og* and *-op* rimes.

NOW OR LATER

■ Repeat the above activities.

■ Show the teacher's copy of Workbook 3 page 25.

Discuss the picture. (*Children may notice that some objects in the picture seem out of place*.)

Point to the first rime *-ot*.

Ask the children to read the rime.

Confirm *-ot*.

Ask: "What is the first word?"

Confirm *got*.

Tell the children to look in the picture for something that rhymes with *got*.

Confirm *pot*.

Ask a child to write *pot* on the first dotted line underneath *got*.

Confirm that *pot* rhymes with *got* and can go with the *-ot* rime.

■ Repeat the procedure for the *-od*, *-og* and *-op* rimes.

EXTENSION

■ Say: "Think of another word that rhymes with *got* and *pot*."

Ask the children to put the chosen word into a rap. For example, "*Got* and *pot*, they rhyme with *dot*."

Ask a child to write the chosen word (*dot*) on the second dotted line below *got* and *pot*.

■ Repeat for *pod* and *rod, jog* and *dog, pop* and *mop*.

■ Children complete Workbook 3 page 25. (*Remember to remove teacher's copy before children complete page*.)

DEVELOPING SKILLS

Some or all of these activities must be done to ensure progress:

■ **Rhyme Picture Cards**

Children sort a selection of Picture Cards into sets according to rhyme.

■ Commercial rhyming games could be used if available.

■ **Flash Cards**

Rhyming words with medial *o*.

rhyming

Rhyming

THE NLF AIMS

- Recognise when words rhyme.
- Identify words that rhyme.
- Read CVC words that rhyme.
- Write CVC words that rhyme.

WHAT YOU NEED

RESOURCES

- *Hector Hedgehog's Big Book of Rhymes (Alphabet)* page 8
- Flash Cards – rhyming: CVC words with medial *u*
- Workbook 3 page 26
- Teacher's copy of Workbook 3 page 26
- Rhyme Picture Cards

KEY LESSON POINTERS

VOCABULARY

below/underneath end rhyme rhyming same/different word

THE CHILDREN should throughout the lesson:

- listen for the rhyme at the end of words.

YOU should throughout the lesson:

- ensure emphasis on the rhyme at the end of words.

THE LESSON

STARTING THE LESSON

- Revisit *Hector Hedgehog's Big Book of Rhymes (Alphabet)* and read page 8.

  Read the rhyme and put emphasis on the rhyming words.

  Ask the children to tell you any words that rhyme in the poem: *fish* and *dish*, *fins* and *tins*.

- Tell the children that you are going to say three words and they have to tell you which two of the words rhyme.

  Suggested words:

out	shout	sing
candle	door	handle
book	cook	paper
snow	brain	rain
pot	got	run
went	sent	give
big	fry	cry
bone	wish	fish

  (*Repeat the correct rhyme when children answer.*)

TEACHING THE LESSON

- Tell the children that you are going to say a word and they have to think of a word that rhymes with it.

  Say *fun*.

  Ask the children for words that rhyme with *fun*. Possible rhymes: *nun, bun, run, sun*.

  If the children have difficulty suggesting words that rhyme, give a clue: a word that rhymes with *fun* and it starts with *r*.

  Say *bug*.

  Ask the children for words that rhyme with *bug*. Possible rhymes: *dug, hug, jug, mug, rug, tug, slug, plug*.

  Say *cut*.

  Ask the children for words that rhyme with *cut*. Possible rhymes: *but, hut, nut, shut*.

  Say *tub*.

  Ask the children for words that rhyme with *tub*. Possible rhymes: *cub, hub, pub, rub, club, grub*.

- Write *bun* on the board.

  Ask the children to read *bun*.

  Ask: "What word rhymes with *bun*?"

  Ask a child to write the chosen word, *fun*, for example.

Ask the children to write the words in a list to show the rhyming pattern.

Say the words *bun, fun.*

Ask: "What other word rhymes with *bun* and *fun*?"

Ask a child to write the chosen word, *run*, for example.

Say the words *bun, fun, run.*

Repeat the procedure for other rhyming words: *sun, nun.*

■ Repeat the procedure for the *-ug, -ut* and *-ub* rimes.

NOW OR LATER

■ Repeat the above activities.

■ Show the teacher's copy of Workbook 3 page 26.

Discuss the picture.

Point to the first rime *-un.*

Ask the children to read the rime.

Confirm *-un.*

Ask: "What is the first word?"

Confirm *nun.*

Tell the children to look in the picture for something that rhymes with *nun.*

Confirm *sun.*

Ask a child to write *sun* on the first dotted line underneath *nun.*

Confirm that *sun* rhymes with *nun* and can go with the *-un* rime.

■ Repeat the procedure for the *-ug, -ut* and *-ub* rimes.

EXTENSION

■ Say: "Think of another word that rhymes with *nun* and *sun.*"

Ask the children to put the chosen word into a rap. For example, "*Nun* and *sun*, they rhyme with *bun.*"

Ask a child to write the chosen word (*bun*) on the second dotted line below *nun* and *sun.*

■ Repeat for *hug* and *jug, but* and *nut, cub* and *tub.*

■ Children complete Workbook 3 page 26. (*Remember to remove teacher's copy before children complete page.*)

DEVELOPING SKILLS

Some or all of these activities must be done to ensure progress:

■ **Rhyme Picture Cards**

Children sort a selection of Picture Cards into sets according to rhyme.

■ Commercial rhyming games could be used if available.

■ **Flash Cards**

Rhyming words with medial *u.*

rhyming

Rhyming

THE NLF AIMS

- Recognise when words rhyme.
- Identify words that rhyme.
- Read CVC words that rhyme.
- Write CVC words that rhyme.

WHAT YOU NEED

RESOURCES

- *Hector Hedgehog's Big Book of Rhymes (Alphabet)* page 18
- Flash Cards – rhyming: CVC words with medial *e*
- Workbook 3 page 27
- Teacher's copy of Workbook 3 page 27
- Rhyme Picture Cards

KEY LESSON POINTERS

VOCABULARY

below/underneath   end   rhyme   rhyming   same/different   word

THE CHILDREN should throughout the lesson:

- listen for the rhyme at the end of words.

YOU should throughout the lesson:

- ensure emphasis on the rhyme at the end of words.

THE LESSON

STARTING THE LESSON

- Revisit *Hector Hedgehog's Big Book of Rhymes (Alphabet)* and read page 18.

  Read the rhyme and put emphasis on the rhyming words.

  Ask the children to tell you any words that rhyme in the poem: *pest* and *vest*, *peas* and *cheese*, *surprise* and *pies*, *huff* and *puff*.

  Tell the children that you are going to say three words and they have to tell you which two of the words rhyme.

  Suggested words:

hook	water	shook
bath	path	bowl
red	pink	sink
night	draw	write
goat	boat	donkey
go	mice	twice
bear	pear	apple
page	book	stage

  (*Repeat the correct rhyme when children answer.*)

TEACHING THE LESSON

- Tell the children that you are going to say a word and they have to think of a word that rhymes with it.

  Say *net*.

  Ask the children for words that rhyme with *net*. Possible rhymes: *wet, bet, get, jet, let, met, pet, vet*.

  If the children have difficulty suggesting words that rhyme, give a clue: a word that rhymes with *net* and it starts with *p*.

  Say *ten*.

  Ask the children for words that rhyme with *ten*. Possible rhymes: *Ben, den, hen, men, pen, when, then*.

  Say *red*.

  Ask the children for words that rhyme with *red*. Possible rhymes: *bed, fed, led, wed, Ted, shed, bread*.

  Say *leg*.

  Ask the children for words that rhyme with *leg*. Possible rhymes: *beg, Meg, peg*.

- Write *let* on the board.

  Ask the children to read *let*.

  Ask: "What word rhymes with *let*?"

Ask a child to write the chosen word, *get*, for example.

Ask the children to write the words in a list to show the rhyming pattern.

Say the words *let*, *get*.

Ask: "What other word rhymes with *let* and *get*?"

Ask a child to write the chosen word, *vet*, for example.

Say the words *let*, *get*, *vet*.

Repeat the procedure for other rhyming words: *bet*, *jet*, *met*, *net*, *pet*, *set*, *wet*.

■ Repeat the procedure for the *-en*, *-eg* and *-ed* rimes.

NOW OR LATER

■ Repeat the above activities.

■ Show the teacher's copy of Workbook 3 page 27.

Discuss the picture. (*Children may notice that some objects in the picture seem out of place.*)

Point to the first rime *-et*.

Ask the children to read the rime.

Confirm *-et*.

Ask: "What is the first word?"

Confirm *wet*.

Tell the children to look in the picture for something that rhymes with *wet*.

Confirm *net*.

Ask a child to write *net* on the first dotted line underneath *wet*.

Confirm that *net* rhymes with *wet* and can go with the *-et* rime.

■ Repeat the procedure for the *-en*, *-ed* and *-eg* rimes.

EXTENSION

■ Say: "Think of another word that rhymes with *wet* and *net*."

Ask the children to put the chosen word into a rap. For example, "*Wet* and *net*, they rhyme with *jet*."

Ask a child to write the chosen word (*jet*) on the second dotted line below *wet* and *net*.

■ Repeat for *men* and *hen*, *fed* and *bed*, *beg* and *peg*.

■ Children complete Workbook 3 page 27. (*Remember to remove teacher's copy before children complete page.*)

FURTHER PRACTICE

DEVELOPING SKILLS

Some or all of these activities must be done to ensure progress:

■ **Rhyme Picture Cards**

Children sort a selection of Picture Cards into sets according to rhyme.

■ Commercial rhyming games could be used if available.

■ **Flash Cards**

Rhyming words with medial *e*.

BLENDING AND SEGMENTING

RHYMING CVC WORDS

rhyming

213

Rhyming

BEFORE YOU START

THE NLF AIMS

- Recognise when words rhyme.
- Identify words that rhyme.
- Read CVC words that rhyme.
- Write CVC words that rhyme.

WHAT YOU NEED

RESOURCES

- *Hector Hedgehog's Big Book of Rhymes (Alphabet)* page 27
- Flash Cards – rhyming: CVC words with medial *i*
- Picture Rhyming Bingo
- Workbook 3 page 28
- Teacher's copy of Workbook 3 page 28

KEY LESSON POINTERS

VOCABULARY

below/underneath   end   rhyme   rhyming
same/different   word

THE CHILDREN should throughout the lesson:

- listen for the rhyme at the end of words.

YOU should throughout the lesson:

- ensure emphasis on the rhyme at the end of words.

THE LESSON

STARTING THE LESSON

- Revisit *Hector Hedgehog's Big Book of Rhymes (Alphabet)* and read page 27.

  Read the rhyme and put emphasis on the rhyming words.

  Ask the children to tell you any words that rhyme in the poem: *man* and *van*, *ill* and *pill*.

- Tell the children that you are going to say three words and they have to tell you which two of the words rhyme.

  Suggested words:

fan	pan	big
go	will	Bill
heel	wheel	boat
down	park	town
sick	quick	big
top	run	hop
hat	trip	slip
sock	clock	watch

  (*Repeat the correct rhyme when children answer.*)

TEACHING THE LESSON

- Tell the children that you are going to say a word and they have to think of a word that rhymes with it.

  Say *tin*.

  Ask the children for words that rhyme with *tin*. Possible rhymes: *bin, din, fin, pin, win, chin, shin, grin*.

  If the children have difficulty suggesting words that rhyme, give a clue: a word that rhymes with *tin* and it starts with *b*.

  Say *tip*.

  Ask the children for words that rhyme with *tip*. Possible rhymes: *dip, hip, lip, pip, rip, sip, zip, ship, chip, whip, trip*.

  Say *six*.

  Ask the children for words that rhyme with *six*. Possible rhymes: *mix, fix*.

  Say *dig*.

  Ask the children for words that rhyme with *dig*. Possible rhymes: *big, fig, jig, pig, wig*.

- Write *win* on the board.

  Ask the children to read *win*.

  Ask: "What word rhymes with *win*?"

  Ask a child to write the chosen word, *fin*, for example.

Ask the children to write the words in a list to show the rhyming pattern.

Say the words *win, fin*.

Ask: "What other word rhymes with *win* and *fin*?"

Ask a child to write the chosen word, *bin*, for example.

Say the words *win, fin, bin*.

Repeat the procedure for other rhyming words: *din, pin, tin, chin, shin, thin*.

■ Repeat the procedure for the *-ip, -ix* and *-ig* rimes.

NOW OR LATER

■ Repeat the above activities.

■ Show the teacher's copy of Workbook 3 page 28.

Discuss the picture. (*Children may notice that some objects in the picture seem out of place.*)

Point to the first rime *-in*.

Ask the children to read the rime.

Confirm *-in*.

Ask: "What is the first word?"

Confirm *fin*.

Tell the children to look in the picture for something that rhymes with *fin*.

Confirm *bin*.

Ask a child to write *bin* on the first dotted line underneath *fin*.

Confirm that *bin* rhymes with *fin* and can go with the *-in* rime.

■ Repeat the procedure for the *-ip, -ix* and *-ig* rimes.

EXTENSION

■ Say: "Think of another word that rhymes with *fin* and *bin*."

Ask the children to put the chosen word into a rap. For example, "*Fin* and *bin*, they rhyme with *pin*."

Ask a child to write the chosen word (*pin*) on the second dotted line below *fin* and *bin*.

■ Repeat for *hip* and *zip*, *fix* and *six*, *fig* and *pig*.

■ Children complete Workbook 3 page 28. (*Remember to remove teacher's copy before children complete page.*)

FURTHER PRACTICE

DEVELOPING SKILLS

■ **Flash Cards**

Rhyming words with medial *i*.

■ **Picture Rhyming Bingo**

Children have a Bingo board on the table. You say a word such as *mix*. Children look for a picture that rhymes with *mix* and cover it.

Suggested words:

hat	prod	fox	mat	trot
pen	flag	jog	flap	pup
hid	ran	shop	mix	hot
big	can	chin	fuss	cut
hug	red	hip	den	leg
fun	men	jog		

rhyming

Rhyming

THE NLF AIMS

- Recognise when words rhyme.
- Identify words that rhyme.
- Read CVC words that rhyme.
- Write CVC words that rhyme.

WHAT YOU NEED

RESOURCES

- *Hector Hedgehog's Big Book of Rhymes (Alphabet)* page 28
- Flash Cards – rhyming: CVC words with medial *a, e, i, o, u*
- Picture Rhyming Bingo
- Workbook 3 pages 29 and 30
- Teacher's copy of Workbook 3 pages 29 and 30
- Assessment 3.4

KEY LESSON POINTERS

VOCABULARY

below/underneath   rhyme   rhyming
word

THE CHILDREN should throughout the lesson:

- listen for the rhyme at the end of words.

YOU should throughout the lesson:

- ensure emphasis on the rhyme at the end of words.

STARTING THE LESSON

■ Revisit *Hector Hedgehog's Big Book of Rhymes (Alphabet)* and read page 28.

Read the rhyme and put emphasis on the rhyming words.

Ask the children to tell you any words that rhyme in the poem: *wok* and *sock, two* and *you.*

Tell the children that you are going to say three words and they have to tell you which two of the words rhyme.

Suggested words:

duck	suck	fish
walk	jump	bump
vest	bird	nest
hang	book	bang
road	river	toad
went	sound	round
back	nose	rose
made	pail	spade

(*Repeat the correct rhyme when children answer.*)

TEACHING THE LESSON

■ Ask: "What other words rhyme with *wok* and *sock?*"

Possible rhymes: *shock, lock, rock, dock, frock, knock, clock.*

Ask: "What other words rhyme with *two* and *you?*"

Possible rhymes: *shoe, do, blue, clue, drew, grew, new, pew, flew, stew, crew.*

■ Write *bat* on the board.

Ask the children to write rhyming words on the board, *hat, rat, fat, cat,* for example.

Ask the children to write the words in a list to show the rhyming pattern.

Ask the children to read their list of written words with emphasis on the rhyme.

Write *hit* on the board.

Ask the children to write rhyming words on the board, *bit, fit, lit, pit, sit, wit,* for example.

Ask the children to read the list of words written with emphasis on the rhyme.

- Repeat the procedure for the *-et* rime, ***bet, get, jet, let, met, net, pet, set, wet***, for example.

- Repeat the procedure for the *-ut* rime, ***but, cut, hut, nut, rut***, for example.

- Repeat the procedure for the *-ot* rime, ***dot, got, hot, lot, not, pot***, for example.

- Show the teacher's copy of Workbook 3 page 29.
  Ask the children to identify the pictures.
  Ask the children to identify the house rimes.
  Confirm *-ap, -up, -op*.
  Tell the children that they have to write the word for each picture in the correct house.
  Ask the children to choose a picture and write the word in the correct house. (*Draw children's attention to the change of vowel.*)

- Repeat the procedure for all the pictures as appropriate.

- Children complete Workbook 3 page 29.
  (*Remember to remove teacher's copy before children complete page.*)

LATER

- Repeat the above lesson before children complete Workbook 3 page 30.

FURTHER PRACTICE

DEVELOPING SKILLS

- **Flash Cards**
  Rhyming words.

- **Picture Rhyming Bingo**
  Children have a Bingo board on the table. You say a word such as *mix*. Children look for a picture that rhymes with *mix* and cover it.

  Suggested words:

hat	prod	fox	mat	trot
pen	flag	jog	flap	pup
hid	ran	shop	mix	hot
big	can	chin	fuss	cut
hug	red	hip	den	leg
fun	men	jog		

ASSESSMENT 3.4

BLENDING AND SEGMENTING

RHYMING CVC WORDS

217

rhyming

UNIT 4

BLENDING AND SEGMENTING

CVC and CVCC words
CV + ck and CV + ng words

INTRODUCTION

Unit 4 of *Fun Phonics* covers the NLF word level work required for Year 1, Term 1 and Term 2 in which pupils should be taught how to:

- discriminate and segment all three sounds in CVC words
- blend sounds to read CVC words
- write the three phonemes in CVC words
- discriminate, read and spell words with final consonant clusters.

While the focus is on CVC words, every opportunity should be taken to read CVC words in context. This should be done in the reading text used in individual schools.

Children should always be encouraged to use the strategies taught to date when reading text.

Dexter Dog's Big Book of Rhymes (CVC) gives the children an opportunity to use the strategies learned to read CVC words in the context of two lively stories. The rhythm and the rhyme of the language help them to predict the words.

When writing stories, children should be encouraged to spell accurately CVC words and CVCC words.

Consonant-vowel-consonant (CVC) words with medial **a**

BEFORE YOU START

THE NLF AIMS

- Read CVC words with medial *a*.
- Write CVC words with medial *a*.

WHAT YOU NEED

RESOURCES

- Flash Cards – CVC words: medial *a*
- Chalkboard/whiteboard
- Workbook 4 page 1
- Teacher's copy of Workbook 4 page 1
- Magnetic letters
- Additional Support 14
- Homework Sheet 4A
- Word List
- Assessment 4.1

KEY LESSON POINTERS

VOCABULARY

alphabet   letter   name   sound
word   vowel   same/different
beginning/middle/end   slow speak

THE CHILDREN should throughout the lesson:

- focus on three-letter words having two consonants and a vowel in the middle (CVC)
- differentiate the final sounds in CVC words
- focus on the correct letter formation.

YOU should throughout the lesson:

- ensure an awareness that CVC words have two consonants and a vowel in the middle
- emphasise that the final sound changes the word
- ensure correct letter formation.

THE LESSON

STARTING THE LESSON

- Flash Cards – Practise reading CVC words with medial *a*.
  Invite class/group response.
  Invite individual response.

TEACHING THE LESSON

- Show three or four CVC words with medial *a*.
  Ask: "How many letters are in each word?"
  Confirm three.
  Slow speak each word to hear the three sounds.
  Ask: "What is the middle sound in each word?"
  Confirm it is the vowel *a*.
  Tell the children that all the words must have a vowel in the middle.

- Slow speak *a* word such as *cat*: *c-a-t*.
  Ask: "What is this word?"
  Confirm *cat*.
  Repeat for other CVC words with medial *a*.
  Suggested words:
  man   bag   sat   bad   fat   tap

- Ask a child to write *bat* on the board. (*Monitor correct letter formation.*)
  Tell the children that you want to write *bad* on the board.
  Ask: "What part of the word *bad* is the same as the word *bat*?"
  Confirm the beginning, *ba* and write *ba* on the board.
  Ask: "What part of the word *bad* is different from the word *bat*?"
  Confirm the ending, *d/t*.
  Write *d* to complete the word *bad*.

- Ask the children to read the words *bat, bad.*

  Ensure that they know the words start the same and have a different ending.

- Repeat the procedure for other groups of words.

  Suggested words:

  cat/can/cap   mad/man/map
  fat/fan/fab   rat/ran/rag
  hat/had/ham   sat/sad/Sam
  pat/pad/pan   tan/tag/tap

NOW OR LATER

- Show the teacher's copy of Workbook 4 page 1.

  Check that the children can identify the pictures.

- Tell the children that they have to write the correct words on the dotted lines.

  Ask the children which words they will write under each picture.

- Children complete Workbook 4 page 1.

LATER

- Repeat the above lesson for further practice.
- Children complete Additional Support 14.

FURTHER PRACTICE

DEVELOPING SKILLS

Some or all of these activities must be done to ensure progress:

- Practise writing CVC words to dictation.

  Dictate by slow speak some words for the children to write (*see Word List*).

  Some children's fine motor skills may not be developed sufficiently to use a pen/pencil for this activity. The same activity can be done using letter cards or magnetic letters.

  Initially it may be necessary to follow these steps:

  1. Slow speak word.
  2. Ask children what sound is at the beginning of the word.
  3. Ask children to write the letter that represents that sound.
  4. Ask children what sound they can hear in the middle of the word.
  5. Ask children to write the letter that represents that sound.
  6. Ask children what sound is at the end of the word.
  7. Ask children to write the letter that represents that sound.
  8. Ask children to read the word they have written.

- **Magnetic letters**

  Children make CVC words with medial *a*.

- **Flash Cards**

  Practise reading CVC words with medial *a*.

- **Suggested activities**

  See Unit 3, page 183.

NOTE

Words like *car, far, jar* have not been included because these are best treated as onset and rime words: *c-ar, f-ar, j-ar.*

ASSESSMENT 4.1

ACTIVITIES AT HOME

Homework Sheet 4A.

CVC medial a

Consonant-vowel-consonant (CVC) words with medial o

BEFORE YOU START

THE NLF AIMS

- Read CVC words with medial *o*.
- Write CVC words with medial *o*.

WHAT YOU NEED

RESOURCES

- Flash Cards – CVC words: medial *o*
- Chalkboard/whiteboard
- Workbook 4 page 2
- Teacher's copy of Workbook 4 page 2
- Magnetic letters
- Homework Sheet 4B
- Word List
- Assessment 4.2

KEY LESSON POINTERS

VOCABULARY

alphabet   letter   name   sound
word   vowel   same/different
beginning/middle/end   slow speak

THE CHILDREN should throughout the lesson:

- focus on three-letter words having two consonants and a vowel in the middle (CVC)
- differentiate the final sounds in CVC words
- focus on the correct letter formation.

YOU should throughout the lesson:

- ensure an awareness that CVC words have two consonants and a vowel in the middle
- emphasise that the final sound changes the word
- ensure correct letter formation.

THE LESSON

STARTING THE LESSON

- Flash Cards – Practise reading CVC words with medial *o*.
  Invite class/group response.
  Invite individual response.

TEACHING THE LESSON

- Show three or four CVC words with medial *o*.
  Ask: "How many letters are in each word?"
  Confirm three.
  Slow speak each word to hear the three sounds.
  Ask: "What is the middle sound in each word?"
  Confirm it is the vowel *o*.
  Remind the children that all the words must have a vowel in the middle.

- Slow speak *o* word such as *dog*: *d-o-g*.
  Ask: "What is this word?"
  Confirm *dog*.
  Repeat for other CVC words with medial *o*.
  Suggested words:
  cot   mop   rod   box   jot   rob

- Ask a child to write **log** on the board. (*Monitor correct letter formation.*)

- Tell the children that you want to write **lot** on the board.

  Ask: "What part of the word **lot** is the same as the word **log**?"

  Confirm the beginning, **lo** and write **lo** on the board.

  Ask: "What part of the word **lot** is different from the word **log**?"

  Confirm the ending, **g/t** and write **t** to complete the word **lot**.

- Ask the children to read the words **log**, **lot**.

  Ensure that they know the words start the same and have a different ending.

- Repeat the procedure for other groups of words.

  Suggested words:

hop/hot/hob	pop/pod/pot
rob/rot/rod	Tom/top/tot
jot/jog	mob/mop

NOW OR LATER

- Show the teacher's copy of Workbook 4 page 2.
  Check that the children can identify the pictures.

- Tell the children that they have to write the correct words on the dotted lines.

  Ask the children which words they will write under each picture.

- Children complete Workbook 4 page 2.

FURTHER PRACTICE

DEVELOPING SKILLS

Some or all of these activities must be done to ensure progress:

- Practise writing CVC words to dictation.

  Dictate by slow speak some words for the children to write (*see Word List*).

  Some children's fine motor skills may not be developed sufficiently to use a pen/pencil for this activity. The same activity can be done using letter cards or magnetic letters.

  Initially it may be necessary to follow these steps:

  1. Slow speak word.
  2. Ask children what sound is at the beginning of the word.
  3. Ask children to write the letter that represents that sound.
  4. Ask children what sound they can hear in the middle of the word.
  5. Ask children to write the letter that represents that sound.
  6. Ask children what sound is at the end of the word.
  7. Ask children to write the letter that represents that sound.
  8. Ask children to read the word they have written.

- **Magnetic letters**

  Children make CVC words with medial *o*.

- **Flash Cards**

  Practise reading CVC words with medial *o*.

- **Suggested activities**

  See Unit 3, page 183.

ASSESSMENT 4.2

ACTIVITIES AT HOME

Homework Sheet 4B.

CVC medial o

Consonant-vowel-consonant (CVC) words: medial **a o**

BEFORE YOU START

THE NLF AIMS

- Read CVC words – medial *a* and medial *o*.
- Write CVC words – medial *a* and medial *o*.

WHAT YOU NEED

RESOURCES

- Flash Cards – CVC words: medial *a*, medial *o*
- Chalkboard/whiteboard
- Workbook 4 page 3
- Teacher's copy of Workbook 4 page 3
- Magnetic letters
- Additional Support 15
- Homework Sheet 4C
- Word List
- Assessment 4.3

KEY LESSON POINTERS

VOCABULARY

alphabet   letter   name   sound
word   vowel   same/different
beginning/middle/end   slow speak

THE CHILDREN should throughout the lesson:

- focus on three-letter words having two consonants and a vowel in the middle (CVC)
- recognise that a vowel change in a CVC word changes the word
- focus on the correct letter formation.

YOU should throughout the lesson:

- ensure an awareness that CVC words have two consonants and a vowel in the middle
- emphasise that a change in vowel in a CVC word changes the word
- ensure correct letter formation.

THE LESSON

STARTING THE LESSON

- Flash Cards – Quick revision of CVC words with medial *a*, medial *o*.

  Invite class/group response.

  Invite individual response.

TEACHING THE LESSON

- Give each child three or four cards of CVC words with medial *a*, medial *o*.

  Tell the children to place the cards face up so that they can see the words. (*More than one child may have the same word.*)

  Say you want all the children who have the word *bat* to show their card.

  (*This could be by pointing to or holding up the identified card.*)

  Scan to check that they have the correct word.

- Tell the children that you want all the children who have the word *cot* to show their card.

  Scan the words to check that they have the correct card.

- At this point some children may show a card with the word *cat*.

  Ask: "What sound is in the middle of *cot*?"

  Confirm *o*.

  Ask: "What sound is in the middle of the word you have chosen?"

  Confirm *a*.

  Ask the children to read their chosen word.

  Confirm *cat*.

  Draw the children's attention to the difference between *cat* and *cot*.

  Confirm that the vowel is different.

- Repeat the procedure for other CVC words.

  (*Ensure children look closely at words and encourage them to correct themselves. For example: "Why can the word* cot *not be* cat*?" Confirm* cot *has* o *in the middle and not* a.)

- Ask a child to write **pot** (*slow speak*) on the board. (*Monitor correct letter formation.*)

- Tell the children that you want to write **pat** on the board.

  Ask: "What part of the word **pat** is different from the word **pot**?"

  Confirm the vowel in the middle, **o/a**.

  Write **pat** on the board.

  Ask the children to read the words **pot, pat**.

  Ensure that they know the words **pot/pat** have different vowels in the middle and that the vowel changes the word.

- Repeat the procedure for other groups of words.

  Suggested words:
hat/hot	rat/rot
cat/cot	tap/top
map/mop	cap/cop

NOW OR LATER

- Show the teacher's copy of Workbook 4 page 3.
  Check that the children can identify the pictures.

- Tell the children that they have to write the correct words on the dotted lines.

  Ask the children which words they will write under each picture.

- Children complete Workbook 4 page 3.

LATER

- Repeat the above lesson for further practice.
- Children complete Additional Support 15.

FURTHER PRACTICE

DEVELOPING SKILLS

Some or all of these activities must be done to ensure progress:

- Practise writing CVC words to dictation – medial *a*, medial *o*.

  You say a word, children write the word (*see Word List*).

  Some children's fine motor skills may not be developed sufficiently to use a pen/pencil for this activity. The same activity can be done using letter cards or magnetic letters.

  Initially it may be necessary to follow these steps:

  1. Slow speak word.
  2. Ask children what sound is at the beginning of the word.
  3. Ask children to write the letter that represents that sound.
  4. Ask children what sound they can hear in the middle of the word.
  5. Ask children to write the letter that represents that sound.
  6. Ask children what sound is at the end of the word.
  7. Ask children to write the letter that represents that sound.
  8. Ask children to read the word they have written.

- **Magnetic letters**

  Children make CVC words with medial *a*, medial *o*.

- **Flash Cards**

  Practise reading CVC words – medial *a*, medial *o*.

- **Suggested activities**

  See Unit 3, page 183.

  Show/give can be extended as:
  Show/give me a word that:
  1. rhymes with *hat*
  2. rhymes with *jog* (and so on).

ASSESSMENT 4.3

ACTIVITIES AT HOME

Homework Sheet 4C.

CVC medial a, o

Consonant-vowel-consonant (CVC) words with medial e

BEFORE YOU START

THE NLF AIMS

- Read CVC words with medial *e*.
- Write CVC words with medial *e*.

WHAT YOU NEED

RESOURCES

- Flash Cards – CVC words: medial *e*
- Chalkboard/whiteboard
- Workbook 4 page 4
- Teacher's copy of Workbook 4 page 4
- Magnetic letters
- Homework Sheet 4D
- Word List
- Assessment 4.4

KEY LESSON POINTERS

VOCABULARY

alphabet   letter   name   sound
word   vowel   same/different
beginning/middle/end   slow speak

THE CHILDREN should throughout the lesson:

- focus on three-letter words having two consonants and a vowel in the middle (CVC)
- differentiate the final sounds in CVC words
- focus on the correct letter formation.

YOU should throughout the lesson:

- ensure an awareness that CVC words have two consonants and a vowel in the middle
- emphasise that the final sound changes the word
- ensure correct letter formation.

THE LESSON

STARTING THE LESSON

- Flash Cards – Practise reading CVC words with medial *e*.

  Invite class/group response.

  Invite individual response.

TEACHING THE LESSON

- Show three or four CVC words with medial *e*.

  Ask: "How many letters are in each word?"

  Confirm three.

  Slow speak each word to hear the three sounds.

  Ask: "What is the middle sound in each word?"

  Confirm it is the vowel *e*.

  Remind the children that all the words must have a vowel in the middle.

- Slow speak *e* word such as *pet*: *p-e-t*.

  Ask: "What is this word?"

  Confirm *pet*.

  Repeat for other CVC words with medial *e*.

  Suggested words:

  leg   men   jet   fed   hem   web

- Ask a child to write *leg* on the board. (*Monitor correct letter formation.*)

- Tell the children that you want to write *let* on the board.

  Ask: "What part of the word *let* is the same as the word *leg*?"

  Confirm the beginning, *le* and write *le* on the board.

  Ask: "What part of the word *let* is different from the word *leg*?"

  Confirm the ending, *g/t*. Write *t* to complete the word *let*.

- Ask the children to read the words *leg*, *let*.

  Ensure that they know the words start the same and have a different ending.

- Repeat the procedure for other groups of words.

  Suggested words:

men/met/Meg	web/wet/wed
peg/pen/pet	bed/beg/bet
hem/hen	Ted/ten

NOW OR LATER

- Show the teacher's copy of Workbook 4 page 4.

  Check that the children can identify the pictures.

- Tell the children that they have to write the correct words on the dotted lines.

  Ask the children which words they will write under each picture.

- Children complete Workbook 4 page 4.

FURTHER PRACTICE

DEVELOPING SKILLS

Some or all of these activities must be done to ensure progress:

- Practise writing CVC words to dictation.

  You say a word (*slow speak*), children write the word (*see Word List*).

  Some children's fine motor skills may not be developed sufficiently to use a pen/pencil for this activity. The same activity can be done using letter cards or magnetic letters.

  Initially it may be necessary to follow these steps:

  1. Slow speak word.
  2. Ask children what sound is at the beginning of the word.
  3. Ask children to write the letter that represents that sound.
  4. Ask children what sound they can hear in the middle of the word.
  5. Ask children to write the letter that represents that sound.
  6. Ask children what sound is at the end of the word.
  7. Ask children to write the letter that represents that sound.
  8. Ask children to read the word they have written.

- **Magnetic letters**

  Children make CVC words with medial *e*.

- **Flash Cards**

  Practise reading CVC words with medial *e*.

- **Suggested activities**

  See Unit 3, page 183.

ASSESSMENT 4.4

ACTIVITIES AT HOME

Homework Sheet 4D.

CVC medial e

Consonant-vowel-consonant (CVC) words: medial a o e

THE NLF AIMS

- Read CVC words – medial *a*, medial *o* and medial *e*.
- Write CVC words – medial *a*, medial *o* and medial *e*.

WHAT YOU NEED

RESOURCES

- Flash Cards – CVC words: medial *a*, medial *o*, medial *e*
- Chalkboard/whiteboard
- Workbook 4 page 5
- Teacher's copy of Workbook 4 page 5
- Magnetic letters
- Additional Support 16
- Homework Sheet 4E
- Word List
- Assessment 4.5

KEY LESSON POINTERS

VOCABULARY

alphabet   letter   name   sound
word   vowel   same/different
beginning/middle/end   slow speak

THE CHILDREN should throughout the lesson:

- focus on three-letter words having two consonants and a vowel in the middle (CVC)
- recognise that a vowel change in a CVC word changes the word
- focus on the correct letter formation.

YOU should throughout the lesson:

- ensure an awareness that CVC words have two consonants and a vowel in the middle
- emphasise that a change in vowel in a CVC word changes the word
- ensure correct letter formation.

THE LESSON

STARTING THE LESSON

- Flash Cards – Quick revision of CVC words with medials *a, o, e*.
  Invite class/group response.
  Invite individual response.

TEACHING THE LESSON

- Give each child three or four cards of CVC words with medials *a, o, e*.
  Tell the children to place the cards face up so that they can see the words. (*More than one child may have the same word.*)
  Say you want all the children who have the word *pet* to show their card.
  (*This could be by pointing to or holding up the identified card.*)
  Scan to check that they have the correct word.

- Tell the children that you want all the children who have the word *leg* to show their card.
  Scan the words to check that they have the correct card.

- At this point some children may show a card with the word *log*.
  Ask: "What sound is in the middle of *leg*?"
  Confirm *e*.
  Ask: "What sound is in the middle of the word you have chosen?"
  Confirm *o*.
  Ask the children to read their chosen word.
  Confirm *log*.
  Draw the children's attention to the difference between *leg* and *log*.
  Confirm that the vowel is different.

- Repeat the procedure for other CVC words.
  (*Ensure children look closely at words and encourage them to correct themselves. For example: "Why can **top** not be **tap**?" Confirm **top** has **o** in the middle and not **a**.*)

- Ask a child to write **get** (*slow speak*) on the board. (*Monitor correct letter formation.*)

- Tell the children that you want to write **got** on the board.

  Ask: "What part of the word **got** is different from the word **get**?"

  Confirm the vowel in the middle, **e/o**.

  Write **get** on the board.

  Ask the children to read the words **get, got**.

  Ensure that they know the words **get/got** have different vowels in the middle and that the vowel changes the word.

- Repeat the procedure for other groups of words.

  Suggested words:

man/men	tan/ten	lot/let
net/not	bat/bet	sat/set
get/got	mat/met	pat/pet/pot

NOW OR LATER

- Show the teacher's copy of Workbook 4 page 5.

  Check that the children can the identify pictures.

- Tell the children that they have to write the correct words on the dotted lines.

  Ask the children which words they will write under each picture.

- Children complete Workbook 4 page 5.

LATER

- Repeat the above lesson for further practice.

- Children complete Additional Support 16.

FURTHER PRACTICE

DEVELOPING SKILLS

Some or all of these activities must be done to ensure progress:

- Practise writing CVC words to dictation – medial *a*, *o*, and *e*.

  You say a word, children write the word (*see Word List*).

  Some children's fine motor skills may not be developed sufficiently to use a pen/pencil for this activity. The same activity can be done using letter cards or magnetic letters.

  Initially it may be necessary to follow these steps:

  1. Slow speak word.
  2. Ask children what sound is at the beginning of the word.
  3. Ask children to write the letter that represents that sound.
  4. Ask children what sound they can hear in the middle of the word.
  5. Ask children to write the letter that represents that sound.
  6. Ask children what sound is at the end of the word.
  7. Ask children to write the letter that represents that sound.
  8. Ask children to read the word they have written.

- **Magnetic letters**

  Children make CVC words with medial *a*, medial *o*, medial *e*.

- **Flash Cards**

  Practise reading CVC words – medial *a*, medial *o*, medial *e*.

- **Suggested activities**

  See Unit 3, page 183.

  Show/give can be extended as:
  Show/give me a word that:
  1. rhymes with *man*
  2. rhymes with *pot*
  3. rhymes with *ten* (and so on).

ASSESSMENT 4.5

ACTIVITIES AT HOME

Homework Sheet 4E.

CVC medial a, e, o

Consonant-vowel-consonant (CVC) words with medial u

BEFORE YOU START

THE NLF AIMS
- Read CVC words with medial *u*.
- Write CVC words with medial *u*.

WHAT YOU NEED

RESOURCES
- Flash Cards – CVC words: medial *u*
- Chalkboard/whiteboard
- Workbook 4 page 6
- Teacher's copy of Workbook 4 page 6
- Magnetic letters
- Homework Sheet 4F
- Word List
- Assessment 4.6

KEY LESSON POINTERS

VOCABULARY
alphabet   letter   name   sound
word   vowel   same/different
beginning/middle/end   slow speak

THE CHILDREN should throughout the lesson:
- focus on three-letter words having two consonants and a vowel in the middle (CVC)
- differentiate the final sounds in CVC words
- focus on the correct letter formation.

YOU should throughout the lesson:
- ensure an awareness that CVC words have two consonants and a vowel in the middle
- emphasise that the final sound changes the word
- ensure correct letter formation.

THE LESSON

STARTING THE LESSON

- Flash Cards – Practise reading CVC words with medial *u*.

  Invite class/group response.

  Invite individual response.

TEACHING THE LESSON

- Show three or four CVC words with medial *u*.

  Ask: "How many letters are in each word?"

  Confirm three.

  Slow speak each word to hear the three sounds.

  Ask: "What is the middle sound in each word?"

  Confirm it is the vowel *u*.

  Remind the children that all the words must have a vowel in the middle.

- Slow speak *u* word such as *sun: s-u-n*.

  Ask: "What is this word?"

  Confirm *sun*.

  Repeat for other CVC words with medial *u*.

  Suggested words:

  bus   rug   hut   fun   pup   mud

- Ask a child to write **tug** on the board. (*Monitor correct letter formation.*)
- Tell the children that you want to write **tub** on the board.

  Ask: "What part of the word **tub** is the same as the word **tug**?"

  Confirm the beginning, **tu** and write **tu** on the board.

  Ask: "What part of the word **tub** is different from the word **tug**?"

  Confirm the ending, **g/b** and write **b** to complete the word **tub**.

  Ask the children to read the words **tug, tub**.

  Ensure that they know the words start the same and have a different ending.
- Repeat the procedure for other groups of words.

  Suggested words:
  cub/cup/cut   mud/mug/mum
  hug/hum/hut   bud/bug/bun/bus/but
  rub/rug/run

NOW OR LATER

- Show the teacher's copy of Workbook 4 page 6.
  Check that the children can identify the pictures.
- Tell the children that they have to write the correct words on the dotted lines.

  Ask the children which words they will write under each picture.
- Children complete Workbook 4 page 6.

FURTHER PRACTICE

DEVELOPING SKILLS

Some or all of these activities must be done to ensure progress:

- Practise writing CVC words to dictation.

  You say a word (*slow speak*), children write the word (*see Word List*).

  Some children's fine motor skills may not be developed sufficiently to use a pen/pencil for this activity. The same activity can be done using letter cards or magnetic letters.

  Initially it may be necessary to follow these steps:

  1. Slow speak word.
  2. Ask children what sound is at the beginning of the word.
  3. Ask children to write the letter that represents that sound.
  4. Ask children what sound they can hear in the middle of the word.
  5. Ask children to write the letter that represents that sound.
  6. Ask children what sound is at the end of the word.
  7. Ask children to write the letter that represents that sound.
  8. Ask children to read the word they have written.

- **Magnetic letters**

  Children make CVC words with medial **u**.

- **Flash Cards**

  Practise reading CVC words with medial **u**.

- **Suggested activities**

  See Unit 3, page 183.

ASSESSMENT 4.6

ACTIVITIES AT HOME

Homework Sheet 4F.

CVC medial u

Consonant-vowel-consonant (CVC) words: medial a o e u

BEFORE YOU START

THE NLF AIMS

- Read CVC words – medial *a*, medial *o*, medial *e* and medial *u*.
- Write CVC words – medial *a*, medial *o*, medial *e* and medial *u*.

WHAT YOU NEED

RESOURCES

- Flash Cards – CVC words: medial *a*, medial *o*, medial *e*, medial *u*
- Chalkboard/whiteboard
- Workbook 4 page 7
- Teacher's copy of Workbook 4 page 7
- Magnetic letters
- Additional Support 17
- Homework Sheet 4G
- Word List
- Assessment 4.7

KEY LESSON POINTERS

VOCABULARY

alphabet letter name sound
word vowel same/different
beginning/middle/end slow speak

THE CHILDREN should throughout the lesson:

- focus on three-letter words having two consonants and a vowel in the middle (CVC)
- recognise that a vowel change in a CVC word changes the word
- focus on the correct letter formation.

YOU should throughout the lesson:

- ensure an awareness that CVC words have two consonants and a vowel in the middle
- emphasise that a change in vowel in a CVC word changes the word
- ensure correct letter formation.

THE LESSON

STARTING THE LESSON

- Flash Cards – Quick revision of CVC words with medials *a, o, e, u*.

  Invite class/group response.

  Invite individual response.

TEACHING THE LESSON

- Give each child three or four cards of CVC words with medials *a, o, e, u*.

  Tell the children to place the cards face up so that they can see the words. (*More than one child may have the same word.*)

  Say you want all the children who have the word **bug** to show their card.

  (*This could be done by pointing to or holding up the identified card.*)

  Scan to check that they have the correct word.

- Tell the children that you want all the children who have the word **but** to show their card.

  Scan the words to check that they have the correct card.

- At this point some children may show a card with the word **bet**.

  Ask: "What sound is in the middle of **but**?"

  Confirm *u*.

  Ask: "What sound is in the middle of the word you have chosen?"

  Confirm *e*.

  Ask the children to read their chosen word.

  Confirm **bet**.

  Draw the children's attention to the difference between **but** and **bet**.

  Confirm that the vowel is different.

- Repeat the procedure for other CVC words.

  (*Ensure children look closely at words and encourage them to correct themselves. For example: "Why can* **ran** *not be* **run**?" Confirm **ran** *has* **a** *in the middle and not* **u**.)

232

- Ask a child to write **bug** (*slow speak*) on the board. (Monitor correct letter formation.)

- Tell the children that you want to write **beg** on the board.

  Ask: "What part of the word **beg** is different from the word **bug**?"

  Confirm the vowel in the middle, **e/u**.

  Write **beg** on the board.

- Ask the children to read the words **bug, beg**.

  Ensure that they know the words **bug/beg** have different vowels in the middle and that the vowel changes the word.

- Repeat the procedure for other groups of words.

  Suggested words:

mud/mad	hum/ham/hem
fun/fan	cup/cap/cop
rug/rag	hut/hat/hot
but/bat/bet	cut/cat/cot
bud/bad/bed	

NOW OR LATER

- Show the teacher's copy of Workbook 4 page 7.

  Check that the children can identify the pictures.

- Tell the children that they have to write the correct words on the dotted lines.

  Ask the children which words they will write under each picture.

- Children complete Workbook 4 page 7.

LATER

- Repeat the above lesson for further practice.

- Children complete Additional Support 17.

FURTHER PRACTICE

DEVELOPING SKILLS

Some or all of these activities must be done to ensure progress:

- Practise writing CVC words to dictation – medial *a, o, e* and *u*.

  You say a word, children write the word (*see Word List*).

  Some children's fine motor skills may not be developed sufficiently to use a pen/pencil for this activity. The same activity can be done using letter cards or magnetic letters.

  Initially it may be necessary to follow these steps:

  1. Slow speak word.
  2. Ask children what sound is at the beginning of the word.
  3. Ask children to write the letter that represents that sound.
  4. Ask children what sound they can hear in the middle of the word.
  5. Ask children to write the letter that represents that sound.
  6. Ask children what sound is at the end of the word.
  7. Ask children to write the letter that represents that sound.
  8. Ask children to read the word they have written.

- **Flash Cards**

  Practise reading CVC words – medial *a*, medial *o*, medial *e*, medial *u*.

- **Suggested activities**

  See Unit 3, page 183.

  Show/give can be extended as:
  Show/give me a word that:
  1. rhymes with *bag*
  2. rhymes with *fox*
  3. rhymes with *web*
  4. rhymes with *bus* (and so on).

ASSESSMENT 4.7

ACTIVITIES AT HOME

Homework Sheet 4G.

CVC medial a, e, o, u

Consonant-vowel-consonant (CVC) words with medial i

BEFORE YOU START

THE NLF AIMS

- Read CVC words with medial *i*.
- Write CVC words with medial *i*.

WHAT YOU NEED

RESOURCES

- Flash Cards – CVC words: medial *i*
- Chalkboard/whiteboard
- Workbook 4 page 8
- Teacher's copy of Workbook 4 page 8
- Magnetic letters
- Rhyming Bingo CVC words
- Homework Sheet 4H
- Word List
- Assessment 4.8

KEY LESSON POINTERS

VOCABULARY

alphabet letter name sound
word vowel same/different
beginning/middle/end slow speak

THE CHILDREN should throughout the lesson:

- focus on three-letter words having two consonants and a vowel in the middle (CVC)
- differentiate the final sounds in CVC words
- focus on the correct letter formation.

YOU should throughout the lesson:

- ensure an awareness that CVC words have two consonants and a vowel in the middle
- emphasise that the final sound changes the word
- ensure correct letter formation.

THE LESSON

STARTING THE LESSON

- Flash Cards – Practise reading CVC words with medial *i*.

  Invite class/group response.

  Invite individual response.

TEACHING THE LESSON

- Show three or four CVC words with medial *i*.

  Ask: "How many letters are in each word?"

  Confirm three.

  Slow speak each word to hear the three sounds.

  Ask: "What is the middle sound in each word?"

  Confirm it is the vowel *i*.

  Remind the children that all the words must have a vowel in the middle.

- Slow speak *i* word such as *sit*: *s-i-t*.

  Ask: "What is this word?"

  Confirm *sit*.

  Repeat for other CVC words with medial *i*.

  Suggested words:

  pin   him   mix   bin   lid   wig

■ Ask a child to write **wig** on the board. (*Monitor correct letter formation.*)

■ Tell the children that you want to write **win** on the board.

Ask: "What part of the word **win** is the same as the word **wig**?"

Confirm the beginning, **wi** and write **wi** on the board.

Ask: "What part of the word **win** is different from the word **wig**?"

Confirm the ending, **n/g**.

Write **n** to complete the word **win**.

Ask the children to read the words **wig, win**.

Ensure that they know the words start the same and have a different ending.

■ Repeat the procedure for other groups of words.

Suggested words:

big/bib/bin   hid/him/hip
dig/did/dip   rib/rip/rim
fin/fix/fit   tig/tin/tip
lid/lip/lit   pig/pin/pit

NOW OR LATER

■ Show the teacher's copy of Workbook 4 page 8. Check that the children can identify the pictures.

■ Tell the children that they have to write the correct words on the dotted lines.

Ask the children which words they will write under each picture.

■ Children complete Workbook 4 page 8.

FURTHER PRACTICE

DEVELOPING SKILLS

Some or all of these activities must be done to ensure progress:

■ Practise writing CVC words to dictation.

Dictate by slow speak some words for the children to write (*see Word List*).

Some children's fine motor skills may not be developed sufficiently to use a pen/pencil for this activity. The same activity can be done using letter cards or magnetic letters.

Initially it may be necessary to follow these steps:

1. Slow speak word.
2. Ask children what sound is at the beginning of the word.
3. Ask children to write the letter that represents that sound.
4. Ask children what sound they can hear in the middle of the word.
5. Ask children to write the letter that represents that sound.
6. Ask children what sound is at the end of the word.
7. Ask children to write the letter that represents that sound.
8. Ask children to read the word they have written.

■ **Flash Cards**

Practise reading CVC words with medial *i*.

■ **Suggested activities**

See Unit 3, page 183.

■ **Rhyming Bingo – CVC words**

Children have Bingo board (*CVC words*) on the table and you say a word, for example, *can*. Children have to look for a word that rhymes with *can* and cover it with a counter.

See suggested words on page 237.

ASSESSMENT 4.8

ACTIVITIES AT HOME

Homework Sheet 4H.

BLENDING AND SEGMENTING

CVC WORDS

CVC medial i

235

Consonant-vowel-consonant (CVC) words: medial a o e u i

THE NLF AIMS

- Read CVC words – medial *a*, medial *o*, medial *e*, medial *i* and medial *u*.
- Write CVC words – medial *a*, medial *o*, medial *e*, medial *i* and medial *u*.

WHAT YOU NEED

RESOURCES

- Flash Cards – CVC words: medial *a*, medial *o*, medial *e*, medial *u*, medial *i*
- Chalkboard/whiteboard
- Workbook 4 page 9
- Teacher's copy of Workbook 4 page 9
- Rhyming Bingo CVC words
- Additional Support 18
- Homework Sheet 4I
- Word List
- Assessment 4.9, 4.10

KEY LESSON POINTERS

VOCABULARY

alphabet   letter   name   sound
word   vowel   same/different
beginning/middle/end   slow speak

THE CHILDREN should throughout the lesson:

- focus on three-letter words having two consonants and a vowel in the middle (CVC)
- recognise that a vowel change in a CVC word changes the word
- focus on the correct letter formation.

YOU should throughout the lesson:

- ensure an awareness that CVC words have two consonants and a vowel in the middle
- emphasise that a change in vowel in a CVC word changes the word
- ensure correct letter formation.

THE LESSON

STARTING THE LESSON

- Flash Cards – Quick revision of CVC words with medials *a, o, e, u, i*.
  Invite class/group response.
  Invite individual response.

TEACHING THE LESSON

- Give each child four or five cards of CVC words with medials *a, o, e, u, i*.
  Tell the children to place the cards face up so that they can see the words. (*More than one child may have the same word.*)
  Say you want all the children who have the word *mix* to show their card.
  (*This could be by pointing to or holding up the identified card.*)
  Scan to check that they have the correct word.

- Tell the children that you want all the children who have the word *sit* to show their card.
  Scan the words to check that they have the correct card.

- At this point some children may show a card with the word *set*.
  Ask: "What sound is in the middle of *sit*?"
  Confirm *i*.
  Ask: "What sound is in the middle of the word you have chosen?"
  Confirm *e*.
  Ask the children to read their chosen word.
  Confirm *set*.
  Draw the children's attention to the difference between *sit* and *set*.
  Confirm that the vowel is different.

- Repeat the procedure for other CVC words.
  (*Ensure children look closely at words and encourage them to correct themselves. For example: "Why can* **pin** *not be* **pan**?" Confirm* **pin** *has* **i** *in the middle and not* **a***.*)

- Ask a child to write *hit* (*slow speak*) on the board. (*Monitor correct letter formation.*)

- Tell the children that you want to write *hat* on the board.

  Ask: "What part of the word *hat* is different from the word *hit*?"

  Confirm the vowel in the middle, *a/i*.

  Write *hat* on the board.

- Ask the children to read the words *hit, hat*.

  Ensure that they know the words *hit/hat* have different vowels in the middle and that the vowel changes the word.

- Repeat the procedure for other groups of words.

  Suggested words:

wig/wag	hip/hop
lid/lad/led	fit/fat
tip/tap/top	tin/tan/ten
lit/lot/let	cut/cat/cot
pat/pet/pit/pot	ham/hem/him/hum
bit/bat/bet/but	bug/bag/beg/big/bog

NOW OR LATER

- Show the teacher's copy of Workbook 4 page 9.

  Check that the children can identify the pictures.

- Tell the children that they have to write the correct words on the dotted lines.

  Ask the children which words they will write under each picture.

- Children complete Workbook 4 page 9.

LATER

- Repeat the above lesson for further practice.

- Children complete Additional Support 18.

- Words with **sh**, **ch**, **wh**, **th** at the beginning or the end should also be practised, for example:

shop	fish	hush	rash
shed	wish	rush	mash
ship	dish		
shut			
chip	rich	thin	when
chin	much	bath	whip
chap	such	with	
chat			

DEVELOPING SKILLS

Some or all of these activities must be done to ensure progress:

- Practise writing CVC words to dictation – medials *a*, *o*, *e*, *i* and *u*.

  You say a word, children write the word (*see Word List*).

  Some children's fine motor skills may not be developed sufficiently to use a pen/pencil for this activity. The same activity can be done using letter cards or magnetic letters.

  Initially it may be necessary to follow these steps:

  1. Slow speak word.
  2. Ask children what sound is at the beginning of the word.
  3. Ask children to write the letter that represents that sound.
  4. Ask children what sound they can hear in the middle of the word.
  5. Ask children to write the letter that represents that sound.
  6. Ask children what sound is at the end of the word.
  7. Ask children to write the letter that represents that sound.
  8. Ask children to read the word they have written.

- **Flash Cards**

  Practise reading CVC words – medial *a*, medial *o*, medial *e*, medial *i*, medial *u*.

- **Rhyming Bingo – CVC words**

  Children have Bingo board (*CVC words*) on the table and you say a word, for example, *lip*. Children have to look for a word that rhymes with *lip* and cover it.

  Suggested words:

lip	fat	when	rag	clap	fun
mix	stop	shut	lot	sat	man
did	big	red	tug	jog	thin
pup	fox	men	got	log	fuss
dug	pan	hen	pod	wet	leg

ASSESSMENT 4.9, 4.10

ACTIVITIES AT HOME

Homework Sheet 4I.

CVC medial a, o, e, u, i

CVC words in context

THE NLF AIMS

- Read CVC words in the context of a story.
- Identify rhyming words in the context of a story.
- Write CVC words in the context of a sentence.
- Begin to understand and use a capital letter and full stop in a sentence.

WHAT YOU NEED

RESOURCES

- Flash Cards – CVC words
- *Dexter Dog's Big Book of Rhymes (CVC)* pages 2 to 11
- Workbook 4 page 10
- Teacher's copy of Workbook 4 page 10
- Homework Sheets 4A to 4I
- Word List
- Read me/Write me Cards
- Magnetic letters

KEY LESSON POINTERS

VOCABULARY

alphabet   letter   name   sound   word
sentence   capital letter   full stop
space/spacing   rhyme

THE CHILDREN should throughout the lesson:

- focus on the rhythm and the rhyme of the language
- practise decoding skills in text
- focus on the content of the story.

YOU should throughout the lesson:

- emphasise the rhythm and the rhyme of the language
- encourage the children to use phonic skills taught to read (decode) text
- encourage referral to the story for answers to questions
- focus on capital letters, full stops and spacing when writing sentences.

STARTING THE LESSON

- Flash Cards – Quick revision of CVC words.

TEACHING THE LESSON

- Show the children *Dexter Dog's Big Book of Rhymes (CVC).*

  (*"The Big Red Box" should be read and discussed in one session or more depending on the needs of the children. The questions about the content in the following lesson are only a guide.*)

  Tell the children to look and listen as you read "The Big Red Box", pages 2 to 11.

  Reread or invite children to read page 2.

  Ask: "Which animals sat on the big red box?"

  Confirm a *cat*, a *dog*, a *hen* and a *fox*.

  Ask: "Which words rhyme?"

  Confirm *fox* and *box*.

  Reread or invite children to read page 3.

  Ask: "Who fell off the box?"

  Confirm the *dog*.

  Ask: "Which words rhyme?"

  Confirm *cat*, *mat* and *sat*.

  Reread or invite children to read pages 4 and 5.

  Ask: "Which animal got the *hat?* the *wig?* the *pen?*"

  Confirm the *cat*, the *pig* and the *hen*.

  Ask: "Which words rhyme?"

  Confirm *hat* and *cat*, *wig* and *pig*, *pen* and *hen*, *fox* and *box*.

  Reread or invite children to read page 6.

  Ask: "What did the fox offer the dog?"

  Confirm a *pin*, a *tin*, a *mug* and a *rug*.

  Ask: "Which words rhyme?"

  Confirm *pin* and *tin*, *mug* and *rug*.

  Reread or invite children to read page 7.

  Ask: "Was the dog happy with what the fox offered him?"

  Ask: "What else did the fox then offer the dog?"

  Confirm a *bat*, a *mat*, a *pan* and a *fan*.

  Ask: "Which words rhyme?"

  Confirm *bat* and *mat*, *pan* and *fan*.

  Reread or invite children to read page 8.

  Ask: "Was the dog happy now?"

  Ask: "What else did the fox offer the dog?"

  Confirm a *tap*, a *map*, a *bag* and a *rag*.

Reread or invite children to read page 9.

Ask: "What did the dog want?"

Confirm the *box*.

Ask: "Why did the dog want the box?"

Confirm for a *bus*.

Reread or invite children to read page 10.

Ask: "Which animals went in the bus?"

Confirm the *dog*, the *pig*, the *hen* and the *cat*.

Reread or invite children to read page 11.

Ask: "Who was going to drive the bus?"

Confirm the *dog*.

Reread the whole story tracking with a pointer and encouraging the children to join in.

NOW OR LATER 1

■ Ask the children to make lists of the rhyming words in the story. They should then see how many other words they can add to each list. (*This could be done as a group or individually.*)

Rhyming words

cat	pig	hen	pin	mug	pan
mat	wig	pen	tin	rug	fan
sat					
hat	tap	bag	bus	me	fox
bat	map	rag	us	see	box

NOW OR LATER 2

■ Show the teacher's copy of Workbook 4 page 10.

Ensure that the children can identify the pictures.

Ask children in turn to read the sentence below the first picture and fill in the missing word. (*Encourage children to use phonic and picture cues.*)

Ask a child to write the missing word.

Tell the children that they have to write the sentence on the dotted line underneath.

Ask: "What kind of letter is at the beginning of a sentence?"

Confirm a capital letter.

Ask: "What comes at the end of a sentence?"

Confirm a full stop.

Write the sentence on the dotted line focusing on the capital letter, the spaces between the words and the full stop at the end.

Repeat the procedure for the second picture.

■ Children complete Workbook 4 page 10. (*Remember to remove teacher's copy before children start work.*)

FURTHER PRACTICE

DEVELOPING SKILLS

Some or all of these activities must be done to ensure progress:

■ Practise writing CVC words and *sh, ch, wh, th* words to dictation.

You say a word, children write the word (*see Word List*).

■ **Magnetic letters**

Children make CVC words and *sh, ch, wh, th* words.

■ **Flash Cards**

Practise reading CVC words and *sh, ch, wh, th* words.

■ **Reading CVC words in context**

– Read me/Write me Cards

– "The Big Red Box"

■ **Dictation: Read me/Write me Cards**

Tell the children that you will read the sentence twice and they must try to remember it.

Read the sentence ensuring that all the sounds are pronounced clearly.

Reread the sentence.

Children write the sentence.

Ask the children to read the written sentence and check for errors such as words missed out or wrong spellings.

Initially it may be necessary to break the sentence down further before the children write. For example, for "Liz is in the cot":

Say "Liz is . . ."

Children write *Liz is* . . .

Say "Liz is in the cot." (*Stress in the cot.*)

Say: "Write in the cot."

NOTE

It is important that the children are encouraged to remember the whole sentence in dictation. However, initially it may be necessary to break down the sentence before the children write. This is especially true for children with poor short-term memories and/or sequencing skills.

ACTIVITIES AT HOME

Homework Sheets 4A to 4I.

CVC words

CVC words in context

BEFORE YOU START

THE NLF AIMS

- Read CVC words in the context of a story.
- Identify rhyming words in the context of a story.
- Write CVC words in the context of a sentence.
- Begin to understand and use a capital letter and full stop in a sentence.

WHAT YOU NEED

RESOURCES

- Flash Cards – CVC words
- *Dexter Dog's Big Book of Rhymes (CVC)* pages 12 to 23
- Workbook 4 page 11
- Teacher's copy of Workbook 4 page 11
- Homework Sheets 4A to 4I
- Word List
- Read me/Write me Cards

KEY LESSON POINTERS

VOCABULARY

alphabet letter name sound word
sentence capital letter full stop
space/spacing rhyme

THE CHILDREN should throughout the lesson:

- focus on the rhythm and the rhyme of the language
- practise decoding skills in text
- focus on the content of the story.

YOU should throughout the lesson:

- emphasise the rhythm and the rhyme of the language
- encourage the children to use phonic skills taught to read (decode) text
- encourage referral to the story for answers to questions
- focus on capital letters, full stops and spacing when writing sentences.

THE LESSON

STARTING THE LESSON

- Flash Cards – Quick revision of CVC words.

TEACHING THE LESSON

- Show the children *Dexter Dog's Big Book of Rhymes (CVC)*.

  (*"The Fit Rat and the Fat Rat" should be read and discussed in one session or more depending on the needs of the children. The questions about the content in the following lesson are only a guide.*)

  Tell the children to look and listen as you read "The Fit Rat and The Fat Rat", pages 12 to 23 with focus on the rhythm and rhyme of the language.

  Reread "The Fit Rat and The Fat Rat" pages 12 and 13.

  Ask: "Who said 'Can I get fit like you?'"

  Confirm the *Fat Rat*.

  Ask: "What did Fit Rat tell Fat Rat to do?"

  Ask: "Which words rhyme?"

  Confirm *you* and *do*, *run*, *fun* and *sun*, *bit*, *fit* and *sit*.

  Reread or invite children to read pages 14 and 15.

  Ask: "What else did Fit Rat tell Fat Rat to do?"

  Ask: "Which words rhyme?"

  Confirm: *hop* and *top*, *bit*, *fit* and *sit*, *day* and *way*.

  Reread or invite children to read pages 16 and 17.

  Discuss the "health warning" that Fit Rat gave Fat Rat.

  Ask: "Which words rhyme?".

  Confirm *bin* and *thin*, *big* and *pig*.

  Reread or invite children to read pages 18 to 21 and discuss how Fat Rat can get fit.

  Ask: "Which words rhyme?"

  Confirm *day* and *way*, *spot* and *got*, *lot* and *got*.

  Encourage the children to predict what Fat Rat might decide to do.

  Reread or invite children to read page 22 and discuss what Fat Rat did decide to do.

  Reread "The Fit Rat and the Fat Rat" tracking with a pointer and encouraging the children to join in.

NOW OR LATER 1

■ Ask the children to make lists of the rhyming words in the story. They should then see how many other words they can add to each list. (*This could be done as a group or individually.*)

Rhyming Words:

fat	you	run	bit	hop
rat	do	fun	fit	top
		sun	sit	

day	bin	big	spot	said
way	thin	pig	got	bed
			lot	

NOW OR LATER 2

■ Show the teacher's copy of Workbook 4 page 11.

Ensure that the children can identify the pictures.

Ask the children to read the sentence below the first picture and fill in the missing word. (*Encourage children to use phonic and picture cues.*)

Ask a child to write the missing word.

Tell the children that they have to write the sentence on the dotted line underneath.

Ask: "What kind of letter is at the beginning of a sentence?"

Confirm a capital letter.

Ask: "What comes at the end of a sentence?"

Confirm a full stop.

Write the sentence on the dotted line focusing on the capital letter, the spaces between the words and the full stop at the end. (*Monitor correct letter formation.*)

Repeat the procedure for the second picture.

Children complete Workbook 4 page 11.
(*Remember to remove teacher's copy before children start work.*)

FURTHER PRACTICE

DEVELOPING SKILLS

Some or all of these activities must be done to ensure progress:

■ Practise writing CVC words and *sh, ch, wh, th* words to dictation.

You say a word, children write the word (*see Word List*).

■ **Flash Cards**

Practise reading CVC words and *sh, ch, wh, th* words.

■ **Reading CVC words in context**

– Read me/Write me Cards

– "The Big Red Box"

– "The Fit Rat and the Fat Rat"

■ **Dictation: Read me/Write me Cards**

Tell the children that you will read the sentence twice and they must try to remember it.

Read the sentence ensuring that all the sounds are pronounced clearly.

Reread the sentence.

Children write the sentence.

Ask the children to read the written sentence and check for errors such as words missed out or wrong spellings.

Initially it may be necessary to break the sentence down further before the children write. For example, for "Liz is in the cot":

Say "Liz is . . ."

Children write *Liz is* . . .

Say "Liz is in the cot." (*Stress <u>in the cot</u>.*)

Say: "Write <u>in the cot</u>."

NOTE

It is important that the children are encouraged to remember the whole sentence in dictation. However, initially it may be necessary to break down the sentence before the children write. This is especially true for children with poor short term memories and/or sequencing skills.

ACTIVITIES AT HOME

Homework Sheets 4A to 4I.

CVC words

CVC words in context

THE NLF AIMS

- Read CVC words in the context of a sentence.
- Write CVC words in the context of a sentence.
- Begin to understand and use a capital letter and full stop in a sentence.

WHAT YOU NEED

RESOURCES

- Flash Cards – CVC words
- Workbook 4 pages 12 to 19
- Homework Sheets 4A to 4I
- Word List
- Read me/Write me Cards

KEY LESSON POINTERS

The following activities should be used for a number of lessons to secure the skills objectives of this section. Encourage children to draw on all of their previous learning and to use strategies already taught.

VOCABULARY

alphabet   letter   name   sound   word
sentence   capital letter   full stop
space/spacing   rhyme

THE CHILDREN should throughout the lesson:

- focus on picture, sound and context cues when reading the sentences
- focus on capital letters, full stops and spacing when writing.

YOU should throughout the lesson:

- encourage the children to focus on picture, sound and context cues when reading
- focus on capital letters, full stops and spacing when writing a sentence.

THE LESSON

SKILLS REVIEW

■ A selection of these activities involving direct teaching should be done before the children complete any of pages 12 to 19 in Workbook 4.

■ Flash Cards – Revision of CVC words.
  Distribute CVC Flash Cards to the children (approximately 5 each).
  Ask the children to indicate if they have the word *bus, dog, wet* and so on.
  Ask the children to indicate if they have a word that rhymes with *ten, box, cup* and so on.

■ Vary the way you gather in the Flash Cards.
  Ask for all the children who have each word you say to give it to you, for example, *bed, dog, sun.*
  Ask for all the children who have a word that rhymes with each word you say to give it to you, for example, a word that rhymes with *cat, pen.*

■ Find the same word – Use Read me/Write me Cards. A list of Read me/Write me Cards with the identified words underlined is on page 243.
  (*This is best done with a group of children to keep the activity quick and snappy.*)

  1. Distribute Read me/Write me Cards to the children, 1, 2 or 3 each.
  2. Tell the children that you will say a word and they have to find the word on one of their cards.
  3. Ask the children to indicate when they find the word, for example, *bag.*
  4. Children who find the identified word read the card with the sentence containing that word to the others in the group.
  5. You scan sentences to check accuracy.

  The children are being asked to find and read identified words in different contexts.

List of Read me/Write me Cards with words you say underlined:

The man is on the <u>bus</u>.	Sam has a <u>red</u> hat.
Ben is in the red <u>bus</u>.	Jon has a <u>red</u> pen.
<u>Mum</u> is in the shop.	Jan has a <u>pet</u> cat.
Get the mop for <u>mum</u>.	Liz fed the <u>pet</u> pig.
Tom is in a <u>big</u> van.	Jim has a <u>mug</u> and a jug.
The <u>big</u> jug is in the bag.	The <u>mug</u> is on the bed.
Liz <u>is</u> in the cot.	The fish <u>is</u> in the net.
Jan <u>is</u> a fat hen.	The net <u>is</u> wet.
Zip up the <u>bag</u>.	Zak is at the <u>vet</u>.
The <u>bag</u> has a big zip.	The <u>vet</u> will get the dog.
The fox <u>hid</u> the cub.	Pat <u>can</u> hop and run.
Sam <u>hid</u> his net.	The cat <u>can</u> sit on the box.
The peg is in the <u>bag</u>.	Ben has a chip <u>pan</u>.
Mum has a red <u>bag</u>.	The lid is on the <u>pan</u>.
Dom hid the <u>bat</u>.	Dan met the <u>men</u>.
A red <u>bat</u> on a red mat.	The <u>men</u> sat in the van.
The <u>dog</u> is in the hut.	Meg is in <u>bed</u>.
Dad has a big <u>dog</u>.	The mug is on the <u>bed</u>.

■ Write CVC words to dictation. (*See Word List*)

■ Children complete one page daily from Workbook 4 pages 12 to 19 during skills practice lessons.

FURTHER PRACTICE

DEVELOPING SKILLS

Some or all of these activities must be done to ensure progress:

■ Practise writing CVC words and *sh, ch, wh, th* words to dictation.

You say a word, children write the word (*see Word List*).

■ **Flash Cards**

Practise reading CVC words and *sh, ch, wh, th* words.

■ **Reading CVC words in context**
  – Read me/Write me Cards
  – "The Big Red Box"
  – "The Fit Rat and the Fat Rat"

■ **Dictation: Read me/Write me Cards**

Tell the children that you will read the sentence twice and they must try to remember it.

Read the sentence ensuring that all the sounds are pronounced clearly.

Reread the sentence.

Children write the sentence.

Ask the children to read the written sentence and check for errors such as words missed out or wrong spellings.

Initially it may be necessary to break the sentence down further before the children write. For example, for "Liz is in the cot":

Say "Liz is . . ."

Children write *Liz is . . .*

Say "Liz is in the cot." (*Stress <u>in the cot</u>.*)

Say: "Write <u>in the cot</u>."

NOTE

It is important that the children are encouraged to remember the whole sentence in dictation. However, initially it may be necessary to break down the sentence before the children write. This is especially true for children with poor short-term memories and/or sequencing skills.

ACTIVITIES AT HOME

Homework Sheets 4A to 4I.

CVC words

The **ck** sound

BEFORE YOU START

THE NLF AIMS

- Hear and identify the sound *ck*.
- Read the letters that represent the sound (*phoneme*) *ck*.
- Write the letters that represent the sound (*phoneme*) *ck* of spoken words.

WHAT YOU NEED

RESOURCES

- Letter Cards *c, k* and *ck*
- Chalkboard/whiteboard
- Workbook 4 page 20
- Teacher's copy of Workbook 4 page 20
- Paper/card
- Homework Sheets 4J and 4K
- Word List
- Assessment 4.11

KEY LESSON POINTERS

VOCABULARY

alphabet   letter   name   sound
letter shape   word   rhyme   join
start/end

THE CHILDREN should throughout the lesson:

- know that two letters can join to make one sound
- focus on spelling patterns *ack, eck, ick, ock* and *uck*

YOU should throughout the lesson:

- emphasise the *ck* sound all the way through
- ensure that the children know that two letters can make one sound
- emphasise spelling patterns *ack, eck, ick, ock* and *uck*.

THE LESSON

STARTING THE LESSON

- Quick revision of *c* and *k*, reading the letter that represents the sound and knowing the sound that the letter represents.

  Show Letter Cards and ask what sound each letter makes.

  Ask the children the names of the letters.

TEACHING THE LESSON

- Remind the children that sometimes two letters join together to make one sound.

- Tell the children that when two letters making one sound come together in words, we only say one sound.

  When *c* and *k* join together they make one sound, *ck*, but both letters must be written.

- Tell the children that *ck* often comes at the end or in the middle of words, but never at the beginning of words.

  Ask the children to tell you words with *ck* at the end.

  Write the words given by the children on pieces of paper/card and stick them on the board.

  Draw the children's attention to the fact that the words have different vowels before the *ck* sound at the end.

- Ask: "Which two letters make the sound *ck* at the end?"

  Confirm *c* and *k*.

- Ask the children to select words with the *ick* rhyme from the words on the board and place them in a list so that the rime is easily seen.

  Ask the children to read *ick* words.

- Ask the children to select words with the *ack* rhyme from the words on the board and place them in a list so that the rime is easily seen.

  Ask the children to read *ack* words.

- Ask children in turn to write *ick* words and *ack* words on the board.

  Suggested words:

kick	rack	lick	pick
back	sack	tick	tack
pack	sick	thick	chick

NOW OR LATER

■ Repeat the procedure for *ock*, *eck* and *uck* rhymes.

Suggested words for writing:

dock	suck	neck	lock
deck	duck	luck	peck
rock	sock	tuck	shock

LATER

■ Show the teacher's copy of Workbook 4 page 20.

Top section of page

Ensure that the children can identify the pictures.

Ask: "What sound is at the end of *sock*?"

Confirm *ck*.

Ask the children to write *ck* to complete the word *sock*.

Ask the children to write *sock* on the dotted line.

Repeat the procedure for the other pictures.

Middle section of page

Ask the children to read the first sentence and fill in the missing word using the words above.

Encourage the children to use sound, picture and context cues and to use the strategy read on and read back.

Ask a child to write the missing word on the teacher's copy.

Ask the children to read the sentence and check that it makes sense.

Repeat the procedure for the other sentences.

Bottom section of page

Ensure that the children know to make rhyming words using the given letters.

FURTHER PRACTICE

DEVELOPING SKILLS

Some or all of these activities must be done to ensure progress:

■ Practise writing *ck* words to dictation.

You say a word, children write the word (*see Word List*).

■ **Flash Cards**

Practise reading *ck* words.

■ Distribute 3 to 5 Flash Cards (*ck* words) to a group and begin the following:

– **Show/Give (word)**
The child who has *lock* shows or gives it to you.

– **Choose/Say**
Children in turn choose a card and tell you what it says.

– **Choose/Ask**
One child chooses a card from the child next to him or her and asks what it says. The questioner must confirm whether or not the answer is correct.

– **Show/Give (rhyme)**
The child who has a word that rhymes with *back* shows or gives it to you.

NOTE

At this point the children should investigate, read and spell words ending in *ss*, *ff* and *ll*. Children need to know the rule that CVC words don't end in an *s*, *f*, or *l*, with the exception of *gas*, *bus*, *pus*, *has*, *his* (*s* in *has* and *his* sounds like *z*).

This jingle will help children remember the *s*, *f* and *l* rule: "These silly, foolish letters don't stand on their own".

Suggested words:

mess	kiss	pass	toss	boss
less	miss	lass	loss	moss
	hiss	mass		

doll	cuff	bell	till	pill
	huff	fell	bill	will
	muff	sell	fill	ill
	puff	tell	hill	
		well		

ASSESSMENT 4.11

ACTIVITIES AT HOME

Homework Sheets 4J and 4K.

ck

The ng sound

THE NLF AIMS

- Hear and identify the sound (phoneme) *ng*.
- Read the letters that represent the sound (phoneme) *ng*.
- Write the letters that represent the sound (phoneme) *ng* of spoken words.

WHAT YOU NEED

RESOURCES

- Letter Cards *n*, *g* and *ng*
- Chalkboard/whiteboard
- Workbook 4 pages 21 and 22
- Teacher's copies of Workbook 4 pages 21 and 22
- Paper/card
- Homework Sheet 4L
- Word List
- Assessments 4.12, 4.13

KEY LESSON POINTERS

VOCABULARY

alphabet   letter   name   sound
letter shape   word   rhyme   join
start/end

THE CHILDREN should throughout the lesson:

- know that two letters can join to make one sound
- focus on spelling patterns *ing*, *ang*, *ong* and *ung*

YOU should throughout the lesson:

- emphasise the *ng* sound all the way through
- ensure that the children know that two letters can make one sound
- emphasise spelling patterns *ing*, *ang*, *ong* and *ung*.

STARTING THE LESSON

■ Quick revision of *n* and *g*, reading the letter that represents the sound and knowing the sound that the letter represents.

Show Letter Cards and ask what sound each letter makes.

Ask the children the names of the letters.

TEACHING THE LESSON

■ Remind the children that sometimes two letters join together to make one sound.

■ Tell the children that when *n* and *g* join together they make the sound *ng*.

Tell the children that it's a nasal sound.

Ask the children to say *ng*.

Ask: "Which two letters make the *ng* sound?"

Confirm *n* and *g* (*sounds and names*).

■ Tell the children that words don't start with *ng*, but *ng* often comes at the end of words.

Ask the children to tell you words with *ng* at the end.

Write the words given by the children on pieces of paper/card and stick them on the board, for example, *song*, *hang*, *ding*, *lung*.

Draw the children's attention to the fact that the words all have different vowels and the *ng* sound at the end.

■ Ask: "Which two letters make *ng*?"

Confirm *n* and *g*.

■ Ask the children to select words with the *ing* rhyme from the words on the board and place them in a list so that the rime is easily seen.

Ask the children to read *ing* words.

■ Ask the children to select words with the *ang* rhyme from the words on the board and place them in a list so that the rime is easily seen.

Ask the children to read *ang* words.

■ Ask children in turn to write *ing* words and *ang* words on the board.

Suggested words:

king	bang	gang	fang
ring	hang	sang	sing
wing	rang	ding	thing

NOW OR LATER

- Repeat the procedure for *ong* and *ung* rhymes.

  Suggested words for writing:

gong	lung	hung	rung	sung
long	song	dong		

- Show the teacher's copy of Workbook 4 page 21.

  Top section of page

  Ensure that the children can identify the pictures.

  Ask: "What sound is at the end of *ring*?"

  Confirm *ng*.

  Ask the children to write *ng* to complete the word *ring*.

  Ask the children to write *ring* on the dotted line.

  Repeat the procedure for the other pictures.

  Middle section of page

  Ask the children to read the first sentence and fill in the missing word using the words above.

  Encourage the children to use sound, picture and context cues and to use the strategy read on and read back.

  Ask a child to write the missing word on the teacher's copy.

  Ask the children to read the sentence and check that it makes sense.

  Repeat the procedure for the other sentences.

  Bottom section of page

  Ensure that the children know to make rhyming words using the given letters.

LATER

- Repeat the above lesson for further practice.

- Children complete Workbook 4 page 22.

  Ensure that children know to find rhyming *ing*, *ong*, *ang* and *ung* words in the word searches.

FURTHER PRACTICE

DEVELOPING SKILLS

Some or all of these activities must be done to ensure progress:

- Practise writing *ng* words to dictation.

  You say a word, children write the word (*see Word List*).

- **Flash Cards**

  Practise reading *ng* words.

- Distribute Flash Cards (*ng* endings) to a group and carry out activities as described on page 245.

  This activity can be extended to include:

  – **Find/Ask**

  A child reads and selects a card, without identifying its position, from the child next to them and asks him or her to find the chosen word, for example, *hang*. The questioner must confirm that the child has found the correct word.

- **What's my sound**

  Children have Letter Cards *n*, *g* and *ng* on the table. You say a word and children hold up the Letter Card that represents the *n*, *g* or *ng* sound at the end of the word.

  Suggested words:

ban	bag	bang
	log	long
	hug	hung
din	dig	ding
	dog	dong
win	wig	wing
ran	rag	rang
run	rug	rung

ASSESSMENTS 4.12, 4.13

ACTIVITIES AT HOME

Homework Sheet 4L.

ng

Consonant clusters at the end of words

THE NLF AIMS

- Identify both sounds in consonant clusters.
- Read CVCC words.
- Spell CVCC words.
- Write CVCC words.

WHAT YOU NEED

RESOURCES

- Flash Cards – CVCC words
- Chalkboard/whiteboard
- Workbook 4 page 23
- Teacher's copy of Workbook 4 page 23
- Homework Sheet 4M
- Word List

KEY LESSON POINTERS

VOCABULARY

alphabet letter name sound vowel
word end

THE CHILDREN should throughout the lesson:

- focus on the final consonant cluster in CVCC words
- identify the two sounds that make the consonant cluster.

YOU should throughout the lesson:

- emphasise both consonants in the final consonant cluster
- ensure an awareness that CVCC words have four letters with a vowel in the "middle"
- ensure correct letter formation.

THE LESSON

TEACHING THE LESSON

■ Tell the children that there will be two sounds at the end of the words that you are going to say.

Ask the children to identify the sounds at the end of the following words: *went, tent, bent, sent, dent, lent, pant, mint, tint.*

(*Emphasise carefully both consonants in the final consonant cluster. In everyday speech one of these often becomes dominant.*)

Confirm *nt*.

Ask: "Which letters make *nt*?"

Confirm *n* and *t*.

■ Tell the children that the two sounds are very close together and they have to listen carefully to hear them both.

■ Ask the children to identify the sounds at the end of the following words: *kilt, wilt, guilt, lilt, belt, felt, melt.*

Confirm *lt*.

Ask: "Which letters make *lt*?"

Confirm *l* and *t*.

■ Write *nt* and *lt* on the board.

Tell the children to listen and tell you if the words end in *lt* or *nt*.

Suggested words:

went	guilt	felt	want
tent	tilt	rent	kilt
bent	sent	wilt	belt
melt	dent	lent	bolt

■ Slow speak the word *bent*.

Ask: "How many sounds can you hear in the word *bent* (*slow speak*)?"

Confirm four, *b e n t*.

Ask a child to write *bent* on the board.

Say the word *tent* (*slow speak*).

Ask: "How many sounds can you hear in the word *tent* (*slow speak*)?"

Confirm four, *t e n t*.

Repeat the procedure for *went, dent, sent, rent, lent*.

Ask: "Which vowel is in the 'middle'?"

Confirm *e*.

Slow speak the word *pant*.

Ask a child to write *pant* on the board.

Ask: "Which vowel is in the 'middle'?"

Confirm *a*.

Slow speak the word *mint*.

Ask a child to write *mint* on the board. (*Some children may find it difficult to hear the i sound in words like* **mint**.)

Ask: "Which vowel is in the middle?"

Confirm *i*.

Repeat the procedure for *tint*.

■ Ask children to read the words, *bent, tent, went, dent, sent, rent, lent, pant, mint, tint*.

■ Ask the children to write down the above words on their paper/jotter. (*Remember to slow speak the words for writing if necessary.*)

NOW OR LATER

■ Repeat the above and focus on writing *lt* words: *melt, belt, felt, kilt, wilt, lilt*.

LATER

■ Repeat the above lesson for words with *st* and *ft* consonant clusters.

Suggested words for the lesson:

fast	last	mast	past	best
test	rest	jest	west	pest
nest	must	fist	just	dust
rust	soft	loft	lift	gift
left	tuft	raft		

■ Show the teacher's copy of Workbook 4 page 23.

Ask the children to identify the pictures.

Ask: "What sound is at the end of *tent*?"

Confirm *nt*.

Ask a child to point to *nt*.

Ask: "What is the other sound?"

Confirm *lt*.

Confirm the procedure: circle the correct sound *nt* and cross out the wrong sound *lt*.

Ask a child to complete the procedure.

Ask a child what to do next.

Confirm they write the whole word (*tent*) on the dotted line.

Ask a child to complete the procedure.

Ask the child to read the word he or she has written.

Confirm *tent*.

■ Children complete Workbook 4 page 23.

DEVELOPING SKILLS

Some or all of these activities must be done to ensure progress:

■ Practise writing CVCC words to dictation.

You say a word, children write the word (*see Word List*).

■ **Flash Cards**

Practise reading CVCC words.

■ Distribute 3 to 5 Flash Cards (CVCC words) to a group and ask them to arrange their cards face up before starting these activities.

– **Show/Give (word)**
The child who has *tent* shows or gives it to you.

– **Choose/Say**
Children in turn choose a card and tell you what it says.

– **Choose/Ask**
One child chooses a card from the child next to him or her and asks what it says. The questioner must confirm whether or not the answer is correct.

– **Show/Give (rhyme)**
The child who has a word that rhymes with *nest* shows or gives it to you.

– **Find/Ask**
A child reads and selects a card, without identifying its position, from the child next to them and asks him or her to find the chosen word, for example, *belt*. The questioner must confirm that the child has found the correct word.

ACTIVITIES AT HOME

Homework Sheet 4M.

Consonant clusters at the end of words

THE NLF AIMS

- Identify both sounds in consonant clusters.
- Read CVCC words.
- Spell CVCC words.
- Write CVCC words.

WHAT YOU NEED

RESOURCES

- Flash Cards – CVCC words
- Chalkboard/whiteboard
- Workbook 4 page 24
- Teacher's copy of Workbook 4 page 24
- Headbands with slits
- Homework Sheet 4M
- Word List

KEY LESSON POINTERS

VOCABULARY

alphabet letter name sound
vowel word sentence end rhyming
spell

THE CHILDREN should throughout the lesson:

- focus on the final consonant cluster in CVCC words
- identify the two sounds that make the consonant cluster.

YOU should throughout the lesson:

- emphasise both consonants in the final consonant cluster
- ensure an awareness that CVCC words have four letters with a vowel in the "middle"
- ensure correct letter formation.

THE LESSON

STARTING THE LESSON

- Flash Cards *nt*, *lt*, *st* and *ft*.
  Give four children headbands with *nt*, *lt*, *st*, *ft* cards to wear.

Ask them to stand in four separate places in front of the group/class.

Explain that the child with the *nt* headband likes words ending with *nt*, and each of the others likes words ending in the letters on their headbands.

- Tell the children that you will call out some words and each of them must decide which set the words belong to by the sound at the end of the word.

Suggested words:

guilt	must	soft	went
sent	lift	dust	lost
melt	belt	last	want
left	salt	halt	raft
best	built	wilt	hint

TEACHING THE LESSON

- Ask a child to write *bent* on board. (*Monitor correct letter formation.*)

  Ask: "Which word would you get if you changed *b* in *bent* to *s*?"

  Confirm *sent*.

  Ask a child to write *sent* under *bent*.

  Ask: "Which word would you get if you changed *s* in *sent* to *t*?"

  Confirm *tent*.

  Ask a child to write *tent* under *sent*.

  Repeat the above procedure for the words *rent*, *went*, *dent*, *lent*, *vent*.

- Ask the children to read the list of *ent* rhyming words.

  Focus the children's attention on the spelling pattern rime. Tell them that if they know how to spell (write) *bent*, they can spell *sent, tent, rent, went, dent, lent, vent*, by changing the first letter.

- Ask a child to write *felt* on board. (*Monitor correct letter formation.*)

  Ask: "Which word would you get if you changed *f* in *felt* to *b*?"

  Confirm *belt*.

  Ask a child to write *belt* under *felt*.

  Ask: "Which word would you get if you changed *b* in *belt* to *m*?"

  Confirm *melt*.

  Ask a child to write *melt* under *belt*.

  Repeat the procedure for *pelt*.

- Ask the children to read the list of *elt* rhyming words.

  Focus the children's attention on the spelling pattern rime and say that if they know how to spell *felt*, they can spell *belt, melt, pelt*, by changing the first letter.

- Repeat the above procedure for *est* rhyming words.

  Suggested words:

best	test	rest	vest
west	pest	nest	

- Repeat the procedure for *oft* and *ift* rhyming words.

  Suggested words:

loft	soft	lift	gift

NOW OR LATER

- Show the teacher's copy of Workbook 4 page 24.

  ### Top section of page

  Ensure that the children can identify the pictures and know the procedure to complete: tick the box for the correct word and put a cross in the box for the wrong word. Write correct word.

  ### Middle section of page

  Ensure that the children know to choose a word from above to complete each sentence.

  ### Bottom section of page

  Ensure that the children know to make rhyming words using the letters given.

FURTHER PRACTICE

DEVELOPING SKILLS

Some or all of these activities must be done to ensure progress:

- Practise writing CVCC words to dictation.

  You say a word, children write the word (*see Word List*).

- **Flash Cards**

  Practise reading CVCC words.

- Distribute 3 to 5 Flash Cards (CVCC words) to a group and ask them to arrange their cards face up before starting these activities.

  – **Show/Give (word)**
  The child who has *went* shows or gives it to you.

  – **Choose/Say**
  Children in turn choose a card and tell you what it says.

  – **Choose/Ask**
  One child chooses a card from the child next to him or her and asks what it says. The questioner must confirm whether or not the answer is correct.

  – **Show/Give (rhyme)**
  The child who has a word that rhymes with *vest* shows or gives it to you.

  – **Find/Ask**
  A child reads and selects a card, without identifying its position, from the child next to them and asks him or her to find the chosen word, for example, *melt*. A questioner must confirm that the child has found the correct word.

ACTIVITIES AT HOME

Homework Sheet 4M.

CVCC

Consonant clusters at the end of words

THE NLF AIMS

- Identify both sounds in consonant clusters.
- Read CVCC words.
- Spell CVCC words.
- Write CVCC words.

WHAT YOU NEED

RESOURCES

- Flash Cards – CVCC words
- Chalkboard/whiteboard
- Workbook 4 page 25
- Teacher's copy of Workbook 4 page 25
- Homework Sheet 4N
- Word List

KEY LESSON POINTERS

VOCABULARY

alphabet letter name sound vowel
word end

THE CHILDREN should throughout the lesson:

- focus on the final consonant cluster in CVCC words
- identify the two sounds that make the consonant cluster.

YOU should throughout the lesson:

- emphasise both consonants in the final consonant cluster
- ensure an awareness that CVCC words have four letters with a vowel in the "middle"
- ensure correct letter formation.

TEACHING THE LESSON

- Tell the children that there will be two sounds at the end of the words that you are going to say.

  Ask the children to identify the sounds at the end of the following words: *camp, damp, lamp, ramp, bump, dump, jump, hump, pump, lump. (Emphasise carefully both consonants in the final consonant cluster. In everyday speech one of these often becomes dominant.)*

  Confirm *mp.*

  Ask: "Which letters make *mp*?"

  Confirm *m* and *p.*

- Tell the children that the two sounds are very close together and they have to listen carefully to hear them both.

- Ask the children to identify the sound at the end of the following words: *band, hand, land, sand, bend, lend, send, mend, pond, fond.*

  Confirm *nd.*

  Ask: "Which letters make *nd*?"

  Confirm *n* and *d.*

- Write *mp* and *nd* on the board.

  Tell the children to listen and tell you if words end in *mp* or *nd.*

  Suggested words:

camp	damp	lamp	ramp	bump
dump	jump	hump	pump	lump
band	hand	land	sand	bend
lend	send	mend	pond	fond

- Slow speak the word *jump.*

  Ask: "How many sounds can you hear in the word *jump* (slow speak)?"

  Confirm four, *j u m p.*

  Ask a child to write *jump* on the board.

  Say the word *lump* (*slow speak*).

  Ask: "How many sounds can you hear in the word *lump* (*slow speak*)?"

  Confirm four, *l u m p.*

  Repeat the procedure for *bump, dump, hump, pump.*

  Ask: "Which vowel is in the middle?"

  Confirm *u.*

Say the word *camp*.

Ask a child to write *camp* on the board.

Repeat the procedure for *damp*, *lamp*, *ramp*.

Ask: "Which vowel is in the middle?"

Confirm *a*.

Say the word *limp*.

Ask a child to write *limp* on the board. (*Some children may find it difficult to hear the* i *sound in words like* **limp***.*)

■ Ask the children to read the words *bump*, *dump*, *jump*, *hump*, *pump*, *lump*, *camp*, *damp*, *lamp*, *ramp*, *limp*.

■ Ask the children to write down the above words on their paper/jotter. (*Remember to slow speak the words for writing if necessary.*)

NOW OR LATER

■ Repeat the above and focus on writing words which end in *nd*.

Suggested words:

| band | hand | land | sand | bend |
| lend | send | mend | pond | fond |

LATER

■ Repeat the above lesson to include words which end in *lf*.

Suggested words:

| elf | self | shelf | golf |

■ Show the teacher's copy of Workbook 4 page 25.

Ensure that the children know the procedure to complete the page: circle the correct sound and cross out the wrong sound. Write the word on the dotted line.

Children complete Workbook 4 page 25.

FURTHER PRACTICE

DEVELOPING SKILLS

Some or all of these activities must be done to ensure progress:

■ Practise writing CVCC words to dictation.

You say a word, children write the word (*see Word List*).

■ **Flash Cards**

Practise reading CVCC words.

■ Distribute 3 to 5 Flash Cards (CVCC words) to a group and ask them to arrange their cards face up before starting these activities.

– **Show/Give (word)**

The child who has *jump* shows or gives it to you.

– **Choose/Say**

Children in turn choose a card and tell you what it says.

– **Choose/Ask**

One child chooses a card from the child next to him or her and asks what it says. The questioner must confirm whether or not the answer is correct.

– **Show/Give (rhyme)**

The child who has a word that rhymes with *band* shows or gives it to you.

– **Find/Ask**

A child reads and selects a card, without identifying its position, from the child next to them and asks him or her to find the chosen word, for example, *golf*. The questioner must confirm that the child has found the correct word.

ACTIVITIES AT HOME

Homework Sheet 4N.

CVCC

Consonant clusters at the end of words

THE NLF AIMS

- Identify both sounds in consonant clusters.
- Read CVCC words.
- Spell CVCC words.
- Write CVCC words.

WHAT YOU NEED

RESOURCES

- Flash Cards – CVCC words
- Chalkboard/whiteboard
- Workbook 4 page 26
- Teacher's copy of Workbook 4 page 26
- Headbands with slits
- Homework Sheet 4N
- Word List

KEY LESSON POINTERS

VOCABULARY

alphabet letter name sound vowel word sentence rhyming end pattern spell

THE CHILDREN should throughout the lesson:

- focus on the final consonant cluster in CVCC words
- identify the two sounds that make the consonant cluster.

YOU should throughout the lesson:

- emphasise both consonants in the final consonant cluster
- ensure an awareness that CVCC words have four letters with a vowel in the "middle"
- ensure correct letter formation.

THE LESSON

STARTING THE LESSON

■ Flash Cards *lf*, *mp* and *nd*.
Give three children headbands with *lf*, *mp*, *nd* cards to wear.

Ask them to stand in three separate places in front of group/class.

Explain that the child with the *lf* headband likes words ending with *lf*, and each of the others likes words ending in the letters on their headbands.

■ Tell the children you will call out words ending in *lf*, *mp* and *nd* and each child must decide which set they go to by the sound at the end of the word.

Suggested words:

elf	self	shelf	golf	
camp	damp	lamp	ramp	bump
dump	jump	hump	lump	limp
band	hand	land	sand	bend
lend	send	mend	pond	fond

TEACHING THE LESSON

■ Ask a child to write *camp* on the board. (*Monitor correct letter formation.*)

Ask: "Which word would you get if you changed *c* in *camp* to *d*?"

Confirm *damp*.

Ask a child to write *damp* under *camp*.

Ask: "Which word would you get if you changed *d* in *damp* to *l*?"

Confirm *lamp*.

Ask a child to write *lamp* under *damp*.

Repeat the above procedure for *ramp*.

■ Ask the children to read the list of *amp* rhyming words.

Focus the children's attention on the spelling pattern rime. Tell them that if they know how to spell (write) *camp*, they can spell *damp*, *lamp*, *ramp*, by changing the first letter.

■ Repeat the procedure for **ump** rhyming words.

Suggested words:

bump   dump   hump
lump   jump   pump

■ Ask a child to write **band** on the board. (*Monitor correct letter formation.*)

Ask: "Which word would you get if you changed **b** in **band** to **h**?"

Confirm **hand**.

Ask a child to write **hand** under **band**.

Ask: "Which word would you get if you changed **h** in **hand** to **l**?"

Confirm **land**.

Ask a child to write **land** under **hand**.

Repeat the procedure for **sand**.

■ Ask the children to read the list of **and** rhyming words.

Focus the children's attention on the spelling pattern rime and say that if they know how to spell **band**, they can spell **hand**, **land**, **sand**, by changing the first letter.

■ Repeat the above procedure for **end** rhyming words.

Suggested words:

bend   lend   send   mend

■ Repeat the above procedure for **elf** rhyming words.

Suggested words:

elf   shelf   self

NOW OR LATER

■ Show the teacher's copy of Workbook 4 page 26.

Top section of page

Ensure that the children can identify the pictures and know the procedure to complete: tick the box for the correct word and put a cross in the box for the wrong word. Write the correct word.

Middle section of page

Ensure that the children know to choose a word from above to complete each sentence.

Bottom section of page

Ensure that the children know to make rhyming words using the letters given.

FURTHER PRACTICE

DEVELOPING SKILLS

Some or all of these activities must be done to ensure progress:

■ Practise writing CVCC words to dictation.

You say a word, children write the word (*see Word List*).

■ **Flash Cards**

Practise reading CVCC words.

■ Distribute 3 to 5 Flash Cards (CVCC words) to a group and ask them to arrange their cards face up before starting these activities.

– **Show/Give (word)**
The child who has *lamp* shows or gives it to you.

– **Choose/Say**
Children in turn choose a card and tell you what it says.

– **Choose/Ask**
One child chooses a card from the child next to him or her and asks what it says. The questioner must confirm whether or not the answer is correct.

– **Show/Give (rhyme)**
The child who has a word that rhymes with *send* shows or gives it to you.

– **Find/Ask**
A child reads and selects a card, without identifying its position, from the child next to them and asks him or her to find the chosen word, for example, *self*. The questioner must confirm that the child has found the correct word.

ACTIVITIES AT HOME

Homework Sheet 4N.

CVCC

Consonant clusters at the end of words

BEFORE YOU START

THE NLF AIMS

- Identify both sounds in consonant clusters.
- Read CVCC words.
- Spell CVCC words.
- Write CVCC words.

WHAT YOU NEED

RESOURCES

- Flash Cards – CVCC words
- Chalkboard/whiteboard
- Workbook 4 page 27
- Teacher's copy of Workbook 4 page 27
- Word List

KEY LESSON POINTERS

VOCABULARY

alphabet letter name sound vowel
word end

THE CHILDREN should throughout the lesson:

- focus on the final consonant cluster in CVCC words
- identify the two sounds that make the consonant cluster.

YOU should throughout the lesson:

- emphasise both consonants in the final consonant cluster
- ensure an awareness that CVCC words have four letters with a vowel in the "middle"
- ensure correct letter formation.

THE LESSON

TEACHING THE LESSON

■ Tell the children that there will be two sounds at the end of the words that you are going to say.

Ask the children to identify the sounds at the end of: *milk, silk, bulk, hulk, sulk.* (*Emphasise carefully both consonants in the final consonant cluster.*
In everyday speech, one of these often becomes dominant.)

Confirm *lk.*

Ask which letters make *lk.*

Confirm *l* and *k.*

■ Tell the children that the two sounds are very close together and they have to listen carefully to hear them both.

■ Ask the children to identify the sound at the end of: *mask, task, risk, tusk, musk, desk.*

Confirm *sk.*

Ask which letters make *sk.*

Confirm *s* and *k.*

■ Write *lk* and *sk* on the board.

Tell the children to listen and tell you if words end in *lk* or *sk.*

Suggested words:

milk	silk	bulk	hulk
sulk	ask	mask	task
risk	tusk	rusk	desk
dusk			

■ Ask a child to write *milk* on the board. (*Monitor correct letter formation.*)

Ask: "Which word would you get if you changed the *m* in *milk* to *s*?"

Confirm *silk.*

Ask a child to write *silk* under *milk.*

Ask the children to read *milk* and *silk* and focus their attention on the spelling pattern rime. Tell them that if they know how to spell *milk*, they can spell *silk* by changing the first letter.

■ Repeat the procedure for *ulk* rhyming words.

Suggested words:

bulk	hulk	sulk

- Repeat the procedure for **ask** rhyming words.

  Ask a child to write **ask** on board. (*Monitor correct letter formation.*)

  Ask: "Which word would you get if you put **m** in front of **ask**?"

  Confirm **mask**.

  Ask a child to write **mask** under **ask**.

  Ask: "Which word would you get if you changed **m** in **mask** to **t**?"

  Confirm **task**.

  Ask a child to write **task** under **mask**.

- Ask the children to read list of **ask** rhyming words.

  Focus the children's attention on the spelling pattern rime and say that if they know how to spell **ask**, they can spell **mask** and **task** by adding **m** or **t** to the beginning.

- Repeat the procedure for **usk** rhyming words.

  Suggested words:
  dusk   rusk   tusk

  Other words to read and investigate:
  risk   desk

NOW OR LATER

- Show the teacher's copy of Workbook 4 page 27.

  Top section of the page

  Ensure that the children can identify the pictures and know the procedure to complete: tick the box for the correct word and put a cross in the box for the wrong word. Write the correct word.

  Middle section of the page

  Ensure that the children know to choose a word from above to complete each sentence.

  Bottom section of the page

  Ensure that the children know to make rhyming words using the letters given.

BLENDING AND SEGMENTING

CVCC WORDS

FURTHER PRACTICE

DEVELOPING SKILLS

Some or all of these activities must be done to ensure progress:

- Practise writing CVCC words to dictation.

  You say a word, children write the word (*see Word List*).

- **Flash Cards**

  Practise reading CVCC words.

- Distribute 3 to 5 Flash Cards (CVCC words) to a group and ask them to arrange their cards face up before starting these activities.

  – **Show/Give (word)**
  The child who has *mask* shows or gives it to you.

  – **Choose/Say**
  Children in turn choose a card and tell you what it says.

  – **Choose/Ask**
  One child chooses a card from the child next to him or her and asks what it says. The questioner must confirm whether or not the answer is correct.

  – **Show/Give (rhyme)**
  The child who has a word that rhymes with *milk* shows or gives it to you.

  – **Find/Ask**
  A child reads and selects a card, without identifying its position, from the child next to them and asks him or her to find the chosen word, for example, *desk*. The questioner must confirm that the child has found the correct word.

CVCC

UNIT 4
LESSON 20

Consonant clusters at the end of words

BEFORE YOU START

THE NLF AIMS

- Identify both sounds in consonant clusters.
- Read CVCC words.
- Spell CVCC words.
- Write CVCC words.

WHAT YOU NEED

RESOURCES

- Flash Cards – CVCC words
- Chalkboard/whiteboard
- Workbook 4 page 28
- Teacher's copy of Workbook 4 page 28
- Homework Sheet 4O
- Word List

KEY LESSON POINTERS

VOCABULARY

alphabet   letter   name   sound   vowel
word   end

THE CHILDREN should throughout the lesson:

- focus on the final consonant cluster in CVCC words
- identify the two sounds that make the consonant cluster.

YOU should throughout the lesson:

- emphasise both consonants in the final consonant cluster
- ensure an awareness that CVCC words have four letters with a vowel in the "middle"
- ensure correct letter formation.

THE LESSON

SKILLS REVIEW

- Flash Cards – CVCC words (*sk, lk*).

TEACHING THE LESSON

- Tell the children that there will be two sounds at the end of the words that you are going to say.

  Ask the children to identify the sounds at the end of the following words: *pink, sink, rink, bank, bunk, junk.*

  Confirm *nk.*

- Tell the children that *nk* sounds as if there is *ng* and *k* but when we write *nk* we miss out the *g.*

  Ask which letters make *nk.*

  Confirm *n* and *k.*

- Ask a child to write *pink* on board. (*Monitor correct letter formation.*)

  Ask: "Which word would you get if you changed *p* in *pink* to *s*?"

  Confirm *sink.*

  Ask a child to write *sink* under *pink.*

  Ask: "Which word would you get if you changed *s* in *sink* to *w*?"

  Confirm *wink.*

  Ask a child to write *wink* under *sink.*

  Repeat the above procedure for *link, mink, rink, think.*

- Ask the children to read the list of *ink* rhyming words.

  Focus the children's attention on the spelling pattern rime and tell them that if they know how to spell (write) *pink*, they can spell *sink, link, mink, kink* and *think*, by changing the first letter.

- Repeat the procedure for *ank* rhyming words.

  Ask a child to write *bank* on board. (*Monitor correct letter formation.*)

  Ask: "Which word would you get if you changed *b* in *bank* to *s*?"

  Confirm *sank*.

  Ask a child to write *sank* under *bank*.

  Ask: "Which word would you get if you changed *s* in *sank* to *t*?"

  Confirm *tank*.

  Ask a child to write *tank* under *sank*.

  Repeat the procedure for *rank* and *thank*.

- Ask the children to read the list of *ank* rhyming words.

  Focus the children's attention on the spelling pattern rime and say that if they know how to spell *bank*, they can spell *sank*, *tank*, *rank* and *thank* by changing the first letter(s).

- Repeat the above procedure for *unk* rhyming words.

  Suggested words:
  bunk   junk   punk

  Focus the children's attention on the fact that the three lists have different vowels, that is, *a*, *i* and *u* and *nk* sound at the end.

- Write *sk*, *lk*, *nk* on the board. Ask the children to listen and tell you if words end in *sk*, *lk* or *nk*.

  Suggested words:

pink	task	milk	wink	bunk
mask	silk	bask	hulk	bank
think	flask	sulk	risk	bulk

NOW OR LATER

- Show the teacher's copy of Workbook 4 page 28.

  Top section of page

  Ensure that the children can identify the pictures and know the procedure to complete: tick the box for the correct word and put a cross in the box for the wrong word. Write the correct word.

  Middle section of page

  Ensure that the children know to choose a word from above to complete each sentence.

  Bottom section of page

  Ensure that the children know to make rhyming words using the letters given.

FURTHER PRACTICE

DEVELOPING SKILLS

Some or all of these activities must be done to ensure progress:

- Practise writing CVCC words to dictation.

  You say a word, children write the word (*see Word List*).

- **Flash Cards**

  Practise reading CVCC words.

- Distribute 3 to 5 Flash Cards (CVCC words) to a group and ask them to arrange their cards face up before starting these activities.

  – **Show/Give (word)**
  The child who has *tank* shows or gives it to you.

  – **Choose/Say**
  Children in turn choose a card and tell you what it says.

  – **Choose/Ask**
  One child chooses a card from the child next to him or her and asks what it says. The questioner must confirm whether or not the answer is correct.

  – **Show/Give (rhyme)**
  The child who has a word that rhymes with *silk* shows or gives it to you.

  – **Find/Ask**
  A child reads and selects a card, without identifying its position, from the child next to them and asks him or her to find the chosen word, for example, *task*. The questioner must confirm that the child has found the correct word.

ACTIVITIES AT HOME

Homework Sheet 4O

CVCC

Consonant clusters at the end of words

BEFORE YOU START

THE NLF AIMS

- Read CVCC words.
- Spell CVCC words.
- Write CVCC words.

WHAT YOU NEED

RESOURCES

- Flash Cards – CVCC words
- Chalkboard/whiteboard
- Workbook 4 pages 29 and 30
- Teacher's copies of Workbook 4 pages 29 and 30
- Assessment 4.14
- Homework Sheets 4M to 4O
- Read me/Write me Cards

KEY LESSON POINTERS

VOCABULARY

alphabet letter name sound word
vowel end phrase rhyming illustrate

THE CHILDREN should throughout the lesson:

- focus on the final consonant cluster in CVCC words
- identify the two sounds that make the consonant cluster.

YOU should throughout the lesson:

- emphasise both consonants in the final consonant cluster
- ensure an awareness that CVCC words have four letters with a vowel in the middle
- ensure correct letter formation.

THE LESSON

SKILLS REVIEW

- Flash Cards – CVCC words.

TEACHING THE LESSON

- The main focus of this lesson is to read CVCC words in context: Read me/Write me Cards.

- Flash Cards – Read me/Write me Cards.

  Invite the children as a group to read Read me/Write me Cards.

  Invite children individually to read Read me/Write me Cards.

- Display Read me/Write me Cards so that the children can see them.

  Ask children in turn to find Read me/Write me Cards which have words that rhyme:

  Cards with rhyming words:

a pink sink	junk on a bunk
a gift in a lift	a hand on the sand
a lamp in the camp	a pump on the dump
a bump and a jump	a vest in the nest

  Encourage the children to focus carefully on the words. The rhyming words need to have the same vowel sound and the same consonant cluster at the end.

- Show the teacher's copy of Workbook 4 page 29.

  Top section of page
  Ensure that the children know to draw a picture to illustrate the phrases.

  Bottom section of page
  Ensure that the children know to choose and write, on the dotted line, the word that rhymes with the given word.

- Children complete Workbook 4 page 29.

LATER

- Repeat the above activities before the children complete Workbook 4 page 30.

FURTHER PRACTICE

DEVELOPING SKILLS

Some or all of these activities must be done to ensure progress:

- Practise writing CVCC words to dictation.
  You say a word, children write the word (*see Word List*).

- Flash Cards
  Practise reading CVCC words.

- Reading: Read me/Write me Cards

- Dictation – Read me/Write me Cards
  Tell the children that you will read the phrase twice and that they must try to remember it.
  Read the phrase to the children ensuring that all the sounds are pronounced clearly.
  Reread the phrase.
  Children write the phrase.
  Ask the children to read written phrase and check for any errors (*words missed out or wrong spellings*).
  Initially it may be necessary to break down the phrase before the children write, for example, for the phrase "A belt on a kilt":
  Say: "A belt . . ."
  Children write "A belt . . ."
  Say: "A belt on a kilt". (*Stress on a kilt.*)
  Say: "Write on a kilt."

NOTE

It is important to encourage the children to remember the whole phrase in dictation. Initially, however, it may be necessary to break down the phrase before the children write. This is especially true for children with poor short term memories or poor sequencing skills, or both.

ASSESSMENT 4.14

ACTIVITIES AT HOME

Homework Sheets 4M to 4O.

CVCC

UNIT 5

BLENDING AND SEGMENTING

CCVC words
Digraphs
Trigraphs

INTRODUCTION

Unit 5 of *Fun Phonics* covers the NLF word level work required for year 1 Terms 2 and 3 moving into Year 2 in which pupils should be taught:

- how to segment, read and spell CCVC words

- that the same phoneme can be represented in more than one way

- that the same spelling can represent more than one sound

- how to segment, read and spell words with digraphs.

The section of the unit that focuses on digraphs develops a crucial skill for successful spelling. Children must have an understanding of the concept that vowels can be represented in more than one way and that the choice of digraph is not random. They should be taught that most vowel spellings have a particular position in words, for example, **ay** appears at the end and **ai** in the middle. Also that spellings such as **ai** and **a-e** which may appear interchangeable are associated with particular consonants. For example, words ending in -**ake**, such as *bake* and *cake*, and -**ate**, such as *late* and *gate* are common, but words ending in -*aik* and -*ait* are less common.

It is also important that children develop a firm grasp of the concept that one spelling can represent more than one sound and that the sense of the text will determine the pronunciation of the word. Children should be encouraged at all times to use text cues as well as phonics. For example, *ow* is pronounced **ou** in *cow* and **oa** in *slow*. Similarly *row*, when used in relation to a boat, is pronounced **oa** and *row*, when referring to a quarrel, is pronounced **ou**.

Consonant clusters at the beginning of words

BEFORE YOU START

THE NLF AIMS

- Hear and identify initial consonant clusters in words.
- Read the letters that represent consonant clusters at the beginning of words.
- Write the letters that represent consonant clusters at the beginning of words.

WHAT YOU NEED

RESOURCES

- Flash Cards – consonant clusters
- Whiteboard/chalkboard
- Workbook 5 pages 1 and 2
- Teacher's copy of Workbook 5 pages 1 and 2
- Quick Cards – consonant clusters
- Word List

KEY LESSON POINTERS

VOCABULARY

alphabet letter name sound
word vowel beginning consonant
consonant cluster

THE CHILDREN should throughout the lesson:

- focus on the initial consonant cluster in CCVC words
- identify the two sounds that make the consonant cluster.

YOU should throughout the lesson:

- emphasise both consonants in the initial consonant cluster
- ensure an awareness that CCVC words have four letters with a vowel in the "middle"
- ensure correct letter formation.

THE LESSON

TEACHING THE LESSON

- Tell the children that there are two sounds very close together at the beginning of the words that you are going to say. Encourage them to listen carefully.

- Ask the children to identify the sounds at the beginning of the following words: **trip**, **trap**, **trod**, **trim**, **trot**. (*Emphasise carefully both consonants in the initial consonant cluster.*)

  Confirm **tr**.

  Ask the children: "Which letters make **tr**?"

  Confirm **t** and **r**.

  Tell the children that the two sounds are very close together and they have to listen carefully to hear them both.

  Ask the children to identify the sounds at the beginning of the following words: **brush**, **brick**, **bring**, **brass**.

  Confirm **br**.

  Ask the children: "Which letters make **br**?"

  Confirm **b** and **r**.

  Repeat for **cr**, **dr**, **pr**, **fr**, **gr**.

  Suggested words:

crab	cry	crown	cross	crust
drawer	drip	dragon	drink	drum
pram	press	present	prize	pretty
friend	frog	frill	frock	fruit
grab	gran	grapes	grin	grass

- Stick **tr**, **br**, **cr**, **dr**, **pr**, **fr**, **gr** cards on the board.

  Tell the children that you will say a word and they have to tell you which sounds the word starts with.

  Invite group/individual responses.

  Suggested words:

train	cracker	bran	dress	prince
frost	grip	bread	problem	fringe
green	tractor	crush	crayon	bridge
prune	fridge	track	crocodile	draw
drill	grizzly			

- Repeat the above activity and ask children in turn to say the sound that the word starts with and point to the card that represents that sound.

■ Show the teacher's copy of Workbook 5 page 1.

Ask the children to identify the pictures.

Ask: "What sound is at the beginning of *tree*?"

Confirm *tr*.

Ask a child to point to *tr*.

Ask: "What is the other sound?"

Confirm *br*.

■ Confirm the procedure: "Circle the correct sound *tr* and cross out the wrong sound *br*."

Ask a child to complete the procedure.

Tell the children that they should write the correct two letters that represent the *tr* sound on the dotted line.

Ask a child to complete the procedure.

■ The children complete Workbook 5 page 1. (*Remember to remove teacher's copy before the children start work.*)

LATER

■ Repeat the above lesson before the children complete Workbook 5 page 2.

FURTHER PRACTICE

DEVELOPING SKILLS

Some or all of these activities must be done to ensure progress:

■ Quick Cards

Children have *br, fr, tr, cr, dr, gr, pr* cards face up on the table.

You call out a word and children point to or hold up the appropriate card.

Suggested words:

bridge	train	drip	fridge
crash	green	prize	trap
crib	dress	gran	pram
grass	prince	drain	crayon
truck	friend	bread	frame

As with initial sounds, some clusters are easily confused: *br/ dr, cr/ gr, dr/ tr, br/ pr*.

It is often difficult for young children to hear the difference between the clusters. Individual speech problems can also cause difficulties. Give plenty of practice.

■ **Practise writing consonant clusters at the beginning of words**

You say a word, children write the initial consonant cluster.

br, fr, tr, cr, dr, gr, pr

Consonant clusters at the beginning of words

THE NLF AIMS

- Hear and identify initial consonant clusters in words.
- Read CCVC words.
- Spell CCVC words.

WHAT YOU NEED

RESOURCES

- *Freda Frog's Big Book of Rhymes (Consonant Clusters)* pages 2 to 13
- Flash Cards – consonant clusters
- Word List
- Whiteboard/chalkboard
- Workbook 5 pages 3 and 4
- Teacher's copy of Workbook 5 pages 3 and 4
- Quick Cards – consonant clusters
- Homework Sheet 5A

KEY LESSON POINTERS

VOCABULARY

alphabet letter name sound
word vowel beginning consonant
consonant cluster

THE CHILDREN should throughout the lesson:

- focus on the initial consonant cluster in CCVC words
- identify the two sounds that make the consonant cluster.

YOU should throughout the lesson:

- emphasise both consonants in the initial consonant cluster
- ensure an awareness that CCVC words have four letters with a vowel in the "middle"
- ensure correct letter formation.

STARTING THE LESSON

- Quick revision of Flash Cards used in Lesson 1.
- Tell the children that you will say a word and they have to tell you what sounds the word starts with.

Suggested words:

bridge	truck	crab	drink	great
France	present	grow	bread	draw
trickle	cream	fry	pram	tray

TEACHING THE LESSON

- Introduce "The Spring Parade" to the children and look at the illustrations on pages 2 and 3 to establish what the book might be about.
- Read page 3 and discuss the content.
- Tell the children that this book has many words starting with the consonant clusters that they have been learning about.

  Write *br*, *tr*, *cr*, *dr*, *pr*, *fr*, *gr* on the board.

  (*Arrange the clusters as headings for word lists.*)

- Tell the children that you will continue to read "The Spring Parade" starting at page 4 and they have to identify the words starting with one of the sounds written on the board.

- Read page 4.

  Discuss the content as appropriate.

  Ask: "Which consonant cluster appears at the beginning of some words on this page?"

  Confirm *fr*.

  Ask the children to identify *fr* words: *front, frog, Freda, friend.*

  You should write the words in the appropriate column as they are identified by the children, or have words previously written on paper or card to stick in the appropriate column.

  Underline the *fr* sound in each word.

- Read page 5 and discuss.

  Ask: "Which consonant cluster appears at the beginning of some words on this page?"

  Confirm *dr*.

  Ask the children to identify *dr* words: *dreamy, dragon, drowned, dress, drags.*

  Write or stick the words in the appropriate column as they are identified by the children.

  Underline the *dr* sound in each word.

266

- Repeat the procedure for pages 6 to 10.

  Page 6: *creaky, crab, creeping, crash, crawling.*

  Page 7: *brown, breaks, break, breathtaking.*

  Page 8: *Grace, grasshopper, grandest, grin.*

  Page 9: *prairie, prances, primrose, proud.*

  Page 10: *trap-door, trying, troublesome, trousers.*

- Ask: "Which alphabet letter do these sounds all have in common?"

  Confirm *r.*

- Read pages 11 to 13 and discuss the ending of the story.

- Focus on CCVC words with *fr, br, tr.*

  Ask children in turn to write CCVC words on the board.

  Suggested words:

brim	bran	trap	trip
trod	trot	frog	from

  Other words to investigate:

brick	brush	brass	frock
frill	trick	track	trash

- Show the teacher's copy of Workbook 5 page 3.

  Ensure that the children can identify the pictures and know how to complete the procedure.

  Top: Tick the box for the correct word. Cross the box for the wrong word. Write the correct word on the dotted line.

  Middle: Complete sentences by choosing a word from the top section. Encourage the children to use the strategy read on/read back.

  Bottom: Use the word given in a sentence.

LATER

- Repeat the above lesson as appropriate before children complete Workbook 5 page 4.

  Focus on *cr, pr, dr* words.

  Suggested words:

crab	crib	cram	pram	prim	prod
prop	drip	drop	drag	drum	

  Other words to investigate:

crack	crush	press	drill	drink	dress

FURTHER PRACTICE

DEVELOPING SKILLS

Some or all of these activities must be done to ensure progress:

- **Quick Cards**

  Children have *br, fr, tr, cr, dr, gr, pr* cards face up on the table.

  You call out a word and children point to or hold up the appropriate card.

  Suggested words:

broom	truck	dry	frozen
crumb	grumble	practise	tree
crown	drive	great	pretty
grey	princess	drink	cradle
treacle	fruit	bride	brick

  As with initial sounds, some clusters are easily confused: *br/ dr, cr/ gr, dr/ tr, br/ pr.*

  It is often difficult for young children to hear the difference between the clusters. Individual speech problems can also cause difficulties. Give plenty of practice.

- **Flash Cards**

  Practise reading CCVC words.

- **Practise writing CCVC words to dictation**

  See Word List.

- **Paint and display**

  Children could make a large frieze showing the parade, to be used as a backdrop to mount CCVC words.

ACTIVITIES AT HOME

Homework Sheet 5A.

CCVC words

Consonant clusters at the beginning of words

BEFORE YOU START

THE NLF AIMS

- Hear and identify initial consonant clusters in words.
- Read the letters that represent consonant clusters at the beginning of words.
- Write the letters that represent consonant clusters at the beginning of words.

WHAT YOU NEED

RESOURCES

- Flash Cards – consonant clusters
- Whiteboard/chalkboard
- Workbook 5 pages 5 and 6
- Teacher's copy of Workbook 5 pages 5 and 6
- Quick Cards – consonant clusters
- Word List

KEY LESSON POINTERS

VOCABULARY

alphabet letter name sound
word vowel beginning consonant
consonant cluster

THE CHILDREN should throughout the lesson:

- focus on the initial consonant cluster in CCVC words
- identify the two sounds that make the consonant cluster.

YOU should throughout the lesson:

- emphasise both consonants in the initial consonant cluster
- ensure an awareness that CCVC words have four letters with a vowel in the "middle"
- ensure correct letter formation.

THE LESSON

STARTING THE LESSON

- Flash Cards – quick revision of consonant clusters covered in Lessons 1 and 2.

TEACHING THE LESSON

- Tell the children that there will be two different sounds very close together at the beginning of the words that you are going to say.

  Ask the children to identify the sounds at the beginning of the following words: *slipper, sleeve, slip, slap*. (*Emphasise carefully both consonants in the initial consonant cluster.*)

  Confirm *sl*.

  Ask: "Which letters make *sl*?"

  Confirm *s* and *l*.

  Tell the children that the two sounds are very close together and they have to listen carefully to hear them both.

  Ask the children to identify the sound at the beginning of the following words: *blouse, blazer, black, blow*.

  Confirm *bl*.

  Ask: "Which letters make *bl*?"

  Confirm *b* and *l*.

- Repeat the above for *cl, pl, fl, gl*.

  Suggested words:

clock	clean	clothes	clap	club
plum	plate	plug	plant	plank
fly	flag	flip	flat	fluffy
glasses	glad	glove	glitter	gloomy

- Stick the *sl, bl, cl, pl, fl, gl* cards on the board.

  Tell the children that you will say a word and they have to tell you what sound the word starts with.

  Invite group/individual responses.

  Suggested words:

sledge	blanket	clogs	flames	plaster
glass	blood	cliff	slug	plop
flop	gloss	flippers	clown	blink
flower	playing	slide	glue	sleeve

- Repeat the above activity and ask children in turn to say the sound that the word starts with and point to the card that represents that sound.

■ Show the teacher's copy of Workbook 5 page 5.
Ask the children to identify the pictures.
Ask: "What sound is at the beginning of *blouse*?"
Confirm *bl*.
Ask a child to point to *bl*.
Ask the child what the other sound is.
Confirm *sl*.

■ Confirm the procedure: "Circle the correct sound *bl* and cross out the wrong sound *sl*."
Ask a child to complete the procedure.

■ Tell the children that they should write the correct two letters that represent the *bl* sound on the dotted line.

■ Ask a child to complete the procedure.

■ Children complete Workbook 5 page 5.
(*Remember to remove teacher's copy before children start to work.*)

LATER

■ Repeat the above lesson before children complete Workbook 5 page 6.

FURTHER PRACTICE

DEVELOPING SKILLS

Some or all of these activities must be done to ensure progress:

■ Quick Cards

Children have *sl*, *bl*, *cl*, *pl*, *fl*, *gl* cards face up on the table.

You call out a word and children point to or hold up the appropriate card.

Suggested words:

glow	slice	blue	clever
float	plastic	play	clean
gladiator	flock	flood	sleep
slide	blister	class	glisten
block	plan	blood	glum

As with initial sounds, some clusters are easily confused: *pl*/*bl*, *cl*/*gl*.

It is often difficult for young children to hear the difference between the clusters. Individual speech problems can also cause difficulties. Give plenty of practice.

■ Practise writing consonant clusters at the beginning of words

You say a word, children write the initial consonant cluster.

sl, bl, cl, pl, fl, gl

UNIT 5
LESSON 4

Consonant clusters at the beginning of words

BEFORE YOU START

THE NLF AIMS

- Hear and identify initial consonant clusters in words.
- Read CCVC words.
- Spell CCVC words.

WHAT YOU NEED

RESOURCES

- *Freda Frog's Big Book of Rhymes (Consonant Clusters)* pages 14 to 22
- Flash Cards – consonant clusters
- Whiteboard/chalkboard
- Workbook 5 pages 7 and 8
- Teacher's copy of Workbook 5 pages 7 and 8
- Quick Cards – consonant clusters
- Word List
- Homework Sheet 5B

KEY LESSON POINTERS

VOCABULARY

alphabet letter name sound
word vowel beginning consonant
consonant cluster

THE CHILDREN should throughout the lesson:

- focus on the initial consonant cluster in CCVC words
- identify the two sounds that make the consonant cluster.

YOU should throughout the lesson:

- emphasise both consonants in the initial consonant cluster
- ensure an awareness that CCVC words have four letters with a vowel in the "middle"
- ensure correct letter formation.

THE LESSON

STARTING THE LESSON

- Quick revision of Flash Cards used in Lesson 3.
- Tell the children that you will say a word and they have to tell you what sounds the word starts with.
  Suggested words:

plastic	glum	clay	clown
blue	flurry	slimy	plums
glue	flop	sledge	blink

TEACHING THE LESSON

- Tell the children that the next section of the Big Book is a collection of rhymes focusing on the consonant clusters *pl, cl, sl, gl, fl, bl.*
  Write *pl, cl, sl, gl, fl, bl* on the board.
  (*Arrange the clusters as headings for word lists.*)
  Tell the children that you will read the first rhyme starting at page 14 and they will have to identify the words starting with one of the sounds written on the board.

- Read pages 14 and 15.
  Discuss the contents as appropriate.

- Ask: "Which consonant cluster appears at the beginning of some words on these pages?"
  Confirm *bl.*
  Ask the children to identify *bl* words: *blazer, blue, blot, blood, blancmange, blob, black, bleach, blame, bluebottle.**
  Write or stick the words in the appropriate column as they are identified by the children.

- Read pages 16 and 17.
  Discuss the contents as appropriate.

- Ask: "Which consonant cluster appears at the beginning of some words on this page?"
  Confirm *cl.*
  Ask the children to identify *cl* words: *Clarabella, clever, clown, clarinet, climbing, clutching, clap.**
  Write or stick the words in the appropriate column as they are identified by the children.

- Repeat the procedure for pages 18 to 22.
  Pages 18 and 19: *Flossy, fleas, flock, flit, flitter, float, flurry, flying, flops, flamenco.**

Pages 20 and 21: *Gloria, Gloop, gloomy, glum, glamorous, glasses, glimpses, gleaming, glee.**

Page 22: *please, platypus, play, plate, plump, plums, plane, plasticine, plant, plink, plonk.**

■ Choose only four or five words from each list* above.

Ask: "Which alphabet letter do these clusters all have in common?"

Confirm *l.*

■ Focus on CCVC words with *pl, cl, gl.*

Ask children in turn to write CCVC words on the board.

Suggested words:

plan	plug	plip	plum	plop
plus	plot	clap	clip	clop
club	clog	glad	glum	clan

Other words to investigate:

| click | cluck | clock | cling | clang | class |
| clasp | glass | gloss | pluck | plant | |

■ Show the teacher's copy of Workbook 5 page 7.

Ensure that the children can the identify pictures and know how to complete the procedure.

Top: Tick the box for the correct word. Cross the box for the wrong word. Write the correct word on the dotted line.

Middle: Complete sentences by choosing a word from the top section. Encourage the children to use the strategy read on/read back.

Bottom: Use the word given in a sentence.

LATER

■ Repeat the above lesson as appropriate before children complete Workbook 5 page 8.

Focus on *sl, fl, bl* words.

Suggested words:

slip	slap	slop	slot	slim	slum
slid	slug	flip	flap	flop	flag
flit	flat	flan	blob	blot	blip

Other words to investigate:

| slush | slack | sling | flash | flush | fling |
| fluff | blush | black | | | |

FURTHER PRACTICE

DEVELOPING SKILLS

Some or all of these activities must be done to ensure progress:

■ **Quick Cards**

Children have *sl, fl, cl, pl, bl, gl* cards face up on the table.

You call out a word and children point to or hold up the appropriate card.

Suggested words:

glad	sledge	black	club
flag	plate	plaster	clock
glow	fly	flap	sleeve
slip	blanket	clasp	glitter
blouse	planet	glum	plop

As with initial sounds, some clusters are easily confused: *pl/ bl, cl/ gl.*

It is often difficult for young children to hear the difference between the clusters. Individual speech problems can also cause difficulties. Give plenty of practice.

■ **Flash Cards**

Practise reading CCVC words.

■ **Practise writing CCVC words to dictation**

See Word List.

■ **Paint and display**

Children could make large pictures of the characters, to be used as backdrops to mount CCVC words.

ACTIVITIES AT HOME

Homework Sheet 5B.

CCVC words

Consonant clusters at the beginning of words

THE NLF AIMS

- Hear and identify initial consonant clusters in words.
- Read the letters that represent consonant clusters at the beginning of words.
- Write the letters that represent consonant clusters at the beginning of words.

WHAT YOU NEED

RESOURCES

- Flash Cards – consonant clusters
- Whiteboard/chalkboard
- Workbook 5 pages 9 and 10
- Teacher's copy of Workbook 5 pages 9 and 10
- Quick Cards – consonant clusters
- Word List

KEY LESSON POINTERS

VOCABULARY

alphabet letter name sound
word vowel beginning consonant
consonant cluster

THE CHILDREN should throughout the lesson:

- focus on the initial consonant cluster in CCVC words
- identify the two sounds that make the consonant cluster.

YOU should throughout the lesson:

- emphasise both consonants in the initial consonant cluster
- ensure an awareness that CCVC words have four letters with a vowel in the "middle"
- ensure correct letter formation.

STARTING THE LESSON

- Flash Cards – quick revision of consonant clusters learned to date.

TEACHING THE LESSON

- Tell the children that there will be two different sounds very close together at the beginning of the words that you are going to say.

  Ask the children to identify the sounds at the beginning of the following words: *snap, snow, snake, snout.* (*Emphasise carefully both consonants in the initial consonant cluster.*)

  Confirm *sn*.

  Ask: "Which letters make *sn*?"

  Confirm *s* and *n*.

- Tell the children that the two sounds are very close together and they have to listen carefully to hear them both.

  Ask the children to identify the sound at the beginning of the following words: *smell, smoke, smooth, smile.*

  Confirm *sm*.

  Ask: "Which letters make *sm*?"

  Confirm *s* and *m*.

- Repeat the above for *sk, sw, st, sp.*

  Suggested words:

skin	skirt	sky	skull
swim	swing	sweat	switch
stop	start	step	stem
spell	speak	spin	spout

- Stick *sn, sm, sk, sw, st, sp* cards on the board

  Tell the children that you will say a word and they have to tell you what sound the word starts with.

  Invite group/individual responses.

  Suggested words:

spider	snack	smart	skip	sweep
stone	smash	spill	snail	stool
sweet	snout	skid	switch	spin
small	skittle	stitch		

- Repeat the above activity and ask children in turn to say the sound that the word starts with and point to the card that represents that sound.

  Invite individual responses.

- Show the teacher's copy of Workbook 5 page 9.

   Ask the children to identify the pictures.

   Ask: "What sound is at the beginning of *snowman*?"

   Confirm *sn*.

   Ask a child to point to *sn*.

   Ask the child what the other sound is.

   Confirm *sk*.

   Confirm the procedure: "Circle the correct sound *sn* and cross out the wrong sound *sk*."

   Ask a child to complete the procedure.

- Tell the children that they should write the correct two letters that represent the *sn* sound on the dotted line.

   Ask a child to complete the procedure.

- Children complete Workbook 5 page 9. (*Remember to remove teacher's copy before children start to work.*)

LATER

- Repeat the above lesson before children complete Workbook 5 page 10.

FURTHER PRACTICE

DEVELOPING SKILLS

Some or all of these activities must be done to ensure progress:

- **Quick Cards**

   Children have *sn*, *sm*, *sk*, *sw*, *st*, *sp* cards face up on the table.

   You call out a word and children point to or hold up the appropriate card.

   Suggested words:

sniff	smoky	skip	swan
stone	spoon	spice	skate
snug	small	swallow	stairs
spade	stand	swift	skid
smell	snore		

   As with initial sounds, some clusters are easily confused: *st*/*sp*, *sn*/*sm*.

   It is often difficult for young children to hear the difference between the clusters. Individual speech problems can also cause difficulties. Give plenty of practice.

- **Practise writing consonant clusters at the beginning of words**

   You say a word, children write the initial consonant cluster.

sn, sm, sk, sw, st, sp

Consonant clusters at the beginning of words

THE NLF AIMS

- Hear and identify initial consonant clusters in words.
- Read CCVC words.
- Spell CCVC words.

WHAT YOU NEED

RESOURCES

- *Freda Frog's Big Book of Rhymes (Consonant Clusters)* pages 23 to 31
- Flash Cards – consonant clusters
- Whiteboard/chalkboard
- Workbook 5 pages 11 and 12
- Teacher's copy of Workbook 5 pages 11 and 12
- Quick Cards – consonant clusters
- Word List
- Assessment 5.1
- Homework Sheet 5C

KEY LESSON POINTERS

VOCABULARY

alphabet letter name sound
word vowel beginning consonant
consonant cluster

THE CHILDREN should throughout the lesson:

- focus on the initial consonant cluster in CCVC words
- identify the two sounds that make the consonant cluster.

YOU should throughout the lesson:

- emphasise both consonants in the initial consonant cluster
- ensure an awareness that CCVC words have four letters with a vowel in the "middle"
- ensure correct letter formation.

STARTING THE LESSON

- Quick revision of Flash Cards used in Lesson 5.
- Tell the children that you will say a word and they have to tell you what sounds the word starts with.

  Suggested words:

swim	skip	stair	smoke
sparrow	snow	snap	swing
stamp	skid	smell	spot

TEACHING THE LESSON

- Tell the children that the next section of the Big Book is a collection of rhymes focusing on the consonant clusters *sw, sk, sl, st, sm, sp, sn*.

  Write *sw, sk, sl, st, sm, sp, sn* on the board.

  (*Arrange the clusters as headings for word lists.*)

  Tell the children that you will read the first rhyme starting at page 23 and they will have to identify the words starting with one of the sounds written on the board.

- Read page 23 and discuss the content.

- Ask: "Which consonant cluster appears at the beginning of some words on this page?"

  Confirm *sk*.

  Ask the children to identify *sk* words: *skunk, Skelly, skateboard, skilful, skater, skims, skids, skitters, skippety.**

  Write the words in the appropriate column as they are identified by the children.

- Read page 24 and discuss the content.

- Ask: "Which consonant cluster appears at the beginning of some words on this page?"

  Confirm *sl*.

  Ask the children to identify *sl* words: *sloppy, slug, slithers, slides, slowly, sleepily, slipslop, slurping, slipper, slime.**

- Repeat the procedure for pages 25 to 31.

  Page 25: *Smoky, smooth, smell, smashing, smelly, smart, small.**

  Page 26: *snoring, Snotter, snail, snooze, snug, sneaks, snake, snack, snatched, snip, snap, snorum.**

  Page 27: *speak, Spanish, spider, spinach, spin.**

  Pages 28 and 29: *starving, Stella, stew, stink, stone, stomach, stoat, sting, starfish, stuffs, stocking, sticks, stands, stove, steaming, stirring, sticky.**

Page 30 and 31: *swan, swish, swoosh, sweeping, swooping, swim.**

■ Choose only four or five words from each list*
above.

Ask: "Which alphabet letter do these clusters all
have in common?"

Confirm *s*.

■ Focus on CCVC words with *sw, sk, st*.

Ask children in turn to write CCVC words on the
board.

Suggested words:

| swim | swam | swag | skim | skin |
| skip | skid | stop | stem | step |

Other words to investigate:

| skill | skull | swish | swell | swing |
| stick | stock | sting | stung | still |

■ Show the teacher's copy of Workbook 5 page 11.

Ensure that the children can identify the pictures
and know how to complete the procedure.

Top: Tick the box for the correct word. Cross the
box for the wrong word. Write the correct word
on the dotted line.

Middle: Complete sentences by choosing a word
from the top section. Encourage the children to
use the strategy read on/read back.

Bottom: Use the word given in a sentence.

LATER

■ Repeat the above lesson as appropriate before
children complete Workbook 5 page 12.

Focus on *sm, sp, sn* words.

Suggested words:

| smut | spit | spot | spin | snap | snip |

Other words to investigate:

| smock | smell | smash | speck | spill |
| spell | snack | sniff | snuff | |

FURTHER PRACTICE

DEVELOPING SKILLS

Some or all of these activities must be done
to ensure progress:

■ **Quick Cards**

Children have *sw, sk, st, sm, sp, sn* cards
face up on the table.

You call out a word and children point to
or hold up the appropriate card.

Suggested words:

swing	skull	stop	smoke
spin	snow	swap	sniff
skeleton	stamp	Spain	smell

As with initial sounds, some clusters are
easily confused: *sn/sm, st/sp*.

It is often difficult for young children to
hear the difference between the clusters.
Individual speech problems can also cause
difficulties. Give plenty of practice.

■ **Flash Cards**

Practise reading CCVC words.

■ **Practise writing CCVC words to dictation**

See Word List.

■ **Paint and display**

Children could make large pictures of the
characters, to be used as backdrops to
mount CCVC words.

■ **Dictation: CCVC/CVCC**

Gran has a long dress.
Greg has a plan.
Brad has a drum.
The pram is on the grass.
The frog can swim.
The fish is in the pond.
Mum went to the bus stop.
Glen can jump and skip.
The plug is in the sink.
A flag is on the cliff.
The crab is on the sand.
The desk has a flat top.

ASSESSMENT 5.1

ACTIVITIES AT HOME

Homework Sheet 5C.

CCVC words

Vowel digraph oo

BEFORE YOU START

THE NLF AIMS

- Hear and identify vowel digraph *oo* in words.
- Read words containing the digraph *oo*.
- Write words containing the digraph *oo*.

WHAT YOU NEED

RESOURCES

- Flash Card *oo*
- Flash Cards *oo* words
- Whiteboard/chalkboard
- Workbook 5 page 13
- Teacher's copy of Workbook 5 page 13
- Magnetic letters
- Assessment 5.2
- Homework Sheet 5D
- Word List

KEY LESSON POINTERS

VOCABULARY

alphabet   letter   name   sound   word
vowel   rhyming   middle   spell   sentence
double   slow speak

THE CHILDREN should throughout the lesson:

- focus on two vowels representing one sound.

YOU should throughout the lesson:

- emphasise that two vowels can make one sound.

THE LESSON

TEACHING THE LESSON

■ Tell the children that they have to listen for the sound in the middle of the words.

Say *room, pool, moon, fool*.

Ask: "What sound can you hear in the middle?"

Confirm *oo*.

■ Ask: "Which letters make the sound *oo*?"

After discussion, tell the children: "There are different ways to write the *oo* sound, but today we are going to talk about two *o*s together making the sound *oo*."

■ Show the *oo* card and ask the children to say *oo*.

Tell the children you want to write the word *cool*.

Ask: "How many sounds can you hear?"

Confirm three.

Slow speak *cool* and clap on sounds *c-oo-l*.

Ask: "What is the first sound?"

Confirm *c* and write on the board.

Ask: "What sound can you hear next?"

Confirm *oo*.

Ask: "Which two letters make the *oo* sound?"

Confirm double *o*.

Write *o* and *o* and ask: "What sound do they make?"

Confirm *oo*.

(At the beginning it may be helpful to underline the *oo* as a reminder to the children that the two letters join to make the one sound.)

Ask: "What sound is at the end of *cool*?"

Confirm *l* and write on the board.

Ask the children to read the word *cool*.

■ Repeat the procedure for *fool, pool, tool, stool, spool*, making a list on the board.

(*Remember to draw children's attention to the consonant cluster at the beginning of* **stool** *and* **spool**.)

- Ask the children to read the list of words.

  Ask: "What do you notice about the list?"

  Confirm that they all have *oo* in the middle; they all end in *l*, and they rhyme.

  Ensure that the children know that if they can read and write *cool*, they can read and write all the other rhyming words as only the first sound(s) change(s).

- Repeat the above procedure for *food, mood*.

  Other words to investigate, read and spell:

moon	soon	noon	spoon	boot
toot	hoot	root	shoot	room
zoom	broom	bloom	groom	gloom

- Flash Cards practice: read *oo* words.

LATER

- Repeat the above lesson as appropriate.

- Show the teacher's copy of Workbook 5 page 13.

  Top: Ensure that the children can read the words and know to draw a picture to illustrate each word.

  Middle: Ensure that the children know to choose a word from the above section to complete each sentence. Encourage the children to use the strategy read on/read back.

  Bottom: Ensure that the children know to make rhyming words using the letters given.

FURTHER PRACTICE

DEVELOPING SKILLS

Some or all of these activities must be done to ensure progress:

- Practise writing single-syllable words with vowel digraph *oo*

  You say a word, children write the word (*see Word List*).

- Magnetic letters

  Children make *oo* words.

- Flash Cards

  Practise reading *oo* words.

ASSESSMENT 5.2

ACTIVITIES AT HOME

Homework Sheet 5D.

BLENDING AND SEGMENTING

VOWEL DIGRAPHS

OO

277

Vowel digraph ee

BEFORE YOU START

THE NLF AIMS

- Hear and identify vowel digraph *ee* in words.
- Read words containing the digraph *ee*.
- Write words containing the digraph *ee*.

WHAT YOU NEED

RESOURCES

- Flash Cards *oo* and *ee*
- Flash Cards *oo* and *ee* words
- Onset and Rime Cards – *c, f, p, t, st, sp* (...ool)
    m, n, s, sp (...oon)
    b, h, t, r, sh (...oot)
    r, z, br, bl, gr, gl (...oom)
- Whiteboard/chalkboard
- Workbook 5 pages 14 and 15
- Teacher's copy of Workbook 5 pages 14 and 15
- Magnetic letters
- Assessment 5.3
- Word List
- Homework Sheet 5E

KEY LESSON POINTERS

VOCABULARY

alphabet   letter   name   sound   word
vowel   rhyming   middle   spell   sentence
double   slow speak   illustrate

THE CHILDREN should throughout the lesson:

- focus on two vowels representing one sound.

YOU should throughout the lesson:

- emphasise that two vowels can make one sound.

THE LESSON

STARTING THE LESSON

- Ask: "Which two letters make the *oo* sound?"
  Confirm two *o*s.

Onset and Rime

- Write *ool* on the board.
  Ask the children to read the rime *ool*.
  Hold up the Onset Cards and ask the children to complete words using the Onset Cards and given rime.
  Invite group/individual responses. (*Keep activity quick and snappy by holding up Onset Cards in quick succession.*)

TEACHING THE LESSON

- Tell the children that they have to listen for the sound in the middle of the words.
  Say *feet, keep, heel, weed.*
  Ask: "What sound can you hear in the middle of the word?"
  Confirm *ee*.
  Ask: "Which letters make the sound *ee*?"
  After discussion, tell the children: "There are different ways to write the *ee* sound, but today we are going to talk about two *e*s together making the sound."

- Ask: "What kind of letter is *e*?"
  Confirm vowel.
  Tell the children that when two vowels come together, the first one usually says its name and the other is silent. We only say one *e* (name).
  A good rhyme to help children remember this rule:
  *When two vowels together play a game
  Only the first one says its name.*

- Show the *ee* card and ask the children to say *ee*.
  Tell the children you want to write the word *feel*.
  Ask: "How many sounds can you hear?"
  Confirm three.
  Slow speak *feel* and clap on sounds *f-ee-l*.
  Ask: "What is the first sound?"
  Confirm *f* and write on the board.
  Ask: "What sound can you hear next?"
  Confirm *ee*.

Ask: "Which two letters make the *ee* sound?"

Confirm double *e*.

Write *e* and *e* and ask: "What sound do they make?"

Confirm *ee*.

Ask: "What sound is at the end of *feel*?"

Confirm *l* and write on the board.

Ask the children to read the word *feel*.

■ Repeat the procedure for *heel, peel, reel, wheel, steel*.

■ Ask the children to read the list of words.

Ask: "What do you notice about the list?"

Confirm that they all have *ee* in the middle and they all end in *l*. They rhyme.

Ensure that the children know that if they can read and write *feel*, they can read and write all the other rhyming words as only the first sound(s) change(s).

■ Repeat the above procedure for *deep, keep, peep, weep, sheep, sleep, steep* and *cheep*.

Other words to investigate, read and spell:

feet	meet	sleet	sheet	sweet	feed
need	seed	weed	greed	tweed	speed
leek	meek	peek	seek	week	cheek

■ Flash Cards practice: read *ee* words.

LATER (1)

■ Repeat the above lesson as appropriate.

■ Show the teacher's copy of Workbook 5 page 14.

Top: Ensure that the children can read the words and know to draw a picture to illustrate the word.

Middle: Ensure that the children know to choose a word from above section to complete each sentence. Encourage the children to use the strategy read on/read back.

Bottom: Ensure that the children know to make rhyming words using the letters given.

LATER (2)

■ Children complete Workbook 5 page 15. (*Ensure that children can identify pictures and know to write the correct word on the dotted line.*)

oo or *ee* in Developing Skills section is a good activity to do before the workbook page.

FURTHER PRACTICE

DEVELOPING SKILLS

Some or all of these activities must be done to ensure progress:

■ **Practise writing single-syllable words with vowel digraph *ee***

You say a word, children write the word (*see Word List*).

■ **Magnetic letters**

Children make *ee* words.

■ **Flash Cards**

Practise reading *ee* words.

■ *oo* or *ee*

Tell the children that you will say some words and they have to say the letters that make the sounds in the middle of the words.

Children should answer double *o* or double *e*.

Invite group/individual responses.

Suggested words:

seed	sweet	soon	seen	moon
fool	feel	hood	look	leek
peel	pool	hoop	stool	steel
wool	wheel	feet	foot	teeth

■ **Dictation:** *oo/ee*

Gran has a big spoon.
Nick is on the stool.
We can feed the sheep.
The bee is in the tree.
We get wool from the sheep.
A sweet stuck in his tooth.
The crab is in the deep pool.
Lee took the wheel to the shed.
I will go to the zoo next week.
Adeel will meet us soon.

ASSESSMENT 5.3

ACTIVITIES AT HOME

■ Homework Sheet 5E.

ee

Vowel digraph ai

THE NLF AIMS

- Hear and identify vowel digraph *ai* in words.
- Read words containing the digraph *ai*.
- Write words containing the digraph *ai*.

WHAT YOU NEED

RESOURCES

- Flash Card *ai*
- Flash Cards *ai* words
- Whiteboard/chalkboard
- Workbook 5 page 16
- Teacher's copy of Workbook 5 page 16
- Magnetic letters
- Assessment 5.4
- Word List
- Poster – Digraphs: *a* (long)
- Homework Sheet 5F

KEY LESSON POINTERS

VOCABULARY

alphabet letter name sound word vowel rhyming middle spell sentence illustrate slow speak

THE CHILDREN should throughout the lesson:

- focus on two vowels representing one sound
- know that the first sound in a vowel digraph usually says its name and the second is silent.

YOU should throughout the lesson:

- emphasise that two vowels can make one sound
- ensure that children know that when two vowels come together in words the first one usually says its name and the second is silent.

THE LESSON

TEACHING THE LESSON

- Tell the children that they have to listen for the sound in the middle of the words.
  Say *rail, pail, wait, paint*.
  Ask: "What sound can you hear in the middle?"
  Confirm *a* (*long*).

- Ask: "Which letters make the sound *a* (*long*)?"
  After discussion, tell the children: "There are different ways to write the *a* (*long*) sound, but today we are going to talk about *a* and *i* together making the sound *a* (*long*)."

- Ask: "What kind of letters are *a* and *i*?"
  Confirm vowels.

  Show the *ai* card and ask the children to say *ai*.

  Remind the children that when two vowels come together, the first one usually says its name and the other is silent.

  A good rhyme to help children remember this rule:

  When two vowels together play a game
  Only the first one says its name.

- Tell the children you want to write the word *pail*.
  Ask: "How many sounds can you hear?"
  Confirm three.
  Slow speak *pail* and clap on sounds *p-ai-l*.
  Ask: "What is the first sound?"
  Confirm *p* and write on the board.
  Ask: "What sound can you hear next?"
  Confirm *ai*.
  Ask: "Which two letters make the *ai* sound?"
  Confirm *a* and *i*.
  Write *a* and *i* and ask: "What sound do they make?"
  Confirm *ai*.
  (*At the beginning it may be helpful to underline the* **ai** *as a reminder to the children that the two letters join to make the one sound.*)
  Ask: "What sound is at the end of *pail*?"
  Confirm *l* and write on the board.
  Ask the children to read the word *pail*.

- Repeat the procedure for *tail, sail, rail, fail, mail, jail* and *snail*.

  (*Remember to draw children's attention to the consonant cluster at the beginning of* **snail**.)

- Ask the children to read the list of words.

  Ask: "What do you notice about the list?"

  Confirm that they all have *ai* in the middle and they all end in *l*. They rhyme.

  Ensure that the children know that if they can read and write *pail*, they can read and write all the other rhyming words as only the first sound(s) change(s).

- Repeat the above procedure for *gain, rain, pain, stain, chain, train, drain, grain, brain* and *Spain*.

  Other words to investigate, read and spell:
  laid   paid   raid   wait
  waist   paint   faint

- Flash Cards practice: read *ai* words.

LATER

- Repeat the above lesson as appropriate.

- Show the teacher's copy of Workbook 5 page 16.

  Top: Ensure that the children can read the words and know to draw a picture to illustrate the word.

  Middle: Ensure that the children know to choose a word from the above section to complete each sentence. Encourage the children to use the strategy read on/read back.

  Bottom: Ensure that the children know to make rhyming words using the letters given.

FURTHER PRACTICE

DEVELOPING SKILLS

Some or all of these activities must be done to ensure progress:

- Practise writing single-syllable words with vowel digraph *ai*

  You say a word, children write the word (*see Word List*).

- Magnetic letters

  Children make *ai* words.

- Flash Cards

  Practise reading *ai* words.

- Dictation: *ai*

  We will wait for the train.
  Mum will need red paint.
  Zack got wet feet in the rain.
  Craig has a pain in his foot.
  The wood has a stain on it.
  Jill can wait at the tree.
  The snail is on the grass.
  Gran paid for the book.
  The chain fell on my foot.
  The dog has a long tail.

ASSESSMENT 5.4

ACTIVITIES AT HOME

Homework Sheet 5F.

BLENDING AND SEGMENTING

VOWEL DIGRAPHS

ai

Vowel digraph oa

BEFORE YOU START

THE NLF AIMS

- Hear and identify vowel digraph *oa* in words.
- Read words containing the digraph *oa*.
- Write words containing the digraph *oa*.

WHAT YOU NEED

RESOURCES

- Flash Card *oa*
- Flash Cards *oa* words
- Whiteboard/chalkboard
- Onset and Rime Cards *t, s, r, f, m, j, sn* (...ail)
  g, r, p, st, ch, tr, dr, gr, br (...ain)
  l, p, r (...aid)
- Workbook 5 page 17
- Teacher's copy of Workbook 5 page 17
- Assessment 5.5
- Word List
- Poster – Digraphs: *o* (long)
- Homework Sheet 5G

KEY LESSON POINTERS

VOCABULARY

alphabet letter name sound
word vowel rhyming
beginning/end/middle slow speak
spell sentence

THE CHILDREN should throughout the lesson:

- focus on two vowels representing one sound
- know that the first sound in a vowel digraph usually says its name and the second is silent.

YOU should throughout the lesson:

- emphasise that two vowels can make one sound
- ensure that children know that when two vowels come together in words the first one usually says its name and the second is silent.

THE LESSON

STARTING THE LESSON

- Ask: "Which two letters make the **ai** sound?"
  Confirm **a** and **i**.

Onset and rime

- Write **ail** on the board.
  Ask: "What is the rime?"
  Confirm **ail**.
  Hold up the Onset Cards and ask the children to complete words using the Onset Cards and given rime. (*Keep activity quick and snappy by holding up Onset Cards in quick succession.*)
- Repeat above activity for **ain** and **aid** rimes.

TEACHING THE LESSON

- Tell the children that they have to listen for the sound in the middle of the words.
  Say **coat, boat, road, soap**.
  Ask: "What sound can you hear in the middle?"
  Confirm **o** (*long*).
  Ask: "Does anyone know which letters make the sound **o** (*long*)?"
  After discussion, tell the children: "There are different ways to write the **o** (*long*) sound, but today we are going to talk about **o** and **a** together making the sound **o** (*long*)."
- Ask: "What kind of letters are **o** and **a**?"
  Confirm vowels.
  Show the **oa** card and ask: "Which letter will say its name when **o** and **a** come together?"
  Confirm **o** and ask: "What does the **a** do?"
  Confirm it stays silent.
  Remind the children that when two vowels come together, the first one usually says its name and the other is silent.
  A good rhyme to help children remember this rule:
  When two vowels together play a game
  Only the first one says its name.
- Tell the children you want to write the word **boat**.
  Ask: "How many sounds can you hear?"
  Confirm three.

Slow speak *boat* and clap on sounds *b-oa-t*.

Ask: "What is the first sound?"

Confirm *b* and write on the board.

Ask: "What sound can you hear next?"

Confirm *oa*.

Ask: "Which two letters make the *oa* sound?"

Confirm *o* and *a*.

Write *o* and *a* and ask: "What sound do they make?"

Confirm *oa*. (*At the beginning it may be helpful to underline the* **oa** *as a reminder to the children that the two letters join to make the one sound.*)

Ask: "What sound is at the end of *boat*?"

Confirm *t* and write on the board.

Ask the children to read the word *boat*.

■ Repeat the procedure for *coat, goat, moat, float, stoat, throat*. (*Remember to draw children's attention to the consonant digraph* **th** *alongside the* **r** *in throat and the consonant cluster at the beginning of* **float** *and* **stoat**.)

■ Ask the children to read the list of words.

Ask: "What do you notice about the list?"

Confirm that they all have *oa* in the middle and they all end in *t*. They rhyme.

Ensure that the children know that if they can read and write *boat*, they can read and write all the other rhyming words as only the first sound(s) change(s).

■ Repeat the above procedure for *coast, roast, toast, boast*.

Other words to investigate, read and spell:

coal   goal   foal
load   road   toad
loan   moan

■ Flash Cards practice: read *oa* words.

LATER

■ Repeat the above lesson as appropriate.

■ Show the teacher's copy of Workbook 5 page 17.

Top: Ensure that the children can read the words and know to draw a picture to illustrate the word.

Middle: Ensure that the children know to choose a word from the above section to complete each sentence. Encourage the children to use the strategy read on/read back.

Bottom: Ensure that the children know to make rhyming words using the letters given.

FURTHER PRACTICE

DEVELOPING SKILLS

Some or all of these activities must be done to ensure progress:

■ **Onset and rime**

Practise making words using Onset and Rime Cards *...ail, ...ain, ...aid*.

■ **Practise writing single-syllable words with vowel digraph *oa***

You say a word, children write the word (*see Word List*).

■ **Flash Cards**

Practise reading *oa* words.

■ **Dictation: *oa***

Joan fell on the road.
The soap is in the sink.
We had toast and milk.
We went in a coach to the zoo.
The toad swam in the pond.
The oak tree is big.
The green coat is in the shop.
We will paint the boat black.

ASSESSMENT 5.5

ACTIVITIES AT HOME

Homework Sheet 5G.

oa

283

Vowel digraph ie

BEFORE YOU START

THE NLF AIMS

- Hear and identify vowel digraph *ie* in words.
- Read words containing the digraph *ie*.
- Write words containing the digraph *ie*.

WHAT YOU NEED

RESOURCES

- Flash Card *ie*
- Flash Cards *ie, ai, oa* words
- Onset and Rime Cards *t, s, r, f, m, j, sn* (...ail); *g, r, p, st, ch, tr, dr, gr, br* (...ain) *l, p, r* (...aid)
- Onset and Rime Cards *b, c, g, m, fl, st* (...oat); *b, c, r, t* (...oast); *l, r, t* (oad) *c, f, g* (...oal)
- Whiteboard/chalkboard
- Workbook 5 page 18
- Teacher's copy of Workbook 5 page 18
- Magnetic letters
- Assessment 5.6
- Word List
- Poster – Digraphs: *i* (long)
- Homework Sheet 5H

KEY LESSON POINTERS

VOCABULARY

alphabet   letter   name   sound
word   vowel   rhyming
beginning/end/middle   slow speak
spell   sentence

THE CHILDREN should throughout the lesson:

- focus on two vowels representing one sound
- know that the first sound in a vowel digraph usually says its name.

YOU should throughout the lesson:

- emphasise that two vowels can make one sound
- ensure that children know that when two vowels come together in words the first one usually says its name and the second is silent.

THE LESSON

STARTING THE LESSON

- Ask: "Which two letters make the *ai* sound?"
  Confirm *a* and *i*.
  Ask: "Which two letters make the *oa* sound?"
  Confirm *o* and *a*.

Onset and rime

- Write *ail* on the board.
  Ask: "What is the rime?"
  Confirm *ail*.
  Hold up the Onset Cards and ask the children to complete words using the Onset Cards and given rime. (*Keep activity quick and snappy by holding up Onset Cards in quick succession.*)
- Repeat the above activity for *ain* and *aid* rimes.
- Repeat the above activity for *oat, oast, oad* and *oal* rimes.

TEACHING THE LESSON

- Tell the children that they have to listen for the sound at the end of the words.
  Say *tie, pie, lie, die*.
  Ask: "What sound can you hear at the end?"
  Confirm *i* (*long*).
  Ask: "Does anyone know which letters make the sound *i* (*long*)?"
  After discussion, tell the children: "There are different ways to write the *i* (*long*) sound, but today we are going to talk about *i* and *e* together making the sound *i* (*long*)."

- Ask: "What kind of letters are *i* and *e*?"
  Confirm vowels.
  Show *ie* card and ask: "Which letter will say its name when *i* and *e* come together?"
  Confirm *i* and ask: "What does the *e* do?"
  Confirm it stays silent.
  Remind the children that when two vowels come together, the first one usually says its name and the other is silent.
  A good rhyme to help children remember this rule:
  When two vowels together play a game
  Only the first one says its name.

- Tell the children you want to write the word *die*.
  Ask: "How many sounds can you hear?"
  Confirm two.
  Slow speak *die* and clap on the sounds *d-ie*.
  Ask: "What is the first sound?"

Confirm **d** and write on the board.

Ask: "What sound can you hear next?"

Confirm **ie**.

Ask: "Which two letters make the **ie** sound?"

Confirm **i** and **e**.

Write **i** and **e** and ask: "What sound do they make?"

Confirm **ie**. (*At the beginning it may be helpful to underline the* **ie** *as a reminder to the children that the two letters join to make the one sound.*)

Ask the children to read the word **die**.

■ Repeat the procedure for **tie**, **lie**, **pie**.

■ Ask the children to read the list of words.

Ask: "What do you notice about the list?"

Confirm that they all have **ie** at the end. They rhyme.

Ensure that the children know that if they can read and write **die**, they can read and write all the other rhyming words as only the first sound(s) change(s).

■ Tell the children that some words have **ie** in the middle, such as **died**, **tied**, **cried**, **fried**, **dried**.

Tell the children you want to write the word **died**.

Ask the children how to write the word **die**.

Confirm **d** at the beginning and then **i** and **e** making the sound **ie**.

Write **die** on the board.

Ask: "How do you change **die** to **died**?"

Confirm add **d** at the end.

Write **d** to complete the word **died**.

Ask: "How many sounds are in **died**?"

Confirm three.

Slow speak **died**, **d-ie-d** and clap on the sounds.

■ Repeat the procedure for **tied**.

Other words to investigate, read and spell:

| cried | fried | dried | tried | | |
| ties | cries | tries | dries | fries | flies |

■ Flash Cards practice: read **ie** words.

LATER

■ Repeat the above lesson as appropriate.

■ Show the teacher's copy of Workbook 5 page 18.

Top: Ensure that the children can read the words and know to draw a picture to illustrate each word.

Middle: Ensure that the children know to choose a word from above section to complete each sentence.

Bottom: Ensure that the children know to make rhyming words using the letters given.

DEVELOPING SKILLS

Some or all of these activities must be done to ensure progress:

■ **Onset and rime**

Practise making words using Onset and Rime Cards *...ail, ...ain, ...aid, ...oat, ...oast, ...oad, ...oal.*

■ **Practise writing single-syllable words with vowel digraph *ie***

You say a word, children write the word (*see Word List*).

■ **Magnetic letters**

Children make *ie* words.

■ **Flash Cards**

Practise reading *ie* words.

■ **Dictation**

ASSESSMENT 5.6

ACTIVITIES AT HOME

Homework Sheet 5H.

ie

Vowel digraph ou

BEFORE YOU START

THE NLF AIMS

- Hear and identify vowel digraph *ou* in words.
- Read words containing the digraph *ou*.
- Write words containing the digraph *ou*.

WHAT YOU NEED

RESOURCES

- Flash Card *ou*
- Flash Cards *ou* words
- Onset and Rime Cards *l, cl, pr* (...oud)
  f, h, r, s, p, gr (...ound)
  m, s (...outh)
  tr, sp, st, sh (...out)
- Whiteboard/chalkboard
- Workbook 5 page 19
- Teacher's copy of Workbook 5 page 19
- Magnetic letters
- Assessment 5.7
- Word List
- Homework Sheet 5I

KEY LESSON POINTERS

VOCABULARY

alphabet   letter   name   sound
word   vowel   rhyming
beginning/end/middle   slow speak
spell   sentence

THE CHILDREN should throughout the lesson:

- focus on two vowels representing one sound.

YOU should throughout the lesson:

- emphasise that two vowels can make one sound.

THE LESSON

TEACHING THE LESSON

- Tell the children that they have to listen for the sound in the middle of the words.

  Say *mouth, loud, round, count.*

  Ask: "What sound can you hear in the middle?"

  Confirm *ou.*

- Ask: "Which letters make the sound *ou*?"

  After discussion, tell the children: "There are different ways to write the *ou* sound, but today we are going to talk about *o* and *u* together making the sound *ou*."

- Ask: "What kind of letters are *o* and *u*?"

  Confirm vowels.

  Tell the children that the two vowels can join together to make one sound.

  Show the *ou* card and ask the children to say *ou.*

- Tell the children you want to write the word *loud.*

  Ask: "How many sounds can you hear?"

  Confirm three.

  Slow speak *loud* and clap on sounds *l-ou-d.*

  Ask: "What is the first sound?"

  Confirm *l* and write on the board.

  Ask: "What sound can you hear next?"

  Confirm *ou.*

  Ask: "Which two letters make the *ou* sound?"

  Confirm *o* and *u.*

  Write *o* and *u* and ask: "What sound do they make?"

  Confirm *ou.*

  (*At the beginning it may be helpful to underline the* **ou** *as a reminder to the children that the two letters join to make the one sound.*)

  Ask: "What sound is at the end of *loud*?"

  Confirm *d* and write on the board.

  Ask the children to read the word *loud.*

■ Repeat the procedure for *cloud, proud*.
(*Remember to draw the children's attention to the consonant clusters at the beginning of* **cloud** *and* **proud**.)

■ Ask the children to read the list of words.

Ask: "What do you notice about the list?"

Confirm that they all have *ou* in the middle and they all end in *d*. They rhyme.

Ensure that the children know that if they can read and write *loud*, they can read and write all the other rhyming words as only the first sound(s) change(s).

■ Repeat the procedure for *found, hound, round, sound, pound, ground*.

Other words to investigate, read and spell:
mouth   south   trout   spout   shout   snout

■ Flash Cards practice: read *ou* words.

LATER

■ Repeat the above lesson as appropriate.

■ Show the teacher's copy of Workbook 5 page 19.

Top: Ensure that the children can read the words and know to draw a picture to illustrate each word.

Middle: Ensure that the children know to choose a word from the above section to complete each sentence. Encourage the children to use the strategy read on/read back.

Bottom: Ensure that the children know to make rhyming words using the letters given.

FURTHER PRACTICE

DEVELOPING SKILLS

Some or all of these activities must be done to ensure progress:

■ **Onset and rime**

Practise making words using Onset and Rime Cards *...oud, ...ound, ...outh, ...out.*

■ **Practise writing single-syllable words with vowel digraph ou**

You say a word, children write the word (*see Word List*).

■ **Magnetic letters**

Children make *ou* words.

■ **Flash Cards**

Practise reading *ou* words.

ASSESSMENT 5.7

ACTIVITIES AT HOME

Homework Sheet 5I.

BLENDING AND SEGMENTING

VOWEL DIGRAPHS

287

ou

Vowel digraph oi

THE NLF AIMS

- Hear and identify vowel digraph *oi* in words.
- Read words containing the digraph *oi*.
- Write words containing the digraph *oi*.

WHAT YOU NEED

RESOURCES

- Flash Cards *ou* and *oi*
- Flash Cards *ou* and *oi* words
- Onset and Rime Cards *l, cl, pr* (...oud)
  f, h, r, s, p, gr (...ound)
  m, s (...outh)
  tr, sp, st, sh (...out)
- Whiteboard/chalkboard
- Workbook 5 page 20
- Teacher's copy of Workbook 5 page 20
- Magnetic letters
- Assessment 5.8
- Word List
- Rhyming Bingo
- Homework Sheet 5J

KEY LESSON POINTERS

VOCABULARY

alphabet   letter   name   sound
word   vowel   rhyming
beginning/end/middle   slow speak
spell   sentence

THE CHILDREN should throughout the lesson:

- focus on two vowels representing one sound.

YOU should throughout the lesson:

- emphasise that two vowels can make one sound.

THE LESSON

STARTING THE LESSON

- Ask: "Which two letters make the *ou* sound?"
  Confirm *o* and *u*.

Onset and rime

- Write *ound* on the board.
  Ask: "What is the rime?"
  Confirm *ound*.
  Hold up the Onset Cards and ask the children to complete the words using the Onset Cards and given rime. (*Keep activity quick and snappy by holding up onset cards in quick succession.*)
- Repeat the activity for *out* rime.

TEACHING THE LESSON

- Tell the children that they have to listen for the sound in the middle of the words.
  Say *coin, boil, join, soil*.
  Ask: "What sound can you hear in the middle?"
  Confirm *oi*.
  Ask: "Which letters make the sound *oi*?"
  After discussion, tell the children: "There are different ways to write the *oi* sound, but today we are going to talk about *o* and *i* together making the sound *oi*."

- Ask: "What kind of letters are *o* and *i*?"
  Confirm vowels.
  Tell the children that the two vowels can join together to make one sound.
  Show *oi* card and ask the children to say *oi*.

- Tell the children you want to write the word *boil*.
  Ask: "How many sounds can you hear?"
  Confirm three.
  Slow speak *boil* and clap on sounds *b-oi-l*.
  Ask: "What is the first sound?"
  Confirm *b* and write on the board.
  Ask: "What sound can you hear next?"
  Confirm *oi*.

Ask: "Which two letters make the *oi* sound?"

Confirm *o* and *i*.

Write *o* and *i* and ask: "What sound do they make?"

Confirm *oi*.

Ask: "What sound is at the end of *boil*?"

Confirm *l* and write on the board.

Ask the children to read the word *boil*.

■ Repeat the procedure for *soil, coil, toil, spoil*. (*Remember to draw the children's attention to the consonant clusters at the beginning of* **spoil**.)

■ Ask the children to read the list of words.

Ask: "What do you notice about the list?"

Confirm that they all have *oi* in the middle and they all end in *l*. They rhyme.

Ensure that the children know that if they can read and write *boil*, they can read and write all the other rhyming words as only the first sound(s) change(s).

Other words to investigate, read and spell:

coin   join   moist   hoist   point   joint

■ Flash Cards practice: read *oi* words.

LATER

■ Repeat the above lesson as appropriate.

■ Show the teacher's copy of Workbook 5 page 20.

Top: Tell the children that they have to make *-oil, -oin, -oint* rhyming words by using the letters in the box above. The children should know that they may use a letter more than once.

Bottom: Ensure that the children can read the phrases and know to draw pictures that illustrate each phrase.

FURTHER PRACTICE

DEVELOPING SKILLS

Some or all of these activities must be done to ensure progress:

■ **Practise writing single-syllable words with vowel digraph *oi***

You say a word, children write the word (*see Word List*).

■ **Magnetic letters**

Children make *oi* words.

■ **Flash Cards**

Practise reading *oi* words.

■ **Rhyming Bingo**

Children have a Bingo board on the table and you say a word, for example *soon*. Children have to look for a picture of a word that rhymes with *soon*, such as *moon*, and cover it with a counter.

Suggested words:

rope	root	join	rail	soot
note	south	float	heel	soon
lie	pain	cook	Spain	nail
die	loud	meet	keep	neat
see	main	noon	pool	boat
look	fool	saint	foal	rain

■ **Dictation:** *ie, ou, oi*

Sam has a red and black tie.
The man found a coin.
A trout is a fish.
The pie has a thick crust.
The oil is on the ground.
The roots are in the soil.
The dog had a stick in his mouth.
The plant will die in the frost.

ASSESSMENT 5.8

ACTIVITIES AT HOME

Homework Sheet 5J.

BLENDING AND SEGMENTING

VOWEL DIGRAPHS

oi

Digraph **ar**

THE NLF AIMS

- Hear and identify digraph *ar* in words.
- Read words containing *ar* in the middle.
- Write words containing *ar* in the middle.

WHAT YOU NEED

RESOURCES

- Flash Card *ar*
- Flash Cards *ar* words
- Letter Card *r*
- Whiteboard/chalkboard
- Workbook 5 page 21
- Teacher's copy of Workbook 5 page 21
- Magnetic letters
- Assessment 5.9
- Word List
- Homework Sheet 5K

KEY LESSON POINTERS

VOCABULARY

alphabet   letter   name   sound
word   vowel   rhyming
beginning/end/middle   slow speak
spell   sentence

THE CHILDREN should throughout the lesson:

- focus on all words having a vowel (or y)
- differentiate between the alphabet name *r* and the written representation of the sound *ar*.

YOU should throughout the lesson:

- emphasise that all words must have a vowel (or y)
- ensure that children know the difference between the alphabet letter *r* and the sound *ar*.

TEACHING THE LESSON

- Show the children the *r* letter card.
  Ask: "What sound does this letter make?"
  Confirm *r*.
  Ask: "What is its name?"
  Confirm *r*.
  Tell the children that when *r* comes after the vowel *a* (*ar*) and is in the middle or at the end of a word, the sound *ar* sounds like the alphabet letter *r* (*name*).

- Say the word *park*.
  Ask: "How many sounds can you hear?"
  Confirm three.
  Ask: "What is the first sound?"
  Confirm *p* and write on the board.
  Ask: "What sound can you hear at the end?"
  Confirm *k* and write on the board.
  Ask: "What sound can you hear in the middle?"
  Confirm *ar*.
  Ask: "How do you write the sound you hear in the middle?"
  You may need to remind the children that *park* must have a vowel in it and ask them where it might be.
  Confirm after the *p* and before the *r*.
  Confirm that *ar* represents the sound they hear between *p* and *k*.

- Repeat the procedure for *dark, bark, hark, lark, mark* and *spark*.
  (*Remember to draw children's attention to the consonant clusters at the beginning of* **spark**.)

- Ask the children to read the list of words.

  Ask: "What do you notice about the list?"

  Confirm that they all have *ar* in the middle and they all end in *k*. They rhyme.

  Ensure that the children know that if they can read and write *park*, they can read and write all the other rhyming words as only the first sound(s) change(s).

- Repeat the procedure for *dart, cart, part, tart, start, car, jar, tar, bar, star*.

  Other words to investigate, read and spell:
  arm   farm   harm   lard   yard   card

- Flash Cards practice: read *ar* words.

- Show the teacher's copy of Workbook 5 page 21.

  Top: Ensure that the children can read the words and know to draw a picture to illustrate each word.

  Middle: Ensure that the children know to choose a word from the above section to complete each sentence. Encourage the children to use the strategy read on/read back.

  Bottom: Ensure that the children know to make rhyming words using the letters given.

FURTHER PRACTICE

DEVELOPING SKILLS

Some or all of these activities must be done to ensure progress:

- **Practise writing single-syllable words with *ar***

  You say a word, children write the word (*see Word List*).

- **Magnetic letters**

  Children make *ar* words.

- **Flash Cards**

  Practise reading *ar* words.

- **Dictation: *ar***

  Beth will start the car.
  It is dark in the loft.
  A dart is sharp.
  My bed is hard.
  The dog is in the yard.
  Mark has a red scarf.
  I sent him a card.
  The goat is in the barn.
  Bart cut his arm.
  The car is in the car park.

ASSESSMENT 5.9

ACTIVITIES AT HOME

Homework Sheet 5K.

Digraph **or**

BEFORE YOU START

THE NLF AIMS

- Hear and identify digraph *or* in words.
- Read words containing *or* in the middle.
- Write words containing *or* in the middle.

WHAT YOU NEED

RESOURCES

- Flash Cards *ar* and *or*
- Flash Cards *ar, or* words
- Whiteboard/chalkboard
- Workbook 5 page 22
- Teacher's copy of Workbook 5 page 22
- Magnetic letters
- Word List
- Assessment 5.10
- Homework Sheet 5L

KEY LESSON POINTERS

VOCABULARY

alphabet   letter   name   sound   word
vowel   rhyming   middle   spell   sentence
illustrate

THE CHILDREN should throughout the lesson:

- focus on *or* in the middle of words
- focus on *o* and *r* representing *or*.

YOU should throughout the lesson:

- emphasise that *or* in the middle of words is represented by *o* and *r*.

THE LESSON

STARTING THE LESSON

- Flash Cards: quick revision of **ar** words.

  Ensure that the children know that the words must have the vowel **a** followed by **r**.

  Invite the children to write **ar** words on the board.

  Suggested words:

park	hard	farm	charm	yard
part	card	mark	harp	star

- Tell the children that today's words will have a different vowel before **r**.

TEACHING THE LESSON

- Say the word **horn**.

  Ask: "How many sounds can you hear?"

  Confirm three.

  Ask: "What is the first sound?"

  Confirm **h** and write on the board.

  Ask: "What sound can you hear at the end?"

  Confirm **n** and write on the board.

  Ask: "What sound can you hear in the middle?"

  Confirm **or**.

  Ask: "How do you write the sound you hear in the middle?"

  You may need to remind the children that **horn** must have a vowel in it and ask them where it might be.

  Confirm after the **h** and before the **r**.

  Confirm that **or** represents the sound they hear between **h** and **n**.

■ Repeat the procedure for *corn, born, worn, torn, thorn*.

(*Remember to draw children's attention to the consonant digraph at the beginning of* **thorn**. *Note: In some accents the word* **torn** *will be pronounced with a long* **o**.)

Ask the children to read the list of words.

Ask: "What do you notice about the list?"

Confirm that they all have *or* in the middle and they all end in *n*. They rhyme.

Ensure that the children know that if they can read and write *horn*, they can read and write all the other rhyming words as only the first sound(s) change(s).

■ Repeat the procedure for *fork, cork, York, stork*.

Other words to investigate, read and spell:
for   cord   storm   sort   snort   short

■ Flash Cards practice: read *or* words.

■ Show the teacher's copy of Workbook 5 page 22.

Top: Ensure that the children can read the words and know to draw a picture to illustrate each word.

Middle: Ensure that the children know to choose a word from the above section to complete each sentence. Encourage the children to use the strategy read on/read back.

Bottom: Ensure that the children know to make rhyming words using the letters given.

FURTHER PRACTICE

DEVELOPING SKILLS

Some or all of these activities must be done to ensure progress:

■ **Practise writing single-syllable words with *or***

You say a word, children write the word (*see Word List*).

■ **Magnetic letters**

Children make *or* words.

■ **Flash Cards**

Practise reading *or* words.

■ **Listening for *ar* and *or***

You say a word and children say if the word has *ar* or *or* in the middle.

Suggested words:

farm	fork	cord	cart	harm
barn	horn	short	thorn	start
yarn	stork	park	sort	card

■ **Dictation: *or***

A stork has long legs.
His coat is torn.
The stem has a thorn on it.
Norma has short socks.
The bus has a loud horn.

ASSESSMENT 5.10

ACTIVITIES AT HOME

Homework Sheet 5L.

or

Digraph ir

BEFORE YOU START

THE NLF AIMS

- Hear and identify digraph *ir* in words.
- Read words containing *ir* in the middle.
- Write words containing *ir* in the middle.

WHAT YOU NEED

RESOURCES

- Flash Cards *ar, or* and *ir*
- Flash Cards *ir* words
- Whiteboard/chalkboard
- Workbook 5 page 23
- Teacher's copy of Workbook 5 page 23
- Magnetic letters
- Word List
- Assessment 5.11
- Homework Sheet 5M

KEY LESSON POINTERS

VOCABULARY

alphabet letter name sound word vowel rhyming middle spell sentence illustrate

THE CHILDREN should throughout the lesson:

- focus on *ir* in the middle of words
- focus on *i* and *r* representing *ir*.

YOU should throughout the lesson:

- emphasise that *ir* in the middle of words is represented by *i* and *r*.

THE LESSON

STARTING THE LESSON

- Tell the children that you are going to say a word and they have to tell you if they hear **ar** or **or** in the middle.

  Invite group/individual responses.

  Suggested words:

part	darn	cork	cart	spark	corn
dark	snort	dart	York	born	bark
storm	mark	tart	torn		

- Tell the children that they are going to look at words with a different vowel and **r**.

TEACHING THE LESSON

- Say the word **girl**.

  Ask: "How many sounds can you hear?"

  Confirm three.

  Ask: "What is the first sound?"

  Confirm **g** and write on the board.

  Ask: "What sound can you hear at the end?"

  Confirm **l** and write on the board.

  Ask: "What sound can you hear in the middle?"

  Confirm **ir**.

  (*Remember that children often find it difficult to hear the* **i** *sound in the middle of words and may want to represent* **ir** *with the* **r** *sound.*)

  Remind the children that **girl** must have a vowel in it and ask them what that vowel might be.

  Confirm **i**.

  Ask: "How can you write the sound **ir** that you hear in the middle of the word **girl**?"

  Confirm **ir**.

  Ask "How do you write **girl**?"

  Confirm and write on the board.

- Repeat the procedure for *twirl, swirl, whirl*. (*Remember to draw children's attention to the consonant clusters at the beginning of* **twirl** *and* **swirl***, and the consonant digraph at the beginning of* **whirl***.*)

- Ask the children to read the list of words.

  Ask: "What do you notice about the list?"

  Confirm that they all have *ir* in the middle and they all end in *l*. They rhyme.

  Ensure that the children know that if they can read and write *girl*, they can read and write all the other rhyming words as only the first sound(s) change(s).

- Repeat the procedure for *dirt, skirt, shirt, squirt*.

  Other words to investigate, read and spell:

bird	third
sir	stir
first	thirst
firm	squirm

- Flash Cards practice: read *ir* words.

- Show the teacher's copy of Workbook 5 page 23.

  Top: Ensure that the children can read the words and know to draw a picture to illustrate each word.

  Middle: Ensure that the children know to choose a word from above section to complete each sentence. Encourage the children to use the strategy read on/read back.

  Bottom: Ensure that the children know to make rhyming words using the letters given.

FURTHER PRACTICE

DEVELOPING SKILLS

Some or all of these activities must be done to ensure progress:

- **Practise writing single-syllable words with *ir***

  You say a word, children write the word (*see Word List*).

- **Magnetic letters**

  Children make *ir* words.

- **Flash Cards**

  Practise reading *ir* words.

- **Listening for *ar, or, ir***

  You say a word and the children say if the word has *ar, or* or *ir* in the middle.

  Suggested words:

barn	girl	fork	cart	short
bird	hard	dart	whirl	horn
first	shirt	harp	thorn	firm
mark	lard	storm	born	

- **Dictation: *ir***

  The bird sang in the tree.
  He has a red shirt.
  Joy has a long skirt.
  The girl is in the shop.
  He has dirt on his boot.

ASSESSMENT 5.11

ACTIVITIES AT HOME

Homework Sheet 5M.

Digraph ay

THE NLF AIMS

- Hear and identify digraph *ay* in words.
- Read words containing the digraph *ay*.
- Write words containing the digraph *ay*.

WHAT YOU NEED

RESOURCES

- Flash Card *ay*
- Flash Cards *ay* words
- Whiteboard/chalkboard
- Workbook 5 page 24
- Teacher's copy of Workbook 5 page 24
- Magnetic letters
- Word List
- Assessment 5.12
- Poster – Digraphs: *a* (long)
- Homework Sheet 5N

KEY LESSON POINTERS

VOCABULARY

alphabet   letter   name   sound   word
vowel   rhyming   middle   spell   sentence
illustrate

THE CHILDREN should throughout the lesson:

- focus on two letters representing one sound
- know that the first sound in a vowel digraph usually says its name. Here *y* is acting as a vowel.

YOU should throughout the lesson:

- emphasise that two letters can make one sound
- ensure children know that when two vowels come together in words the first one usually says its name and the second is silent.

TEACHING THE LESSON

- Tell the children that they have to listen for the sound at the end of the words.

  Say *day, tray, say, clay*.

  Ask: "What sound can you hear at the end of the words?"

  Confirm *a* (long).

- Ask: "Which letters represent the sound *a* (*long*)?"

  Confirm *ai* (previously taught).

  Tell the children that there is another way to write *a* (*long*), that is, *a* and *y*.

  Show the children the *ay* card and ask them to say *ay*.

  Tell the children that if the *a* (*long*) sound is in the middle of a word it is usually represented by *ai*, but if it is at the end of a word it is represented by *ay*. (*This applies to single-syllable words.*)

- Tell the children you want to write the word *day*.

  Ask: "How many sounds can you hear?"

  Confirm two.

  Slow speak *day* and clap on sounds *d-ay*.

  Ask: "What is the first sound?"

  Confirm *d* and write on the board.

  Ask: "What sound can you hear next?"

  Confirm *ay*.

  Ask: "Where can you hear the *a* (*long*) sound, in the middle or at the end?"

  Confirm at the end.

  Ask: "How should you write the *a* (*long*) sound when it comes at the end?"

  Confirm *ay*.

  Ask the children to read the word *day*.

- Repeat the procedure for *bay, day, hay, may, pay, ray, say, way*.

- Ask the children to read the list of words.

  Ask: "What do you notice about the list?"

  Confirm that they all have *ay* at the end. They rhyme.

  Ensure that the children know that if they can read and write *day*, they can read and write all the other rhyming words – only the first sound(s) change(s).

- Repeat the above procedure for *play, tray, stay.* (*Remember to draw children's attention to the consonant clusters at the beginning of* **play**, **tray** *and* **stay**.)

- Flash Cards practice: read *ay* words.

- Show the teacher's copy of Workbook 5 page 24.

  Tell the children to make 10 *ay* rhyming words and write them on the lines. Demonstrate and explain the procedure:

  1. Cross out the vowels (*ay* doesn't follow a vowel).
  2. Cross out *q* (as it is always followed by *u* in English).
  3. Cross out *x* (it is usually at the end of a word).
  4. Try the remaining letters as onsets with the *ay* rime to make real words.

  (*Note: Some children may want to make the proper names Fay and Jay. Say that this is not acceptable in this case because proper names need to start with a capital letter. Jay with a lower case is a bird and fay with a lower case, though unfamiliar, is a fairy.*)

  Ensure that the children can read the phrases and know to draw pictures that illustrate each phrase.

LATER

- Name the letters:

  Ask the children the two different ways of making the *a* (*long*) sound.

  Confirm *ai* and *ay*.

  Stick the *ai* and *ay* cards on the board for the children to see.

  Ask: "Where would you usually find the *a* (*long*) sound written as *ai*?"

  Confirm in the middle of a word.

  Ask: "Where would you usually find the *a* (*long*) sound written as *ay*?"

  Confirm at the end of a word.

  Tell the children that you will say a word and they have to answer *ai* or *ay* and point to the correct card, that is the one that represents the sound.

  Invite group/individual responses.

  Suggested words:

day	gain	tray	clay	train	may
stain	rain	wait	hay	spray	nail
pail	play	sail	drain	stay	way
paint	tail	pay			

FURTHER PRACTICE

DEVELOPING SKILLS

Some or all of these activities must be done to ensure progress:

- Practise writing single-syllable words with vowel digraph *ay*

  You say a word, children write the word (*see Word List*).

- Magnetic letters

  Children make *ay* words.

- Flash Cards

  Practise reading *ay* words.

- **Dictation:** *ay*

  Sanjay and Kay went out to play.
  Gran will pay on the bus.
  The milk jug is on the tray.
  We ran a long way.
  It was a wet day.

ASSESSMENT 5.12

ACTIVITIES AT HOME

Homework Sheet 5N.

ay

Split digraph a—e

THE NLF AIMS

- Read words containing the split digraph *a-e*.
- Write words containing the split digraph *a-e*.

WHAT YOU NEED

RESOURCES

- Flash Card *a-e*
- Flash Cards *a-e* words
- Whiteboard/chalkboard
- Workbook 5 page 25
- Teacher's copy of Workbook 5 page 25
- Magnetic letters
- Word List
- Assessment 5.13
- Poster – Digraphs: *a* (long)
- Homework Sheet 5O

KEY LESSON POINTERS

VOCABULARY

alphabet letter name sound word
vowel rhyming middle spell sentence
illustrate short long end silent

THE CHILDREN should throughout the lesson:

- focus on two vowels being separated by another letter (consonant)
- focus on the first vowel saying its name and the *e* at the end being silent.

YOU should throughout the lesson:

- emphasise the two vowels being separated by another letter (consonant)
- emphasise the first vowel says its name and the *e* at the end is silent.

THE LESSON

TEACHING THE LESSON

- Write *tape* on the board.

  Ask the children to read the word *tape*.

  Tell the children that when *e* comes at the end of a word, as in *tape*, the vowel in the middle says its name and not its sound, and the vowel *e* at the end is silent.

- Show examples of how *e* at the end of a word changes the *a* to *a* (*long*).

  Write *cap* on the board.

  Ask the children to read the word *cap*.

  Ask: "What is the sound in the middle?"

  Confirm *a*.

  Write *e* at the end of *cap*.

  Ask the children to read the word *cape*.

  Ask: "What sound is in the middle?"

  Confirm *a* (*long*).

- Repeat for other words:

  tap → tape   man → mane
  can → cane   mad → made
  hat → hate   mat → mate

  Ensure that the children know that *e* at the end of a word is silent and it makes *a* in the middle say its name.

- Write *a* on the board.

  Ask: "What sounds can the letter *a* represent?"

  Confirm *a* and *a* (*long*).

  Ask: "Which letter goes at the end of a word to make the *a* long?"

  Confirm *e*.

- Tell the children that you will say a word and they have to say whether the word has *e* at the end or not.

  Encourage the children to tell you how they know that the word has an *e* at the end or not, that is, whether the given word has a short/long vowel in the middle.

  Invite group/individual responses.

  Suggested words:

cat	Kate	plate	pat	date	same
Sam	mat	cake	fad	fade	made
mad	ran	name	tap	tape	wave
fan	bag	safe	grape	shake	hat
hate					

- Tell the children that you want to write the word *came*.

Ask: "How many sounds can you hear?"

Confirm three.

Slow speak *came* and clap on sounds *c-a* (*long*)-*m*.

Ask: "What is the first sound?"

Confirm *c* and write on the board.

Ask: "What sound can you hear next?"

Confirm *a* (*long*).

Ask: "How do you write the *a* (*long*) sound in *came*?"

Confirm *a* with a silent *e* at the end.

Write *a* on the board.

Ask: "What sound can you hear at the end of *came*?"

Confirm *m* and write on the board.

Ask: "What must you remember to write at the end of the word to make the *a* say *a* (*long*)?"

Confirm *e*.

Ask the children to read the word *came*.

■ Repeat the above procedure for *fame, game, lame, name, same, tame*.

■ Ask the children to read the list of words.

Ask: "What do you notice about the list?"

Confirm that they all have *e* at the end making the *a* say *a* (*long*) and that the words rhyme.

Ensure that the children know that if they can read and write *came*, they can read and write all the other rhyming words as only the first sound(s) change(s).

■ Repeat the above procedure for *bake, cake, lake, make, cake, take, wake, shake, flake, snake; date, gate, hate, late, mate, plate, skate; cave, gave, save, wave, grave*.

■ Point out that *a-e* is more often used to make the *a* (*long*) sound where the consonant is *m* (...*ame*), *k* (...*ake*), *v* (...*ave*) or *t* (...*ate*). While *ai* represents the same sound, it is not as common with these consonants. Exceptions are *wait, bait* and *gait*.

■ Flash Cards practice: read *a-e* words.

■ Show the teacher's copy of Workbook 5 page 25.

Top: Ensure that the children can read the words and know to draw a picture to illustrate each word.

Middle: Ensure that the children know to choose a word from the above section to complete each sentence. Encourage the children to use the strategy read on/read back.

Bottom: Ensure that the children know to make rhyming words using the letters given.

FURTHER PRACTICE

DEVELOPING SKILLS

Some or all of these activities must be done to ensure progress:

■ **Practise writing single-syllable words with split digraph *a–e***

You say a word, children write the word (*see Word List*).

■ **Magnetic letters**

Children make *a-e* words.

■ **Flash Cards**

Practise reading *a-e* words.

■ **Dictation: *a–e***

Dad left a cake on a plate.
Gran came to the park with me.
I gave Jade a book.
The dog hid in the cave.
The snake is on the rock.

ASSESSMENT 5.13

ACTIVITIES AT HOME

Homework Sheet 5O.

a—e

Digraphs ai, ay, a—e

THE NLF AIMS

- Hear and identify long *a* in words.
- Read words containing *ai*, *ay* or *a-e*.
- Write words containing *ai*, *ay* or *a-e*.

WHAT YOU NEED

RESOURCES

- Flash Cards *ai*, *ay*, *a-e*
- Flash Cards *ai*, *ay*, *a-e* words
- Whiteboard/chalkboard
- Workbook 5 page 26
- Teacher's copy of Workbook 5 page 26
- Magnetic letters
- Word List
- Assessment 5.14
- Poster – Digraphs: *a* (long)

KEY LESSON POINTERS

VOCABULARY

alphabet letter name sound word
vowel rhyming middle spell sentence
illustrate short long end silent

THE CHILDREN should throughout the lesson:

- focus on the fact that *a* (long) can be represented in three different ways.

YOU should throughout the lesson:

- emphasise the three different ways of writing *a* (long) sound.

TEACHING THE LESSON

- Tell the children that you want them to think of the different ways of representing the *a* (*long*) sound.

  Discuss and confirm *ai*, *ay*, *a-e*.

- Ask: "Where is *ai* usually found in words?"
  Confirm in the middle.
  Ask: Where is *ay* usually found in words?"
  Confirm at the end.

- Tell the children that you will say a word and they have to answer *ai* or *ay*.

  Invite group/individual responses.

  Suggested words:

way	hail	fail	bay	jail	mail
say	snail	ray	fray	laid	paid
tray	brain	play	Spain	grain	waist
hay	faint				

- Write *cake* on the board.

  Ask: "What is special about *e* at the end of the word *cake*?"

  Confirm it stays silent and makes the short *a* say *a* (*long*).

  Elicit from the children which consonants usually have a silent *e* to make the *a* (*long*) sound.

  Confirm *k*, *m* and *v* (*t* could be included here).

- Tell the children that you will say a word and they have to say whether the word has silent *e* at the end or not, that is, whether the *a* is long or short.

  Invite group or individual responses.

  Suggested words:

gave	bad	bake	cape	cap	spade
cave	sad	lake	wag	game	late
gas	save	shake	map	wax	make
tap	tape	skate	van	maze	case
jam	rake	fame			

- Flash Cards: quick practice of words with *a* (*long*) represented in three different ways.

  Invite group/individual responses.

- Tell the children that you want them to write words with the *a* (*long*) sound.

  Suggested words:

tray	train	cake	cave	pain	clay
day	name	say	plate	pay	stain
chain	faint	hay	may	same	bake
waist	wave	snail			

  (*Help children understand that the same sound can be written in more than one way. Encourage them to apply this knowledge to spelling and not to approach spelling in a random way.*)

- Show the teacher's copy of Workbook 5 page 26.

  Ensure that the children can identify the pictures and know to write the words in the appropriate column.

FURTHER PRACTICE

DEVELOPING SKILLS

Some or all of these activities must be done to ensure progress:

- **Practise writing single-syllable words with *ai*, *ay* and *a-e***

  You say a word, children write the word (*see Word List*).

- **Magnetic letters**

  Children make *ai*, *ay* and *a-e* words.

- **Flash Cards**

  Practise reading *ai*, *ay*, *a-e* words.

- **Dictation: *ai*, *ay*, *a-e***

  We went a long way on the train.
  Meg will wait at the gate.
  Ben has a cake on the tray.
  They went out to play in the rain.
  The snail is on the rake.
  Dad will take the paint to Scott.

ASSESSMENT 5.14

BLENDING AND SEGMENTING

DIGRAPHS, LONG A

ai, ay, a—e

Digraph ow

BEFORE YOU START

THE NLF AIMS

- Hear and identify the digraph *ow* in words.
- Read words containing the digraph *ow*.
- Write words containing the digraph *ow*.

WHAT YOU NEED

RESOURCES

- Flash Card *ow*
- Flash Cards *ow* words
- Whiteboard/chalkboard
- Workbook 5 page 27
- Teacher's copy of Workbook 5 page 27
- Magnetic letters
- Word List
- Assessment 5.15
- Poster – Digraphs: *o* (long)
- Homework Sheet 5P

KEY LESSON POINTERS

VOCABULARY

alphabet   letter   name   sound   word
vowel   rhyming   rhyme   spell   sentence
middle   end

THE CHILDREN should throughout the lesson:

- focus on two letters representing one sound.

YOU should throughout the lesson:

- emphasise that two letters can make one sound.

THE LESSON

TEACHING THE LESSON

■ Tell the children that they have to listen for the sound at the end of the words.

Say *snow, show, blow, row*.

Ask: "What sound can you hear at the end of the words?"

Confirm *o* (*long*).

■ Ask: "Which letters represent the *o* (*long*) sound?"

Confirm *oa* (previously taught).

Tell the children there is another way to write *o* (*long*), which is *o* and *w*.

Show the children the *ow* card and ask them to say *ow*.

Tell the children that if the *o* (*long*) sound is in the middle of a word it is usually represented by *oa*. (*This applies to single-syllable words. Exceptions are* **own**, **bowl**, **grown**.)

■ Tell the children you want to write the word *bow*.

Ask: "How many sounds can you hear?"

Confirm two.

Slow speak *bow* and clap on sounds *b-ow*.

Ask: "What is the first sound?"

Confirm *b* and write on the board.

Ask: "What sound can you hear next?"

Confirm *o* (*long*).

Ask: "Where can you hear the *o* (*long*) sound, in the middle or at the end?"

Confirm at the end.

Ask: "How should you write the *o* (*long*) sound?"

Confirm *ow*.

Ask the children to read the word *bow*.

■ Repeat the procedure for *low, mow, row, sow, tow*.

■ Ask the children to read list of words.

Ask: "What do you notice about the list?"

Confirm that they all have *ow* at the end. They rhyme.

Ensure that the children know that if they can read and write *bow*, they can read and write all the other rhyming words – only the first sound(s) change(s).

- Repeat the above procedure for *snow, blow, flow, crow, grow, show*.

  (*Remember to draw children's attention to the consonant clusters at the beginning of* **blow**, **flow**, **crow** *and* **grow** *and the consonant digraph at the beginning of* **show**.)

- Flash Cards practice: read *ow* words.

- Show the teacher's copy of Workbook 5 page 27.

  Top: Ensure that the children can read the words and know to draw a picture to illustrate each word.

  Middle: Ensure that the children know to choose a word from the above section to complete each sentence. Encourage the children to use the strategy read on/read back.

  Bottom: Ensure that the children know to make rhyming words using the letters given.

LATER

- Name the letters:

  Ask the children what the two different ways are of making the *o* (*long*) sound.

  Confirm *oa* and *ow*.

  Ask: "Where would you usually find the *o* (*long*) sound written as *oa*?"

  Confirm in the middle of a word.

  Ask: "Where would you usually find the *o* (*long*) sound written as *ow*?"

  Confirm at the end of a word.

  Tell the children that you will say a word and they have to answer *oa* or *ow* and point to the correct card, that is the one that represents the sound.

  Invite group/individual responses.

  Suggested words:

coat	goal	low	float	snow
show	flow	boat	moat	row
coal	sow	bow	goat	road
moan	grow	blow	loaf	tow
crow	toast	cloak	soap	boast

  Exceptions to *ow* at the end of words are *toe, foe, hoe, Joe*.

FURTHER PRACTICE

DEVELOPING SKILLS

Some or all of these activities must be done to ensure progress:

- Practise writing single-syllable words with vowel digraph *ow*

  You say a word, children write the word (*see Word List*).

- Magnetic letters

  Children make *ow* words.

- Flash Cards

  Practise reading *ow* words.

- Dictation: *ow*

  The snow is deep.
  A crow is black.
  The seeds will grow in the pots.
  The stool is low.
  The wind will blow the flag.
  The clock is slow.

ASSESSMENT 5.15

ACTIVITIES AT HOME

Homework Sheet 5P.

BLENDING AND SEGMENTING

DIGRAPHS

OW

Split digraph o–e

THE NLF AIMS

- Read words containing the split digraph *o-e*.
- Write words containing the split digraph *o-e*.

WHAT YOU NEED

RESOURCES

- Flash Card *o-e*
- Flash Cards *o-e* words
- Whiteboard/chalkboard
- Workbook 5 page 28
- Teacher's copy of Workbook 5 page 28
- Magnetic letters
- Word List
- Assessment 5.16
- Poster – Digraphs: *o* (long)
- Homework Sheet 5Q

KEY LESSON POINTERS

VOCABULARY

alphabet   letter   name   sound   word
vowel   rhyming   middle   spell   sentence
short   long   end   silent

THE CHILDREN should throughout the lesson:

- focus on two vowels being separated by another letter (consonant)
- focus on the first vowel saying its name and the *e* at the end being silent.

YOU should throughout the lesson:

- emphasise the two vowels being separated by another letter (consonant)
- emphasise the first vowel says its name and the *e* at the end is silent.

TEACHING THE LESSON

- Write **hole** on the board.

  Ask the children to read the word **hole**.

  Tell the children that when **e** comes at the end of a word, as in **hole**, the vowel in the middle says its name **o** (*long*) and not its sound, and the vowel **e** at the end is silent.

- Show examples of how **e** at the end of a word changes the **o** to **o** (*long*).

  Write **cod** on the board.

  Ask the children to read the word **cod**.

  Ask: "What is the sound in the middle?"

  Confirm **o**.

  Write **e** at the end of **cod**.

  Ask the children to read the word **code**.

  Ask: "What sound is in the middle?"

  Confirm **o** (*long*).

- Repeat for other words:

  hop → hope   rob → robe
  rod → rode   not → note

  Ensure that the children know that **e** at the end of a word is silent and it makes **o** in the middle say its name.

- Write **o** on the board.

  Ask: "What sounds can the letter **o** represent?"

  Confirm **o** and **o** (*long*).

  Ask: "Which letter goes at the end of a word to make the **o** long?"

  Confirm **e**.

- Tell the children that you will say a word and they have to say whether the word has **e** at the end or not.

  Encourage the children to tell you how they know whether the word has an **e** at the end or not, that is, whether the given word has a short/long vowel in the middle.

  Invite group/individual responses.

  Suggested words:

cod	code	dog	lot	pole
stone	top	hop	woke	hope
mole	mop	cot	rose	bone
rope	rod	choke	dot	cone
fog	job	hole	smoke	hot

- Tell the children that you want to write the word **pole**.

  Ask: "How many sounds can you hear?"

Confirm three.

Slow speak *pole* and clap on sounds *p-o* (*long*) *-l.*

Ask: "What is the first sound?"

Confirm *p* and write on the board.

Ask: "What sound can you hear next?"

Confirm *o* (*long*).

Ask: "How do you write the *o* (long) sound in *pole*?"

Confirm *o* with a silent *e* at the end.

Write *o* on the board.

Ask: "What sound can you hear at the end of *pole*?"

Confirm *l* and write on the board.

Ask: "What must you remember to write at the end of the word to make the *o* say *o* (*long*)?"

Confirm *e*.

Ask the children to read the word *pole*.

■ Repeat the above procedure for *mole* and *stole*.

■ Ask the children to read the list of words.

Ask: "What do you notice about the list?"

Confirm that they all have *e* at the end making the *o* say *o* (*long*) and that the words rhyme.

Ensure that the children know that if they can read and write *pole*, they can read and write all the other rhyming words – only the first sound(s) change(s).

■ Repeat the above procedure for *joke, poke, woke, broke, spoke, smoke, choke; bone, stone, cone; hose, nose, rose.*

■ While *oa* and *o-e* represent the same sound, point out that *oke, ose* and *ope* are more common than *oak, oas* and *oap*, that is, if the consonant is *k, s* or *p*, the *o* (long) with silent *e* usually applies.

■ Flash Cards practice: read *o-e* words.

■ Show the teacher's copy of Workbook 5 page 28.

Top: Ensure that the children can read the words and know to draw a picture to illustrate each word.

Middle: Ensure that the children know to choose a word from the above section to complete each sentence. Encourage the children to use the strategy read on/read back.

Bottom: Ensure that the children know to make rhyming words using the letters given.

FURTHER PRACTICE

DEVELOPING SKILLS

Some or all of these activities must be done to ensure progress:

■ Practise writing single-syllable words with split digraph *o-e*

You say a word, children write the word (*see Word List*).

■ **Magnetic letters**

Children make *o-e* words.

■ **Flash Cards**

Practise reading *o-e* words.

■ **Dictation:** *o-e*

The rope is long.
Joe broke his arm.
I fell on a stone and cut my hand.
The rose has a strong smell.
The smoke is thick and black.

ASSESSMENT 5.16

ACTIVITIES AT HOME

Homework Sheet 5Q.

BLENDING AND SEGMENTING

SPLIT DIGRAPHS

o—e

Digraphs oa, ow, o—e

THE NLF AIMS

- Hear and identify the long *o* in words.
- Read words containing *oa*, *ow* or *o-e*.
- Write words containing *oa*, *ow* or *o-e*.

WHAT YOU NEED

RESOURCES

- Flash Cards *oa, ow, o-e*
- Flash Cards *oa, ow, o-e* words
- Whiteboard/chalkboard
- Workbook 5 page 29
- Teacher's copy of Workbook 5 page 29
- Magnetic letters
- Word List
- Assessment 5.17
- Poster – Digraphs: *o* (long)

KEY LESSON POINTERS

VOCABULARY

alphabet letter name sound word
vowel rhyming middle spell sentence
short long end silent

THE CHILDREN should throughout the lesson:

- focus on the fact that *o* (long) can be represented in three different ways.

YOU should throughout the lesson:

- emphasise the three different ways of writing *o* (long) sound.

TEACHING THE LESSON

- Tell the children that you want them to think of the different ways of representing the *o* (*long*) sound.

  Discuss and confirm *oa, ow, o-e*.

- Ask: "Where is *oa* usually found in words?"

  Confirm in the middle.

  Ask: Where is *ow* usually found in words?"

  Confirm at the end.

- Tell the children that you will say a word and they have to answer *oa* or *ow*.

  Invite group/individual responses.

  Suggested words:

load	mow	throat	foam	crow	toad
throw	snow	foal	coast	show	coach
low	loan	roast	blow	tow	coat
grow	boast	groan	flow	road	bow

- Write *note* on the board.

  Ask: "What is special about *e* at the end of the word *note*?"

  Confirm it stays silent and makes the short *o* say *o* (long).

  Ask: "What letter goes at the end of a word to make the *o* long?"

  Confirm *e*.

■ Tell the children that you will say a word and they have to say whether or not the word has a silent *e* at the end, making the *o* say *o* (*long*).

Invite group or individual responses.

Suggested words:

stole	job	joke	mop	hose	poke
pot	nose	broke	cone	code	cod
log	spoke	hop	hope	pop	stone
jog	rope	rob	robe		

■ Flash Cards: quick practice of words with *o* (*long*) represented in three different ways.

Invite group/individual responses.

■ Tell the children that you want them to write words with the *o* (long) sound.

Suggested words:

snow	coat	joke	foal	woke	blow
show	toad	choke	grow	boat	hole
low	mow	moan	rope	road	crow

(*Help children understand that the same sound can be written in more than one way. Encourage them to apply this knowledge to spelling, and not to approach spelling in a random way.*)

■ Show the teacher's copy of Workbook 5 page 29.

Ensure that the children can identify the pictures and know to write the words in the appropriate column.

DEVELOPING SKILLS

Some or all of these activities must be done to ensure progress:

■ **Practise writing single-syllable words with *oa*, *ow* and *o-e***

You say a word, children write the word (*see Word List*).

■ **Magnetic letters**

Children make *oa*, *ow* and *o-e* words.

■ **Flash Cards**

Practise reading *oa*, *ow*, *o-e* words.

■ **Dictation: *oa*, *ow*, *oe***

My coat has a hole in it.
A stone is on the road.
We will tow the car with the rope.
I hope the raft will float.
Joan will row the boat.
A bone stuck in his throat.

ASSESSMENT 5.17

oa, ow, o—e

Vowel digraph ea

THE NLF AIMS

- Hear and identify the long *e* in words.
- Read words containing the digraph *ea*.
- Write words containing the digraph *ea*.

WHAT YOU NEED

RESOURCES

- Flash Card *ea*
- Flash Cards *ea* words
- Word List
- Whiteboard/chalkboard
- Workbook 5 page 30
- Teacher's copy of Workbook 5 page 30
- Magnetic letters
- Assessment 5.18
- Poster – Digraphs: *e* (long)
- Homework Sheet 5R

KEY LESSON POINTERS

VOCABULARY

alphabet letter name sound word
vowel rhyming rhyme middle spell
sentence end

THE CHILDREN should throughout the lesson:

- focus on two letters representing one sound
- know that the first sound in a vowel digraph usually says its name and the second is silent.

YOU should throughout the lesson:

- emphasise that two letters can make one sound
- ensure that the children know that when two vowels come together in words the first one usually says its name and the second is silent
- ensure that the children know that one sound can be represented in more than one way.

STARTING THE LESSON

■ Tell the children that they have to listen for the sound in the middle of the words.

Say *heat, seat, meat.*

Ask: "What sound can you hear in the middle?"

Confirm *e* (*long*).

TEACHING THE LESSON

■ Ask: "Which letters represent the sound *e* (*long*)?"

Confirm *ee* (previously taught).

Tell the children that there is another way to write the *e* (*long*), that is, *e* and *a*.

Show the children the *ea* card.

Remind the children that when two vowels come together the first one usually says its name and the other is silent.

Ask the children what rhyme helps them remember this.

Confirm:
When two vowels together play a game
Only the first one says its name.

■ Tell the children that the sound *e* (*long*) is almost always written *ee* or *ea* but there are no rules to help them remember which one to use in spelling.

Say: "You have to learn to know which word looks right."

■ Show the *ea* card and ask the children to say *ea.*

Tell the children you want to write the word *heat.*

Ask: "How many sounds can you hear?"

Confirm three.

Slow speak *heat* and clap on sounds *h-ea-t.*

Ask: "What is the first sound?"

Confirm *h* and write on the board.

Ask: "What sound can you hear next?"

Confirm *e* (*long*).

Ask: "Which two letters make the *e* (*long*) sound?"

Confirm *e* and *a.*

Write *e* and *a* and ask: "What sound do these letters make?"

Confirm *ea*.

Ask: "What sound is at the end of **heat**?"

Confirm *t* and write on the board.

Ask the children to read the word **heat**.

■ Repeat the procedure for **beat, meat, peat, seat, wheat, pleat**.

(*Remember to draw children's attention to the consonant digraph at the beginning of* **wheat** *and the consonant cluster at the beginning of* **pleat**.)

■ Ask the children to read the list of words.

Ask: "What do you notice about the list?"

Confirm that they all have *ea* in the middle and they all end in *t*. They rhyme.

Ensure that the children know that if they can read and write **heat**, they can read and write all the other rhyming words – only the first sound(s) change(s).

Other words to investigate, read and spell:

bead	lead	read	each	reach	beach
teach	peach	team	seam	cream	dream
meal	real	deal	steal		

■ Flash Cards practice: read *ea* words.

Encourage the children to learn and chant the words in rhyming groups.

Hold up the Flash Card and say *each*.

Children say *each, beach, peach, reach, teach*.

Hold up the Flash Card and say *eat*.

Children say *eat, beat, heat, meat, neat, seat*.

■ Repeat for *team, cream, steam, dream; lean, mean, clean; bead, lead, read*.

This is helpful to children whose visual memory is poor but whose auditory memory is better.

■ Show the teacher's copy of Workbook 5 page 30.

Top: Ensure that the children can read the phrases and know they have to draw a picture to illustrate each phrase.

Middle: Ensure that the children know to choose a word from the above section to complete each sentence. Encourage the children to use the strategy read on/read back.

Bottom: Ensure that the children know to make rhyming words using the letters given.

FURTHER PRACTICE

DEVELOPING SKILLS

Some or all of these activities must be done to ensure progress:

■ Practise writing single-syllable words with vowel digraph *ea*

You say a word, children write the word (*see Word List*).

The multisensory approach of Look, Say, Think*, Cover, Write and Check is a good strategy for learning how to spell words.

■ Magnetic letters

Children make *ea* words.

■ Flash Cards

Practise reading *ea* words.

■ Dictation: *ea*

We had a cup of tea.
The fish swam in the sea.
Gran will cook meat for tea.
Rose will read the book to Jean.
Grant will teach me to skate.
Jay had a bad dream.
Mum sat on a seat in the park.
The dog is not real.

* It is very important that children are encouraged to think about the tricky parts of words when they use this strategy.

ASSESSMENT 5.18

ACTIVITIES AT HOME

Homework Sheet 5R.

BLENDING AND SEGMENTING

VOWEL DIGRAPHS

ea

Vowel digraphs ee and ea

THE NLF AIMS

- Hear and identify the long *e* in words.
- Read words containing the digraph *ee* or *ea*.
- Spell words containing the digraph *ee* or *ea*.

WHAT YOU NEED

RESOURCES

- Flash Cards *ee* and *ea*
- Flash Cards *ee*, *ea* words
- Large paintings of peach and wheel (prepared previously)
- Whiteboard/chalkboard
- Workbook 5 page 31
- Teacher's copy of Workbook 5 page 31
- Magnetic letters
- Word List
- Assessment Sheet 5.19
- Poster – Digraphs: *e* (long)
- Collection of *ea* and *ee* pictures
- Homework Sheet 5R

KEY LESSON POINTERS

VOCABULARY

alphabet letter name sound word vowel rhyming middle spell sentence double homophone* meaning

*This word should only be used with children if appropriate.

THE CHILDREN should throughout the lesson:

- focus on the fact that *e* (long) can be represented in two different ways.

YOU should throughout the lesson:

- emphasise the two different ways of writing the *e* (long) sound.

STARTING THE LESSON

■ Tell the children that you want them to think of the different ways of representing the long *e*.

Discuss and confirm *ee* and *ea*.

TEACHING THE LESSON

■ Tell the children that they have to learn to use the correct spelling *ee* or *ea*. The wrong choice of spelling will change the meaning of the sentence.

Ask the children to write the words *see* and *sea*.

Through discussion, elicit how important it is to use the correct spelling in the sentences:

I can *see* the book.
I can swim in the *sea*.

The children will come across two other commonly used homophones in their everyday reading and writing: *week/ weak*, *meet/ meat*.

Establish the correct use of each.

Write the sentence:

Last *week/ weak* I went to the park.

Ask the children to read the sentence and spell both *week* and *weak*.

Ask: "Which is correct in the sentence?"

Confirm *week*.

Ask: "What does *week* mean?"

Confirm a duration of time: seven days.

Ask: "What does *weak* mean?"

Confirm 'not strong'.

Ensure that the children know when to use *week/ weak*.

■ Repeat for *meet/ meat*.

■ Common homophones where the *ee* word is probably more used at this stage are *been/ bean*, *seem/ seam*, *peel/ peal*.

Establish the correct use of each.

Common homophones where the *ea* word is probably more used at this stage are *reed/read reel/ real*, *tee/ tea*, *beech/ beach*, *steel/ steal*, *deer/ dear*.

Establish the correct use of each.

- Display the large pictures of a peach and a wheel.
- Distribute the Flash Cards of *ea* words and *ee* words.

  Ask: "Which letters make the *e* (*long*) sound?"

  Confirm *ee* and *ea*.

  Ask a child to read aloud their word without the others seeing it and then to put it into a sentence.

  Invite the other children to say if the word will go on the wheel or on the peach.

  Encourage the children to say: "It will go on the wheel because it has a double *e*" or, "It will go on the peach because it has an *e* and an *a* together."

- Invite the children to stick their word on the correct picture.

  Suggested words:

tea	sea	see	weak	week
meat	meet	bean	been	seem
peel	reed	read	beach	bead
deer	dear	tree	sheet	dream

- Encourage the children to learn and chant *ea* rhymes:

each	beach	peach	reach	teach	
eat	beat	heat	meat	neat	seat
team	cream	dream	steam		
lean	mean	clean			
bead	lead	read			

- Now encourage the children to learn and chant *ee* rhymes:

bee	see	free	tree	three
been	seen	green	queen	
deep	keep	sleep	sheep	
feet	meet	sweet	sheet	street
feed	need	seed	speed	
feel	heel	wheel		

  Children need a lot of exposure to seeing these words in context so you should take every opportunity to focus on them in Guided Reading.

- Show the teacher's copy of Workbook 5 page 31.

  Top: Ensure that the children can identify the pictures and know to write the word for each picture under the correct vowel digraph *ee* or *ea*.

  Bottom: Ensure that the children can read the sentences and know to choose the sentence with the correct spelling of the identified word according to the context.

FURTHER PRACTICE

DEVELOPING SKILLS

Some or all of these activities must be done to ensure progress:

- Practise writing single-syllable words with vowel digraphs *ee*, *ea*

  You say a word, children write the word (*see Word List*).

- Magnetic letters

  Children make *ee*, *ea* words.

- Flash Cards

  Practise reading *ee*, *ea* words.

- Dictation: *ee, ea*

  I got meat from the shop.
  We have been in the sea.
  Glen had beans on toast.
  Gran feels weak.
  I am five next week.
  We will meet at the bus stop.
  I can see the beads.
  Dad will make a cup of tea.

ASSESSMENT 5.19

ACTIVITIES AT HOME

Homework Sheet 5R (as appropriate) or use blank wall to make up your own.

ee/ea

Trigraph **igh**

THE NLF AIMS

- Hear and identify the long *i* in words.
- Read words containing the trigraph *igh*.
- Write words containing the trigraph *igh*.

WHAT YOU NEED

RESOURCES

- Flash Card *igh*
- Flash Cards *igh* words
- Whiteboard/chalkboard
- Workbook 5 page 32
- Teacher's copy of Workbook 5 page 32
- Magnetic letters
- Word List
- Assessment Sheet 5.20
- Poster – Digraphs: *i* (long)

KEY LESSON POINTERS

VOCABULARY

alphabet letter name sound word
vowel rhyming middle spell sentence
silent

THE CHILDREN should throughout the lesson:

- focus on three letters representing one sound
- know that *i* says its name and *g* and *h* are silent
- know that one sound can be represented in more than one way.

YOU should throughout the lesson:

- emphasise that three letters can make one sound
- ensure that the children know that *i* says its name and *g* and *h* are silent
- ensure that the children know that one sound can be represented in more than one way.

THE LESSON

TEACHING THE LESSON

- Tell the children that they have to listen for the sound in the middle of the words.
  Say *fight, light, might*.
  Ask: "What sound can you hear in the middle?"
  Confirm *i* (*long*).

- Ask: "Which letters represent the sound *i* (*long*)?"
  Confirm *ie* (previously taught).
  Tell the children that there is another way to write *i* (*long*), which is *igh*.
  Show the children the *igh* card and ask them to say *i* (*long*).
  Tell the children that if the sound *i* (*long*) is in the middle of a word it is usually represented by *igh*.

- Tell the children that you want to write the word *night*.
  Ask: "How many sounds can you hear?"
  Confirm three.
  Slow speak *night* and clap on sounds *n-igh-t*.
  Ask: "What is the first sound?"
  Confirm *n* and write on the board.
  Ask: "What sound can you hear next?"
  Confirm *i* (*long*).
  Ask: "Which letters make the *i* (*long*) sound?"
  Confirm *i, g* and *h*.
  Write *i, g* and *h* and ask: "What sound do these letters make?"
  Confirm *i* (*long*).
  Ask: "What sound is at the end of *night*?"
  Confirm *t* and write on the board.
  Ask the children to read the word *night*.

- Repeat the procedure for *fight, might, light, right, sight, bright, flight, fright.*

  (*Remember to draw children's attention to the consonant clusters at the beginning of* **bright**, **flight** *and* **fright**.)

- Ask the children to read the list of words.

  Ask: "What do you notice about the list?"

  Confirm that they all have *igh* in the middle and they all end in *t*. They rhyme.

  Ensure that the children know that if they can read and write *night*, they can read and write all the other rhyming words as only the first sound(s) change(s).

- Flash Cards: read *igh* words.

- Encourage the children to learn and chant the words in rhyming groups.

  Hold up the Flash Card and say *fight*.

  Children say *fight, light, might, night, right, sight*.

  Repeat for *bright, fright, flight, plight*.

  This is helpful to children whose visual memory is poor but whose auditory memory is better.

NOW OR LATER

- Show the teacher's copy of Workbook 5 page 32.

  Top: Ensure that the children can read the phrases and know to draw a picture to illustrate each phrase.

  Middle: Ensure that the children know to choose a word from the words above to complete each sentence.

  Bottom: Ensure that the children know to make rhyming words using the letters given.

FURTHER PRACTICE

DEVELOPING SKILLS

Some or all of these activities must be done to ensure progress:

- Practise writing single-syllable words with trigraph *igh*

  You say a word, children write the word (*see Word List*).

  The multisensory approach of Look, Say, Think*, Cover, Write, Check is a good strategy for learning how to spell words.

- **Magnetic letters**

  Children make *igh* words.

- **Flash Cards**

  Practise reading *igh* words.

- **Dictation:** *igh*

  Can you turn off the light?
  It is a bright day.
  I might go to the shops.
  It is not good to fight.
  I went to sleep last night.
  The flight was late.
  Lee fell and cut her right hand.
  The loud bang gave them a fright.

* It is very important that children are encouraged to think about the tricky parts of words when they use this strategy.

ASSESSMENT 5.20

igh

Long i represented by y

THE NLF AIMS

- Hear and identify the long *i* in words.
- Read words with the long *i* represented by *y*.
- Spell words with the long *i* represented by *y*.

WHAT YOU NEED

RESOURCES

- Flash Card *y*
- Flash Cards *y* words
- Whiteboard/chalkboard
- Workbook 5 page 33
- Teacher's copy of Workbook 5 page 33
- Magnetic letters
- Word List
- Assessment Sheet 5.21
- Poster – Digraphs: *i* (long)
- Homework Sheet 5S

KEY LESSON POINTERS

VOCABULARY

alphabet letter name sound word vowel rhyming rhyme middle spell sentence first/end

THE CHILDREN should throughout the lesson:

- focus on long *i* at the end of words being represented by *y*.

YOU should throughout the lesson:

- ensure that the children know that long *i* can be represented by *y* at the end of words.

THE LESSON

STARTING THE LESSON

■ Tell the children that they have to listen for the sound at the end of the words.

Say *my, by, shy, cry*.

Ask: "What sound can you hear at the end of the words?"

Confirm *i* (*long*).

TEACHING THE LESSON

■ Ask: "Which letters represent the sound *i* (*long*)?"

Confirm *igh* (previously taught).

Tell the children that there is another way to write *i* (*long*), that is, *y*.

Tell the children that if the *i* (*long*) sound is in the middle of a word it is usually represented by *igh*, but if it is at the end of a word it is represented by *y*.

Exceptions are *high, sigh, die, lie, pie, tie*.

■ Tell the children you want to write the word *my*.

Ask: "How many sounds can you hear?"

Confirm two.

Slow speak *my* and clap on sounds *m-y*.

Ask: "What is the first sound?"

Confirm *m* and write on the board.

Ask: "What sound can you hear next?"

Confirm *i* (*long*).

Ask: "How should you write the *i* (*long*) sound?"

Confirm *y*.

Write *y* and ask: "What sound does this letter make at the end of a word?"

Confirm *i* (*long*).

Ask the children to read the word *my*.

Repeat the procedure for *by, cry, dry, fry, try*. (*Remember to draw the children's attention to the consonant cluster at the beginning of* cry, dry, fry *and* try.)

■ Ask the children to read the list of words.

Ask: "What do you notice about the list?"

Confirm that they all have *y* at the end. They rhyme.

Ensure that the children know that if they can read and write *my*, they can read and write all the other rhyming words – only the first sound(s) change(s).

- Repeat the above procedure for *fly, sly, sky, sty, spy, why*.

  (*Remember to draw the children's attention to the consonant clusters at the beginning of* **fly**, **sly**, **sky**, **sty** *and* **spy** *and the consonant digraph at the beginning of* **why**.)

- Flash Cards practice: read *i* (*long*) represented by *y* words.

  Encourage the children to learn and chant the words in rhyming groups.

  Hold up the Flash Card and say **by**.

  Children say **by**, **my**

- Repeat the procedure for *shy, why*; *cry, dry, fry, try*; *sky, sly, spy, sty*.

- Show the teacher's copy of Workbook 5 page 33.

  Top: Ensure that the children can read the phrases and know to draw a picture to illustrate each phrase.

  Middle: Ensure that the children know to choose a word from the words above to complete each sentence. Encourage the children to use the strategy read on/read back.

  Bottom: Ensure that the children know to make rhyming words using the letters given.

LATER

- Name the letters:

  Ask the children what the two different ways are of making the *i* (*long*) sound.

  Confirm *igh* and *y*.

  Ask: "Where would you usually find the *i* (*long*) sound written as *igh*?"

  Confirm in the middle of a word.

  Ask: "Where would you usually find the *i* (*long*) sound written as *y*?"

  Confirm at the end of a word.

  Tell the children that you will say a word and they have to answer *igh* or *y*.

  Invite group/individual responses.

  Suggested words:

night	shy	cry	tight	bright	light
why	by	flight	fly	fright	my
try	might	right	sky		

  Exceptions to *y* at the end of words are *tie, lie, pie, die, high, sigh, thigh*.

FURTHER PRACTICE

DEVELOPING SKILLS

Some or all of these activities must be done to ensure progress:

- Practise writing single-syllable words with *y* at the end

  You say a word, children write the word (*see Word List*).

  The multisensory approach of Look, Say, Think*, Cover, Write, Check is a good strategy for learning how to spell words.

- Magnetic letters

  Children make *y* ending words.

- Flash Cards

  Practise reading *y* ending words.

- Dictation

  The fly is on the cake.
  My mum went to see my Gran.
  We will fry the fish for tea.
  Why did you cry?
  The class will try to sing the song.

* It is very important that children are encouraged to think about the tricky parts of words when they use this strategy.

ASSESSMENT 5.21

ACTIVITIES AT HOME

Homework Sheet 5S.

y (long)

Split digraph i–e

THE NLF AIMS

- Hear and identify the long *i* in words.
- Read words containing the split digraph *i-e*.
- Write words containing the split digraph *i-e*.

WHAT YOU NEED

RESOURCES

- Flash Card *i-e*
- Flash Cards *i-e* words
- Whiteboard/chalkboard
- Workbook 5 page 34
- Teacher's copy of Workbook 5 page 34
- Magnetic letters
- Word List
- Assessment 5.22
- Poster – Digraphs: *i* (long)
- Homework Sheet 5T

KEY LESSON POINTERS

VOCABULARY

alphabet   letter   name   sound   word
vowel   rhyming   middle   spell   sentence
illustrate   short   long   silent

THE CHILDREN should throughout the lesson:

- focus on two vowels being separated by a consonant
- focus on the first vowel saying its name and the final *e* being silent.

YOU should throughout the lesson:

- emphasise the two vowels being separated by a consonant
- emphasise that the first vowel says its name and the final *e* is silent.

THE LESSON

TEACHING THE LESSON

- Write **hide** on the board.

  Ask the children to read the word **hide**.

  Remind the children that when **e** comes at the end of a word, as in **hide**, the vowel in the middle says its name and not its sound, and the final **e** is silent.

- Show examples of how **e** at the end of a word changes the **i** to **i** (*long*).

  Write **slid** on the board.

  Ask the children to read the word **slid**.

  Ask: "What is the sound in the middle?"

  Confirm **i**.

  Write **e** at the end of **slid**.

  Ask the children to read the word **slide**.

  Ask: "What sound is in the middle?"

  Confirm **i** (*long*).

- Repeat for other words:

pip	→ pipe	rip	→ ripe	din → dine
fin	→ fine	bit	→ bite	pin → pine
win	→ wine	twin	→ twine	
shin	→ shine	kit	→ kite	

- Ask: "What does the **e** at the end of a word do to the vowel in the middle?"

  Confirm **e** makes the middle vowel say its name and **e** stays silent.

  Ask: "What does **a** become when **e** is at the end?"

  Confirm **a** (*long*).

  Write examples on the board: **hat/hate**.

  Ask: "What does **o** become when **e** is at the end?"

  Confirm **o** (*long*).

  Write examples on the board: **hop/hope**.

- Write **i** on the board.

  Ask: "What sounds can the letter **i** represent?"

  Confirm **i** and **i** (*long*).

  Ask: "Which letter goes at the end of a word to make the **i** long?"

  Confirm **e**.

  Tell the children that you will say a word and they have to say whether the word has **e** at the end or not.

  Encourage the children to tell you how they know whether the word has an **e** at the end or not. (*The middle vowel says or does not say its name.*)

Invite group/individual responses.

Suggested words:

sit	hide	pin	pine	mine	shine
shin	rip	ripe	pipe	din	pip
dine	like	write	tip	ride	mine

■ Tell the children that you want to write the word *ripe*.

Ask: "How many sounds can you hear?"

Confirm three.

Slow speak *ripe* and clap on sounds *r-i* (*long*)-*p*.

Ask: "What is the first sound?"

Confirm *r* and write on the board.

Ask: "What sound can you hear next?"

Confirm *i* (*long*).

Ask: "How do you write the *i* (*long*) sound in *ripe*?"

Confirm *i* (*long*) with a silent *e* at the end.

Write *i* on the board.

Ask: "What sound can you hear at the end of *ripe*?"

Confirm *p* and write on the board.

Ask: "What must you remember to write at the end of the word to make the *i* say *i* (*long*)?"

Confirm *e*.

Ask the children to read the word *ripe*.

■ Repeat the above procedure for *pipe*, *wipe*, *swipe*.

■ Ask the children to read the list of words.

Ask: "What do you notice about the list?"

Confirm that they all have *e* at the end making the *i* say *i* (*long*) and that the words rhyme.

Ensure that the children know that if they can read and write *ripe*, they can read and write all the other rhyming words – only the first sound(s) change(s).

■ Repeat the above procedure for *hide, ride, tide, side, wide, slide, bride; dine, fine, line, mine, nine, pine, wine, twine, shine; mime, time, chime; file, pile, tile, smile, while; bite, kite, white; like, bike, hike, trike*.

(*While* **igh** *and* **i-e** *represent the same sound, point out that* **i-e** *is more commonly used and* **igh** *is usually used before* **t** *as in* **sight** *and* **right**.)

■ Show the teacher's copy of Workbook 5 page 34.

Top: Ensure that the children can read the phrases and know to draw a picture to illustrate each phrase.

Middle: Ensure that the children know to choose a word from the above section to complete each sentence.

Bottom: Ensure that the children know to make rhyming words using the letters given.

FURTHER PRACTICE

DEVELOPING SKILLS

Some or all of these activities must be done to ensure progress:

■ Practise writing single-syllable words with split digraph *i-e*

You say a word, children write the word (*see Word List*).

The multisensory approach of Look, Say, Think*, Cover, Write, Check is a good strategy for learning how to spell words.

■ **Magnetic letters**

Children make *i-e* words.

■ **Flash Cards**

Practise reading *i-e* words.

■ **Dictation**

The plum is ripe.
The tile fell off the roof.
Hector can ride his bike.
Rosa has white sheets on the bed.
I like green grapes.

* It is very important that children are encouraged to think about the tricky parts of words when they use this strategy.

ASSESSMENT 5.22

ACTIVITIES AT HOME

Homework Sheet 5T (as appropriate) or use blank wall to make up your own.

i—e

Long i represented by ie, igh, y, i-e

THE NLF AIMS

- Read words containing *ie, igh, y, i-e*.
- Spell words containing *ie, igh, y, i-e*.

WHAT YOU NEED

RESOURCES

- Flash Cards *ie, igh, y* and *i-e*
- Flash Cards *ie, igh, y* and *i-e* words
- Whiteboard/chalkboard
- Workbook 5 page 35
- Teacher's copy of Workbook 5 page 35
- Magnetic letters
- Word List
- Assessment 5.23
- Poster – Digraphs: *i* (long)
- Homework Sheets 5S and 5T
- Large pictures: light(bulb), pie, fly, kite (prepared previously)

KEY LESSON POINTERS

VOCABULARY

alphabet letter name sound word vowel rhyming middle spell sentence short long end silent consonant

THE CHILDREN should throughout the lesson:

- focus on the fact that long *i* can be represented in four different ways.

YOU should throughout the lesson:

- emphasise the four different ways of writing the long *i* sound.

THE LESSON

STARTING THE LESSON

- Tell the children that you want them to think of the different ways of representing the *i* (*long*) sound.

  Discuss and confirm *ie, igh, y, i-e*.

TEACHING THE LESSON

- Ask: "Where is *igh* usually found in words?"

  Confirm in the middle.

  Ask: "Where is *y* usually found in words?"

  Confirm at the end.

  Tell the children that you will say a word and they have to answer *igh* or *y*.

  Invite group/individual responses.

  Suggested words:

fly	night	bright	shy	sky
flight	by	might	sty	slight
my	cry	fry	fright	flight

- Write *i* on the board.

  Ask: "What sounds can the letter *i* represent?"

  Confirm *i* and *i* (*long*).

  Ask: "Which letter goes at the end of a word to make the *i* long?"

  Confirm *e*.

  Ask the children: "What is special about an *e* at the end of a word?"

  Confirm it stays silent and makes the *i* say *i* (*long*).

  Tell the children that you will say a word and they have to say whether or not the word has *e* at the end, making the *i* say *i* (*long*).

  Invite group/individual responses.

  Suggested words:

fin	fine	twine	shine	thin
pine	fine	sit	kite	bin
big	bride	slide	tin	white
pip	pin	file	lid	dig

- Flash Cards practice: quick practice of words with *i* (*long*) represented in four different ways.

  Invite group/individual responses.

  Ask: "Which letters make the sound *i* (*long*)?":

  Display the large pictures of the pie, light(bulb), fly and kite.

- Distribute the Flash Cards of *ie*, *igh*, *y* and *i-e* words.

  Suggested words:

slide	tie	fright	bike	nine	cry
lie	die	time	tight	shy	drive
smile	why	high	bright		

  Children in turn read aloud their word without the others seeing it.

  Invite the other children to say if it will go on the picture of the pie, light, fly or kite.

  Encourage the children to say: "It will go on the pie because it has *ie*" or, "It will go on the fly because it ends in *y*."

  Invite the children to stick their word on the correct picture.

- Tell the children that you want them to write some words with the *i* (*long*) sound.

  Suggested words:

my	fight	mine	pie	might
bright	shy	bride	kite	tie
cry	night	pie	ride	why
light	fright	fry	nine	

  (*Help children understand that the same sound can be written in more than one way. Encourage them to apply this knowledge to spelling and not to approach spelling in a random way.*)

- Show the teacher's copy of Workbook 5 page 35.

  Top: Ensure that the children can read the words and know to underline the words with *i* (*long*).

  Middle: Ensure that the children know to choose a word from those underlined above to complete each sentence. Encourage the children to use the strategy read on/read back.

  Bottom: Ensure that the children can read the phrases and know to draw a picture to illustrate each phrase.

FURTHER PRACTICE

DEVELOPING SKILLS

Some or all of these activities must be done to ensure progress:

- **Practise writing single-syllable words with *ie*, *igh*, *y* and *i-e***

  You say a word, children write the word (*see Word List*).

  The multisensory approach of Look, Say, Think*, Cover, Write, Check is a good strategy for learning how to spell words.

- **Magnetic letters**

  Children make *ie*, *igh*, *y*, *i-e* words.

- **Flash Cards**

  Practise reading words with *ie*, *igh*, *y*, *i-e*.

- **Dictation**

  Last night we saw the moon in the sky.
  I lost my tie.
  I might cry.
  Why did you fight with him?
  My bike has a bright light.
  The white shirt is dry.

* It is very important that children are encouraged to think about the tricky parts of words when they use this strategy.

ASSESSMENT 5.23

ACTIVITIES AT HOME

Homework Sheets 5S and 5T (as appropriate) or use blank wall to make up your own.

BLENDING AND SEGMENTING

DIGRAPHS, LONG I

ie, igh, y, i—e

Long **u** represented by **ew**

THE NLF AIMS

- Hear and identify the long *u* in words.
- Read words with the long *u* represented by *ew*.
- Spell words with the long *u* represented by *ew*.

WHAT YOU NEED

RESOURCES

- Flash Card *ew*
- Flash Cards *ew* words
- Whiteboard/chalkboard
- Workbook 5 page 36
- Teacher's copy of Workbook 5 page 36
- Magnetic letters
- Word List
- Assessment Sheet 5.24
- Poster – Digraphs: *u* (long)

KEY LESSON POINTERS

VOCABULARY

alphabet   letter   name   sound   word
vowel   rhyming   rhyme   middle   spell
sentence   double

THE CHILDREN should throughout the lesson:

- focus on long *u* at the end of words being represented by *ew*.

YOU should throughout the lesson:

- ensure that the children know that long *u* can be represented by *ew* at the end of words.

TEACHING THE LESSON

- Tell children the that they have to listen for the sound at the end of the words.
  Say *few, pew, stew, grew*.
  Ask: "What sound can you hear at the end of the words?"
  Confirm *u* (*long*).

- Ask: "Which letters represent the sound *u* (*long*)?"
  Confirm *oo* (previously taught).
  Tell the children that there is another way to write *u* (*long*), that is, *ew*.
  Tell the children that if the sound *u* (*long*) is in the middle of a word it is usually represented by *oo*, but if it is at the end of a word it is represented by *ew*.
  Exceptions are *blue, clue, due, glue, Sue* and *true*. (*Note* ue *is usually used at the end of words of more than one syllable.*)

- Tell the children you want to write the word *new*.
  Ask: "How many sounds can you hear?"
  Confirm two.
  Slow speak *new* and clap on sounds *n-ew*.
  Ask: "What is the first sound?"
  Confirm *n* and write on the board.
  Ask: "What sound can you hear next?"
  Confirm *u* (*long*).
  Ask: "Which letters make the *u* (*long*) sound?"
  Confirm *e* and *w*.
  Write *ew* and ask: "What sound do these letters make at the end of a word?"
  Confirm *u* (*long*).
  Ask the children to read the word *new*.

- Repeat the procedure for *dew, few, pew*.

- Ask the children to read the list of words.
  Ask: "What do you notice about the list?"
  Confirm that they all have *ew* at the end. They rhyme.
  Ensure that the children know that if they can read and write *new* they can read and write all the other rhyming words – only the first sound(s) change(s).

- Repeat the above procedure for **blew, crew, drew, flew, grew.**

  (*Remember to draw children's attention to the consonant clusters at the beginning of the words.*)

  Other words to investigate, read and spell:
  screw   chew   threw

- Flash Cards practice: read **u** (*long*) represented by **ew** words.

  Encourage the children to learn and chant the words in rhyming groups.

  Hold up the Flash Card and say **new**.

  The children say **new, dew, few, pew**.

  Hold up the Flash Card and say **blew**.

  The children say **blew, crew, drew, flew, grew, screw, chew, threw**.

  This is helpful to children whose visual memory is poor but whose auditory memory is better.

- Show the teacher's copy of Workbook 5 page 36.

  Top: Ensure that the children can read the phrases and know to draw a picture to illustrate each phrase.

  Middle: Ensure that the children know to choose a word from the words above to complete each sentence.

  Bottom: Ensure that the children know to make rhyming words using the letters given.

LATER

- Ask the children: "What are the two different ways of making the **u** (*long*) sound?"

  Confirm **oo** and **ew**.

  Ask: "Where would you usually find the **u** (*long*) sound written as **oo**?"

  Confirm in the middle of a word.

  Ask: "Where would you usually find the **u** (*long*) sound written as **ew**?"

  Confirm at the end of a word.

  Tell the children that you will say a word and they have to answer **oo** or **ew**.

  Invite group/individual responses.

  Suggested words:

fool	cool	stew	stool	drew	crew
room	loop	threw	spoon	boot	flew
few	moon	grew	good		

FURTHER PRACTICE

DEVELOPING SKILLS

Some or all of these activities must be done to ensure progress:

- **Practise writing single-syllable words with *ew* at the end**

  You say a word, children write the word (*see Word List*).

  The multisensory approach of Look, Say, Think*, Cover, Write, Check is a good strategy for learning how to spell words.

- **Magnetic letters**

  Children make *ew* ending words.

- **Flash Cards**

  Practise reading *ew* ending words.

- **Dictation**

  A few girls came to tea.
  I have a new coat.
  Drew made a pot of stew.
  I sat on a pew in a church.
  The wind blew my hat off.
  The crew are on the ship.
  My dog likes to chew a bone.
  The plants grew well.

* It is very important that children are encouraged to think about the tricky parts of words when they use this strategy.

ASSESSMENT 5.24

ew

Split digraph u–e

THE NLF AIMS

- Hear and identify the long *u* in words
- Read words containing the split digraph *u-e*.
- Write words containing the split digraph *u-e*.

WHAT YOU NEED

RESOURCES

- Flash Card *u-e*
- Flash Cards *u-e* words
- Whiteboard/chalkboard
- Workbook 5 page 37
- Teacher's copy of Workbook 5 page 37
- Magnetic letters
- Word List
- Assessment 5.25
- Poster – Digraphs: *u* (long)

KEY LESSON POINTERS

VOCABULARY

alphabet letter name sound word vowel rhyming middle spell sentence short/long vowels end silent consonant rule separated

THE CHILDREN should throughout the lesson:

- focus on two vowels being separated by a consonant
- focus on the first vowel saying its name and the final *e* being silent.

YOU should throughout the lesson:

- emphasise the two vowels being separated by a consonant
- emphasise the first vowel says its name and the final *e* is silent.

THE LESSON

TEACHING THE LESSON

■ Write *cute* on the board.

Ask the children to read the word *cute*.

Ask: "What rule applies here?"

The children should use their previous knowledge of silent *e* at the end of words making *a* say *a* (*long*), *o* say *o* (*long*) and *i* say *i* (*long*).

Show examples of how *e* at the end of a word changes the *u* to *u* (*long*).

Write *cub* on the board.

Ask the children to read the word *cub*.

Ask: "What is the sound in the middle?"

Confirm *u*.

Write *e* at the end of *cub*.

Ask the children to read the word *cube*.

Ask: "What sound is in the middle?"

Confirm *u* (*long*).

■ Repeat for other words:

tub	→ tube	cut →	cute
plum	→ plume	us →	use

■ Ask: "What does the *e* at the end of a word do to the vowel in the middle?"

Confirm it makes the middle vowel say its name and also that it stays silent.

Ask: "What does *a* become when *e* is at the end?"

Confirm *a* (*long*).

Ask: "What does *o* become when *e* is at the end?"

Confirm *o* (*long*).

Ask: "What does *i* become when *e* is at the end?"

Confirm *i* (*long*).

■ Write *u* on the board.

Ask: "What sounds can the letter *u* represent?"

Confirm *u* and *u* (*long*).

Ask: "Which letter goes at the end of a word to make the *u* (*long*)?"

Confirm *e*.

■ Tell the children that you will say a word and they have to say whether or not the word has *e* at the end.

Encourage the children to tell you how they know whether or not the word has an *e* at the end. (*The middle vowel says or does not say its name.*)

Invite group/individual responses.

Suggested words:

sun	June	flume	rug	bus	flute
rude	fun	prune	tune	mug	rub
rule	cube	jug	tube	mum	fun

■ Tell the children that you want to write the word *June*.

Ask: "How many sounds can you hear?"

Confirm three.

Slow speak *June* and clap on sounds *j-u* (*long*)-*n*.

Ask: "What is the first sound?"

Confirm *J* and write on the board.

Ask: "What sound can you hear next?"

Confirm *u* (*long*).

Ask: "How do you write the *u* (*long*) sound in *June*?"

Confirm *u* with a silent *e* at the end.

Write *u* on the board.

Ask: "What sound can you hear at the end of *June*?"

Confirm *n* and write on the board.

Ask: "What must you remember to write at the end of the word to make the *u* say *u* (*long*)?"

Confirm *e*.

Ask the children to read the word *June*.

■ Repeat the above procedure for *tune, prune*.

■ Ask the children to read the list of words.

Ask: "What do you notice about the list?"

Confirm that they all have *e* at the end making the *u* say *u* (*long*) and that the words rhyme.

Ensure that the children know that if they can read and write *June*, they can read and write all the other rhyming words – only the first sound(s) change(s).

■ Other words to investigate, read and spell:
rude   flute   rule   cube   tube   pure   cure

(*While* oo *and* u-e *represent the same sound, point out that* u-e *is more commonly used.*)

■ Children complete Workbook 5 page 37.

FURTHER PRACTICE

DEVELOPING SKILLS

Some or all of these activities must be done to ensure progress:

■ Practise writing single-syllable words with split digraph *u-e*

You say a word, children write the word (*see Word List*).

The multisensory approach of Look, Say, Think*, Cover, Write, Check is a good strategy for learning how to spell words.

■ Magnetic letters

Children make *u-e* words.

■ Flash Cards

Practise reading *u-e* words.

■ Dictation

Luke has a tube of paint.
A cube has six sides.
Tara can play the flute.
June is the month after May.
A prune is a dried plum.

* It is very important that children are encouraged to think about the tricky parts of words when they use this strategy.

ASSESSMENT 5.25

u—e

Long **u** represented by
ue, oo, ew, u–e

THE NLF AIMS

- Read words containing *ue, oo, ew, u-e*.
- Spell words containing *ue, oo, ew, u-e*.

WHAT YOU NEED

RESOURCES

- Flash Cards *ue, oo, ew* and *u-e*
- Flash Cards *ue, oo, ew* and *u-e* words
- Whiteboard/chalkboard
- Workbook 5 page 38
- Teacher's copy of Workbook 5 page 38
- Magnetic letters
- Word List
- Assessment 5.26
- Poster – Digraphs: *u* (long)
- Homework Sheet 5U
- Large pictures: screw, blue (paper), moon, tube (prepared previously)

KEY LESSON POINTERS

VOCABULARY

alphabet letter name sound word vowel rhyming middle spell sentence end

THE CHILDREN should throughout the lesson:

- focus on the fact that long *u* can be represented in four different ways.

YOU should throughout the lesson:

- emphasise the four different ways of writing the long *u* sound.

THE LESSON

STARTING THE LESSON

- Tell the children that you want them to think of the different ways of representing the long *u* sound.

  Discuss and confirm *ue, oo, ew, u-e*.

TEACHING THE LESSON

- Ask: "Where is *oo* usually found in words?"

  Confirm in the middle.

  Ask: "Where is *ew* usually found in words?"

  Confirm at the end.

  Tell the children that you will say a word and they have to answer *oo* or *ew*.

  Invite group/individual responses.

  Suggested words:

chew	broom	shoot	threw	new	noon
grew	school	room	dew	stool	flew

  Ask: "What is special about an *e* at the end of a word?"

  Confirm it stays silent and makes the *u* vowel in the middle say its name.

- Write *u* on the board.

  Ask: "What sounds can the letter *u* represent?"

  Confirm *u* and *u* (*long*).

  Ask: "Which letter goes at the end of a word to make the *u* long?"

  Confirm *e*.

  Tell the children that you will say a word and they have to say whether the word has *e* at the end or not; whether the *u* is long or short.

  Invite group/individual responses.

  Suggested words:

pup	prune	flume	fuss	duke
huff	cut	cube	June	but
tug	plume	fuse	mud	rude

- Flash Cards practice: quick practice of words with *u* (*long*) represented in four different ways.

  Invite group/individual responses.

  Ask: "Which letters make the sound *u* (*long*)?"

  Confirm *ue, oo, ew, u-e*.

  Display the large pictures of a screw, blue (paper), moon and tube.

- Distribute the Flash Cards of *ue*, *oo*, *ew* and *u-e* words.

Suggested words:

grew	cube	stool	blue	threw
groom	food	flew	rule	glue
true	drew	loop	tube	use

Children in turn read aloud their word without the others seeing it.

Invite the other children to say if it will go on the picture of the screw, blue, moon or tube.

Encourage the children to say: "It will go on the screw because it has *ew*" or, "It will go on the moon because it has *oo* in the middle."

Invite the children to stick their word on the correct picture.

- Tell the children that you want them to write some words with the long *u* sound.

(*Children should know that the same sound can be written in more than one way. Encourage them to apply this knowledge to spelling.*)

Suggested words:

glue	stool	rude	flew	true	hoof
cube	new	tune	grew	clue	flute
mood	soon	chew	use	room	tube

- Show the teacher's copy of Workbook 5 page 38.

Top: Ensure that the children can read the words and know to underline the words with the *u* (*long*) sound.

Middle: Ensure that the children know to choose a word from those underlined above to complete each sentence. Encourage the children to use the strategy read on/read back.

Bottom: Ensure that the children can read the phrases and know to draw a picture to illustrate each phrase.

FURTHER PRACTICE

DEVELOPING SKILLS

Some or all of these activities must be done to ensure progress:

- **Practise writing single-syllable words with *ue*, *oo*, *ew* and *u-e***

You say a word, children write the word (*see Word List*).

The multisensory approach of Look, Say, Think*, Cover, Write, Check is a good strategy for learning how to spell words.

- **Magnetic letters**

Children make *ue*, *oo*, *ew*, *u-e* words.

- **Flash Cards**

Practise reading words with *ue*, *oo*, *ew*, *u-e*.

- **Dictation**

Sue stood on the new stool.
He blew a tune on a flute.
Bob can use my tube of glue.
He drew with a blue pen.
We will look for a clue.

* It is very important that children are encouraged to think about the tricky parts of words when they use this strategy.

ASSESSMENT 5.26

ACTIVITIES AT HOME

Homework Sheet 5U.

ue, oo, ew, u—e

oi and oy representing the same sound

BEFORE YOU START

THE NLF AIMS

- Hear and identify the sound represented by *oi* and *oy* in words.
- Read words containing *oi* or *oy*.
- Write words containing *oi* or *oy*.

WHAT YOU NEED

RESOURCES

- Flash Cards *oi* and *oy*
- Flash Cards *oi* and *oy* words
- Whiteboard/chalkboard
- Workbook 5 page 39
- Teacher's copy of Workbook 5 page 39
- Magnetic letters
- Word List
- Assessment 5.27
- Homework Sheet 5V

KEY LESSON POINTERS

VOCABULARY

alphabet   letter   name   sound   word
vowel   rhyming   middle   spell
sentence   end

THE CHILDREN should throughout the lesson:

- focus on *oi* and *oy* representing the same sound
- know that *oi* usually appears in the middle of words and *oy* at the end of words.

YOU should throughout the lesson:

- ensure that the children know that *oi* and *oy* represent the same sound
- know that *oi* usually appears in the middle of words and *oy* at the end of words.

THE LESSON

TEACHING THE LESSON

- Tell the children that they have to listen for the sound at the end of the words. Say *boy, toy, joy, coy*.
  Ask: "What sound can you hear at the end?"
  Confirm the sound represented by *oy*.

- Ask: "Which letters represent the sound *oi* in the middle of words?"
  Confirm *o* and *i* (previously taught).
  Tell the children there is another way to write the sound when it is at the end of words, that is, *oy*.
  Tell the children that if the sound is in the middle of a word it is usually represented by *oi*, but if it is at the end of a word it is represented by *oy*.
  Exceptions are *royal, loyal, oyster, voyage*.

- Tell the children you want to write the word *boy*.
  Ask: "How many sounds can you hear?"
  Confirm two.
  Slow speak *boy* and clap on sounds *b-oy*.
  Ask: "What is the first sound?"
  Confirm *b* and write on the board.
  Ask: "What sound can you hear next?"
  Confirm *oy*.
  Ask: "Which letters make the *oy* sound?"
  Confirm *o* and *y*.
  Write *oy* and ask: "What sound does this make at the end of a word?"
  Confirm *oy*.
  Ask the children to read the word *boy*.

- Repeat the procedure for *toy, joy, coy, Roy*.

- Ask the children to read the list of words.
  Ask: "What do you notice about the list?"
  Confirm that they all have *oy* at the end and that the words rhyme.
  Ensure that the children know that if they can read and write *boy*, they can read and write all the other rhyming words – only the first sound(s) change(s).
  Other words to investigate, read and spell:
  annoy   enjoy   employ   destroy

■ Flash Cards practice: read *oy* words.

Encourage the children to learn and chant the words in rhyming groups.

Hold up the Flash card and say ***boy***.

Children say ***coy, joy, toy, Roy***.

This is helpful to children whose visual memory is poor but whose auditory memory is better.

LATER

■ Name the letters:

Ask the children: "What are the two different ways of making ***oi***?"

Confirm ***oi*** and ***oy***.

Ask: "Where will you usually find the ***oi*** sound written as ***oi***?"

Confirm in the middle of a word.

Ask: "Where will you usually find the ***oy*** sound written as ***oy***?"

Confirm at the end of a word.

Tell the children that you will say a word and they have to answer ***oi*** or ***oy***.

Invite group/individual responses.

Suggested words:

boil	boy	coy	foil	join
toy	point	coin	enjoy	Roy
joint	soil	annoy	spoil	hoist

■ Show the teacher's copy of Workbook 5 page 39.

Top: Ensure that the children can read the phrases and know to draw a picture to illustrate each phrase.

Bottom: Ensure that the children know they have to check the spelling of the words and correct them if wrong. Ensure they know that not all the words are spelled wrong.

FURTHER PRACTICE

DEVELOPING SKILLS

Some or all of these activities must be done to ensure progress:

■ **Practise writing words with *oi* and *oy***

You say a word, children write the word (*see Word List*).

The multisensory approach of Look, Say, Think*, Cover, Write, Check is a good strategy for learning how to spell words.

■ **Magnetic letters**

Children make *oi* and *oy* words.

■ **Flash Cards**

Practise reading *oi* and *oy* words.

■ **Dictation**

The coin is in the bank.
Joy can boil eggs for tea.
The coil was made of steel.
My car needs oil.
The spike has a sharp point.
The soil in the tub is wet.
The boy came to play with me.
The toy is in the toy box.
Roy and his dog went to the park.
I enjoy a good film.
Lareb and Lee jump for joy.

* It is very important that children are encouraged to think about the tricky parts of words when they use this strategy.

ASSESSMENT 5.27

ACTIVITIES AT HOME

Homework Sheet 5V.

oi/oy

Digraph ow

THE NLF AIMS

- Hear and identify digraph *ow* in words.
- Read words containing the digraph *ow*.
- Write words containing the digraph *ow*.

WHAT YOU NEED

RESOURCES

- Flash Card *ow*
- Whiteboard/chalkboard
- Workbook 5 pages 40 to 42
- Teacher's copy of Workbook 5 pages 40 to 42
- Magnetic letters
- Word List
- Assessment 5.28
- Homework Sheet 5W

KEY LESSON POINTERS

VOCABULARY

alphabet letter name sound word vowel rhyming middle spell sentence illustrate

THE CHILDREN should throughout the lesson:

- focus on two letters representing one sound
- know that one sound can be represented two different ways
- know that *ow* can represent two different sounds.

YOU should throughout the lesson:

- emphasise that two letters can make one sound
- ensure that the children know that one sound can be represented in two different ways
- ensure that the children know that *ow* can represent two different sounds.

THE LESSON

TEACHING THE LESSON

■ Tell the children that they have to listen for the sound at the end of the words.

Say *cow, how, now, row*.

Ask: "What sound can you hear at the end of the words?"

Confirm *ow*.

■ Ask: "Which letters represent the sound *ow* when it is in the middle of words like *round, loud, proud*?"

Confirm *o* and *u* (previously taught).

Tell the children that there is another way to write the sound represented by *ou*, that is *ow*.

Show the children the *ow* card and ask them to say *ow*.

Tell the children that *ow* can come at the end of words or in the middle.

■ Tell the children you want to write the word *bow*.

Ask: "How many sounds can you hear?"

Confirm two.

Slow speak *bow* and clap on sounds *b-ow*.

Ask: "What is the first sound?"

Confirm *b* and write on the board.

Ask: "What sound can you hear next?"

Confirm *ow*.

Ask: "Which letters make the *ow* sound here?"

Confirm *o* and *w*.

Write *ow* on the board.

Ask the children to read the word *bow*.

■ Repeat the procedure for *cow, how, row, now*.

■ Ask the children to read the list of words.

Ask: "What do you notice about the list?"

Confirm that they all have *ow* at the end. They rhyme.

Ensure that the children know that if they can read and write *bow*, they can read and write all the other rhyming words as only the first sound(s) change(s).

■ Tell the children you want to write the word *town*.

Ask: "How many sounds can you hear?"

Confirm three.

Slow speak *t-ow-n*.

Ask: "Where can you hear the *ow* sound this time?"

Confirm in the middle.

Ask: "What is the first sound?"

Confirm **t** and write on the board.

Ask: "What sound is in the middle?"

Confirm **ow** and write on the board.

Ask: "What sound is at the end?"

Confirm **n** and write on the board.

Ask the children to read the word **town**.

- Repeat the procedure for **down, gown, frown, drown, brown, crown, clown**.

  Other words to investigate, read and spell:

owl	howl	fowl	growl	tower
power	flower	shower	towel	vowel
crowd	powder			

- Flash Cards practice: read **ow** words.

- Children complete Workbook 5 page 40.

LATER

It is not as easy to know when to use **ou** and when to use **ow** as it is for **ai** and **ay**. Help children to recognise that **ou** rarely comes at the end of a word (exception **thou**). We should always use **ow** at the end of a word, but **ou** and **ow** can both be used in the middle of a word. Children should learn that it is usually correct to use **ou** before **t, se, th, nd, nt**.

- Ask: "What sound do **ou** and **ow** make?"

  Confirm **ou**.

  Stick the **ou** and **ow** cards on the board.

  Tell the children that you will say a word and they have to answer **ou** or **ow** and point to the correct card, that is, the one that represents the sound.

  Invite group/individual responses.

  Suggested words:

house	growl	cloud	towel	clown	mouth
ground	drown	owl	count	brown	shout

- Show the teacher's copy of Workbook 5 page 41.

  Top: Ensure that the children can read the phrases and know to draw a picture to illustrate the phrase.

  Bottom: Ensure that the children know that they have to check the spelling of the words, that is, to see if there are any errors and correct them. Ensure that the children know that not all the words have the wrong spelling.

  Children will now know that **ow** can represent two different sounds as in **cow** and **slow**. The context of the sentence will tell them which way to read the word.

  Workbook 5 page 42 gives practice in this.

FURTHER PRACTICE

DEVELOPING SKILLS

Some or all of these activities must be done to ensure progress:

- Practise writing single-syllable words with vowel digraph **ow**

  You say a word, children write the word (*see Word List*).

  The multisensory approach of Look, Say, Think*, Cover, Write and Check is a good strategy for learning how to spell words.

- **Magnetic letters**

  Children make **ow** and **ou** words.

- **Flash Cards**

  Practise reading **ow** and **ou** words.

- **Dictation**

  The shower is hot.
  We get milk from a cow.
  The brown dog ran in the park.
  Can I play now?
  The owl flew up in the tree.
  The towel is on the shelf.

* It is very important that children are encouraged to think about the tricky parts of words when they use this strategy.

ASSESSMENT 5.28

ACTIVITIES AT HOME

Homework Sheet 5W.

OW

Digraph **aw**

BEFORE YOU START

THE NLF AIMS

- Read words containing digraph *aw*.
- Spell words containing digraph *aw*.

WHAT YOU NEED

RESOURCES

- Flash Card *aw*
- Flash Cards *aw* words
- Whiteboard/chalkboard
- Workbook 5 pages 43 and 44
- Teacher's copy of Workbook 5 pages 43 and 44
- Magnetic letters
- Word List
- Assessment 5.29

KEY LESSON POINTERS

VOCABULARY

alphabet   letter   name   sound   word
vowel   rhyming   middle   spell   sentence

THE CHILDREN should throughout the lesson:

- focus on two letters making one sound.

YOU should throughout the lesson:

- emphasise that two letters can make one sound
- ensure the children know that one sound can be represented in more than one way.

THE LESSON

STARTING THE LESSON

- Say the word *got*.

  Ask: "What sound can you hear in the middle of the word *got*?"

  Confirm *o*.

  Ask a child to write *got* on the board.

  Focus the children's attention on the fact that the sound *o* in *got* is represented by the letter *o*.

TEACHING THE LESSON

- Tell the children that there is another way to write the *o* sound.

  Write *saw* on the board.

  Ask: "Which letters represent the *o* sound this time?"

  Confirm *a* and *w*.

- Tell the children you want to write the word *jaw*.

  Ask: "How many sounds can you hear?"

  Confirm two.

  Slow speak *jaw* and clap on sounds *j-aw*.

  Ask: "What is the first sound?"

  Confirm *j* and write it on the board.

  Ask: "What sound can you hear next?"

  Confirm *o*.

  Ask: "Which letters make the *o* sound?"

  Confirm *a* and *w* and write them on the board.

  Ask the children to read the word *jaw*.

- Repeat the procedure for *jaw, law, paw, raw, claw, draw, flaw, straw* on the board.

  Ensure that the children know that if they can read and write *saw* they can read and write all the other rhyming words – only the first sound(s) change(s).

- Repeat the procedure for *dawn, fawn, lawn, yawn, shawl*.

- Flash Cards practice: *aw* words.

- Show the teacher's copy of Workbook 5 page 43.

  Top: Ensure that the children can read the phrases and know to draw a picture to illustrate each phrase.

  Middle: Ensure that the children know to choose a word from the words above to complete each sentence.

  Bottom: Ensure that the children know to make rhyming words using the letters given.

LATER

- Point out that *o* can also be represented by *au*. *August* and *because* are high frequency words which will have been taught as sight vocabulary.

  Workbook page 44 has been included to give practice in these words. *Autumn* and *author* have been included on this page as these are words used by children at this stage.

FURTHER PRACTICE

DEVELOPING SKILLS

Some or all of these activities must be done to ensure progress:

- **Practise writing *aw* words**

  You say a word, children write the word (*see Word List*).

  The multisensory approach of Look, Say, Think*, Cover, Write and Check is a good strategy for learning how to spell words.

- **Magnetic letters**

  Children make *aw* words.

- **Flash Cards**

  Practise reading *aw* words.

- **Dictation**

  I saw a plane in the sky.
  The boy lay on the lawn.
  Rita can draw a cat.
  The dog has a sore paw.
  Ali can use a saw.

* It is very important that children are encouraged to think about the tricky parts of words when they use this strategy.

ASSESSMENT 5.29

aw

Digraphs
ur and er

BEFORE YOU START

THE NLF AIMS

- Hear and identify digraph *ur* in words and digraph *er* in words.
- Read words containing *ur* and words containing *er*.
- Write words containing *ur* and words containing *er*.

WHAT YOU NEED

RESOURCES

- Flash Cards *ar, or, ir, ur* and *er*
- Flash Cards *ar, or, ir, ur* and *er* words
- Whiteboard/chalkboard
- Workbook 5 page 45
- Teacher's copy of Workbook 5 page 45
- Magnetic letters
- Word List
- Assessment 5.30

KEY LESSON POINTERS

VOCABULARY

alphabet letter name sound word vowel rhyming middle spell sentence illustrate

THE CHILDREN should throughout the lesson:

- focus on *ur* in words
- focus on *u* and *r* representing *ur*
- focus on *er* in words
- focus on *e* and *r* representing *er*.

YOU should throughout the lesson:

- emphasise that *ur* in words is represented by *u* and *r*
- emphasise that *er* in words is represented by *e* and *r*.

THE LESSON

STARTING THE LESSON

- Flash Cards: quick revision of *ar, or, ir* words.

  Ask the children which vowels they can hear in *park, cord, girl*.

  Confirm *a, o* and *i* respectively.

  Further practice may be needed.

  Suggested words:
  yard   born   bird   farm   cork   twirl

TEACHING THE LESSON

- Say the word *burn*.

  Ask: "How many sounds can you hear?"

  Confirm three.

  Ask: "What sound do you hear first?"

  Confirm *b* and write on the board.

  Ask: "What sound do you hear at the end?"

  Confirm *n* and write on the board.

  Ask: "What sound do you hear in the middle?"

  Confirm *ur*.

  Ask: "How can you write the sound you hear in the middle?"

  Confirm *u* and *r*.

  Ask the children to read the word *burn*.

- Repeat the procedure for *turn*.

- Ask the children to read the words.

  Ask: "What do you notice about the two words?"

  Confirm that they have *ur* in the middle and they end in *n*. They rhyme.

  Ensure that the children know that if they can read and write *burn*, they can read and write *turn*.

- Other words to investigate, read and spell:
  fur   curl   hurl   nurse   purse   hurt   burst
- Flash Cards practice: read **ur** words.
- Say the word **herb**.

  Ask: "How many sounds can you hear?"

  Confirm three.

  Ask: "What sound do you hear first?"

  Confirm **h** and write on the board.

  Ask: "What sound do you hear at the end?"

  Confirm **b** and write on the board.

  Ask: "What sound do you hear in the middle?"

  Confirm **er**.

  Ask: "How can you write the sound you hear in the middle?"

  Confirm **e** and **r**.

  Ask the children to read the word **herb**.

  Other words to investigate, read and spell:

her	herd	fern	stern	verb	term
nerve	serve	verse	father	sister	silver

- Show the teacher's copy of Workbook 5 page 45.

  Top: Ensure that the children can read the phrases and know to draw a picture to illustrate each phrase.

  Bottom: Ensure that the children know to choose a word from the box above to complete each sentence.

FURTHER PRACTICE

DEVELOPING SKILLS

Some or all of these activities must be done to ensure progress:

- **Practise writing words with vowel-consonant digraphs *ur* and *er***

  You say a word, children write the word (*see Word List*).

- **Magnetic letters**

  Children make *ur* and *er* words.

- **Flash Cards**

  Practise reading vowel-consonant digraph *ur* and *er* words.

- **Listening for *ur* or *er***

  You say a word and children say if the word has *ur* or *er* in the middle.

  Suggested words:

burn	herd	burst	curl	verb
turn	nurse	serve	hurt	term
purse	fern	herb		

- **Dictation**

  My feet hurt.
  We had a burst pipe.
  Jock had to turn around to see.
  Molly stood at the kerb.
  She took her books home.

ASSESSMENT 5.30

ur/er

Trigraphs **air** and **ear**

BEFORE YOU START

THE NLF AIMS

- Hear and identify trigraphs *air* and *ear* in words.
- Read words containing *air* and words containing *ear*.
- Write words containing *air* and words containing *ear*.

WHAT YOU NEED

RESOURCES

- Flash Cards *ar, or, ir, ur, er, air* and *ear*
- Flash Cards *ar, or, ir, ur, er, air* and *ear* words
- Whiteboard/chalkboard
- Workbook 5 page 46
- Teacher's copy of Workbook 5 page 46
- Magnetic letters
- Word List
- Assessment 5.31

KEY LESSON POINTERS

VOCABULARY

alphabet letter name sound word vowel rhyming middle spell sentence illustrate followed by

THE CHILDREN should throughout the lesson:

- focus on *air* in words
- focus on *ai* and *r* representing *air*
- focus on *ear* in words
- focus on *ea* and *r* representing *ear*.

YOU should throughout the lesson:

- emphasise that *air* in words is represented by *ai* and *r*
- emphasise that *ear* in words is represented by *ea* and *r*.

THE LESSON

STARTING THE LESSON

- Flash Cards practice: quick revision of *ar, or, ir, ur, er* words.

  Ask the children which vowels they can hear in *yard, sort, twirl, burn, herd.*

  Confirm *a, o, i, u, e* respectively.

- You say a word and children say if the word has *ar, or, ir, ur* or *er* in the middle.

  Suggested words:

lark	corn	third	charm	fork
term	burn	bark	stern	herd
farm	cord	girl	march	north
serve	burst	herb	skirt	curl
hurt	shirt	turn	first	hard

TEACHING THE LESSON

- Show the card *ai* and ask: "What sound is this?"

  Confirm *ai*.

  Remind the children of the rhyme:

  When two vowels together play a game
  Only the first one says its name.

- Show the card *ea* and ask: "What sound is this?"

  Confirm *ea*.

  Remind the children of the rhyme:

  When two vowels together play a game
  Only the first one says its name.

- Tell the children that *ai* and *ea* are often followed by *r* and that *air* and *ear* are common spelling patterns in the English language.

  Write the word *air* on the board.

  Write *ch, f, h, p, st* on the board.

  Tell the children that you want to use the letters to make new words with the *air* rime.

  Ask children in turn to write a word on the board.

  Encourage the children to write the words in a list so that the rhyming pattern can be seen.

  Ensure that the children know that if they can read and write *air*, they can read and write all the other rhyming words.

- Encourage the children to learn and chant the words in rhyming groups.

  Hold up the Flash Card and say *air*.

  Children say *air, fair, hair, pair, stair, chair*.

- Write the word *ear* on the board.

  Write *d, f, g, h, n, y, cl, sp* on the board.

  Tell the children that you want to use the letters to make new words with the *ear* rime.

  Ask children in turn to write a word on the board.

  Encourage the children to write the words in a list so that the rhyming pattern can be seen.

  Ensure that the children know that if they can read and write *ear*, they can read and write all the other rhyming words.

- Encourage the children to learn and chant the words in rhyming groups.

  Hold up the Flash Card and say *ear*.

  Children say *ear, dear, fear, gear, hear, near, year, clear, spear*.

- Flash Cards practice: **air** words and **ear** words.

- Show the teacher's copy of Workbook 5 page 46.

  Top: Ensure that the children can read the phrases and know to draw a picture to illustrate each phrase.

  Middle: Ensure that the children know to choose a word from the box above to complete each sentence. Encourage the children to use the strategy read on/read back.

  Bottom: Ensure that the children know to make rhyming words using the letters given.

FURTHER PRACTICE

DEVELOPING SKILLS

Some or all of these activities must be done to ensure progress:

- Practise writing single-syllable words with *air* and words with *ear*

  You say a word, children write the word (*see Word List*).

  The multisensory approach of Look, Say, Think*, Cover, Write, Check is a good strategy for learning how to spell words.

- **Magnetic letters**

  Children make *air* words and *ear* words.

- **Flash Cards**

  Practise reading words with *air* and words with *ear*.

- **Listening for *air* or *ear***

  You say a word and children say if the word has *air* or *ear* in the middle.

  Suggested words:

chair	clear	hear	stair	hair
fair	dear	pair	near	tear

- **Dictation**

  Jack sat on a high chair.
  He has a new pair of boots.
  Max has short hair.
  She sits near to me in the class.
  I can hear the sound of the bells.

* It is very important that children are encouraged to think about the tricky parts of words when they use this strategy.

ASSESSMENT 5.31

BLENDING AND SEGMENTING

TRIGRAPHS

air/ear

WORD LISTS

GLOSSARY

WORD LISTS

UNIT 3

1. CVC rhyming words

bag	bad	ban	bat	cap
rag	dad	fan	cat	gap
sag	had	man	fat	lap
tag	lad	pan	hat	map
wag	mad	ran	mat	nap
jag	sad	tan	pat	tap
		van	rat	
			sat	

bid	big	bin	bit	dip
did	dig	din	fit	hip
hid	fig	fin	hit	lip
lid	jig	pin	kit	nip
rid	pig	tin	lit	pip
	rig	win	pit	rip
	tig		sit	sip
	wig		wit	tip
				zip

bed	beg	den	bet
fed	leg	hen	get
led	peg	men	jet
red		pen	let
wed		ten	met
			net
			pet
			set
			wet

hob	dog	hop	dot
job	fog	mop	got
rob	jog	pop	hot
sob	log	top	lot
			not
			pot

cub	but	bug	bun
hub	gut	dug	fun
pub	hut	hug	gun
rub	jut	jug	nun
tub	nut	mug	run
	rut	rug	sun
	tut	tug	

UNITS 3 and 4

2. CVC words

Medial *a*

bat	man
bad	mat
ban	map
cat	nab
can	nap
cap	pad
dab	pan
dad	pad
fab	pat
fad	rag
fat	ran
fan	rat
gas	ram
gap	sad
had	sag
hat	sat
ham	tab
jam	tag
jab	tan
jag	tap
lab	van
lad	vat
lag	wax
lap	wag
mad	

Medial *e*

bed	men
beg	met
bet	net
den	peg
fed	pen
get	pet
hem	red
hen	set
jet	vet
led	web
leg	wed
let	wet

Medial *i*

bid	lit
bib	mix
big	nip
bin	nib
bit	pig
did	pin
dig	pip
dim	pit
din	rib
dip	rid
fib	rig
fig	rim
fin	rip
fit	sin
fix	sip
hid	sit
him	tig
hip	tin
hit	tip
jig	wig
kid	win
kit	wit
lid	wig
lip	zip

Medial *o*

box	log
cod	lot
cop	mob
cot	mop
dog	not
dot	pod
fog	pop
fox	pot
got	rob
hob	rod
hop	rot
hot	sob
job	top
jog	

Medial *u*

bud	jug
bug	jut
bun	mud
bus	mug
but	mum
cub	nut
cup	nun
cut	pub
dug	pup
dud	rub
fun	rug
gum	run
gun	rut
gut	sum
hub	sun
hug	tub
hum	tug
hut	tut

3. sh words

shop	dish	bash	hush	mesh
ship	fish	cash	mush	fresh
shed	wish	mash	rush	
shell		rash	crush•	
shelf		dash	brush•	
sharp•		crash•	flush•	
short•		smash•		
shirt•				

4. ch words

chin	chimp*	much
chip	champ*	such
chop	chest*	rich
chap	chick*	
chill	church•	

5. th words

thin	bath	moth	with
thick	path	cloth•	
think*	maths	broth•	
thank*		froth•	
thump*			
third•			
thorn•			

6. wh words

when
whip
whisk*
whiff
which

7. Word list ck

back	neck	kick	dock	duck
sack	deck	lick	lock	luck
tack	peck	pick	sock	suck
rack	fleck•	sick	rock	tuck
pack	speck•	tick	shock	pluck•
whack		thick	dock•	stuck•
black•		click•	block•	truck•
crack•		stick•	flock•	
track•		trick•	frock•	
		brick•		
		flick•		

UNIT 4

8. Double letter endings

ill	bell	hiss	egg
till	fell	kiss	add
bill	sell	miss	odd
fill	tell	mess	off
hill	well	less	buzz
pill		pass	mitt
sill	cuff	lass	doll
will	huff	mass	
	muff	toss	
	puff	loss	
		boss	
		moss	

9. ng words

king	bang	gong	hung
ring	gang	long	lung
sing	hang	song	rung
wing	rang	dong	sung
thing	sang	pong	clung•
swing•	clang•		slung•
sting•	slang•		flung•
fling•			stung•
bring•			
sling•			

* Unit 4
• Unit 5

10. CVCC words

st	sk	lk	nk	ft
fast	ask	milk	bank	soft
last	bask	silk	sank	loft
mast	mask	bulk	tank	lift
past	task	hulk	link	gift
best	desk	sulk	pink	rift
lest	risk		rink	sift
test	busk		sink	left
rest	dusk		wink	tuft
vest	tusk		bunk	raft
west	rusk		junk	daft
pest			hunk	
nest				
mist				
fist				
just				
must				
dust				
rust				
lost				
cost				

nt	lt	mp	nd
bent	melt	camp	band
tent	felt	damp	hand
sent	belt	lamp	land
rent	pelt	ramp	sand
went	kilt	bump	bend
lent	wilt	dump	lend
dent	tilt	jump	send
vent		hump	mend
tint		lump	fend
lint		pump	tend
pant		rump	pond
rant		limp	fond
		romp	bond
		pomp	

UNIT 5

11. CCVC words
(plus double consonant endings)

cl	fl	sl
clap	flip	slim
clip	flap	slam
club	flat	slip
cliff	fluff	slap
clog	flit	slum
	flag	slug

gl	pl	bl
glad	plum	blot
glum	plug	blip
glass	plus	
	plan	
	plot	
	plod	

br	fr	pr	tr
brim	from	pram	trap
bran	frog	prop	trim
brass	frill	prod	trip
		press	trot
			trod

gr	dr	cr
grab	drag	crib
gran	drip	crab
grip	drop	crop
grin	drug	cross
grass	drum	
	dress	
	drill	

sp	st	sk	sw
spin	stem	skin	swim
spot	step	skip	swam
spit	stop	skid	swell
spill	still	skim	

sl	sn	sm
slim	snap	smut
slip	snip	smell
slap	snug	
	snob	

12. c–c at beginning and ending

crisp	brand
crust	grand
frost	stand
blast	spend
blink	clamp
stink	cramp
drink	stamp
plonk	stomp
trend	tramp
stump	plant
plump	spent
grump	flint
	print
	blunt
	grunt
	stunt

13. oo words

moon	food	boot
noon	mood	hoot
soon		root
spoon		toot
		shoot
		scoot

too	hoop	cool	room
zoo	loop	tool	zoom
	troop	wool	gloom
	stoop	fool	bloom
	scoop	pool	broom
		stool	groom
		spool	

14. ee words

bee	beef	feel	deep
see	reef	heel	keep
tree		peel	peep
free		reel	weep
		steel	sleep
		wheel	steep
			bleep
			cheep
			sheep

feet	need	week	teeth
meet	weed	seek	
sleet	seed	leek	
sweet	feed	meek	
greet	tweed	cheek	
sheet	greed		
	breed		
	speed		

15. ai words

fail	laid	gain
hail	paid	rain
jail	raid	pain
mail		stain
nail		train
pail		grain
rail		brain
sail		Spain
tail		chain
snail		
trail		

wait	paint
waist	faint

16. oa words

oat	coal	load	loan	coast
boat	foal	road	moan	roast
coat	goal	toad	groan	toast
goat				boast
moat				
float				
stoat				
throat				

oak	oat	oar	soap	loaf
soak	oats	oars	coach	foam
cloak				

17. ie words

die	died	ties
tie	tied	cries
pie	cried	tries
lie	fried	dries
	dried	fries
	tried	flies

18. ou words

loud	found	mouth	grout
cloud	hound	south	snout
proud	mound		stout
	round		trout
	sound		spout
	wound		scout
	pound		shout
	ground		

count	foul
mount	

19. oi words

coin	joint	moist	oil
join	point	hoist	boil
		joist	soil
			coil
			toil
			spoil

20. ar words

car	art	arm	yarn
far	dart	farm	barn
jar	cart	harm	darn
bar	part	charm	
tar	tart		
star	start		

ark	card	sharp
park	hard	
bark	lard	
dark	yard	
hark		
lark		
mark		
spark		
shark		

21. or words

horn	fork	cord	sort	storm
corn	cork	lord	snort	
born	York		short	
morn	stork			
torn				
thorn				

22. ir words

bird	twirl	first
third	whirl	thirst
	swirl	

dirt	birth	smirk
skirt	mirth	chirp
shirt		
squirt		

23. ay words

bay	pay	clay
day	ray	play
gay	say	tray
lay	way	stay
hay		fray
may		sway
		pray

24. a-e words

bake	came	ate	fade	cave
cake	fame	date	made	gave
lake	game	gate	spade	save
make	lame	hate		rave
take	same	mate		wave
wake	tame	plate		grave
flake	shame	skate		
snake		grate		
shake				

sale	daze	tape	cane
tale	maze	grape	mane
male	blaze	shape	pane
whale			

safe	case

25. ow words

bow	blow	arrow	shadow	yellow
low	snow	narrow	shallow	pillow
mow	flow	barrow	elbow	window
row	glow	sparrow	follow	
sow	grow			
tow	crow			
	throw			
	know			

26. o-e words

hole	coke	hose
mole	joke	nose
pole	poke	rose
sole	woke	close
stole	broke	
	spoke	
	smoke	
	choke	

bone	hope	code
cone	rope	
stone	slope	

27. ea words

eat	bean	each
heat	lean	teach
meat	mean	reach
seat		beach
pleat		peach
bleat		
wheat		

seam	meal	bead
team	seal	read
cream	real	
dream	steal	
steam		

28. igh words

high	fight
sigh	might
thigh	light
	night
	right
	sight
	tight
	bright
	flight
	fright

29. y (long) words

cry	my	fly	sky
dry	by	sly	sty
fry			spy
try			why
			shy

30. i-e words

hide	pipe	dine	mime
ride	ripe	fine	time
tide	wipe	line	chime
side	swipe	mine	
wide		nine	
slide		pine	
bride		wine	
		twine	
		spine	
		shine	

file	bite	bike	wife
pile	kite	like	
tile	white		
smile			
while			

31. ew words

dew	flew	threw
few	blew	knew
new	grew	screw
pew	crew	chew
stew	drew	

32. u-e words

cube	mule	use	June	cute
tube	rule	fuse	tune	flute
			prune	

33. ue words

blue
true
clue
glue

34. oy words

coy
boy
joy
toy
annoy
enjoy
cowboy
tomboy

35. ow words

bow	town	owl	towel	crowd
cow	down	howl	vowel	
how	gown	fowl	tower	
row	frown	growl	power	
now	drown		flower	
	brown		shower	
	crown		powder	

36. aw words

jaw	claw	crawl	fawn	hawk
law	flaw	shawl	dawn	
saw	draw		lawn	
paw			yawn	

37. ur words

curl	urn	burst	church	blur
hurl	burn	blur		
furl	turn			

38. er words

her	fern
herd	term

39. air words

air
fair
hair
stair
chair

40. ear words

ear
fear
dear
gear
hear
near
tear
spear
clear
shear

GLOSSARY

alliteration
The use of the same initial sound in words which are close together: e.g. *Dexter dog digs deep* while *digging* for his *dinner*.

analogy
The use of a word pattern, that is the rime, as a basis for reading and spelling other words with the same rime, e.g. if you can read and write *hand*, you can read and write *band*, *sand*, *land*.

auditory discrimination
An ability to detect the differences or similarities between individual speech sounds when presented orally (e.g. *d/b/p*).

auditory memory
An ability to remember material presented orally.

blending
A merging of phonemes together to pronounce a word. In order to read an unfamiliar word phonemically, a child must attribute a phoneme to each letter or letter combination in the word and then merge the phonemes together to pronounce the word.

cluster
Consonant cluster – two consonants occuring close together each retaining their own alphabet sound e.g. *cl, sp, nt, lk*. (Clusters are sometimes referred to as blends)

consonant
A sound which is produced when the speaker uses lips, tongue and teeth to cause some sort of friction, or burst of air. All letters of the alphabet except '*a*', '*e*', '*i*' ,'*o*', '*u*' are consonants.

Contrast with vowel sounds, which are formed by changing the shape of the mouth and airway. The letter 'y' can act as a vowel or a consonant.

digraph
A combination of two letters used to make a single speech sound such as *ch* and *ai*.

decoding
Pronunciation of a word from the visual code of the letters.

encoding
Producing a written word for a spoken word.

grapheme
A written representation of a speech sound.

homophone
Words which sound the same but have different meaning or different spelling: *read/reed; pair/pear; right/write/rite.*

letter
Character of the alphabet.

motor skills
Muscle movements controlled by the brain.

- **gross motor**: large movements involving the body, legs, hands and arms.
- **fine motor**: small movements involving the fingers, e.g. pencil control, use of scissors.

multisensory
The simultaneous use of as many senses as possible including – hearing, seeing, touching and involving saying and writing.

onset and rime
Onset is the initial consonant or consonant cluster of letters in words which precedes the vowel, e.g. **b**ag, **cl**ock.

Rime refers to the vowel and final consonant(s) e.g. *-at* in *cat*, *-ing* in *string*, or the final digraph e.g. *ow* in *cow, how, now*.

When using onset and rime, words are grouped by final sound(s):

e.g.	man	best	new
	can	vest	few
	ran	test	grew
	van	nest	flew
	fan	pest	

phoneme
The smallest unit of sound in a word. There are approximately 44 phonemes in the English language. A phoneme can be formed by one, two, three or four letters e.g.

cot – one letter	*chat* – two letters
high – three letters	*station* – four letters

cat has three phonemes *c-a-t*, but *chat* also has three phonemes *ch-a-t*.

phonics
Usually taken to mean a strategy for teaching reading and spelling where an understanding of the correspondence between speech sounds (phonemes) and letters (graphemes) is taught.

phonological awareness
An explicit awareness of the sounds in words – demonstrated by the ability to identify onset, generate rime and segment syllables in words.

rap
A form of oral rhyme/poem which has a very strong rhythm and rapid pace.

rhyme / rime
Rhymes and rimes are not identical. Rhymes have word endings which sound the same but are not necessarily spelled in the same way, e.g. *socks/fox*. Rimes are word endings which always retain the same spelling pattern, e.g. *box/fox*.

segment
to break a word or part of a word down into its component phonemes, for example, *c-a-t, sh-o-p*

short–term working memory
A system of temporarily holding information for a brief period while the individual processes information to carry out an intellectual task.

slow speak
Pronunciation of words in a slow, deliberate way, segmenting the component phonemes.

split digraph
Two vowels representing one sound but separated by a consonant. The final vowel always being *e*.

trigraph
Three letters representing one phoneme.

visual discrimination
The ability to detect the differences in shape, size and orientation of letters e.g. *d/b; p/q, n/u*.

vowel
a phoneme produced without audible friction or closure. Every syllable contains a vowel or *y*.